SAVING THE INTERNATIONAL JUSTICE REGIME

While resistance to international courts is not new, what is new, or at least newly conceptualized, is the politics of backlash against these institutions. *Saving the International Justice Regime: Beyond Backlash against International Courts* is at the forefront of this new conceptualization of backlash politics. It brings together theories, concepts, and methods from the fields of international law, international relations, human rights and political science, and case studies from around the globe to pose – and answer – three questions related to backlash against international courts: What is backlash and what forms does it take? Why do states and elites engage in backlash against international human rights and criminal courts? What can stakeholders and supporters of international justice do to meet these contemporary challenges?

Courtney Hillebrecht is the Samuel Clark Waugh Distinguished Professor of International Relations and an Associate Professor of Political Science at the University of Nebraska-Lincoln. She is the author of *Domestic Politics and International Human Rights Tribunals: The Problem of Compliance* (Cambridge University Press, 2014).

Saving the International Justice Regime

BEYOND BACKLASH AGAINST INTERNATIONAL COURTS

COURTNEY HILLEBRECHT

University of Nebraska-Lincoln

CAMBRIDGE
UNIVERSITY PRESS

CAMBRIDGE
UNIVERSITY PRESS

University Printing House, Cambridge CB2 8BS, United Kingdom

One Liberty Plaza, 20th Floor, New York, NY 10006, USA

477 Williamstown Road, Port Melbourne, VIC 3207, Australia

314–321, 3rd Floor, Plot 3, Splendor Forum, Jasola District Centre, New Delhi – 110025, India

103 Penang Road, #05–06/07, Visioncrest Commercial, Singapore 238467

Cambridge University Press is part of the University of Cambridge.

It furthers the University's mission by disseminating knowledge in the pursuit of education, learning, and research at the highest international levels of excellence.

www.cambridge.org
Information on this title: www.cambridge.org/9781316511411
DOI: 10.1017/9781009052610

First published 2021

A catalogue record for this publication is available from the British Library.

Library of Congress Cataloging-in-Publication Data
NAMES: Hillebrecht, Courtney, author.
TITLE: Saving the international justice regime : beyond backlash against international courts / Courtney Hillebrecht, University of Nebraska-Lincoln.
DESCRIPTION: Cambridge, United Kingdom ; New York, NY : Cambridge University Press, 2022. | Includes bibliographical references and index.
IDENTIFIERS: LCCN 2021024122 | ISBN 9781316511411 (hardback) | ISBN 9781009055642 (paperback) | ISBN 9781009052610 (ebook)
SUBJECTS: LCSH: International criminal courts – Political aspects. | International Criminal Court.
CLASSIFICATION: LCC KZ7230 .H55 2022 | DDC 345/.01–dc23
LC record available at https://lccn.loc.gov/2021024122

ISBN 978-1-316-51141-1 Hardback
ISBN 978-1-009-05564-2 Paperback

To Carrick, Nola, and Willa

Contents

Tables

Acknowledgments

This book is the result of many years of work, as well as the support, encouragement, and generosity of countless colleagues and friends.

I am forever indebted to Hannah Read for her exceedingly capable research assistance. Her insightful comments, keen eye for detail, and deep understanding of the literature made this book immeasurably better.

My editor, Tom Randall, has been a supportive and knowledgeable shepherd of this project, and I am grateful for his help in shaping this manuscript. I am also thankful to the anonymous reviewers whose incisive feedback strengthened the book's argument and approach.

I am so fortunate to be part of a community of generous human rights, international law, and political science scholars and students. They have read drafts, provided thoughtful feedback, sparked new ideas, and, above all, been a source of friendship and camaraderie.

This book would not have been possible without the many practitioners at international human rights and criminal courts, nongovernmental organizations, and the United Nations who opened their doors to me, answered countless questions, and provided key insights into the challenges they face every day in their work. Beyond their generosity, these practitioners provided a constant source of inspiration and hope. Despite working day in and day out on some of the most crushing contemporary human rights atrocities and facing the full effects of backlash politics, these dedicated human rights professionals continue to work tirelessly to build a world characterized by justice, peace, and equality.

Finally, I owe an eternal debt of gratitude to my family: to my parents, Moose and Jane Hillebrecht, for their unflagging support; to my husband Carrick, for being a true partner in this life; and to my daughters, Nola and Willa, for bringing me countless moments of joy and wonder.

Abbreviations

ACN	Advisory Committee on Nominations of Judges
ACJHR	African Court of Justice and Human Rights
ACmHPR	African Commission on Human and Peoples' Rights
ACtHPR	African Court on Human and Peoples' Rights
AHPRS	African Human and Peoples' Rights System
ASP	Assembly of States Parties
AU	African Union
C90-NM	Cambio 90-Nueva Mayoría
CAN	Comunidad Andina/Andean Community
CAT	Convention against Torture
CCJ	Community Court of Justice
CEJIL	Center for Justice and International Law
CICC	Coalition for the ICC
CIDH	Comisión Interamericana de Derechos Humanos/IACmHR
COE	Council of Europe
DPRK	Democratic Republic of Korea/North Korea
DRC	Democratic Republic of the Congo
EACJ	East African Court of Justice
EALA	East African Legislative Assembly
ECCC	Extraordinary Chambers in the Courts of Cambodia
ECHR	European Convention on Human Rights
ECOWAS	Economic Community of West African States
ECtHR	European Court of Human Rights
ELN	Ejército de Liberación Nacional/National Liberation Army
EU	European Union
FARC	Fuerzas Armadas Revolucionarias de Colombia/ Revolutionary Armed Forces of Colombia

FIDH	Fédération internationale des ligues des droits de l'homme/ International Federation for Human Rights
G7	Group of Seven
GRECO	Group of States against Corruption
GR-PBA	Group on Programme, Budget and Administration
IACmHR	Inter-American Commission on Human Rights
IACtHR	Inter-American Court of Human Rights
IAHRS	Inter-American Human Rights System
ICC	International Criminal Court
ICTR	International Criminal Tribunal for Rwanda
ICTY	International Criminal Tribunal for the former Yugoslavia
IJRC	International Justice Resource Center
IO	international organization
IT	information technology
LBA	Lima Bar Association
MERCOSUR	Mercado Común del Sur/Southern Common Market
NACLA	North American Congress on Latin America
NGO	nongovernmental organization
OAS	Organization of American States
OAU	Organization of African Unity
OTP	Office of the Prosecutor (International Criminal Court)
P-5	Permanent five members of the United Nations Security Council
PACE	Parliamentary Assembly of the Council of Europe
PTCII	Pre-Trial Chamber II of the International Criminal Court
SADC	South African Development Community
SCSL	Special Court for Sierra Leone
SNI	Servicio de Inteligencia Nacional/National Intelligence Service
STL	Special Tribunal for Lebanon
TFV	Trust Fund for Victims (International Criminal Court)
UK	United Kingdom
UN	United Nations
UNASUR	Union of South American Nations
UNHCHR	UN High Commissioner for Human Rights
UNIIIC	UN International Independent Investigation Commission
UNSC	United Nations Security Council
USA	United States of America
V-Dem	Varieties of Democracy

Legal Cases

EUROPEAN COURT OF HUMAN RIGHTS

Case of Anchugov and Gladkov *v.* Russia. No. 11157/04 and 15162/05 (European Court of Human Rights, 2013).

Case of OAO Neftyanaya Kompaniya Yukos *v.* Russia. No. 14902/04 (European Court of Human Rights, 2014).

Case of Varvara *v.* Italy. No. 17475/09 (European Court of Human Rights, 2013).

Maggio and Others *v.* Italy. No. 4628/09, 52851/08, 53727/08, 54486/08, and 56001/08

(European Court of Human Rights, 2011).

HOUSE OF LORDS (UK)

Regina *v.* Bartle and the Commissioner of Police for the Metropolis and others ex parte Pinochet/Regina *v.* Evans and another and the Commissioner of Police for the Metropolis and others ex parte Pinochet (House of Lords, Great Britain, November 25, 1998).

INTER-AMERICAN COMMISSION ON HUMAN RIGHTS

Comunidades Indígenas da Bacia do Rio Xingu, Pará, Brasil. MC 382/10 (Inter-American Commission on Human Rights, April 1, 2011).

Juan Carlos Abella *v.* Argentina. Report No. 55/97, Case 11.137 (Inter-American Commission on Human Rights, November 18, 1997).

INTERNATIONAL CRIMINAL COURT

Afghanistan

Burundi

Democratic Republic of the Congo

Myanmar

INTERNATIONAL COURT OF JUSTICE

RUSSIAN FEDERATION

Case of OAO Neftyanaya Kompaniya Yukos *v.* Russia in Connection with the Request of the Ministry of Justice of the Russian Federation (Constitutional Court of the Russian Federation, January 19, 2017).

VENICE COMMISSION

Venice Commission. *Opinion No. 832/2015 Russian Federation Final Opinion on the Amendments to the Federal Constitutional Law on the Constitutional Court, Adopted by the Venice Commission at Its 107th Plenary Session (Venice, 10–11 June 2016).* Strasbourg: Council of Europe, 2016. https://www.venice.coe.int/webforms/documents/default.aspx?pdffile=CDL-AD(2016)016-e.

Resolutions, Statutes, and Treaties

COUNCIL OF EUROPE

Committee of Ministers of the Council of Europe. "Brighton Declaration" (European Court of Human Rights, April 2012).

Committee of Ministers of the Council of Europe. "Brussels Declaration" (European Court of Human Rights March 27, 2015).

Committee of Ministers of the Council of Europe. "Copenhagen Declaration" (European Court of Human Rights, April 13, 2018).

EUROPEAN TREATY SERIES

"European Convention for the Protection of Human Rights and Fundamental Freedoms, as amended by Protocol Nos. 11 and 14." Opened for signature November 4, 1950. *European Treaty Series* no. 5.

"European Convention on State Immunity." Opened for signature May 16, 1972. *European Treaty Series* no. 74.

"Protocol 11 to the European Convention for the Protection of Human Rights and Fundamental Freedoms, Restructuring the Control Machinery Established Thereby." Opened for signature May 11, 1994. *European Treaty Series* no. 155.

"Protocol 14 to the European Convention for the Protection of Human Rights and Fundamental Freedoms Amending the Control System of the Convention." Opened for signature May 13, 2004. *European Treaty Series* no. 194.

"Protocol No. 15 amending the European Convention for the Protection of Human Rights and Fundamental Freedoms." Opened for signature June 24, 2013. *European Treaty Series* no. 213.

ITALY

La sentenza n. 49 of 2015 (Corte Costituzionale, 2015).

ORGANIZATION OF AFRICAN UNITY/AFRICAN UNION TREATIES/ RESOLUTIONS

"African [Banjul] Charter on Human and Peoples' Rights." Adopted June 27, 1981. *Organization of African Unity/African Union Treaties, Conventions, Protocols & Charters*, CAB/LEG/67/3 rev. 5, 21 I.L.M. 58.

African Union. "Assembly of the African Union: Thirteenth Ordinary Session 1–3 July 2009 Sirte, Great Socialist People's Libyan Arab Jamahiriya: Decisions and Declarations." July 3, 2009.

African Union. "Assembly of the Union: Twenty-Fourth Ordinary Session 30–31 January 2015 Addis Ababa, Ethiopia: Decisions, Declarations, and Resolutions." January 31, 2015.

"Protocol to the African Charter on Human and Peoples' Rights on the Establishment of an African Court on Human and Peoples' Rights." Adopted June 10, 1998. *Organization of African Unity/African Union Treaties, Conventions, Protocols & Charters*.

"Protocol on Amendments to the Protocol on the Statute of the African Court of Justice and Human Rights (Malabo Protocol)." Adopted June 27, 2014. *Organization of African Unity/African Union Treaties, Conventions, Protocols & Charters*.

"Protocol on the Statute of the African Court of Justice and Human Rights." Adopted July 1, 2008. *Organization of African Unity/African Union Treaties, Conventions, Protocols & Charters*.

ORGANIZATION OF AMERICAN STATES

"American Convention on Human Rights." Entered into force July 18, 1978. *Organization of American States*.

"Declaración Sobre El Sistema Interamericano de Derechos Humanos" (La República Argentina, La República Federativa del Brasil, La República de Chile, La República de Colombia, and La República del Paraguay, April 23, 2019).

PARLIAMENTARY ASSEMBLY OF THE COUNCIL OF EUROPE

Parliamentary Assembly of the Council of Europe. "Resolution 1990 (2014): Reconsideration on Substantive Grounds of the Previously Ratified Credentials of the Russian Delegation" (Council of Europe, April 10, 2014).

PERU

Law No. 26,627, Law on the Authentic Interpretation of Article 112 of the Constitution, "Interpretation Law" (The Peruvian Congress, 1996).

República del Perú Constitución Política de 1993 (Republic of Peru 1993 Political Constitution) (The Peruvian Congress, 1993).

UNASUR

"Tratado Constitutivo de La Unión de Naciones Suramericanas." Adopted May 23, 2008. *UNASUR.*

UNITED NATIONS SECURITY COUNCIL

United Nations Security Council Resolution 1593 (United National Security Council, 2005).

United Nations Security Council Resolution 1595 (United Nations Security Council, 2005).

United Nations Security Council Resolution 1664 (United Nations Security Council, 2006).

United Nations Security Council Resolution 1757 (United Nations Security Council, 2007).

United Nations Security Council Resolution 1970 (United Nations Security Council, 2011).

UNITED NATIONS TREATY SERIES

"Rome Statute of the International Criminal Court." Entered into force July 1, 2002. *United Nations Treaty Series* 2187 no. 38544.

"United Nations Convention on Jurisdictional Immunities of States and Their Property." Adopted December 2, 2004. *United Nations Treaty Series* A/RES/ 59/38.

"Vienna Convention on the Law of Treaties (with Annex)." Adopted May 22, 1969. *United Nations Treaty Series* No. 18232.

1

Progress and Pushback in the Judicialization of Human Rights

INTRODUCTION

In 2016, Burundi, The Gambia, and South Africa all made moves to withdraw from the International Criminal Court (ICC).[1] They were not alone. Kenya, Uganda, Rwanda, and a number of other African Union (AU) member states sought to orchestrate a mass withdrawal from the ICC.[2] This withdrawal was precipitated by the ICC's casework in Africa, including indictments against Kenyan President Uhuru Kenyatta and Deputy President William Ruto, as well as former Sudanese President Omar al-Bashir.[3] While mass withdrawal never came to pass, the damage that these sustained rhetorical and political attacks caused continues to reverberate around the international criminal justice sphere. Indeed, efforts to undermine and assail the ICC are not unique to African Union member states. In 2019, the ICC inched closer to opening a case against the president of the Philippines, Rodrigo Duterte. President Duterte had some choice words to express his discontent with international justice: "I will never, never, never answer any question coming from you. It's bullshit to me. I am only

---

[1] Ian Sprouse, "The Gambia's Unsurprising Renunciation of the ICC, or the So-Called 'International Caucasian Court,'" *Africa at LSE* (blog), November 10, 2016, http://blogs .lse.ac.uk/africaatlse/2016/11/10/the-gambias-unsurprising-renunciation-of-the-icc-or-the-so-called-international-caucasian-court/.

[2] Dap Akande, "The African Union Takes on the ICC Again: Are African States Really Turning from the ICC?" *EJIL: Talk!* (blog), July 26, 2011, www.ejiltalk.org/the-african-union-takes-on-the-icc-again/; Laurence R. Helfer and Anne E. Showalter, "Opposing International Justice: Kenya's Integrated Backlash Strategy against the ICC," *International Criminal Law Review* 17, no. 1 (February 2017): 1–46, https://doi.org/10.1163/15718123-01701005.

[3] "Case Information Sheet: Situation in the Republic of Kenya, The Prosecutor v. Uhuru Muigai Kenyatta, Case No. ICC-01/09-02/11 (ICC-PIDS-CIS-KEN-02-014/15_Eng)," International Criminal Court, March 13, 2015, https://www.icc-cpi.int/CaseInformationSheets/kenyattaEng .pdf.

responsible to the Filipino[s]. Filipinos will judge."[4] The Philippines went on to become only the second country ever to withdraw from the ICC.[5]

While the ICC has faced some of the more extreme and showy examples of backlash against international justice, it is far from alone in trying to navigate this current wave of attacks. In Lebanon, Hezbollah has undertaken a nearly decade-long – and quite successful – campaign to undermine the Special Tribunal for Lebanon (STL), a hybrid, domestic–international court designed to investigate and try the perpetrators responsible for the 2005 attack that killed Prime Minister Rafic Hariri. Since the STL opened for business in 2009, Hezbollah and its allies in Iran have systematically tried to subvert it, endangering witnesses and dismantling cases.[6]

In Europe, the United Kingdom (UK) has blustered about withdrawing from the European Court of Human Rights (ECtHR) for many years. Long before "Brexit," British political leaders complained about the ECtHR whenever it handed down a politically unpopular decision and advanced the idea of withdrawing from the Court as a way of drumming up domestic political support.[7] Meanwhile, the Inter-American Court of Human Rights (IACtHR) has undergone a significant structural reform process in order to address systematic noncompliance and outright rejection of the Court by major regional players.[8] At the same time, member states have nearly bankrupted the Inter-American Commission on Human Rights (IACmHR), threatening to disrupt the entire Inter-American Human Rights System (IAHRS).[9]

Taken together, I refer to international human rights and criminal tribunals as the international justice regime.[10] These courts and the international justice

---

[4] "Jail Me, Hang Me: Philippines' Duterte Says Won't Answer to ICC," *Reuters*, December 20, 2019, https://www.reuters.com/article/us-philippines-drugs/jail-me-hang-me-philippines-duterte-says-wont-answer-to-icc-idUSKBN1YO184.

[5] Jason Gutierrez, "Philippines Officially Leaves the International Criminal Court," *The New York Times*, March 17, 2019, https://www.nytimes.com/2019/03/17/world/asia/philippines-international-criminal-court.html.

[6] Meira Svirsky, "Hezbollah Intimidates Witnesses in Hariri Murder Tribunal," *Clarion Project*, March 14, 2013, www.clarionproject.org/news/hezbollah-intimidates-witnesses-hariri-murder-tribunal.

[7] Alice Donald, Jane Gordon, and Philip Leach, *The UK and the European Court of Human Rights* (Manchester: Equality and Human Rights Commission, 2012), https://www.equalityhumanrights.com/sites/default/files/83._european_court_of_human_rights.pdf.

[8] "Understanding the IACHR Reform Process," International Justice Resource Center, last modified November 20, 2012, https://ijrcenter.org/2012/11/20/iachr-reform-process/.

[9] Par Engstrom, Paola Limón, and Clara Sandoval, "#CIDHenCrisis: Urgent Action Needed to Save the Regional Human Rights System in the Americas," *openDemocracy*, May 27, 2016, https://www.opendemocracy.net/en/democraciaabierta/cidhencrisis-urgent-action-needed-to-save-/.

[10] I also use the terms "court" and "tribunal" interchangeably.

regime more broadly have long experienced serious and sustained opposition.[11] This opposition has come in many forms, from the United States' early pledge to do anything in its power to stop the International Criminal Court[12] to Canada's nearly fifty-year-long refusal to join the Inter-American Court of Human Rights.[13] Despite these protestations, since the end of World War II, international human rights and criminal accountability have become both highly legalized and judicialized.[14] International courts and their legalistic language and methods have become fundamental for the negotiation of political questions surrounding human rights. Moreover, international human rights and criminal law are now central parts of discussions about war and peace.[15]

---

[11] Gary Jonathan Bass, *Stay the Hand of Vengeance: The Politics of War Crimes Tribunals* (Princeton, NJ: Princeton University Press, 2000); Christopher Rudolph, "Constructing an Atrocities Regime: The Politics of War Crimes Tribunals," *International Organization* 55, no. 3 (Summer 2001): 655–691, https://doi.org/10.1162/00208180152507588; Jo M. Pasqualucci, *The Practice and Procedure of the Inter-American Court of Human Rights* (Cambridge, UK: Cambridge University Press, 2003); Michael D. Goldhaber, *A People's History of the European Court of Human Rights* (New Brunswick, NJ: Rutgers University Press, 2007); Jelena Subotić, *Hijacked Justice: Dealing with the Past in the Balkans* (Ithaca, NY: Cornell University Press, 2009).

[12] Henry A. Kissinger, "The Pitfalls of Universal Jurisdiction," *Foreign Affairs* 80, no. 4 (July–August 2001): 86–96, https://doi.org/10.2307/20050228.

[13] Bernard Duhaime, "Canada and the Inter-American Human Rights System: Time to Become a Full Player," *International Journal* 67, no. 3 (Summer 2012): 639–659, https://doi.org//10.1177/0020702012067000306.

[14] See, among many others, Laurence R. Helfer, "Overlegalizing Human Rights: International Relations Theory and the Commonwealth Caribbean Backlash against Human Rights Regimes," *Columbia Law Review* 102, no. 7 (November 2002): 1832–1911, https://doi.org/10.2307/1123662; Yuval Shany, "No Longer a Weak Department of Power? Reflections on the Emergence of a New International Judiciary," *European Journal of International Law* 20, no. 1 (February 2009): 73–91, https://doi.org/10.1093/ejil/chn081; Karen J. Alter, *The New Terrain of International Law: Courts, Politics, Rights* (Princeton, NJ: Princeton University Press, 2014); Andreas Follesdal and Geir Ulfstein, eds., *The Judicialization of International Law: A Mixed Blessing?* (Oxford: Oxford University Press, 2018); Courtney Hillebrecht and Alexandra Huneeus, with Sandra Borda, "The Judicialization of Peace," *Harvard International Law Journal* 59, no. 2 (Summer 2018): 279–330, https://ssrn.com/abstract=3227107.

[15] C. Neal Tate and Torbjörn Vallinder, eds., *The Global Expansion of Judicial Power* (New York: New York University Press, 1995); James Meernik, "Justice and Peace? How the International Criminal Tribunal Affects Societal Peace in Bosnia," *Journal of Peace Research* 42, no. 3 (May 2005): 271–289, https://doi.org/10.1177/0022343305052012; Ran Hirschl, "The Judicialization of Mega-Politics and the Rise of Political Courts," *Annual Review of Political Science* 11 (2008): 93–118, https://10.1146/annurev.polisci.11.053006.183906; Payam Akhavan, "Are International Criminal Tribunals a Disincentive to Peace? Reconciling Judicial Romanticism with Political Realism," *Human Rights Quarterly* 31, no. 3 (August 2009): 624–654, https://doi.org/10.1353/hrq.0.0096; Paul K. Huth, Sarah E. Croco, and Benjamin J. Appel, "Does International Law Promote the Peaceful Settlement of International Disputes? Evidence from the Study of Territorial Conflicts since 1945," *American Political Science*

Proponents of these trends hold up international human rights and criminal tribunals as proof of a growing normative consensus around accountability, the rule of law, and human rights. These same proponents hail the growing authority and capacity of international tribunals to investigate allegations of abuse, to try the accused, and to offer accountability and reparations to victims.[16] Yet, opponents, both new and old, of the international human rights and criminal law regimes point to the judicialization and increased legalization of human rights and accountability as examples of Western bias, elitism, and the inefficient bureaucratization of global politics.

Overview of the Problem

While resistance to international courts is not new, what is new, or at least newly conceptualized, is the politics of backlash to these institutions. This book asks – and answers – three main questions about backlash politics:

1. What is backlash and what forms does it take?
2. Why do states and elites engage in backlash against international human rights and criminal courts?
3. What can stakeholders and supporters of international justice do about these contemporary challenges?

To answer these questions, I take a broad theoretical and empirical scope. Building on the research from the human rights, international law, international relations, and political science fields, this book offers a multidimensional theoretical framework that guides our understanding of what backlash is, how it

---

Review 105, no. 2 (May 2011): 415–436, https://doi.org/10.1017/S0003055411000062; Hillebrecht and Huneeus, with Borda "The Judicialization of Peace."

[16] See, among many others, Payam Akhavan, "The International Criminal Court in Context: Mediating the Global and Local in the Age of Accountability," *The American Journal of International Law* 97, no. 3 (July 2003): 712–721, https://doi.org/10.2307/3109871; Clara Sandoval-Villalba, "The Concepts of 'Injured Party' and 'Victim' of Gross Human Rights Violations in the Jurisprudence of the Inter-American Court of Human Rights: A Commentary on Their Implications for Reparations," in *Reparations for Victims of Genocide, War Crimes and Crimes against Humanity: Systems in Place and Systems in the Making*, eds. Carla Ferstman, Mariana Goetz, and Alan Stephens (Leiden, The Netherlands: Koninklijke Brill NV, 2009), 243–282; Philipp Kastner, "Towards Internalized Legal Obligations to Address Justice and Accountability? A Novel Perspective on the Legal Framework of Peace Negotiations," *Criminal Law Forum* 23, no. 1–3 (September 2012): 193–221, https://doi.org/10.1007/s10609-012-9174-4; Kate Cronin-Furman, "Managing Expectations: International Criminal Trials and the Prospects for Deterrence of Mass Atrocity," *International Journal of Transitional Justice* 7, no. 3 (November 2013): 434–454, https://doi.org/10.1093/ijtj/ijt016; James Meernik, "The International Criminal Court and the Deterrence of Human Rights Atrocities," *Civil Wars* 17, no. 3 (2015a): 318–339, https://doi.org/10.1080/13698249.2015.1100350.

manifests, and why it occurs, all based on the concept of authority in international adjudication. Moving well beyond the single case studies that have thus far dominated much of the discussion of backlash against human rights and criminal tribunals, *Saving the International Justice Regime* examines backlash politics across two legal regimes – the international human rights and criminal regimes; three court systems – the European Court of Human Rights, the Inter-American Human Rights System, and the ICC; and three continents and nearly a dozen countries. Chapter 2 provides in-depth information about the book's theoretical framework, empirical approach, and case selection.

Through this broad set of cases and interdisciplinary theoretical framework, this book advances the current thinking about backlash to international courts. In particular, *Saving the International Justice Regime* makes three contributions related to the study of backlash:

1. It provides a new definition and typology of backlash against international human rights and criminal tribunals.
2. It offers an interdisciplinary, multipronged theoretical framework that guides the empirical discussion of backlash politics across a broad scope of cases.
3. It generates a set of concrete policy recommendations to help international justice stakeholders safeguard international human rights and criminal tribunals.

Backlash, as I understand it, is more than noncooperation and noncompliance. It is a sustained attack on the tribunals that fundamentally challenges their structural, adjudicative, and moral authority. I take backlash to mean the politics of states and individual political leaders' seeking to undermine and subvert the tribunals by working within the judicialized and legalized landscape of international human rights and criminal law.

Backlash politics threaten both the institutional capacity of the tribunals as well as the norms upon which they are built. At its core, backlash is the result of Western liberal democracies and the tribunals' stakeholders simultaneously overestimating the ability of human rights and criminal courts to restrain state power and underestimating the ability of other powerful actors to usurp these institutions.[17] A global retrenchment of democratic norms has only exacerbated these trends.[18]

---

[17] Daniel Abebe and Tom Ginsburg, "The Dejudicialization of International Politics?" *International Studies Quarterly* 63, no. 3 (September 2019): 521–530, https://doi.org/10.1093/isq/sqz032.

[18] Eric A. Posner, "Liberal Internationalism and the Populist Backlash," *University of Chicago Public Law & Legal Theory Paper Series*, no. 606 (2017), https://doi.org/10.2139/ssrn.2898357; Bruce Jones and Torrey Taussig, "Democracy & Disorder: The Struggle for Influence in the

RESISTANCE, RESENTMENT, AND RETRENCHMENT IN GLOBAL POLITICS

While the end of the Cold War brought with it a certain optimism about the future of democracy and human rights, the global war on terror and the more recent turn to populism has threatened the gains made in those areas. From Viktor Orbán in Hungary to Jair Bolsonaro in Brazil to Donald Trump in the United States (USA), leaders across the world have abandoned global governance and the liberal democratic order upon which it rests. This includes, but is not limited to, the international justice regime.

Resistance and retrenchment in global politics reflects a broader rejection of – and disdain for – the rule of law, democratic principles, and basic human rights. The World Justice Project's Rule of Law Index indicates that declines in the rule of law marked nearly every corner of the globe between 2015 and 2020.[19] Growing disaffected with democracy and its unmet promises, voters in Asia, Europe, Latin America, the United States, and beyond have ushered in a wave of populist governments, intent on reversing the democratic gains of the last century.[20] According to the Varieties of Democracy (V-Dem) project, in 2019, for the first time in nearly twenty years, the number of autocracies exceeded that of democracies.[21] Rates of repression against civil society have increased, as have restrictions on the media and free speech.[22] Attacks on democratic liberal institutions and on the procedural consensus upon which democracy is built have only escalated in recent years.[23]

Attacks against liberal institutions and norms have been met with resistance. Although V-Dem described 2019 as a year in which major democracies risked sliding into autocracies, their data also revealed that 2019 brought more resistance and prodemocratic protests than in previous years. Nearly half of

---

New Geopolitics," *Brookings Institute*, February 2019, https://www.brookings.edu/research/democracy-disorder-the-struggle-for-influence-in-the-new-geopolitics/.

[19] "WJP Rule of Law Index 2020," World Justice Project, n.d., https://worldjusticeproject.org/rule-of-law-index/.

[20] Yun-han Chu et al., "A Lost Decade for Third-Wave Democracies?" *Journal of Democracy* 31, no. 2 (April 2020): 166–181, https://journalofdemocracy.org/articles/a-lost-decade-for-third-wave-democracies/.

[21] Anna Lührmann et al., "Authoritarian Surges–Resistance Grows: Democracy Report 2020," *Varieties of Democracy (V-Dem)*, 2020, https://www.v-dem.net/en/publications/democracy-reports/.

[22] Lührmann et al., "Authoritarian Surges."

[23] Claudia Landwehr, "Backlash against the Procedural Consensus," *The British Journal of Politics and International Relations* 22, no. 4 (November 2020): 598–608, https://doi.org/10.1177/1369148120946981.

all countries were host to prodemocratic protests in 2019, up from only a quarter in 2009.[24]

It is against this backdrop of democratic retrenchment and resistance that backlash against the international justice regime plays out. Backlash against international human rights and criminal courts can, of course, be part of a larger, wholesale rejection of the rule of law, democratic liberalism, and global governance. But, backlash against the international justice regime also can be more restrained in both targets and tactics. The definition and typology of backlash below offer guiding principles for how backlash against international human rights and criminal tribunals fits into both the extraordinary politics of existential threats to the global order as well as more restrained – and even mundane – assaults on specific norms, ideals, and institutions.

Understanding Backlash: A Guide to the Chapter

The rest of this chapter proceeds as follows. It begins by outlining how international human rights and criminal tribunals work and from whence international courts derive their authority. It is only by understanding international courts' authority, and its precariousness, that scholars and stakeholders can understand what backlash against these courts is, how it manifests, why it occurs, and what to do about it. The centerpiece of the chapter is the unique and novel definition and typology of backlash against human rights and criminal tribunals that follows the discussion of authority. This typology also provides the organizational schema for the empirical chapters in the book. Following a discussion of the definition and typology, the chapter turns to a preview of the remainder of the book.

HOW INTERNATIONAL HUMAN RIGHTS AND CRIMINAL TRIBUNALS WORK: AUTHORITY IN CONTEXT

The international justice regime is fertile ground for exploring various forms of backlash, the multiple drivers of backlash politics, and the variety of actors that can engage in backlash against international courts. International human rights and criminal courts occupy a unique nexus between the international and domestic spheres. International human rights courts litigate the relationship between states and constituents. International criminal courts, meanwhile, attempt to hold domestic political elites accountable based on ineffable international accountability norms. This positioning makes the international

---

[24] Lührmann et al., "Authoritarian Surges."

justice regime an easy target for populist, nationalist, and authoritarian leaders. Moreover, because of their focus on liberal democratic human rights and accountability norms, international human rights and criminal courts are the crown jewels of the liberal democratic world order, and are thus especially vulnerable to backlash politics.

The international justice regime has experienced a panoply of backlash politics, from threatened withdrawals to near bankrupting to doctrinal challenges and more. International human rights and criminal courts are regularly on the receiving end of toxic vitriol and are the subject of countless angry op-eds. Understanding backlash against the international justice regime is critical for scholars, stakeholders, and supporters alike. Not only is the international justice regime important in its own right, but its experience with such a wide array of backlash politics can prove instructive for better understanding backlash against the global order more broadly.

The International Justice Regime: An Overview

The international human rights and criminal justice regime is expansive, covering nearly all corners of the globe and a wide array of individual and collective rights. All of the courts that are embedded in this regime, broadly speaking, share a set of common goals: demanding accountability for human rights abuses, whether during times of war or peace; providing reparations for victims; deterring future violence; and upholding normative standards of human rights and dignity. Both international human rights and criminal courts promote a vision of (nearly) universal human rights, one in which individuals are endowed with inherent and inalienable rights, regardless of how much power their state yields.

The regional human rights courts in Africa, the Americas, and Europe have their roots in international human rights law, including both civil and political rights, as well as economic, social, and cultural rights. The tribunals' legal ambit is broad and the list of rights protected by these courts is long, ranging from the right to fair trial to intellectual property rights. These courts are part of regional organizations, like the African Union, the Council of Europe (COE), and the Organization of American States (OAS). States ratify regional human rights conventions, which then bind them to the jurisdictional powers of the tribunals. In doing so, states open themselves up for the adjudication of complaints brought by individuals against their government.[25]

---

[25] Vanda Lamm, *Compulsory Jurisdiction in International Law* (Cheltenham, UK: Edward Elgar, 2014).

These tribunals reconceive the very notion of state sovereignty. While other forms of international law, such as international trade or security law, are based on the principle of reciprocity and address how governments treat each other, international human rights law concerns how governments treat their citizens. Human rights courts, however, upend that relationship by allowing individuals to file petitions against their governments at these courts. States, in turn, agree to be subject to rulings based on petitions brought by an individual plaintiff and handed down by an international court. While the regional courts are now a staple of international human rights law, it is important not to lose sight of the radical experiment with sovereignty that they represent.[26]

International criminal tribunals have a different objective, of course, but one that is related to the broader mandate of upholding individuals' rights when governments fail to do so. International criminal tribunals are focused on individual criminal responsibility rather than state responsibility. The range of violations over which they have jurisdiction is often much narrower than those adjudicated at the human rights tribunals and typically includes war crimes, crimes against humanity, and genocide.[27] International criminal courts aim to convict the worst perpetrators of the worst crimes. Underlying their mission is the idea that some human rights norms are inviolate. These *jus cogens* norms are few and far between (e.g., genocide, torture, and war crimes), but given their severity and the fact that they "deeply shock the conscience of humanity"[28] these norms, advocates argue, cannot be limited by time or space. They can be tried anywhere, from the halls of the ICC to the Extraordinary Chambers in the Courts of Cambodia (ECCC).[29] Sovereignty and head of state immunity cannot shelter perpetrators from accountability for the crimes they committed, or so the thinking goes.[30]

---

[26] Jost Delbrück, "International Protection of Human Rights and State Sovereignty," *Indiana Law Journal* 57, no. 4 (Fall 1982): 567–578, https://www.repository.law.indiana.edu/cgi/view content.cgi?article=2302&context=ilj; Michael P. Donnelly, "Democracy and Sovereignty vs International Human Rights: Reconciling the Irreconcilable?" *The International Journal of Human Rights* (April 2018): 1–22, https://doi.org/10.1080/13642987.2018.1454904; Daniel W. Hill, "Why Governments Cede Sovereignty: Evidence from Regional Human Rights Courts," *Foreign Policy Analysis* 14, no. 3 (July 2018): 299–325, https://doi.org/10.1093/fpa/orwo31.

[27] Collectively I refer to these as "atrocity crimes."

[28] "Rome Statute of the International Criminal Court," entered into force July 1, 2002, *United Nations Treaty Series* 2187 no. 38544.

[29] This is to say nothing of the principle of universal jurisdiction as it manifests in national trials.

[30] Kenneth Roth, "The Case for Universal Jurisdiction," *Foreign Affairs* 80, no. 5 (September–October 2001): 150–154, https://doi.org/10.2307/20050258; Ellen L. Lutz and Caitlin Reiger, eds., *Prosecuting Heads of State* (Cambridge, UK: Cambridge University Press, 2009).

The international criminal tribunals' relationship to states is also different than that of the regional human rights tribunals. In the case of the ICC, states can ratify the Rome Statute, which then means that the ICC can bring their leaders to trial, either through self-referrals from the states or the referral powers of the ICC Prosecutor. The United Nations Security Council (UNSC) also can refer cases, a process I discuss in more detail below.[31] In the case of the International Criminal Tribunal for Rwanda (ICTR) and the International Criminal Tribunal for the former Yugoslavia (ICTY), the United Nations (UN) created and paid for the tribunals, with varying levels of state consent. For the so-called hybrid tribunals in Cambodia, Lebanon, and Sierra Leone, the state and the UN collaborated on creating and running the courts.[32]

From Whence the Power of International Courts

There is a broad and lively scholarly debate about the authority of international courts, as well as about the very concept of authority itself. While there are multiple ways of categorizing this scholarly dialogue, the scholarship on the authority of international courts generally falls into three categories: formalist and structural accounts of authority; accounts of authority derived from the courts' performance; and normative and sociolegal approaches to authority.[33] Formalist and structural approaches suggest that international courts derive their authority from the basic tenets of principal–agent theory. The principals, which are the member states, create international courts to adjudicate on their behalf. Scholars operating in this tradition emphasize the structural relationship between states and international courts, particularly the degree of independence international courts enjoy.[34]

---

[31] The ways in which cases get brought to the ICC complicates, somewhat, this relationship.

[32] "International and Hybrid Criminal Courts and Tribunals," United Nations and the Rule of Law, n.d., https://www.un.org/ruleoflaw/thematic-areas/international-law-courts-tribunals/international-hybrid-criminal-courts-tribunals/.

[33] This understanding of authority collapses and modifies Alter, Helfer, and Madsen's typology into three categories down from four. Karen Alter, Laurence R. Helfer, and Mikael Rask Madsen, "How Context Shapes the Authority of International Courts," *Law and Contemporary Problems* 79, no. 1 (2016): 1–36, https://scholarship.law.duke.edu/lcp/vol79/iss1/1/; Karen Alter, Laurence R. Helfer, and Mikael Rask Madsen, eds., *International Court Authority* (Oxford: Oxford University Press, 2018).

[34] Barbara Koremenos, Charles Lipson, and Duncan Snidal, "The Rational Design of International Institutions," *International Organization* 55, no. 4 (Autumn 2001): 761–799, https://doi.org/10.1162/002081801317193592; Judith Goldstein et al., "Introduction: Legalization and World Politics," *International Organization* 54, no. 3 (Summer 2000): 385–399, https://doi

The second camp of rationalist scholars views international courts' authority as stemming from their performance. Do states comply with their judgments? Participate in the processes? In these academic debates, authority is often linked to, if not equated with, effectiveness.[35] While it might be unlikely for a court lacking in authority to induce compliance or to be "effective," these ideas are conceptually and practically distinct and need to be treated as such.

Normative and sociolegal approaches to international court authority shift the emphasis from the structure and performance of international tribunals to the practice and shared meaning between the courts and their constituents. Courts derive their authority through their perceived legitimacy from stakeholders and participants. Authority is contingent on both context and usage. Scholars writing in this vein suggest that the authority of international courts is predicated on the types of obligations, or duties, they impose on states and participants and the degree to which those obligations are deemed obligatory and "fair" in a given context.[36]

In their recent edited volume, Alter, Helfer, and Madsen advance a definition of court authority that is practice-based, taking into account the political, legal, and social impacts of the tribunals on their audiences.[37] Their emphasis on the de facto authority of the courts, as reflected in the observable behaviors of courts' audiences, is an amalgamation of the three aforementioned approaches with an eye toward generalizability and empirical applications.

.org/10.1162/002081800551262; Ronald B. Mitchell and Patricia M. Keilbach, "Situation Structure and Institutional Design: Reciprocity, Coercion, and Exchange," *International Organization* 55, no. 4 (Autumn 2001): 891–917, https://doi.org/10.1162/002081801317193637; B. Peter Rosendorff, "Stability and Rigidity: Politics and Design of the WTO's Dispute Settlement Procedure," *American Political Science Review* 99, no. 3 (August 2005): 389–400, https://doi.org/10.1017/S0003055405051737.

35 Yuval Shany, *Assessing the Effectiveness of International Courts* (Oxford: Oxford University Press, 2014).

36 Başak Çali, *The Authority of International Law: Obedience, Respect, and Rebuttal* (Oxford: Oxford University Press, 2015); Başak Çali, Anne Koch, and Nicola Bruch, "The Legitimacy of Human Rights Courts: A Grounded Interpretivist Analysis of the European Court of Human Rights," *Human Rights Quarterly* 35, no. 4 (November 2013): 955–984, https://doi.org/10.1353/hrq.2013.0057; Kamari M. Clarke, Abel S. Knottnerus, and Eefje de Volder, "Africa and the ICC: An Introduction," in *Africa and the ICC: Perceptions of Justice*, eds. Kamari M. Clarke, Abel S. Knottnerus, and Eefje de Volder (Cambridge, UK: Cambridge University Press, 2016), 1–36; Kieran McEvoy, "Beyond Legalism: Towards a Thicker Understanding of Transitional Justice," *Journal of Law and Society* 34, no. 4 (December 2007): 411–440, https://doi.org/10.1111/j.1467-6478.2007.00399.x; Kamari Maxine Clarke, *Fictions of Justice: The International Criminal Court and the Challenge of Legal Pluralism in Sub-Saharan Africa* (New York: Cambridge University Press, 2009).

37 Alter, Helfer, and Madsen, *International Court Authority*.

This book takes a similar approach, although rather than trying to assess how authority is expressed or measured, I emphasize the sources, or origins, of international courts' authority. Broadly speaking, the goal of the attacks on the liberal world order is to undermine the authority of the norms and institutions that support it, including international human rights and criminal courts. As such, any analysis of backlash must begin by asking: from whence do these institutions derive their authority?

Building on the existing scholarship on international courts' authority, this book focuses on three sources of court authority: (1) their structural relationship with states, including both their independence from member states as well as their abiding reliance on those principals; (2) the act of adjudicating and the subsequent state responses; and (3) their normative high ground, drawn from both the norms on which they adjudicate as well as their legal expertise, which generates and advances human rights and criminal accountability norms.[38] This typology of authority provides a wide-angle view of the origin of courts' authority and, relatedly, the dimensions of international courts' authority that are most vulnerable to backlash politics. In the remainder of this section, I discuss each source of authority in turn.

Principals and Agents: Power from Structure

As noted above, formalist, also called structuralist or functionalist, approaches to international adjudication suggest that international courts, like other international organizations, derive their authority from their relationship to member states. States, acting as principals, contract with the agents – the tribunals – to solve collective action problems.[39] This means that states design

---

[38]   See, among others, Tate and Vallinder, *The Global Expansion of Judicial Power*; Ian Hurd, "Legitimacy and Authority in International Politics," *International Organization* 53, no. 2 (Spring 1999): 379–408, https://doi.org/10.1162/002081899550913; Karen J. Alter, "Agents or Trustees? International Courts in Their Political Context," *European Journal of International Relations* 14, no. 1 (March 2008): 33–63, https://doi.org/10.1177/1354066107087769; Laurence R. Helfer and Karen J. Alter, "Legitimacy and Lawmaking: A Tale of Three International Courts," *Theoretical Inquiries in Law* 14, no. 2 (July 2013): 479–504, https://doi.org/10.1515/til-2013-024; Ingo Venzke, "Understanding the Authority of International Courts and Tribunals: On Delegation and Discursive Construction," *Theoretical Inquiries in Law* 14, no. 2 (2013): 381–410, https://doi.org/10.1515/til-2013-020; Alter, Helfer, and Madsen, "How Context Shapes the Authority of International Courts"; Leslie Vinjamuri, "The International Criminal Court and the Paradox of Authority," *Law and Contemporary Problems* 79, no. 1 (2016): 275–287, https://scholarship.law.duke.edu/lcp/vol79/iss1/10.

[39]   Karen J. Alter, "Who Are the Masters of the Treaty? European Governments and the European Court of Justice," *International Organization* 52, no. 1 (Winter 1998): 121–147, https://doi.org/10.1162/002081898550572; Alter, "Agents or Trustees?"; Rachel Cichowski,

and engage with courts that have the independence and authority to try cases concerning their policies and practices. By delegating authority to such a court, states not only signal a credible commitment to conflict resolution but also bind their own hands in the case of future disputes.[40]

One way that international courts fulfill their credible commitment function is through the principle of compulsory jurisdiction. Compulsory jurisdiction is the understanding that once a state accepts the authority of a court, it cannot pick and choose which cases it will allow the court to hear and must instead abide by all of the courts' rulings.[41] States are bound by the courts that they create.

In practice, compulsory jurisdiction means states must formally accept the jurisdiction of international courts, which then adjudicate disputes between member states, and, in the case of human rights courts, between member states and constituents. In the case of the Inter-American Court of Human Rights, for example, a handful of states, including the United States, Canada, and much of the English-speaking Caribbean, have *not* agreed to the jurisdiction of the Inter-American Court of Human Rights. This means that although these states are part of the Organization of American States, which is the umbrella organization under which the Inter-American Court of Human Rights operates, the IACtHR cannot entertain petitions against them, nor are they bound by any *erga omnes partes* effects of the IACtHR's jurisprudence.

Much like the regional courts, the conflict-specific international criminal tribunals also require that states grant them the authority to pursue cases against suspected perpetrators. The principal–agent dynamic is somewhat less evident here than in the case of the regional courts. Often, but not always, the individual political elites negotiating with the United Nations about the creation of a criminal court are the victors of a conflict, and thus not likely to

"Civil Society and the European Court of Human Rights," APSA 2010 *Annual Meeting Paper* (2010), https://papers.ssrn.com/abstract=1643604.

40   Laurence R. Helfer and Anne-Marie Slaughter, "Toward a Theory of Effective Supranational Adjudication," *Yale Law Journal* 107 (1997): 273–392, http://papers.ssrn.com/sol3/papers.cfm?abstract_id=131409; Goldstein et al., "Introduction: Legalization and World Politics"; Koremenos, Lipson, and Snidal, "The Rational Design of International Institutions"; Anne-Marie Slaughter, "A Global Community of Courts," *Harvard International Law Journal* 44, no. 1 (Winter 2003): 191–219, https://heinonline.org/HOL/P?h=hein.journals/hilj44&i=197; Laurence R. Helfer, "Why States Create International Tribunals: A Theory of Constrained Independence," in *Conferences on New Political Economy: Vol. 23: International Conflict Resolution*, eds. Stefan Voigt, Max Albert, and Dieter Schmidtchen (Tübingen, Germany: Mohr Siebeck, 2006), 253–276.

41   Lamm, *Compulsory Jurisdiction in International Law*. See Chapters 2 and 3 for a more in-depth discussion of compulsory jurisdiction.

be held accountable by the tribunal to which they are agreeing.[42] In some cases, such as the Special Tribunal for Lebanon, a lack of domestic political consensus on the creation of the court paved the way for a UN-initiated tribunal, the very fact of which has been a rallying cry for the court's opponents over the years.[43]

The International Criminal Court takes this principal–agent relationship and complicates it further. As noted above, the ICC can garner cases through three mechanisms: self-referrals, which abide by the basic tenets of the aforementioned principal–agent relationship; the ICC Prosecutor's so-called *propio motu* powers; and UN Security Council referrals. The majority of situations get to the ICC by way of states' self-referrals. This is when states ask the ICC to investigate abuses that they are unable or unwilling to investigate and adjudicate domestically. Self-referrals are also avenues for deploying the international legal lasso to remove potential political spoilers.[44]

A second mechanism by which cases get to the ICC is the Office of the Prosecutor's (OTP's) ability to bring cases through the *propio motu* mechanism. This mechanism allows the Prosecutor to open an investigation into allegations of atrocity crimes in member states. When states ratify the Rome Statute and accept the jurisdiction of the ICC, they also accept the OTP's *propio motu* powers.

The third mechanism of generating ICC cases is through UN Security Council referral, which allows the UNSC to refer any situation it deems necessary to the ICC, even if the alleged crimes do not take place within or by a Rome Statute member state. In this instance, then, states that have not accepted the jurisdiction of the ICC may still find their leaders called before the court. To date, this has happened only

---

[42] Public Information and Communication Section, "STL Close-Up," *Special Tribunal for Lebanon*, May 30, 2007, www.stl-tsl.org/images/stories/About/STL_Close-up_EN.pdf; Victor Peskin, *International Justice in Rwanda and the Balkans: Virtual Trials and the Struggle for State Cooperation* (New York: Cambridge University Press, 2008); Tessa Allebas, "The ICC and Victor's Justice: How to Move Away from the Stigma?" *The Hague Institute for Global Justice*, July 19, 2013, www.thehagueinstituteforglobaljustice.org/latest-insights/latest-insights/commentary/the-icc-and-victors-justice-how-to-move-away-from-the-stigma/; Courtney Hillebrecht and Scott Straus, "Who Pursues the Perpetrators?: State Cooperation with the ICC," *Human Rights Quarterly* 39, no. 1 (February 2017): 162–188, https://doi.org/10.1353/hrq.2017.0006.

[43] Benedetta Berti, "Peace vs. Justice in Lebanon: The Domestic and Regional Implications of the UN Special Tribunal," *Strategic Assessment* 13, no. 4 (January 2011): 101–111, https://strategicassessment.inss.org.il/en/articles/peace-vs-justice-in-the-domestic-and-regional-implications-of-the-un-special-tribunal/.

[44] Hillebrecht and Straus, "Who Pursues the Perpetrators?"

twice, first with respect to the situation in Darfur[45] and, second, with respect to the situation in Libya.[46] In both instances, the leadership in Sudan and Libya, as well as their allies across Africa and beyond, pointed to the ways in which these courts violate sovereignty rights and do not have the legal or moral authority to pursue this form of justice. The UNSC referral mechanism operates outside of the principal–agent framework, as these states have expressly not agreed to the ICC's authority. It is precisely because of this arrangement that these two UNSC-initiated cases have erupted in such a firestorm. For those indicted and their allies, the authority of the ICC has been corrupted by the power of the UNSC.[47]

The structural relationships between international courts and states endow the courts with authority to rule on cases against their principals. At the same time, however, this relationship creates the tribunals' abiding dependence on states. While courts vary in their independence from member states, no court, and particularly no human rights or criminal court, can ever fully escape its reliance on its member states. This dependency, in turn, becomes a major driver of backlash politics.

Authority through the Act of Adjudicating

In addition to their structural power, human rights and criminal tribunals derive their authority from the act of adjudicating.[48] This approach to understanding international courts' authority is similar to the aforementioned

---

45 United Nations Security Council Resolution 1593 (United Nations Security Council, 2005).

46 United Nations Security Council Resolution 1970 (United Nations Security Council, 2011).

47 Bethel Aregawi, "The Politicisation of the International Criminal Court by United Nations Security Council Referral," *Conflict Trends*, ACCORD, no. 2 (2017), https://www.accord.org.za /conflict-trends/politicisation-international-criminal-court-united-nations-security-council- referrals/.

48 Allison Marston Danner, "Enhancing the Legitimacy and Accountability of Prosecutorial Discretion at the International Criminal Court," *The American Journal of International Law* 97, no. 3 (July 2003): 510–552, https://doi.org/10.2307/3109838; Armin von Bogdandy, "The Democratic Legitimacy of International Courts: A Conceptual Framework," *Theoretical Inquiries in Law* 14, no. 2 (2013): 361–380, https://doi.org/10.1515/til-2013-019; Armin von Bogdandy and Ingo Venzke, "On the Functions of International Courts: An Appraisal in Light of Their Burgeoning Public Authority," *Leiden Journal of International Law* 26, no. 1 (March 2013): 49–72, https://doi.org/10.1017/S0922156512000647; Andreas Follesdal, "The Legitimacy Deficits of the Human Rights Judiciary: Elements and Implications of a Normative Theory," *Theoretical Inquiries in Law* 14, no. 2 (2013): 339–360, https://doi.org/10 .1515/til-2013-018; Helfer and Alter, "Legitimacy and Lawmaking"; Yonatan Lupu, "International Judicial Legitimacy: Lessons from National Courts," *Theoretical Inquiries in Law* 14, no. 2 (2013): 437–454, https://doi.org/10.1515/til-2013-022; Shany, *Assessing the Effectiveness of International Courts*.

scholarship on international courts' performance.[49] It is not enough for a court to simply exist on paper. Rather, by exercising their power to try cases and hold states and perpetrators to account, international courts generate adjudicative authority. This adjudicative authority includes upholding due process and prioritizing robust legal standards, handing down judgments and punishments, issuing reparations, facilitating compliance, and serving as a deterrent against future abuses.

While a court's adjudicative authority is central to its role as a judicial institution, this form of authority is easily undermined. For example, when the courts experience major breaches in their legal procedures, whether that means an ICC judge holding a diplomatic post at the same time as serving on the bench or Hezbollah breaching the confidentiality of witnesses and victims at the STL, the implications reach far beyond that particular case.[50]

In a similar vein, courts garner adjudicative authority through enforcing compliance orders and meting out punishments. In the case of international criminal tribunals, however, the punishments are often laughably lax, at least from the perspective of outsiders and victims. Consider, for example, the ICC's first conviction against Thomas Lubanga Dyilo. Despite being convicted for conscripting child soldiers into a long and bloody conflict in the Democratic Republic of the Congo (DRC), Mr. Lubanga was sentenced to only fourteen years in prison.[51] Meanwhile, compliance with international court rulings often remains elusive.[52] When the courts can coerce or convince states to pay reparations to victims, change their human rights policies or hand over suspects, they demonstrate to a wider audience that they have power vis-à-vis the state. And, of course, the opposite is true – and arguably more common.[53] When cases are disrupted, reparations go unpaid, policies go unchanged, and wanted perpetrators walk freely without fear of arrest, the courts' adjudicative authority is diminished.

---

[49] See Shany, *Assessing the Effectiveness of International Courts.*

[50] Mark Leon Goldberg, "Special Tribunal for Lebanon Files Indictment. Hezbollah on Notice," *UN Dispatch* (blog), January 17, 2011, https://www.undispatch.com/special-tribunal-for-lebanon-files-indictment-hezbollah/; Svirsky, "Hezbollah Intimidates Witnesses in Hariri Murder Tribunal"; Kevin Jon Heller, "Judge Ozaki Must Resign – Or Be Removed," *Opinio Juris*, March 29, 2019, http://opiniojuris.org/2019/03/29/judge-ozaki-must-resign-or-be-removed/.

[51] Situation in the Democratic Republic of the Congo in the Case of the *Prosecutor* v. *Thomas Lubanga Dyilo*, Decision on Sentence Pursuant to Article 76 of the Statute, No. ICC-01/04-01/06 (Trial Chamber I of the International Criminal Court, July 10, 2012).

[52] Clifford James Carrubba and Matthew Joseph Gabel, "Courts, Compliance, and the Quest for Legitimacy in International Law," *Theoretical Inquiries in Law* 14, no. 2 (2013): 505–542, https://doi.org/10.1515/til-2013-025.

[53] See, for example, Subotić, *Hijacked Justice.*

Authority through the Normative High Ground

In addition to their adjudicative capacity, human rights and criminal tribunals possess a certain moral and normative authority. The tribunals derive their normative and moral authority from their technical knowledge of the law, which advances and generates human rights and accountability norms, as well as the (near) consensus around the norms upon which they are founded.[54]

International human rights and criminal tribunals are based on shared norms about rights and accountability. They share a collective belief that the perpetrators of human rights and atrocity crimes should be held accountable; that victims should receive reparations; that the rule of law should be upheld; and that international institutions can and should deter future atrocities. Of course, the normative consensus upon which the international justice regime is built is not without cracks in its foundation.[55] States, political elites, and other stakeholders do not all agree about the scope of rights that should fall under these courts' jurisdictions, nor do they agree about precisely how these courts should adjudicate cases. The interpretation of international law and the courts' mandates on the domestic level is rife with contestation and negotiation.[56] The "consensus" then is actually quite fragile, and the fissures within the normative framework are ripe for exploitation.

In addition to preserving the norms on which they were built, the tribunals continuously enhance those normative foundations. The tribunals and the lawyers, judges, and bureaucrats who work there are keepers of a vast, collective wealth of knowledge about human rights and criminal accountability. The courts guard massive archives of information about particular cases as well as

[54] Hurd, "Legitimacy and Authority in International Politics"; Michael Barnett and Martha Finnemore, *Rules for the World: International Organizations in Global Politics* (Ithaca, NY: Cornell University Press, 2004); Başak Çali, "Perceptions of the Authority of the European Court of Human Rights amongst Apex Court Judges in the UK, Germany, Ireland, Turkey and Bulgaria: Summary of Findings," *University College London*, 2011, https://ecthrproject.files.wordpress.com/2011/05/domestic-judges-ecthr-summary-findingsbw.pdf; Helfer and Alter, "Legitimacy and Lawmaking"; Alter, Helfer, and Madsen, "How Context Shapes the Authority of International Courts"; Vinjamuri, "The International Criminal Court and the Paradox of Authority."

[55] Courtney Hillebrecht, "Normative Consensus and Contentious Practice: Challenges to Universalism in International Human Rights Courts," *Human Rights Quarterly* 41, no. 1 (February 2019): 190–194, https://doi.org/10.1353/hrq.2019.0010.

[56] Clarke, *Fictions of Justice*; Phil Clark, *Distant Justice: The Impact of the International Criminal Court on African Politics* (Cambridge, UK: Cambridge University Press, 2018); Sally Engle Merry, "Beyond Compliance: Toward an Anthropological Understanding of International Justice," in *Mirrors of Justice: Law and Power in the Post-Cold War Era*, eds. Kamari Maxine Clarke and Mark Goodale (New York: Cambridge University Press, 2010), 28–42.

broader technical knowledge about human rights and international criminal law.[57] In collecting, adjudicating on, and communicating this technical know-how, the tribunals advance and update human rights and criminal accountability norms.

While this expertise can enhance the international courts' legitimacy and authority, this highly rarefied world of international human rights and international accountability also isolates the courts from the constituents they are meant to protect. Indeed, the judicialization of human rights is self-reinforcing and further increases the courts' power by excluding non-judicial actors. While, on the one hand, this creates a barrier between the courts, their principals, and the perpetrators they are meant to try, it also serves to alienate the tribunals from the very people they aim to serve, almost none of whom understand international human rights law, never mind the Byzantine process of adjudicating cases before an international court. This gap can be easy fodder for states and elites looking to undermine the courts and delegitimize them in the eyes of voters, supporters, and even allies.

Summary

International courts derive their authority from three main sources. The first of these, their structural relationship with states, both endows courts with the power to adjudicate but also ties them inextricably to the demands of their stakeholders. This relationship can set the stage for backlash politics. The second source of international courts' authority is through the act of adjudicating. By investigating, hearing, and adjudicating on cases, international courts can bolster their authority, both real and perceived. The challenge comes when states and elites disrupt, dismantle, or disregard the courts' adjudicative functions. Finally, international courts derive their authority from their normative power. What the tribunals and their supporters might view as the moral high ground, however, opponents of international justice view as narratives of neocolonialism and elitism. In brief, it is precisely from the very same avenues that international courts derive their authority that they can be subject to intense backlash.

DEFINING BACKLASH

While concern over the eroding authority of international courts is nearly universal across the human rights and criminal court landscape, scholars, policymakers, and other stakeholders do not share a common definition of

---

[57]   Barnett and Finnemore, *Rules for the World.*

what constitutes backlash. Absent a clear definition of *what* backlash is and a typology of *how* backlash manifests, scholars and stakeholders alike are unable to assess backlash across a range of cases or provide generalizable explanations for why backlash occurs and what to do about it. To put it differently, if the concept of backlash is not clearly defined and operationalized, theorizing about what drives backlash politics is impossible. In this section, I provide a definition of backlash politics and in the section that follows, I offer a novel typology of how it materializes.

Briefly, I conceptualize backlash as having three defining features. First, backlash is neither normatively "bad behavior" nor any and every instance of pushback. Instead, backlash is a sustained effort to undermine international courts' authority. The second defining feature of backlash is that it targets the roots of international courts' authority. Third, backlash against international human rights and criminal courts must be more nuanced than wholesale rejections of the liberal democratic order and traditional sovereignty claims. Fiery rhetoric alone is insufficient; it must be accompanied by action that targets the tribunals' authority. The following discussion elaborates on each of these three features.

The Content of Backlash: Neither Everyday Pushback Nor "Bad Behavior"

In common parlance, the term backlash can cover any manner of sins, and as such, it is easy for stakeholders, scholars, and observers to use the term whenever states fail to comply with a ruling, when political elites bristle at a court's decision, when civil society groups protest a judgment, or when vociferous critics of the liberal democratic world order take to the stage to denounce the very construct of human rights or accountability. Yet, it is important to differentiate between backlash and these adjacent concepts and behaviors.

First, backlash is not necessarily the same as normatively bad behavior. Backlash cannot be any singular incident of noncompliance or noncooperation. Instead, backlash represents a systematic, organized approach that states and political elites take in dealing with the tribunals. It is a concentrated effort to undermine the courts' authority, whether that is through the courts' relationship with states, the act of adjudicating, or the tribunals' normative framework. To put it differently, backlash cannot be reserved to label actions that we, as observers, apply post hoc to behavior that we deem normatively distasteful.

In addition to differentiating between backlash and "bad behavior," it is important to differentiate between backlash and other forms of resistance, pushback, and normative debate. This distinction is arguably more difficult but also more important. International courts are, by definition, sites of contentious politics and normative indeterminacy.[58] Disagreement is a feature, not a bug, of the contentious relationships inherent in international law.[59] Not every instance of pushback or debate is backlash. The following discussion differentiates between backlash against international human rights and criminal courts and the routine forms of resistance that are innate in international adjudication.

Pushback, Resistance, and Backlash

In their definition of backlash to international human rights courts, Madsen, Cebulak, and Wiebusch attempt to disentangle the concepts of backlash and pushback, arguing that individual states' efforts to alter the course of the law (e.g., pushback) is conceptually distinct from backlash (a concerted effort to change or dismantle international courts).[60] It is quite easy to imagine a scenario in which a state fully subscribes to the idea of international human rights adjudication in general and international human rights and criminal courts in particular, and yet disagrees with a specific ruling or set of rulings. Lovat would refer to this type of response to international human rights and criminal adjudication as "common or garden variety" resistance.[61] Soley and Steininger similarly differentiate

---

[58] Martti Koskenniemi, *The Politics of International Law* (Oxford: Hart Publishing, 2011).

[59] For more examples, see Karen J. Alter, James T. Gathii, and Laurence R. Helfer, "Backlash against International Courts in West, East and Southern Africa: Causes and Consequences," *European Journal of International Law* 27, no. 2 (May 2016): 293–328, https://doi.org/10.1093/ejil/chw019; Vinjamuri, "The International Criminal Court and the Paradox of Authority"; Mikael Rask Madsen, Pola Cebulak, and Micha Wiebusch, "Backlash against International Courts: Explaining the Forms and Patterns of Resistance to International Courts," *International Journal of Law in Context* 14, no. 2 (June 2018): 197–220, https://doi.org/10.1017/S1744552318000034; Wayne Sandholtz, Yining Bei, and Kayla Caldwell, "Backlash and International Human Rights Courts," in *Contracting Human Rights: Crisis, Accountability, and Opportunity*, eds. Alison Brysk and Michael Stohl (Cheltenham, UK: Edward Elgar, 2018), 159–178.

[60] Madsen, Cebulak, and Wiebusch, "Backlash against International Courts".

[61] Henry Lovat, "International Criminal Tribunal Backlash," in *The Oxford Handbook of International Criminal Law*, eds. Kevin Jon Heller, Frédéric Mégret, Sarah M. H. Nouwen, Jens David Ohlin, and Darryl Robinson (Oxford: Oxford University Press, 2020). See also Cass R. Sunstein, "Backlash's Travels," *Harvard Civil Rights-Civil Liberties Law Review* 42, no. 2 (Summer 2007): 435–450, https://heinonline.org/HOL/P?h=hein.journals/hcrcl42&i=439; Andreas Hofmann, "Resistance against the Court of Justice of the European Union," *International Journal of Law in Context* 14, no. 2 (June 2018): 258–274, https://doi.org/10.1017

between objection and contestation related to an individual judgment, and resistance and backlash to an institution.[62] In brief, while a pattern of resistance or pushback against a tribunal's rulings can become a form of backlash politics, not every incident of pushback is the conceptual equivalent to backlash.

Noncompliance and Noncooperation

Much like resistance and pushback, noncompliance and noncooperation are ubiquitous in international adjudication. No single example of noncompliance or noncooperation is sufficient to be considered backlash. However, a long-term strategy of noncompliance and noncooperation could fit under the definition of backlash outlined above, assuming that noncompliance or noncooperation was the result of an intentional strategy to undermine an international court and not the lack of domestic implementation capacity.[63] That said, regardless of the reason behind sustained noncompliance or noncooperation, these patterns can spell trouble for international human rights and criminal courts. Repeated noncompliance makes the tribunals appear impotent to enforce the laws that they are designed to enforce, while repeated noncooperation hampers the tribunals' ability to actually conduct the work that they need to do, and leads to more cases and violations.[64]

Norm Contestation

Just as backlash is not the same as pushback or noncompliance, backlash is not the same as norm contestation. A discussion of backlash against international human rights and criminal courts should not take a legal regime without normative debate as the ideal starting point. As noted above, international law is, by definition, contentious. It represents a panoply of ideas, norms, and institutions that are in constant contestation and flux.[65] Not only has international law evolved over time, but it engages nearly 200 individual

/S174455231800006X; Ximena Soley and Silvia Steininger, "Parting Ways or Lashing Back? Withdrawals, Backlash and the Inter-American Court of Human Rights," *International Journal of Law in Context* 14, no. 2 (June 2018): 237–257, https://doi.org/10.1017/S1744552318000058.

[62] Soley and Steininger, "Parting Ways or Lashing Back?"

[63] Madsen, Cebulak, and Wiebusch, "Backlash against International Courts"; Sandholtz, Bei, and Caldwell, "Backlash and International Human Rights Courts"; Erik Voeten, "Populism and Backlashes against International Courts," *Perspectives on Politics* 18, no. 2 (June 2020): 407–422, https://doi.org/10.1017/S1537592719000975.

[64] Peskin, *International Justice in Rwanda and the Balkans.*

[65] Koskenniemi, *The Politics of International Law.*

states, each offering their own experience, preferences, and geopolitical positions. Moreover, reasonable participants can disagree about particular human rights and accountability norms or how they are expressed. In fact, norm contestation can serve to advance the goals of the tribunals and strengthen existing norms by putting them through a rigorous debate and evaluation process.[66]

With that in mind, in Chapter 2, I discuss how normative schisms can lead to backlash politics. In brief, when normative schisms are widened intentionally, core tenets of human rights, accountability, and the rule of law are called into question. When normative discontent is part of a larger campaign to undermine the moral and adjudicative authority of the tribunals, normative contestation tips into backlash. But, as with resistance and pushback, each example of norm contestation is not necessarily backlash. The target of the efforts can help to differentiate between norm contestation and backlash.

The Target: The Authority of International Courts

The second defining feature of backlash is that it must be aimed at a court's authority. This means that backlash politics must be targeted at exploiting the tribunals' relationship to member states, its ability to adjudicate, and/or its normative framework. Sandholtz, Bei, and Caldwell understand backlash much like I do, as a sustained effort to undermine the authority of international courts.[67] Manifestations of backlash, as I discuss in the following section, can take many forms, but they share a similar target: the authority of an international court.

Alter and Zürn argue that one defining feature of backlash is that it has a retrograde objective.[68] They contend that retrograde and regressive are distinctive concepts. The former, they claim, simply means returning to

---

[66]   Nicole Deitelhoff, "What's in a Name? Contestation and Backlash against International Norms and Institutions," *The British Journal of Politics and International Relations* 22, no. 4 (November 2020): 715–727, https://doi.org/10.1177/1369148120945906; Nicole Deitelhoff and Lisbeth Zimmermann, "Things We Lost in the Fire: How Different Types of Contestation Affect the Robustness of International Norms," *International Studies Review* 22, no. 1 (March 2020): 51–76, https://doi.org/10.1093/isr/viy080; Nicole Deitelhoff and Lisbeth Zimmermann, "Norms under Challenge: Unpacking the Dynamics of Norm Robustness," *Journal of Global Security Studies* 4, no. 1 (January 2019): 2–17, https://doi.org/10.1093/jogss/ogy041.

[67]   Sandholtz, Bei, and Caldwell, "Backlash and International Human Rights Courts."

[68]   Karen J. Alter and Michael Zürn, "Conceptualising Backlash Politics: Introduction to a Special Issue on Backlash Politics in Comparison," *The British Journal of Politics and International Relations* 22, no. 4 (November 2020): 563–584, 564, https://doi.org/10.1177/1369148120947958.

a prior condition and is thus stripped of the normative implications of the latter, which can be more easily construed as "backward-looking."[69] This semantic difference, however, is not significant enough to provide real traction on the concept of backlash. As the rest of this book illustrates, a more concrete conceptualization of backlash is that it must be aimed at challenging the authority of international courts and the principles on which they are built, regardless of the directionality – regressive, progressive, retrograde, or otherwise – of the effort.

Undermining Courts' Authority through Action

As the previous discussion outlined, backlash must be a sustained effort targeted at undermining an international human rights or criminal courts' authority. The third defining feature of backlash is that efforts to weaken international courts authority must be based in (costly) action, not just fiery rhetoric about sovereignty or the ills of globalism.

Strong emotions, and particularly indignation and resentment, are frequently attendant to backlash politics.[70] Indeed, both genuine and performative indignation often characterizes the rhetoric that accompanies backlash. While these emotive performances can gain purchase with a domestic or international audience, we should be careful not to consider righteous indignation as a clear calling card for backlash against international human rights and criminal courts. Bluster without action is not enough to constitute backlash against international norms and laws. This is not to say that words and rhetoric do not matter. Rather, it is to call attention to the fact that for threats against the international justice regime to be credible, those states and elites making the threats need to be willing to pay real political, reputational, or even material costs. Otherwise, the threats are just hot air.

This means, for example, that the same arguments that states have advanced for decades about the ways in which international tribunals could potentially violate the sovereignty of their member states would not, alone, be considered backlash. These claims need to be met with specific assertions about and actions taken against the courts' authority. In a related vein, backlash is not simply populist or anti-globalization rhetoric. While populist politics and the

---

[69]   Alter and Zürn, "Conceptualising Backlash Politics," 566.
[70]   Roger Petersen, "Emotions and Backlash in US Society and Politics," *The British Journal of Politics and International Relations* 22, no. 4 (November 2020): 609–618, https://doi.org/10.1177/1369148120948726.

world-razing language that accompanies it can be a motivating factor of backlash politics, backlash need not be limited to these efforts.[71]

Relatedly, Alter and Zürn argue that backlash must reach some level of public consciousness and take the shape of extraordinary politics.[72] While there is, indeed, a clear connection between backlash and public consciousness through provocative, out-of-the ordinary politics, backlash also can take place under a cloak of secrecy and with mind-numbing mundanity. While some public spectacle might advance backlash politics, in other instances, particularly when it is justice insiders engaging in the backlash, backlash politics are not publicly salient – by design. The typology outlined in the following section illustrates both extraordinary forms of backlash politics, as well as those manifestations that are very ordinary indeed.

Courts as (Re-)Active Actors

Before turning to the typology of backlash politics, it is important to note that the courts are not passive actors. The courts and their supporters can both respond to and preempt backlash. This can take a variety of forms, from dejudicializing hot-button topics that could spark backlash to watering down judgments to induce compliance.[73] Throughout the case studies presented in the following chapters, I highlight the ways in which the tribunals, their supporters, and their umbrella organizations prevent and react to backlash politics.

OPERATIONALIZING BACKLASH: EXTRAORDINARY AND ORDINARY POLITICS

Beyond defining backlash, it is important to identify a set of manifestations of backlash politics that share its defining characteristics: sustained action that targets the tribunals' structural, adjudicative, and normative authority by challenging the status quo. In this book, I identify four different manifestations of backlash that match these criteria. These include: (1) withdrawals from

---

[71] Voeten, "Populism and Backlashes against International Courts."

[72] Alter and Zürn, "Conceptualising Backlash Politics."

[73] Shai Dothan, "Judicial Deference Allows European Consensus to Emerge," *Chicago Journal of International Law* 18, no. 2 (2018): 393–418; Jed Odermatt, "Patterns of Avoidance: Political Questions before International Courts," *International Journal of Law in Context* 14, no. 2 (June 2018): 221–236, https://doi.org/10.1017/S1744552318000046; Øyvind Stiansen and Erik Voeten, "Backlash and Judicial Restraint: Evidence from the European Court of Human Rights," *International Studies Quarterly* 64, no. 4 (December 2020): 770–784, https://doi .org/10.2139/ssrn.3166110.

international human rights and criminal tribunals; (2) advancing alternate or substitute justice mechanisms; (3) imposing financial and bureaucratic restrictions on the courts; and (4) posing doctrinal challenges to the principles on which the tribunals are based.

While this typology shares some similarities with the typology set out by Sandholtz, Bei, and Caldwell it is unique in its breadth and inclusion of high-profile structural attacks on the courts, as well as subtler – yet no less damaging – assaults, such as internal bureaucratic and budgetary maneuvers and conceptual challenges.[74] This typology reflects the spectrum of backlash behaviors that target all three sources of international courts' authority: (1) their relationship with states; (2) their adjudicative capacity; and (3) their moral high ground.

In the following discussion, I explain each manifestation of backlash and provide some brief examples. Table 1.1 provides a brief summary of each form of backlash politics.

Withdrawal

The first type of backlash I explore in this book is states' withdrawals from international courts. Threats of withdrawal are not new, but they have become more prevalent over the past decade, even if actualized withdrawals remain quite rare. As discussed earlier, member states of the AU have threatened to withdraw from the Rome Statute and thus the ICC and to create an alternative forum for international criminal accountability. To date, however, the only AU member state to withdraw from the Rome Statute has been Burundi.[75] Russia has repeatedly threatened to withdraw from the European Court of Human Rights. Meanwhile, in Latin America, Venezuela withdrew from the Inter-American Court of Human Rights in 2013 and submitted its withdrawal from the OAS and, by extension, the Inter-American Commission on Human Rights in 2017.[76] Other countries, including Brazil, have made similar threats.

---

[74] Sandholtz, Bei, and Caldwell, "Backlash and International Human Rights Courts."

[75] Jina Moore, "Burundi Quits International Criminal Court," *The New York Times*, October 27, 2017, https://www.nytimes.com/2017/10/27/world/africa/burundi-international-criminal-court.html.

[76] "On April 26, 2017, Maduro announced Venezuela would withdraw from the Organization of American States (OAS), a process that requires two years. This decision was reversed by Interim President Guaido and the National Assembly. On January 10, 2019, the OAS Permanent Council voted not to recognize the second term of former President Nicolas Maduro and on April 9, 2019 the OAS Permanent Council approved a resolution to accept interim President Guaido's nominee Gustavo Tarre as Venezuela's representative to the Permanent Council on April 9."

TABLE 1.1 *Typologizing backlash against international human rights and criminal courts*

Form of Backlash	Definition and Description
Withdrawing from International Human Rights and Criminal Courts	States and elites withdraw from, or threaten to withdraw from, international human rights and criminal courts. These efforts undermine the tribunals' structural authority, as well as their ability to adjudicate on cases that otherwise would fall under their jurisdiction. Withdrawals and threatened withdrawals also subvert the courts' normative and moral authority, as these efforts are almost always associated with narratives alleging bias at the courts.
Advancing Alternative Justice Mechanisms	States and elites propose and/or create new human rights mechanisms to supplant the court or tribunal they are seeking to undermine. These new tribunals have less structural independence and weaker human rights and criminal accountability standards than the original court. These efforts exploit the structural dependency of tribunals on states and further exacerbate allegations of bias at the original tribunals. States and elites often propose alternate justice mechanisms in combination with threatened or realized withdrawals.
Enacting Bureaucratic and Budgetary Restrictions	States and elites work within the tribunals' legal system to impose a set of bureaucratic and/or budgetary restrictions that incapacitate the court. Over time, these restrictions can undermine the courts' ability to adjudicate and threaten its moral authority. These budgetary and bureaucratic restrictions exploit the structural relationship between tribunals and states and undermine the courts' structural independence.
Challenges to Court Doctrine	States and elites mount conceptual or doctrinal challenges to the legal system embodied by the court they are working to undermine. These challenges aim to dilute the impact of the courts on domestic politics and to weaken the ability of the court to

TABLE 1.1 *(continued)*

Form of Backlash	Definition and Description
	force policy change. These efforts limit the courts' adjudicative authority while also calling into question the courts' normative high ground. As with the other forms of backlash, the tribunals' structural relationship with states is both a source of the tribunals' authority vis-à-vis states as well as source of vulnerability,

Withdrawals represent a particularly potent form of backlash because they expose the fact that the tribunals' authority over states is conditional on states' acceptance of that authority. International courts derive their structural power from member states, but withdrawals threaten to undermine that authority. Withdrawals – or even threats thereof – emphasize the primacy of place of state sovereignty and suggest that the principle of compulsory jurisdiction is not so compulsory after all, if states can simply walk away from a court.[77]

Withdrawals and threatened withdrawals also attack the tribunals' adjudicative and moral authority. Courts cannot adjudicate on states or cases over which they have no jurisdiction. Withdrawing from a court is a blunt instrument for thwarting its adjudicative authority. Moreover, withdrawals threaten the normative authority of courts. Not only do they question the principle of compulsory jurisdiction, but they also force a stark conversation about the universality of the norms on which the tribunals rest. If, in fact, there were a consensus about the value of these human rights and accountability norms, then withdrawal would not be an option.

I consider withdrawals, or threatened withdrawals, from international human rights and criminal courts as a form of backlash because they target, via costly action, the courts' structural, adjudicative, and moral authority. Withdrawing from a court exceeds routine resistance, and while it might be

(Bureau of Western Hemisphere Affairs, "U.S. Relations with Venezuela: Bilateral Relations Fact Sheet," *U.S. Department of State*, July 6, 2020, https://www.state.gov/u-s-relations-with-venezuela /#:~:text=Venezuela's%20Membership%20in%20International%20Organizations&text=Venezu ela%20is%20a%20founding%20member,(CELAC)%2C%20and%20PetroCaribe).

77 See, for example, *Case Concerning Military and Paramilitary Activities in and against Nicaragua (Nicaragua v. United States of America); Merits*, International Court of Justice, June 27, 1984.

considered "bad behavior," when it is a systematized effort to undermine a court's authority, it also constitutes backlash.

Alternative Justice Mechanisms

The second manifestation of backlash I consider in this book is the creation of substitute or alternative justice mechanisms. This occurs when states and political elites create alternative courts or quasi-courts to the international tribunals they seek to subvert. Substitutions can happen on the domestic level with the creation of domestic criminal courts meant to negate international jurisdiction. In addition, regional or subregional organizations can create their own tribunals or quasi-judicial mechanisms to try human rights and atrocity crimes.

The rationale behind substitutions is often to demonstrate that the instigators of backlash are not against justice as such, but rather are opposed to the "biased" justice handed down by international courts. This form of backlash is often accompanied by rhetoric alleging that the international justice system is a tool of neocolonialism and inherently biased. For instance, the threatened walkout of the African Union from the ICC prompted a number of plans to create an African criminal court, while opponents of the Inter-American Court of Human Rights have relied on MERCOSUR (the Common Market of the South, comprised of Argentina, Brazil, Paraguay, Uruguay, and Venezuela)[78] and other subregional organizations to promote a Bolivarian sense of justice. Neither regional initiative, it should be noted, would fully replace the scope of accountability offered by the tribunals they were meant to undermine.

Ostensibly, states and elites could create alternate justice mechanisms as a way to advance, rather than undermine, the goals of human rights and accountability. Such instances would not be considered backlash. The creation of alternate or substitute justice mechanisms becomes a form of backlash, however, when it takes aim at subverting or undermining the authority of the court in question. Substitute justice mechanisms, much like withdrawals, pose a threat to the structural authority of international courts because they illustrate that states are not bound by the courts they create and instead can abandon courts with which they disagree in favor of courts that they can control. They also threaten the ability of human rights and criminal courts

---

[78]   MERCOSUR suspended the Bolivarian Republic of Venezuela in 2017. (Silvio Cascione, "Mercosur Suspends Venezuela, Urges Immediate Transition," *Reuters*, August 5, 2017, https://www.reuters.com/article/us-venezuela-politics-mercosur-idUSKBN1AL0IB.)

to fulfill their adjudicative role by taking their cases elsewhere, and they undermine the normative authority of the court by openly creating an institution that privileges a different vision of human rights and accountability.

Bureaucratic and Budgetary Restrictions

The third type of backlash discussed in this book is far less ostentatious but equally damaging. It is the imposition of bureaucratic and budgetary restrictions that hamstring international courts. The tribunals require funding from member states – and occasionally outside donors – to support their work. They also need well-functioning bureaucracies to process petitions, gather evidence, hold trials, and track compliance. When their funding is restricted and their bureaucracies strangled, the tribunals cannot do their work. This affects them in many ways, but one of the most significant ways that these restrictions undermine the tribunals is by creating delays in the adjudication of cases. These delays, in turn, make the courts less efficient and less competent. Of course, severe financial restrictions and bureaucratic roadblocks can even portend the end of the tribunals, although such a fate has not yet befallen any of the courts.

In addition to the very practical problems that financial and bureaucratic backlash can precipitate, imposing financial and bureaucratic restrictions on the tribunals reasserts the notion that even the most independent tribunals are not, in fact, independent. US legal scholars have long identified the power of bureaucratic and budgetary restrictions as a way of handicapping courts.[79] The fact that international courts require the continued financial, logistical, and political support of member states and donors makes their structural authority particularly vulnerable to backlash politics. That also means that this form of backlash politics is difficult for the courts to combat.

When states and elites impose bureaucratic and budgetary restrictions on international human rights and criminal courts, they also threaten the courts' adjudicative authority. Without the proper resources and systems in place, courts cannot operate as courts, meaning that they cannot try cases, hold perpetrators accountable, or monitor compliance. Bureaucratic and budgetary restrictions also weaken the courts' normative authority, as it suggests that the courts can be easily manipulated. These efforts illustrate that the courts

---

[79] See, for example, Pauline T. Kim, "Beyond Principal-Agent Theories: Law and Judicial Hierarchy," *Northwestern University Law Review* 105, no. 2 (2015), https://scholarlycommons .law.northwestern.edu/nulr/vol105/iss2/3/.

might be keepers of a vast treasure trove of technical knowledge and moral authority, but it is states who hold the key.

Of course, not all bureaucratic or budgetary crises constitute backlash. The tribunals, much like the member states that fund them, can fall on hard times. Even the most well-intentioned bureaucrats can mismanage the inner workings of an international tribunal and its budget. It is when states and elites enact budgetary and bureaucratic restrictions as part of an assault on the tribunals' ability to complete its work that these restrictions can be classified as backlash.

Challenges to Court Doctrine

The fourth and final type of backlash I discuss in this book consists of threatening courts' authority through doctrinal challenges. Doctrinal challenges limit the adjudicative authority of international courts vis-à-vis domestic politics. States and elites can use – and usurp – the concepts of complementarity or subsidiarity/margin of appreciation to circumscribe the courts' ability to change or curb domestic policy and legislation. All international human rights and criminal courts have doctrinal expectations about when and to what degree the court should defer to domestic politics. For example, complementarity, a principle central to the ICC, suggests that the ICC only has jurisdiction when domestic courts fail to prosecute perpetrators to the standards set out in the Rome Statute.[80] In the regional human rights courts, the principles of subsidiarity and the margin of appreciation advance the notion that states have a fair amount of latitude when it comes to implementing international human rights courts' rulings.[81] These doctrines acknowledge the inherently contentious nature of international adjudication.

---

[80] See, for example, William W. Burke-White, "Proactive Complementarity: The International Criminal Court and National Courts in the Rome System of International Justice," *Harvard International Law Journal* 49, no. 1 (Winter 2008): 53–108, https://scholarship.law.upenn.edu /faculty_scholarship/138/; Michael A. Newton, "The Complementarity Conundrum: Are We Watching Evolution or Evisceration?" *Santa Clara Journal of International Law* 8 (2010): 115–164, https://scholarship.law.vanderbilt.edu/faculty-publications/642; Chris Stephen, "Clarifying the Principle of Complementarity: The ICC Confirms Admissibility of Case despite Investigation by Kenya," *EJIL: Talk!* (blog), September 14, 2011, https://www .ejiltalk.org/clarifying-the-principle-of-complementarity-the-icc-confirms-admissibility-of-case-despite-investigation-by-kenya/; Sarah M. H. Nouwen, *Complementarity in the Line of Fire: The Catalysing Effect of the International Criminal Court in Uganda and Sudan* (Cambridge, UK: Cambridge University Press, 2013).

[81] Michael R. Hutchinson, "The Margin of Appreciation Doctrine in the European Court of Human Rights," *International & Comparative Law Quarterly* 48, no. 3 (July 1999): 638–650, https://doi.org/10.1017/S0020589300063478; Paolo G. Carozza, "Subsidiarity as a Structural

Doctrinal challenges become backlash, however, when they are part of a strategic, organized campaign that prevents the courts from carrying out the full scope of their adjudicative work.

Undermining the courts' legal frameworks has a doubly negative effect on court authority. On the one hand, it means that the courts cannot proceed with their casework as they were designed to do. Diluting or diminishing the courts' ability to rule on domestic policies and practices endangers victims and leaves them without recourse. It limits the ability of the courts to effect domestic policy change and casts doubt on their ability to run effective trials.

Moreover, when the tribunals' ability to adjudicate is limited, it also affects their normative authority. When courts provide more deference to their original stakeholders, or indeed to any constituency, in order to keep them in the fold,[82] they apply the law unevenly, further exacerbating claims of judicial bias. Moreover, efforts to limit or circumscribe the adjudicative and normative authority of international courts also illustrate the courts' vulnerability to their member states, thus highlighting the tenuous nature of their structural authority, as well.

Doctrinal challenges generally take place within the general confines of the tribunals' legal structures and processes. As noted above, courts can – and do – act strategically in order to de-escalate potential sources of conflict.[83] It is when the states and elites undermining the courts drive the dejudicialization process as part of a larger campaign against international courts, that judicial deference can quickly become symptomatic of backlash politics.[84]

Summary

The typology of backlash offered here is not exhaustive, nor is it meant to be. Rather, this typology of backlash is designed to illustrate a set of manifestations

---

Principle of International Human Rights Law," *American Journal of International Law* 97, no. 1 (January 2003): 38–79, https://scholarship.law.nd.edu/law_faculty_scholarship/564/; Dean Spielmann, "Allowing the Right Margin: The European Court of Human Rights and the National Margin of Appreciation Doctrine: Waiver or Subsidiarity of European Review?" *Cambridge Yearbook of European Legal Studies* 14 (2012): 381–418, https://doi.org/10.5235/152 88871280558057o; Andreas Follesdal, "Squaring the Circle at the Battle at Brighton: Is the War between Protecting Human Rights or Respecting Sovereignty Over, or Has It Just Begun?" in *Shifting Centres of Gravity in Human Rights Protection: Rethinking Relations between the ECHR, EU, and National Legal Orders,* eds. Oddný Mjöll Arnardóttir and Antoine Buyse (London: Routledge, 2016).

[82] Dothan, "Judicial Deference Allows European Consensus to Emerge"; Stiansen and Voeten, "Backlash and Judicial Restraint."

[83] Abebe and Ginsburg, "The Dejudicialization of International Politics?"

[84] Stiansen and Voeten, "Backlash and Judicial Restraint."

of backlash politics that share three defining characteristics: (1) they are neither normatively "bad behavior" nor routine pushback; (2) they target the structural, adjudicative, and normative authority of international courts; and (3) they are action-oriented. Each of the forms of backlash outlined above can be part of a larger, fiery campaign against the global order, but that is neither necessary nor sufficient for backlash. As the rest of the book illustrates, backlash can take the form of both extraordinary and ordinary politics. Only by understanding the broad spectrum of backlash politics can scholars, stakeholders, and supporters work to save the international justice regime.

ROADMAP TO THE BOOK

The rest of the book is organized according to the typology of backlash politics outlined above, with each of the empirical chapters dedicated to one form of backlash. Before presenting the empirical work, however, Chapter 2 provides a deeper investigation of the theoretical framework that guides the case studies that follow. This chapter draws on the human rights, international law, international relations, and political science literatures to provide an explanatory framework for understanding why and how backlash politics unfolds.

The theoretical framework in Chapter 2 contends that backlash politics can best be explained by four main factors. These include:

1. the tribunals' unrelenting dependency on member states;
2. fundamental, normative schisms about using international human rights and criminal adjudication;
3. the domestic "distributional" consequences of international adjudication; and
4. states and elites' likelihood of engaging in future violence and repression.

These four factors, or drivers, of backlash cover the ideational, functional, and material debates at the heart of backlash politics. They capture both nearly omnipresent factors, such as the tribunals' dependency on states and normative debates, as well as factors that assume more urgency, such as the distributional consequences of international adjudication and the likelihood of future violence. These drivers are both specific enough to provide analytical insight into a wide range of backlash politics while also broad enough to be generalizable to a variety of cases and courts.

After the exposition of the theoretical framework, the book turns to the empirical analyses, using the typology presented above as a guide. Chapters 3 and 4 examine two of the most visible and ostentatious forms of backlash against international human rights and criminal tribunals: withdrawals (or threatened withdrawals) from international courts, and proposals for replacing or supplanting international justice mechanisms. Chapter 3 begins by considering the case of the Inter-American Court of Human Rights and investigates Peru and Venezuela's threatened and actualized withdrawals, respectively. The attention then shifts to Colombia as a counterexample: a country that has faced both widespread domestic violence and intense scrutiny by the IACtHR and, yet, has leaned into the IACtHR rather than pulled out of it.

Chapter 4 explores the African Union's efforts to withdraw from and supplant the ICC. This chapter focuses on the role of a small set of instigators, such as Kenya, in pushing for the creation of an alternate justice mechanism, while also highlighting the importance of a small but vocal group of African Union member states that pushed back against backlash politics. The chapter ends by returning to the experience of Venezuela and its efforts to supplant the IACtHR with a weaker form of accountability within MERCOSUR.

Chapters 5 and 6 examine subtler forms of backlash politics. Chapter 5 considers two cases of bureaucratic and budgetary restrictions designed to hamstring international human rights and criminal tribunals. The first case study is the intentional bankrupting of the Inter-American Commission on Human Rights in retaliation for the domestic consequences of the IACmHR's adjudicative and outreach work. The second half of the chapter considers how judge selection in the Assembly of States Parties (ASP) to the ICC has become a way for states and elites to hamstring the work of the International Criminal Court.

Chapter 6 turns to doctrinal challenges, such as challenges to the principle of the margin of appreciation. This chapter considers the example of Russia's work to expand the margin of appreciation at the ECtHR, such that its rulings have no real domestic effect. The chapter also examines the implications of stakeholder states, such as Denmark and the United Kingdom, engaging in similar activities.

The final chapter of the book, Chapter 7, turns from these empirical examples to offer readers both a summary of the main arguments of the project as well as a discussion of the steps that steward states and stakeholders can take to shore up the international justice regime. I suggest that supporters of international justice can take three main steps: (1) managing public opinion by engaging in targeted and effective self-marketing campaigns as a way to make their case to a broader audience; (2) improving the rule of law and the functioning of the tribunals as judicial institutions; and (3) reaffirming the fundamental norm(s) of criminal accountability and human rights. By providing concrete, actionable advice, Chapter 7, and this book more broadly, suggest that while the challenges that international human rights and criminal courts face are indeed real and sustained, they are not inevitable. Instead, a clear definition and typology of backlash, together with a guiding theoretical framework, can assist scholars and stakeholders alike in not just better understanding backlash against international human rights and criminal courts, but also in fighting back against it.

***

At a moment when it is easy to decry the end of human rights and accountability, it is important to remember the audacious goal of a world characterized by peace, justice, and accountability.[85] As such, this book answers the call of human rights optimists and skeptics alike. It provides systematic analyses of when and why states and elites engage in backlash against international human rights and criminal tribunals. By examining a wide range of courts and cases, and evaluating both the successes and failures of the international justice regime, the research that follows suggests that the answer to this era of backlash is not more courts or more laws or even more cases, or in burning down the international justice regime, but, rather, in improving the way that existing institutions function. It provides clear, policy-relevant practices based on extensive research to protect human rights and criminal tribunals and the norms they espouse. It does not ignore the faults in the international justice system nor does it exaggerate a sense of predetermined doom. Instead, the discussion that follows is rooted firmly in the messy, imperfect and changeable politics of the courts, their member states, and the international system.

---

[85] Stephen Hopgood, *The Endtimes of Human Rights* (Ithaca, NY: Cornell University Press, 2013), 95; Samuel Moyn, *Not Enough: Human Rights in an Unequal World* (Cambridge, MA: Belknap Press of Harvard University Press, 2018); Eric A. Posner, *The Twilight of Human Rights Law* (New York: Oxford University Press, 2014); Kathryn Sikkink, *Evidence for Hope: Making Human Rights Work in the 21st Century* (Princeton, NJ: Princeton University Press, 2017).

2

Backlash in Theoretical Context

INTRODUCTION

ICC President Chile Eboe-Osuji is no stranger to what he has called "negative sentiment" toward international human rights and criminal tribunals.[1] Nigerian-born Eboe-Osuji joined the ICC in 2012 following turns as the Principal Appeals Counsel for the Prosecution in the Charles Taylor Case at the Special Court for Sierra Leone (SCSL), the Head of Chambers and Lead Prosecution Trial Counsel at the ICTR, an advisor to the UN High Commissioner for Human Rights (UNHCHR), and as a barrister in Nigeria and Canada. He has been an outspoken supporter of the ICC and has stood firm in the face of a number of recent challenges: the Philippines' withdrawal from the Rome Statute;[2] the Trump administration's decision to revoke a visa for Fatou Bensouda, the ICC Chief Prosecutor, in retaliation for the Court's investigation into possible war crimes in Afghanistan;[3] and continued criticism of the Court's handling of the conflict in Myanmar/Burma.[4]

In March 2019, Mr. Eboe-Osuji gave the keynote address to the American Society of International Law. In the address, he invoked the legacy of Robert H. Jackson, a former United States Supreme Court Justice, US Attorney General and the United States Solicitor General. Mr. Jackson was also the

[1] Michael Peel, "US Threats over Afghan War Probe 'Troubling', Says ICC," *Financial Times*, December 22, 2019, https://www.ft.com/content/ecb682ec-231a-11ea-b8a1-584213ee7b2b.

[2] Regine Cabato, "Philippines Leaves International Criminal Court as Duterte Probe Is Underway," *Washington Post*, March 18, 2019, https://www.washingtonpost.com/world/asia_pacific/philippines-leaves-international-criminal-court-as-duterte-probe-underway/2019/03/18/f929d1b6-4952-11e9-93d064dbcf38ba41_story.html.

[3] Marlise Simons and Megan Specia, "U.S. Revokes Visa of I.C.C. Prosecutor Pursuing Afghan War Crimes," *The New York Times*, April 5, 2019, https://www.nytimes.com/2019/04/05/world/europe/us-icc-prosecutor-afghanistan.html.

[4] Al Jazeera, "Myanmar Rejects ICC Probe into Alleged Crimes against Rohingya," November 15, 2019, https://www.aljazeera.com/news/2019/11/myanmar-rejects-icc-probe-alleged-crimes-rohingya-191115180754984.html.

Chief United States Prosecutor at the International Military Tribunal (i.e., the Nuremberg Trials) and an early architect of international criminal law.[5] Like Mr. Eboe-Osuji, Mr. Jackson was intimately familiar with hostility toward and skepticism about international accountability. At the top of his keynote address, Mr. Eboe-Osuji harkened back to a speech that Mr. Jackson made in 1945 about the value and challenges of international law and courts. Mr. Jackson wrote – and Mr. Eboe-Osuji reiterated – "Those who best know the deficiencies of international law are those who also know the diversity and permanence of its accomplishments and its indispensability to a world that plans to live in peace."[6] Both in Nuremberg in 1945 and in The Hague in 2020, not to mention in Strasbourg, San José, Banjul, and beyond, the deficiencies of international criminal and human rights courts are quite evident. Enumerating them is less interesting, perhaps, than understanding why and how states and political elites take advantage of them and how the courts and their supporters can assure the "diversity and permanence" of their successes.

This chapter builds on the introduction by addressing the second question at the core of this book: *why* do states engage in backlash politics? The theoretical framework advanced in this chapter identifies four conditions, or driving factors, that lead states and elites to engage in backlash politics. The first is that international human rights and criminal tribunals are dependent on states. This dependency is a function of their structural relationship with states, which, as discussed in Chapter 1, both endows the courts with authority while also making them reliant on states for material, procedural, and normative support. Second, this framework builds on the understanding that international human rights and criminal courts do not enjoy a normative consensus, even from their member states, about the role of international adjudication in mediating disputes or even about the human rights and criminal accountability norms on which the courts are based.

Beyond the tribunals' dependency on states and normative discontent, I suggest that backlash to international human rights and criminal courts is driven by the fact that international human rights and criminal adjudication

5   "Robert H Jackson Biography," Robert H. Jackson Center, n.d., https://www
    .roberthjackson.org/article/robert-h-jackson-biography/.
6   "Rule of Law Among Nations," Robert H. Jackson Center, n.d., https://www
    .roberthjackson.org/speech-and-writing/rule-of-law-among-nations/; Chile Eboe-Osuji, "ICC
    President's Keynote Speech 'A Tribute to Robert H Jackson – Recalling America's
    Contributions to International Criminal Justice' at the Annual Meeting of American Society
    of International Law," *International Criminal Court*, March 29, 2019, https://www.icc-cpi.int
    /Pages/item.aspx?name=190329-stat-pres.

creates domestic political winners and losers. When the tribunals hand down adverse judgments, by definition they find fault with past and present policies and practices. In doing so, they empower the opposition vis-à-vis a sitting government. One response that the government might have to this newly empowered opposition is, of course, repression. Relatedly, then, the fourth driver of backlash that I examine in this chapter is the likelihood of states resorting to (further) violence and thus, wanting to "blind the watchdog," that is, the international justice regime. Even if international courts cannot exact clear punishments, they can draw attention to human rights violations and atrocity crimes and inspire domestic mobilization against sitting governments.

These four factors provide a theoretical framework that reflect the structural, adjudicative, and normative dimensions of international human rights and criminal courts' authority, as well as their positioning at the intersection of international and domestic politics. For example, the flip side of international courts' structural relationship with states is their dependency on them, which makes international courts vulnerable to backlash. Similarly, the courts' normative authority is always predicated on the context in which it operates.[7] Normative schisms can leave international human rights and criminal courts open to attack. Meanwhile, the domestic implications of international human rights and criminal adjudication are a direct function of the courts' adjudicative authority. It is through the act – or threat – of adjudication, that international courts create domestic winners and losers and serve as human rights and accountability watchdogs. Particular rulings can generate steep domestic political costs, causing states and elites to lash out at international courts. Similarly, the prospect of reaching for repression as a tool to maintain the domestic status quo can incentivize efforts to undermine the courts' adjudicative authority through backlash politics.

The remainder of this chapter addresses each of the four main components of the theoretical framework in turn. Then, the chapter offers a consideration of when and why states engage in particular forms of backlash, stressing, however, that the different modes of backlash are not mutually exclusive. Before concluding, this chapter explains the methodological and empirical approach used throughout the remainder of the book.

---

[7]   Karen Alter, Laurence Helfer, and Mikael Rask Madsen, "How Context Shapes the Authority of International Courts," *Law and Contemporary Problems* 79, no. 1 (2016): 1–36, https://scholarship.law.duke.edu/lcp/vol79/iss1/1/.

DEPENDENCE ON STATES AND THE COURTS' SUSCEPTIBILITY TO SUBVERSION

As discussed in Chapter 1, one of the main ways that international courts derive their authority is through their structural relationship with member states. Despite the courts' structural and judicial independence, they rely on states for material support, such as their staff and operating budgets; help with their day-to-day judicial work, such as access to witnesses and evidence; and normative affirmation, including advocating for international justice norms and the courts themselves. As Jacob Katz Cogan argues, courts can have plenty of structural independence and guarantee the fair rights of the accused on paper, but they might lack the political and financial wherewithal to actually implement their written due process guarantees.[8] Indeed, it is impossible to escape the tribunals' reality: they are dependent on states for material, procedural, and normative support, and these dependencies put the courts at risk for backlash. In this section, I consider each of these dependencies in turn, discussing how each form of dependency sets the stage for backlash.

Material Support

International courts, like other international organizations, rely on member states for their operating budgets. While the courts' financial positions vary dramatically, what is consistent across all of the international human rights and criminal courts discussed in this book is that the courts need to ask their umbrella organizations for funds. These crucial funds pay the mortgages on the courts' buildings, pay staff salaries, and keep the lights on, both literally and figuratively. This process means that there is political oversight over the courts' budgets and, thus, their activities. Even the most independent court on paper needs to subject itself to a budgetary overview, often by the very same states and elites that the court aims to try.[9]

---

8 Jacob Katz Cogan, "International Criminal Courts and Fair Trials: Difficulties and Prospects," *Yale Journal of International Law* 27, no. 1 (Winter 2002): 111–140, https://digitalcommons .law.yale.edu/yjil/vol27/iss1/5/.

9 "Budget and Finance Background," Coalition for the International Criminal Court, n.d., http:// iccnow.org/?mod=budgetbackground; "The Council of Europe," Europe's Human Rights Watchdog, n.d., https://www.europewatchdog.info/en/council-of-europe/; Jo M. Pasqualucci, *The Practice and Procedure of the Inter-American Court of Human Rights* (Cambridge, UK: Cambridge University Press, 2003); Marlise Simons, "In The Hague's Lofty Judicial Halls, Judges Wrangle Over Pay," *The New York Times*, January 20, 2019, https://www.nytimes.com/ 2019/01/20/world/europe/hague-judges-pay.html; Theresa Squatrito, "Resourcing Global Justice: The Resource Management Design of International Courts," *Global Policy* 8, no. S5 (August

In addition to their dependency on states and donors for their budgets, international human rights and criminal courts also rely on member states for their staff.[10] Although international bureaucrats working at these institutions do not represent their member states (they are bureaucrats, not diplomats), states can still exert influence over international courts by encouraging or discouraging their citizens from taking positions at these international tribunals. Take, for example, the case of Japan and the ICC. The cornerstone of Japan's policy toward the ICC is to incorporate as many Japanese bureaucrats into the ICC's workforce as possible. Japan is also the ICC's biggest donor. Through its influence over the ICC's budget and bureaucrats, Japan can exert quiet but meaningful guidance over the ICC's bureaucracy and budget.[11] More broadly, these subtle levers of influence serve to deepen the courts' dependency on member states and, thus, increase their susceptibility to backlash.[12]

Procedural Dependencies

In addition to their dependency on states for operating budgets and staff, the tribunals require daily support from, and cooperation with, states in order to perform their most basic judicial tasks: gathering evidence, holding trials, and monitoring compliance. Peskin calls these day-to-day interactions "trials of cooperation" or "virtual trials."[13] These trials of cooperation pertain to the routine ways in which tribunals ask states to participate in the judicial process.

These "trials of cooperation" are central to the courts' work. Consider the case of international criminal tribunals. Without state cooperation to secure access to witnesses and evidence, arrest suspects, and provide information in

---

2017): 62–74, https://doi.org/10.1111/1758-5899.12452; Carsten Stahn, ed., *The Law and Practice of the International Criminal Court* (Oxford: Oxford University Press, 2015).

[10] See, for example, Inter-American Commission on Human Rights, "Inter-American Commission on Human Rights Annual Report 2017," https://www.oas.org/en/IACHR/reports/IA.asp?Year=2017; Pasqualucci, *The Practice and Procedure of the Inter-American Court*; William Schabas, *An Introduction to the International Criminal Court*, 3rd ed. (Cambridge, UK: Cambridge University Press, 2007); Stahn, *The Law and Practice of the International Criminal Court*.

[11] Interview #783, 2016.

[12] Assembly of States Parties, *Report of the Court on Human Resources Management* (The Hague: International Criminal Court, 2015), https://asp.icc-cpi.int/iccdocs/asp_docs/ASP14/ICC-ASP-14-7-ENG.pdf#search=Japan%28DetectedLanguage%3D%22en%22%29; Interview #783, 2016; Sayo Sasaki, "Japan Praised for ICC Backing," *The Japan Times*, November 21, 2006, www.japantimes.co.jp/news/2006/11/21/national/japan-praised-for-icc-backing/.

[13] Victor Peskin, *International Justice in Rwanda and the Balkans: Virtual Trials and the Struggle for State Cooperation* (New York: Cambridge University Press, 2008).

a timely and transparent manner, international criminal courts cannot hold trials. For example, the ICC does not have the authority to arrest suspects, nor can it force states to turn over documents or require that they have unfettered access to witnesses or sites of mass atrocity. While expectations about cooperation on these grounds are clearly spelled out in the Rome Statute, the Court lacks the capacity and legal authority to actually enforce these expectations and depends on states' good will to fulfill their judicial mandate.[14]

International human rights courts also rely on state cooperation. While there are no suspects, as such, to arrest, states still need to respond to the allegations presented against them, show up to trials, and commit to complying with any reparation measures following adverse judgments. While each of these steps are outlined in the courts' statutes, the human rights courts, much like their international criminal counterparts, lack the enforcement capacity to see that states follow-through with them and that they do so in a timely manner.[15]

Beyond the material implications that these procedural dependencies have for backlash politics, there are significant reputational consequences.[16] The tribunals' dependency on member states puts their ability to mount robust legal cases at risk. This increased margin of error can lead to long delays in cases. Prolonged back-and-forths with states over procedural issues cast significant and potentially catastrophic doubt on the tribunals' ability to function as courts, undermining their adjudicative authority.

Normative Support

In addition to material and procedural support, international human rights and criminal courts rely on states for normative support. When states, and particularly influential states, advocate for the courts in political forums, they

[14] "Non-Cooperation," International Criminal Court, last modified June 28, 2019, https://asp .icc-cpi.int/en_menus/asp/non-cooperation/Pages/default.aspx; "Cooperation Agreements," International Criminal Court, n.d., https://www.icc-cpi.int/news/seminarBooks/Cooperati on_Agreements_Eng.pdf; "Recommendations on States' Cooperation with the International Criminal Court (ICC): Experiences and Priorities," International Criminal Court, n.d., https:// www.icc-cpi.int/news/seminarBooks/66%20Recommendations%20Flyer%20(ENG).pdf; "Rome Statute of the International Criminal Court," entered into force July 1, 2002, *United Nations Treaty Series* 2187 no. 38544, http://hrlibrary.umn.edu/instree/Rome_Statute_ICC/Rome_ICC_ toc.html.

[15] Jillienne Haglund, Regional Courts, *Domestic Politics and the Struggle for Human Rights* (New York: Cambridge University Press, 2020); Courtney Hillebrecht, *Domestic Politics and International Human Rights Tribunals: The Problem of Compliance* (New York: Cambridge University Press, 2014).

[16] Peskin, *International Justice in Rwanda and the Balkans.*

can bolster the courts' perceived authority and counter the narratives that the courts are incompetent.[17] Human rights and criminal courts generally espouse pro-Western values and are largely politically and financially supported by powerful Western states. This makes them easy scapegoats for elites and states looking to justify their own human rights practices that run counter to the international justice regime. Allegations of neocolonialism and Western hegemony are common explanations for noncompliance and noncooperation with international human rights and criminal courts, as the following empirical chapters highlight.[18]

While for many, particularly in the Western academic and policy communities, the "international justice as neo-colonialism" narrative rings hollow, in some domestic contexts, these allegations are compelling.[19] Without powerful states coming to international courts' aid, other states can use the guise of the tribunals' bias and incompetence as a way of justifying backlash politics. This means that the courts are dependent on their supporters to stick up for them in international forums, to mainstream international adjudication into other issue areas, and to support the broader goal of international justice. I discuss the importance of stakeholder support in more detail in Chapter 7.

NORMATIVE DISCONTENT: DEBATING HUMAN RIGHTS NORMS

The high ratification rates of human rights and international criminal law instruments – and their attendant tribunals and quasi-tribunals – obfuscates deep disagreements about basic human rights principles. International human rights and criminal tribunals have become spaces to debate these rights issues. At the same time, the very idea of international adjudication for rights claims is also subject to dispute. Normative disputes continue along a number of axes, including individual rights versus collective rights;

---

[17] Kirsten Ainley, "The International Criminal Court on Trial," *Cambridge Review of International Affairs* 24, no. 3 (September 2011): 309–333, https://doi.org/10.1080/09557571.2011.558051; Dancy et al., "What Determines Perceptions of Bias toward the International Criminal Court? Evidence from Kenya," *Journal of Conflict Resolution* 64, no. 7–8 (2020): 1443–1469, https://doi.org/10.1177/0022002719893740; Sara McLaughlin Mitchell and Emillia Justyna Powell, *Domestic Law Goes Global: Legal Traditions and International Courts* (New York: Cambridge University Press, 2011); Interview #520, 2014; Interview #827, 2014; Interview #959, 2014.

[18] Interview #930, 2014.

[19] Courtney Hillebrecht, "International Criminal Accountability and the Domestic Politics of Resistance: Case Studies from Kenya and Lebanon," *Law & Society Review* 54, no. 2 (June 2020): 453–486, https://doi.org/10.1111/lasr.12469; Erik Voeten, "Populism and Backlashes against International Courts," *Perspectives on Politics* 18, no. 2 (June 2020): 407–422, https://doi.org/10.1017/S1537592719000975.

progressive political rights versus traditional values and/or socioeconomic rights; and accountability versus sovereignty and head of state immunity, all of which I discuss in more detail below. Of course, the tribunals also experience normative discord over the fundamental question of whether or not courts are the right place to take political disputes about human rights and accountability in the first place.

The research on states' ratification of human rights treaties demonstrates quite clearly that states often enter treaties, including those backed by international human rights or criminal courts, with few expectations of enforcement.[20] While some scholars argue that ratification is minimally expressive of a state's human rights values, few scholars or observers would consider ratification a foolproof test of a state's commitment to human rights and criminal accountability norms.[21]

As discussed in Chapter 1, normative contestation is nothing new in the human rights or criminal accountability spheres. When the international justice project began in the wake of World War II, it was more of an ambitious, ambiguous dream than a political reality. For example, in Europe, the European Court of Human Rights was created to serve as "the conscience of Europe"[22] but, due to internal contestation about the value of regional human rights adjudication, the Court's jurisdiction was not compulsory for Council of Europe member states until decades later. Meanwhile, in its earliest years, the IAHRS was hamstrung by the region's military dictatorships, which operated in direct contrast to the professed norms of the IAHRS. Even after democratization

[20] See, for example, George W. Downs, David M. Rocke, and Peter N. Barsoom, "Is the Good News about Compliance Good News about Cooperation?" *International Organization* 50, no. 3 (Summer 1996): 379–406, https://doi.org/10.1017/S0020818300033427; James Fearon, "Bargaining, Enforcement and International Cooperation," *International Organization* 52, no. 2 (Spring 1998): 296–305, https://doi.org/10.1162/002081898753162820; Emilie M. Hafner-Burton and Kiyoteru Tsutsui, "Justice Lost! The Failure of International Human Rights Law to Matter Where Needed Most," *Journal of Peace Research* 44, no. 4 (July 2007): 407–425, https://doi.org/10.1177/0022343307078942; Oona Hathaway, "Do Human Rights Treaties Make a Difference?" *Yale Law Journal* 111, no. 8 (2002): 1935–2041, https://digitalcommons .law.yale.edu/cgi/viewcontent.cgi?article=1852&context=fss_papers.

[21] Beth A. Simmons, *Mobilizing for Human Rights: International Law in Domestic Politics* (New York: Cambridge University Press, 2009); Beth A. Simmons and Hyeran Jo, "Measuring Norms and Normative Contestation: The Case of International Criminal Law," *Journal of Global Security Studies* 4, no. 1 (January 2019): 18–36, https://doi.org/10.1093/jogss/ ogy043.

[22] Robert Clarke, *The "Conscience of Europe?": Navigating Shifting Tides at the European Court of Human Rights* (Vienna: Kairos Publications, 2017); Michael Goldhaber, *A People's History of the European Court of Human Rights* (New Brunswick, NJ: Rutgers University Press, 2007); Jonathan Sharpe, ed., *The Conscience of Europe: 50 Years of the European Court of Human Rights* (London: Third Millennium Publishing, 2011).

in the 1990s, the Inter-American Human Rights System was, in the words of Thomas Farer, "no longer a unicorn [but] not yet an ox."[23] International criminal justice also took shape amidst normative contestation, with both the Nuremburg and Tokyo trials in the 1940s plagued by critiques of victors' justice.[24]

Divisions between the East and West slowed much of the progress on human rights, both in terms of law and in terms of building a normative consensus. The development of the international human rights and criminal accountability regimes were marked by disputes about *which* basket of rights should – or should not – be protected. While the dissolution of the Soviet Union and the relative calm of the 1990s reignited the spark of international justice, it did not resolve these fundamental debates.[25] Furthermore, even though the march to democratization in the 1990s was intertwined with a growing call for accountability for atrocity crimes and systemic human rights abuses, there was – and is – no real consensus about head of state immunity. The high-profile Augusto Pinochet and Hissène Habré cases of the early 2000s underscored the *possibility* of, and legal grounds for, head of state accountability, but they did not result in any degree of unanimity about the political or even normative desirability of accountability.[26] In fact, these cases only served to highlight the lack of normative consensus about these principles.

Indeed, any presumption about human rights and criminal accountability norms' status as universally accepted disguises deep divides over which rights matter, for whom, and under which circumstances. Presumptions of universality exacerbate, rather than mitigate, international courts' risk for backlash politics, as these assumptions become the powder keg for accusations of pro-Western bias and neocolonialism. As Reza Afshari notes:

---

[23] Tom Farer, "The Rise of the Inter-American Human Rights Regime: No Longer a Unicorn, Not Yet an Ox," *Human Rights Quarterly* 19, no. 3 (August 1997): 510–546, https://doi.org/10 .1353/hrq.1997.0025.

[24] Gary Jonathan Bass, *Stay the Hand of Vengeance: The Politics of War Crimes Tribunals* (Princeton, NJ: Princeton University Press, 2000).

[25] Daniel Charles Thomas, *The Helsinki Effect: International Norms, Human Rights, and the Demise of Communism* (Princeton, NJ: Princeton University Press, 2001); Zehra F. Kabasakal Arat, "Global Normative Encounters: Human Rights and Their Rivals," *APSA 2020 Annual Meeting Paper* (2020).

[26] Reed Brody, "Victims Bring a Dictator to Justice: The Case of Hissène Habré," *Brot für die Welt*, June 2017, https://www.brot-fuer-die-welt.de/fileadmin/mediapool/2_Downloads/Fachi nformationen/Analyse/Analysis70-The_Habre_Case.pdf; Renée Jeffery, *Amnesties, Accountability, and Human Rights* (Philadelphia: University of Pennsylvania Press, 2014); Naomi Roht-Arriaza, *The Pinochet Effect: Transnational Justice in the Age of Human Rights* (Philadelphia: University of Pennsylvania Press, 2006); Kathryn Sikkink, *The Justice Cascade: How Human Rights Prosecutions Are Changing World Politics* (New York: W. W. Norton & Company, Inc., 2011).

One of the main issues that the current historiography has to grapple with is the apparent disparity between the often-celebrated normative global achievements in codifying human rights values among the UN member states and the often-lamented failures to enforce them . . . . I argue that the link should not be seen as mechanical or procedural. Weaknesses so obviously apparent in the enforcement process signify the lack of vigor in the normative consensus; the vim and vigor by which the face was adorned by high-flying colors might in fact have masked a frail body.[27]

Normative Schisms at International Human Rights and Criminal Tribunals

The normative schisms at international human rights and criminal courts are plentiful. All states and leaders have their own particular idiosyncrasies, preferences, and token causes, so it is nearly impossible to enumerate all of the normative divides that emerge at the international tribunals. Broadly speaking, however, these divisions cluster around three issues: individual rights versus collective rights; progressive political rights versus traditional values and/or socioeconomic rights; and sovereignty and head of state immunity versus accountability. The courts are not always consistent in deciding these debates. International judges, like their domestic counterparts, do not always apply their reasoning uniformly, and the courts' rulings change over time and place. This inconsistency is, of course, a cause and a consequence of backlash politics.[28]

Individual Rights versus Collective Rights

One of the main normative tensions at the international tribunals is the long-held division between individual and collective or traditional group rights. Individual rights refer to those rights that each person, by virtue of being human, can enjoy. Collective rights, in contrast, refer to the rights of

---

[27] Reza Afshari, "On Historiography of Human Rights Reflections on Paul Gordon Lauren's The Evolution of International Human Rights: Visions Seen," *Human Rights Quarterly* 29, no. 1 (February 2007): 1–67, https://doi.org/10.1353/hrq.2007.0000; Courtney Hillebrecht, "Normative Consensus and Contentious Practice: Challenges to Universalism in International Human Rights Courts," *Human Rights Quarterly* 41, no. 1 (February 2019): 190–194, https://doi.org/10.1353/hrq.2019.0010.

[28] See, for example, Yehuda Z. Blum, "Consistently Inconsistent: The International Court of Justice and the Former Yugoslavia (Croatia v. Serbia)," *The American Journal of International Law* 103, no. 2 (April 2009): 264–271, https://doi.org/10.2307/20535149; Nancy Combs, "Seeking Inconsistency: Advancing Pluralism in International Criminal Sentencing," *Yale Journal of International Law* 41, no. 1 (Winter 2016): 1–49, https://digitalcommons.law.yale.edu/yjil/vo l41/iss1/2.

a group. While some supporters of collective rights argue that they protect minority groups, others contend that they are a ruse to violate individual rights.[29]

Both the human rights and international criminal law regimes emphasize individual rights and responsibilities. This emphasis on individual rights and responsibilities is rooted, in many ways, in Western political philosophy and has been a long-standing point of contention in the development of international human rights law and adjudicative bodies.[30] In the case of the human rights courts, they are designed to adjudicate individuals' rights vis-à-vis the state. The international criminal courts, meanwhile, emphasize individual criminal responsibility. The individual, as opposed to the collective, is the main focus. In the words of one interviewee and international justice skeptic, the courts promote one sense of justice and it's not "ours."[31]

Some international courts, such as the Inter-American Court of Human Rights and the African Court on Human and Peoples' Rights (ACtHPR), have generated a significant amount of attention and jurisprudence on collective rights, and particularly the collective land rights of indigenous groups. Nevertheless, this body of jurisprudence remains quite small in the shadow of decades of individual rights adjudication.[32]

Political Rights versus Socioeconomic Rights

In keeping with the tension between individual rights and responsibilities as opposed to collective rights and responsibilities, the tribunals also tend to privilege (progressive) political rights. The rights are "progressive" insofar as they are generally incremental. That is, particularly at the human rights courts, the cases incrementally push the interpretation of the human rights

---

[29] Peter Jones, "Human Rights, Group Rights and Peoples' Rights," *Human Rights Quarterly* 21, no. 1 (February 1999): 80–107, https://doi.org/10.1353/hrq.1999.0009; Miodrag A. Javonoviç, "Recognizing Minority Identities through Collective Rights," *Human Rights Quarterly* 27, no. 2 (May 2005): 625–651, https://doi.org/10.1353/hrq.2005.0019.

[30] Louis Henkin, "International Human Rights as 'Rights,'" *Nomos* 23 (1981): 257–280, https://heinonline.org/HOL/P?h=hein.journals/cdozo1&i=435; Louis Henkin, "The Universality of the Concept of Human Rights," *Annals of the American Academy of Political and Social Science* 506 (November 1989): 10–16, https://doi.org/10.1177/0002716289506001002; Paul Gordon Lauren, *The Evolution of International Human Rights: Visions Seen* (Philadelphia: University of Pennsylvania Press, 2003).

[31] Interview #930, 2014.

[32] Michael Talbot, "Collective Rights in the Inter-American and African Human Rights Systems," *Georgetown Journal of International Law* 49 (2018): 163–189, https://www.law.georgetown.edu/international-law-journal/wp-content/uploads/sites/21/2018/07/GT-GJIL 180005-1.pdf.

covenants to more and more expansive understandings of human rights. This is not to say that every case has a more progressive interpretation of the law than the case that preceded it, but rather, that over time, the judges' interpretations have moved the jurisprudence in a progressive way. Similarly, the jurisprudence at the international criminal tribunals has, over time, expanded the scope of judiciable crimes. An ever-evolving jurisprudence on wartime sexual violence, for example, has led to a more expansive, and arguably more progressive, definition of war crimes.[33]

Immunity versus Accountability

At their most fundamental level, international criminal courts challenge the idea of head of state immunity. Largely established by customary international law, head of state immunity protects heads of state from accountability in other countries and, typically, in their own.[34] International criminal tribunals, however, argue that head of state immunity does not extend to these *jus cogens* norms, nor is the question of accountability confined to domestic politics.[35] Rather, the courts and their supporters assert that heads of states can be held accountable anywhere and anytime for violations of the norms against genocide; war crimes; and torture and crimes against humanity.[36] The courts' jurisdiction over *sitting* heads of state remains a normative fault line.

---

[33] "Jurisprudence of Sexual Violence Cases," Dr. Denis Mukwege Foundation, n.d., https://www.mukwegefoundation.org/jurisprudence-sexual-violence/; Chiseche Salome Mibenge, *Sex and International Tribunals: The Erasure of Gender from the War Narrative* (Philadelphia: University of Pennsylvania Press, 2013).

[34] See, as exceptions, the "European Convention on State Immunity," opened for signature May 16, 1972, *European Treaty Series* no. 74; and the "United Nations Convention on Jurisdictional Immunities of States and Their Property," adopted December 2, 2004, *United Nations Treaty Series* A/RES/59/38. Both the UN and Council of Europe Treaties suffer from low ratification rates and the UN Convention, which opened for signature in 2004, has not yet received enough ratifications to enter into force. For more on the nexus between comity law and hard law on the question of sovereignty immunity, see, among others: Jasper Finke, "Sovereign Immunity: Rule, Comity or Something Else?" *European Journal of International Law* 21, no. 4 (November 2010): 853–881, https://doi.org/10.1093/ejil/chq068; Dapo Akande and Sangeeta Shah, "Immunities of State Officials, International Crimes, and Foreign Domestic Courts," *European Journal of International Law* 21, no. 4 (November 2010): 815–852, https://doi.org/10.1093/ejil/chq080.

[35] See for example, the scholarship on sovereignty immunity and *jus cogens* norms, including but not limited to, Akande and Shah, "Immunities of State Officials"; and Lee M. Caplan, "State Immunity, Human Rights, and Jus Cogens: A Critique of the Normative Hierarchy Theory," *The American Journal of International Law* 97, no. 4 (October 2003): 741–781, https://doi.org/10.2307/3133679.

[36] *Regina v. Bartle and the Commissioner of Police for the Metropolis and Others Ex Parte Pinochet/Regina v. Evans and Another and the Commissioner of Police for the Metropolis and Others Ex Parte Pinochet* (House of Lords, Great Britain, November 25, 1998).

Indeed, head of state accountability, rendered through treaty law rather than custom, clearly illustrates how the legalization and judicialization of rights has obscured deep-seated normative disagreements.[37]

Debating the Adjudication Process

The judicialization of politics, or the use of law and courts to settle political questions,[38] privileges one vision of human rights and accountability: rights and accountability as justiciable facts. This precludes, in many ways, the idea of human rights as a vision of a shared way of being because it prioritizes the relationship between the rights holder and the duty bearer and says that this relationship can and should be debated in a court of law.[39] This is very different than, for example, a human security or a collective rights framework, both of which would prioritize the idea of a community's well-being and lived experience, whether or not such could be adjudicated in court.[40] The legalization of rights has been part of the evolution of the international human rights and criminal justice regime and has been spurred on by a growing number of actors, from states to international organizations (IOs) to nongovernmental organizations (NGOs).[41] At the same time, this process has been exclusionary. The language and privileging of law is not shared equally across different states and cultures.[42] This is a double-edged sword.

---

[37] J. Patrick Kelly, "Naturalism in International Adjudication," *Duke Journal of Comparative & International Law* 18, no. 2 (Spring 2008): 395–421; Widener Law School Legal Studies Research Paper No. 08–29, https://ssrn.com/abstract=1103289.

[38] Ran Hirschl, "The Judicialization of Mega-Politics and the Rise of Political Courts," *Annual Review of Political Science* 11 (2008): 93–118, https://10.1146/annurev.polisci.11.053006.183906.

[39] Rotem Litinski, "Economic Rights: Are They Justiciable, and Should They Be?" *Human Rights Magazine*, November 30, 2019, https://www.americanbar.org/groups/crsj/publications/human_rights_magazine_home/economic-justice/economic-rights-are-they-justiciable-and-should-they-be-/; "Key Concepts on ESCRs–Can Economic, Social and Cultural Rights Be Litigated at Courts?" United Nations Office of the High Commissioner on Human Rights, n.d., https://www.ohchr.org/EN/Issues/ESCR/Pages/CanESCRbelitigatedatcourts.aspx.

[40] Dorothy Estrada-Tanck, *Human Security and Human Rights Under International Law: The Protections Offered to Persons Confronting Structural Vulnerability* (New York: Bloomsbury Publishing, 2016); Rhoda E. Howard-Hassmann, "Human Security: Undermining Human Rights?" *Human Rights Quarterly* 34, no. 1 (February 2012): 88–112, https://doi.org/10.1353/hrq.2012.0004.

[41] Laurence R. Helfer, "Overlegalizing Human Rights: International Relations Theory and the Commonwealth Caribbean Backlash against Human Rights Regimes," *Columbia Law Review* 102, no. 7 (November 2002): 1832–1911, https://doi.org/10.2307/1123662.

[42] Kamari Maxine Clarke, *Fictions of Justice: The International Criminal Court and the Challenge of Legal Pluralism in Sub-Saharan Africa* (New York: Cambridge University Press, 2009); Kamari Maxine Clarke, Abel S. Knottnerus, and Eefje de Volder, "Africa and the ICC: An Introduction,"

As discussed in Chapter 1, international human rights and criminal courts derive much of their moral and legal authority from their technical expertise. There is tremendous power that comes from creating, interpreting, and adjudicating human rights and criminal accountability using legal language and concepts.[43] On the other hand, however, the legalization of human rights and accountability provides ammunition for those looking to undermine the tribunals. It is easy to claim that highly legalistic courts, borrowing from the legal tools of colonial powers, are biased and imperialistic.

INTERNATIONAL COURTS, DOMESTIC CONSEQUENCES

While the tribunals' dependency on states and normative discontent can set the stage for backlash politics, I suggest that two additional factors can be the matches that ignite the flame. The first of these impetuses is the creation of domestic winners and losers as a result of international adjudication. This can generally take two forms. The first is the removal, or threatened removal, of heads of state and other political elites from office following indictments at international criminal courts. The second form is the mobilization of domestic opposition in light of international courts' rulings on a state's human rights policies and practices. This also includes domestic mobilization sparked by international criminal courts' indictments and requests for cooperation. Because of the tribunals' dependencies on states, incumbents and state apparatuses are almost always privileged at the tribunals. They can marshal resources that their domestic opponents cannot. At the same time, however, these same leaders and state bodies are the main targets of international human rights and criminal adjudication because they wield the most power. Sitting regimes and incumbents might have large arsenals at their disposal to push back against the tribunals, but they also have the most to lose.

in *Africa and the ICC: Perceptions of Justice*, eds. Kamari Maxine Clarke, Abel S. Knottnerus, and Eefje de Volder (Cambridge, UK: Cambridge University Press, 2016), 1–36; Sally Engle Merry, *Human Rights and Gender Violence: Translating International Law into Local Justice* (Chicago: University of Chicago Press, 2006); Sally Engle Merry, "Transnational Human Rights and Local Activism: Mapping the Middle," *American Anthropologist* 108, no. 1 (March 2006): 38–51, https://doi.org/10.1525/aa.2006.108.1.38.

43　Bas de Gaay Fortman, "'Adventurous' Judgments: A Comparative Exploration into Human Rights as a Moral Political Force in Judicial Law Development," *Utrecht Law Review* 2, no. 2 (December 2006): 22–43, https://ssrn.com/abstract=991091; Laurence R. Helfer and Karen J. Alter, "Legitimacy and Lawmaking: A Tale of Three International Courts," *Theoretical Inquiries in Law* 14, no. 2 (July 2013): 479–504, https://doi.org/10.1515/til-2013-024; Henry J. Steiner, Philip Alston, and Ryan Goodman, *International Human Rights in Context: Law, Politics, Morals*, 3rd ed. (Oxford: Oxford University Press, 2008).

The Threat of Individual Elite Accountability

Perhaps the most obvious way in which international human rights and criminal courts create domestic distributional consequences is through individual international criminal adjudication. In this process, individuals are held accountable for their perpetration of atrocity crimes and lose their positions and political power as a result. Sitting leaders, too, can be called to stand trial in international courts. While the international relations and international law literatures are divided about the actual likelihood of an incumbent's being removed from power by an international criminal tribunal indictment, most scholars and observers would suggest that the threat thereof is higher today than ever before.[44] In other words, international criminal accountability can create domestic winners and losers by removing the losers, quite literally, from the domestic political sphere.

That being said, the safest place for perpetrators to be in the face of international criminal tribunal indictments is in the executive mansion. From there they are able thwart or delay adjudication or deploy the international legal lasso to send their domestic opponents to stand trial in The Hague before the spotlight gets turned on them.[45]

International Courts and Domestic Policy Preferences: Who Wins?

International justice can create domestic political consequences in other ways, too. International human rights and criminal courts rule on specific allegations of human rights abuse, but in so doing, their jurisprudence touches on bigger issues related to domestic human rights policies and practices. Jurisprudence on issues as diverse as legal accountability or gay rights can prove divisive domestically, alienating some constituencies and advancing the policy agendas of others. Perhaps more importantly for understanding the courts' jurisprudence and its domestic consequences as a trigger for backlash politics, international court rulings can provide a lightning rod for domestic

---

[44] See, for example, Jeffery, *Amnesties, Accountability, and Human Rights*; Daniel Krcmaric, "Should I Stay or Should I Go? Leaders, Exile, and the Dilemmas of International Justice," *American Journal of Political Science* 62, no. 2 (April 2018): 486–498, https://doi.org/10.1111/ajps .12352; Ellen L. Lutz and Caitlin Reiger, eds., *Prosecuting Heads of State* (Cambridge, UK: Cambridge University Press, 2009); Roht-Arriaza, *The Pinochet Effect*; Sikkink, *The Justice Cascade*.

[45] Hillebrecht, "International Criminal Accountability and the Domestic Politics of Resistance"; Courtney Hillebrecht and Scott Straus, "Who Pursues the Perpetrators?: State Cooperation with the ICC," *Human Rights Quarterly* 39, no. 1 (February 2017): 162–188, https://doi.org/10 .1353/hrq.2017.0006.

mobilization.[46] This mobilization, in turn, can threaten the status quo and the executive's control over the policy agenda or even over the government as a whole.

International courts' rulings do not take immediate effect in the domestic context. Instead, states must implement and comply with them.[47] When international human rights and criminal courts issue requests for cooperation or hand down rulings, they interact directly with the executive branch, largely through their ministry or office of foreign affairs. Executives, then, have a great deal of control over if, when, and how international courts' requests and rulings are handled domestically.[48] While executives have the upper hand, domestic actors, from NGOs to legislators and judges, can form compliance coalitions. These compliance coalitions can mobilize around the courts' judgments and requests for cooperation and push for compliance.[49] It is through this process of compliance – or even considering compliance – that the international justice regime can privilege the priorities and politics of some domestic constituencies over others, and particularly over those of the incumbent.[50]

[46] Courtney Hillebrecht, "The Domestic Mechanisms of Compliance with International Law: Case Studies from the Inter-American Human Rights System," *Human Rights Quarterly* 34, no. 4 (November 2012): 959–985, https://doi.org/10.1353/hrq.2012.0069; Simmons, *Mobilizing for Human Rights*.

[47] Jillienne Haglund and Courtney Hillebrecht, "Overlapping International Human Rights Institutions: Introducing the Women's Rights Recommendations Digital Database (WR2D2)," *Journal of Peace Research* 57, no. 5 (September 2020): 648–657, https://doi.org/10.1177/0022343319897954.

[48] Haglund, *Regional Courts, Domestic Politics and the Struggle for Human Rights*; Hillebrecht, *Domestic Politics and International Human Rights Tribunals*.

[49] Hillebrecht, *Domestic Politics and International Human Rights Tribunals*.

[50] Briefly, I understand compliance to mean the degree to which states follow through with the orders handed down by the tribunal. Compliance with international human rights tribunals is a political process that is comprised of (1) financial reparations; (2) symbolic measures such as apologies and recognition for wrongs done; (3) accountability for perpetrators; (4) general measures that change policy and practice; and (5) individual measures that address the specific needs of individual victims. Xinyuan Dai, "Why Comply? The Domestic Constituency Mechanism," *International Organization* 59, no. 2 (Spring 2005): 363–398, https://doi.org/10.1017/S0020818305050125,; Jay Goodliffe and Darren G. Hawkins, "Explaining Commitment: States and the Convention against Torture," *The Journal of Politics* 68, no. 2 (May 2006): 358–371, https://doi.org/10.1111/j.1468-2508.2006.00412.x; Ryan Goodman and Thomas Pegram, eds., *Human Rights, State Compliance, and Social Change* (New York: Cambridge University Press, 2011); Courtney Hillebrecht, "Rethinking Compliance: The Challenges and Prospects of Measuring Compliance with International Human Rights Tribunals," *Journal of Human Rights Practice* 1, no. 3 (November 2009): 362–379, https://doi.org/10.1093/jhuman/hup018; Rachel Murray, "The ESCR Human Rights Law Implementation Project (HRLIP)," University of Bristol Law School, n.d., https://www.bristol.ac.uk/law/hrlip/.

The literature on compliance provides a range of factors for why states comply with international law in general and international courts in particular. While some international-level factors, such as the role of coercion and the design of international institutions, have long been regarded as explanatory factors for compliance with international law, more recent literature has emphasized domestic explanations for compliance.[51] Additional factors that affect a state's level of compliance include the role of NGOs and transnational advocacy networks focusing on cooperation and accountability,[52] the robustness of formal and informal domestic institutions vis-à-vis international courts,[53] and the enforcement structure of the international court itself.[54] What remains constant in all of these explanations is that, first, while the

[51] See, among many others: Sonia Cardenas, *Conflict and Compliance: State Responses to International Human Rights Pressure* (Philadelphia: University of Pennsylvania Press, 2007); Clifford J. Carrubba, "Courts and Compliance in International Regulatory Regimes," *Journal of Politics* 67, no. 3 (August 2005): 669–689, https://doi.org/10.1111/j.1468-2508.2005.00334.x; Courtney Hillebrecht, "Implementing International Human Rights Law at Home: Domestic Politics and the European Court of Human Rights," *Human Rights Review* 13, no. 3 (2012): 279–301, https://doi.org/10.1007/s12142-012-0227-1; Hillebrecht, "The Domestic Mechanisms of Compliance with International Law"; Hillebrecht, *Domestic Politics and International Human Rights Tribunals*; Courtney Hillebrecht, "The Power of Human Rights Tribunals: Compliance with the European Court of Human Rights and Domestic Policy Change," *European Journal of International Relations* 20, no. 4 (December 2014): 1100–1123, https://doi.org/10.1177/1354066113508591; Andreas von Staden, *Strategies of Compliance with the European Court of Human Rights: Rational Choice within Normative Constraints* (Philadelphia: University of Pennsylvania Press, 2018); Øyvind Stiansen, "Directing Compliance? Remedial Approach and Compliance with European Court of Human Rights Judgments," *British Journal of Political Science* (2019): 1–9, https://doi.org/10.1017/S0007123419000292; Øyvind Stiansen, "Delayed but Not Derailed: Legislative Compliance with European Court of Human Rights Judgments," *The International Journal of Human Rights* 23, no. 8 (2019): 1221–1247, https://doi.org/10.1080/13642987.2019.1593153.

[52] Hunjoon Kim and Kathryn Sikkink, "Explaining the Deterrence Effect of Human Rights Prosecutions for Transitional Countries," *International Studies Quarterly* 54, no. 4 (December 2010): 939–963, https://doi.org/10.1111/j.1468-2478.2010.00621.x; Francesca Lessa and Leigh A. Payne, eds., *Amnesty in the Age of Human Rights Accountability: Comparative and International Perspectives* (New York: Cambridge University Press, 2012).

[53] Lisa J. Conant, *Justice Contained: Law and Politics in the European Union* (Ithaca, NY: Cornell University Press, 2002); Javier Couso, Alexandra Huneeus, and Rachel Sieder, eds., *Cultures of Legality: Judicialization and Political Activism in Latin America* (New York: Cambridge University Press, 2010); Hillebrecht, *Domestic Politics and International Human Rights Tribunals*; Alexandra Huneeus, "Courts Resisting Courts: Lessons from the Inter-American Court's Struggle to Enforce Human Rights," *Cornell International Law Journal* 44, no. 3 (Fall 2011): 493–533, https://scholarship.law.cornell.edu/cilj/vol44/iss3/2; Alexandra Huneeus, "Compliance with Judgments and Decisions," in *The Oxford Handbook of International Adjudication*, eds. Cesare P. R. Romano, Karen J. Alter, and Yuval Shany (Oxford: Oxford University Press, 2014), 437–463.

[54] Karen J. Alter, "Who Are the Masters of the Treaty? European Governments and the European Court of Justice," *International Organization* 52, no. 1 (Winter 1998): 121–147, https://doi.org/10

tribunals and their oversight bodies monitor compliance with and implementation of these mandates, compliance remains an almost inherently domestic affair; and second, domestic compliance coalitions can mobilize around international courts' work to try to change the status quo.

Given that the international justice system takes root at the domestic level, it stands that one of the main impetuses for backlash politics is how the courts and their rulings affect domestic politics. From altering the domestic policy agenda, to changing domestic policy and practices, to strengthening domestic courts, to using international courts' rulings and cooperation requests to "name and shame" the government, international human rights and criminal tribunals' work creates domestic winners and losers.

Consider, for example, the IAHRS's jurisprudence on accountability, which has held that immunity for perpetrators of human rights violations runs counter to the Inter-American Convention on Human Rights, and that all perpetrators must be held accountable for their crimes.[55] In some cases, such as in Argentina, Uruguay, and to a lesser extent Peru, these rulings and recommendations led to the overturning of amnesties and pardons and much public debate about accountability for former heads of state.[56] In these instances, the winners (prodemocratic political elites) and the losers (former military leaders sentenced to time in prison) were clear, but the domestic ramifications of international court rulings extend far beyond this black-and-white outcome.

International human rights courts' judgments also can mobilize and empower domestic opposition groups and undermine the government's policy agenda. Take, for example, the ECtHR's rulings on abortion rights. Catholic and conservative governments across Europe have been resistant to heed the ECtHR's rulings on abortion rights, as they run counter to the Catholic Church's position on the issue.[57] Or, consider the case of the Belo Monte

---

.1162/002081898550572; Helfer and Alter, "Legitimacy and Lawmaking"; Laurence R. Helfer and Anne-Marie Slaughter, "Toward a Theory of Effective Supranational Adjudication," *Yale Law Journal* 7, no. 2 (November 2005): 273–391, http://papers.ssrn.com/sol3/papers.cfm?abstract_id=131409.

[55] *Barrios Altos* v. *Perú*, Ser. C. No. 75 Inter-Am. Ct. H.R. (March 14, 2001).

[56] "Peru's Ex-President Fujimori Ordered to Stand Trial Again," *BBC*, February 20, 2018, www.bbc.com/news/world-latin-america-43122187; Lucas Colonna, "El Indulto Alcanza a Ocho Militares y 17 Guerrilleros," *La Nación*, May 22, 2003, https://www.lanacion.com.ar/politica/el-indulto-alcanza-a-ocho-militares-y-17-guerrilleros-nid497951/; *Case of Gelman* v. *Uruguay, Monitoring Compliance with Judgment*, Inter-Am. Ct. H.R. (March 20, 2013); *Juan Carlos Abella* v. *Argentina*, Report No. 55/97, Case 11.137 Inter-Am. Comm'n H.R. (November 18, 1997).

[57] Press Unit, European Court of Human Rights, "Factsheet–Reproductive Rights," *Council of Europe*, December 2019, https://www.echr.coe.int/Documents/FS_Reproductive_ENG.pdf.

Dam in Brazil. This development project ran afoul of indigenous and land rights groups, and activists successfully lobbied the Inter-American Commission on Human Rights for precautionary measures.[58] These precautionary measures ordered the state to stop construction of the dam, threatening the Belo Monte Dam project and eliciting the ire of the Dilma Rousseff regime. This, in turn, directly prompted Brazil's attempts to underfund and thus undermine the IACmHR.[59]

By serving as a lightning rod for domestic mobilization on issues that undercut the status quo, international human rights and criminal tribunals' rulings can be the spark that sets off the flames of backlash against them. In the following section, I examine the fourth and final impetus for backlash politics: the anticipated use of violence and states' need to "blind the watchdog."

BLINDING THE WATCHDOG: ANTICIPATING FUTURE VIOLENCE

International human rights and criminal tribunals serve as watchdogs for the commission of human rights abuses and atrocity crimes, and they can advertise those abuses to a global audience. States and elites engage in backlash politics, in part, to blind these watchdogs. This driver of backlash politics is particularly salient when governments expect that there will be significant domestic mobilization against them and that international adjudication will only further empower this domestic dissent, perhaps even up to the point of destabilizing or overturning the regime.

The literature on state repression assumes that the decision to repress – or not to repress – is a strategic calculation on the part of the state[60] that is conditioned by the ability of the state to coordinate among the agents charged with engaging in repression,[61] the constraining power of domestic institutions,[62] and the effects

[58] *Comunidades Indígenas da Bacia do Rio Xingu, Pará, Brasil*, MC 382/10 Inter-Am. Comm'n H.R. (April 1, 2011).

[59] Mari Hayman, "Brazil Breaks Relations with Human Rights Commission over Belo Monte Dam," *Latin America News Dispatch*, May 3, 2011, http://latindispatch.com/2011/05/03/brazil-breaks-relations-with-human-rights-commission-over-belo-monte-dam/.

[60] Jacqueline H. R. DeMeritt, "The Strategic Use of State Repression and Political Violence," in *Oxford Research Encyclopedia of Politics*, ed. William R. Thompson (October 2016), https://doi.org/10.1093/acrefore/9780190228637.013.32.

[61] Tiberiu Dragu and Yonatan Lupu, "Collective Action and Constraints on Repression at the Endgame," *Comparative Political Studies* 51, no. 8 (July 2018): 1042–1073, https://doi.org/10.1177/0010414017730077.

[62] Daniel W. Hill and Zachary M. Jones, "An Empirical Evaluation of Explanations for State Repression," *American Political Science Review* 108, no. 3 (August 2014): 661–687, https://doi.org/10.1017/S0003055414000306.

of international law more generally.[63] More broadly, the research on repression posits that the more dissent a regime faces, the more likely it is to rely on repressive tactics to squash dissent and retain power.[64] As Ritter finds, executive stability reduces the likelihood of repression, although it can make repression more dangerous when it does happen.[65] Similarly, autocratically elected or appointed legislatures can reduce the likelihood of repression but opposition parties within legislatures increase the risk of repression.[66] One way for governments to break this cycle, of course, is to engage in backlash politics. While backlash is obviously not a panacea, it can be used to buy a flagging regime or an indicted war criminal a little latitude and to signal to the opposition that it fully intends to stay in power, regardless of the costs.

Regimes without meaningful domestic opposition do not need to fear any distributional consequences of international human rights or criminal accountability, as the risks of domestic mobilization or legislative or judicial action in response to a tribunal's ruling or indictment are low.[67] Thus, the real

---

[63]   See, among many others: Daniel W. Hill, "Estimating the Effects of Human Rights Treaties on State Behavior," *The Journal of Politics* 72, no. 4 (October 2010): 1161–1174, https://doi.org/10.1017/s0022381610000599"; Emily Hencken Ritter and Courtenay R. Conrad, "Human Rights Treaties and Mobilized Dissent against the State," *The Review of International Organizations* 11, no. 4 (December 2016): 449–475, https://doi.org/10.1007/s11558-015-9238-4.

[64]   See, for example, Sabine C. Carey, "The Dynamic Relationship between Protest and Repression," *Political Research Quarterly* 59, no. 1 (March 2006): 1–11, https://doi.org/10.1177/1065912906059100101; Courtenay R. Conrad and Emily Hencken Ritter, "Treaties, Tenure, and Torture: The Conflicting Domestic Effects of International Law," *The Journal of Politics* 75, no. 2 (April 2013): 397–409, https://doi.org/10.1017/S0022381613000091; Christian Davenport, ed., *Paths to State Repression* (Lanham, MD: Rowman & Littlefield, 2000); Christopher M. Sullivan, "Undermining Resistance: Mobilization, Repression, and the Enforcement of Political Order," *Journal of Conflict Resolution* 60, no. 7 (October 2016): 1163–1190, https://doi.org/10.1177/0022002714567951.

[65]   Emily Hencken Ritter, "Policy Disputes, Political Survival, and the Onset and Severity of State Repression," *Journal of Conflict Resolution* 58, no. 1 (February 2014): 143–168, https://doi.org/10.1177/0022002712468724; DeMeritt, "The Strategic Use of State Repression and Political Violence."

[66]   Courtenay R. Conrad, "Constrained Concessions: Beneficent Dictatorial Responses to the Domestic Political Opposition," *International Studies Quarterly* 55, no. 4 (December 2011): 1167–1187, https://doi.org/10.1111/j.1468-2478.2011.00683.x; Mauricio Rivera, "Authoritarian Institutions and State Repression: The Divergent Effects of Legislatures and Opposition Parties on Personal Integrity Rights," *Journal of Conflict Resolution* 61, no. 10 (November 2017): 2183–2207, https://doi.org/10.1177/0022002716632301.

[67]   See, among many others: Jean Allain, *A Century of International Adjudication: The Rule of Law and Its Limits* (The Hague: T.M.C. Asser Press, 2000); Michael J. Gilligan, "Is Enforcement Necessary for Effectiveness? A Model of the International Criminal Regime," *International Organization* 60, no. 4 (October 2006): 935–967, https://doi.org/10.1017/S0020818306060310; Victor Peskin, "Caution and Confrontation in the International Criminal Court's Pursuit of Accountability in Uganda and Sudan," *Human Rights Quarterly* 31, no. 3 (August 2009): 655–691, https://doi.org/10.1353/hrq.0.0093.

threat of backlash comes when a regime, facing instability, relies on repression to stay in power and manage domestic dissent, all under the watchful eye of an international human rights or criminal court.[68]

BACKLASH, BUT WHICH FORM?

While the analytical framework outlined in this chapter provides a guide for understanding the drivers and scope conditions of backlash politics, it does not speak to a related question: *which* form of backlash will states and elites choose to deploy? This is an important, if difficult, question to answer. First, it is important to note that the various manifestations of backlash described in Chapter 1 and elaborated on in further detail throughout the remainder of the book are not mutually exclusive. Nor are some forms of backlash inherently "worse" than others. While some forms of backlash, like withdrawals, are more outwardly ostentatious than other manifestations, such as tightening the tribunals' budgets, both modes of backlash can do irreparable harm to international human rights and criminal courts and their authority. Indeed, one could very easily make the argument that the subtler forms of backlash that go largely unnoticed by the media, donors, or other stakeholders can do more to hamper the ability of a tribunal to perform its duties than a recalcitrant state walking out of an international court. Perhaps more importantly, states and political elites can – and do – engage in multiple forms of backlash politics at the same time.

With that in mind, the factors that help to explain *why* states and elites engage in backlash politics also help to explain *which* types of backlash they use. Take, for example, the first two factors that explain backlash politics: the tribunals' dependence on member states and normative discontent. Even though normative discontent is a consistent feature of international adjudication, there has been sufficient normative development in human rights and criminal accountability over the past three decades that most states have some material and social incentives to at least appear to care about human rights and accountability.[69] Further, for those states that *are* the main supporters of these tribunals and on whom international justice depends, it is politically

[68] Abel Escribà-Folch, "Repression, Political Threats, and Survival under Autocracy," *International Political Science Review* 34, no. 5 (November 2013): 543–560, https://doi.org/10 .1177/0192512113488259.

[69] Emilie M. Hafner-Burton, *Forced to Be Good: Why Trade Agreements Boost Human Rights* (Ithaca, NY: Cornell University Press, 2009); Kim and Sikkink, "Explaining the Deterrence Effect of Human Rights Prosecutions for Transitional Countries"; Simmons and Jo, "Measuring Norms and Normative Contestation."

untenable to simply walk away from the international justice regime or to try to supplant it. For these states and their leaders, breaking from the international justice regime that they established and support politically, materially, and normatively is complicated.[70] This is not to say that these states will agree with each and every decision that the tribunals make. Rather, this is to suggest that these states will find value in keeping backlash "low-profile," opting for the subtler forms of backlash, such as budgetary and bureaucratic restrictions, and slowly circumscribing the courts' authority.

In contrast, for states and elites that seek to demonstrate that the normative schisms embedded within the tribunals are insurmountable and that the international justice regime is a biased outfit, the more dramatic approaches to backlash, such as withdrawals and the creation of alternatives, can prove more beneficial in the domestic political sphere.[71] Indeed, states and elites can enjoy political gains *by attacking* the tribunals. As Erik Voten describes in more detail, populist leaders, in particular, might find political headway in outwardly rejecting international courts. This is especially true if these populist leaders are able to weave the courts into their narratives about the exploitative nature of multilateralism.[72] For these states, outwardly lambasting the tribunals can be particularly important in garnering domestic support. Quietly restricting the tribunals' bureaucracy does not launch a public relations campaign that labels the courts as imperialistic and frame backlash politics as a way of rejecting Western dominance.

The third and fourth drivers of backlash politics – the domestic consequences of international adjudication and the likelihood of future violence – also can help to explain the forms of backlash politics that states and elites deploy. International courts' adverse judgments can empower the opposition vis-à-vis sitting governments. When those governments seek to limit or dilute the potential effects of these courts without inspiring more domestic dissent, subtler forms of backlash, like bureaucratic and budgetary restrictions or expanding the margin of appreciation, can serve them well. These forms of backlash limit the impact of international courts on domestic politics but do so in a way that escapes the public's general notice.

When, however, the threat of domestic dissent grows too significant, and the prospect of relying on repression in the future becomes more and more likely, states and elites might be swayed by the more outward-facing forms of backlash, such as withdrawals and substitutions. This might be their gamble

---

[70] Simmons, *Mobilizing for Human Rights.*
[71] Hillebrecht, "International Criminal Accountability and the Domestic Politics of Resistance."
[72] Voeten, "Populism and Backlashes against International Courts."

for resurrection, their one last effort to gain control over both domestic opponents and international justice. By blinding the watchdogs and rejecting international justice in these definitive ways, states and elites can buy themselves at least a little insulation from the scrutiny of international justice institutions.

To put it simply, I expect that states and political elites that (a) are not the core normative or material supporters of international courts and (b) can make domestic headway by positioning themselves against the tribunals will engage in the "louder" behaviors of withdrawing from the tribunals or working to supplant them. There is, of course, obvious overlap here with those states that are most threatened by the domestic implications of international justice and those states most likely to rely on repression in the future. These are also the same states who are most likely to rally against the liberal democratic world order. Meanwhile, those states that are (a) central to the operation of the international justice regime and adhere to and advocate for their normative foundation and (b) cannot, for either domestic or foreign policy reasons, fully reject the tribunals will engage in bureaucratic, budgetary, and legal methods of restricting the tribunals' work and circumscribing the tribunals' authority.

In the chapters that follow, I leverage the theoretical framework above mainly to explain *why* states engage in backlash and *how* different forms of backlash politics unfold. In doing so, however, I also discuss the choices that states make in deploying different forms of backlash and the consequences of those choices for international justice.

METHODOLOGICAL APPROACH AND CASE SELECTION

The theoretical framework outlined in this chapter guides the empirical analyses that follow in Chapters 3 through 6. The four drivers of backlash explained above do not constitute hypotheses; rather, they are signpost and guides for understanding how and why states and elites engage in backlash against international courts. Because the purpose of this book is not hypothesis testing, the empirical analyses rely on comparative case studies and process tracing to better understand what backlash is, how it unfolds, and why it occurs.[73] As such, the cases were selected on the dependent variable, that is,

---

[73] Nathaniel Beck, "Is Causal-Process Observation an Oxymoron?" *Political Analysis* 14, no. 3 (Summer 2006): 347–352, https://doi.org/10.1093/pan/mpj015; David Collier, "Understanding Process Tracing," *PS: Political Science & Politics* 44, no. 4 (October 2011): 823–830, https://doi.org/10.1017/S1049096511001429; James Mahoney, "The Logic of Process Tracing Tests in the Social Sciences," *Sociological Methods & Research* 41, no. 4 (November 2012): 570–597, https://doi.org/10.1177/0049124112437709.

backlash. Readers should note that while this empirical strategy limits causal inference, it facilitates a deep investigation of the shape that backlash politics takes and how it unfolds. The case studies provide illustrations of the different forms of backlash and show how those forms of backlash undermine international courts' authority. Each case study also highlights the role of the drivers of backlash identified in the theoretical framework.

The data for the case studies in the following chapters were collected from a wide range of sources. The data come from interviews with stakeholders; content analysis of thousands of newspaper articles across eight different country studies; deep engagement with policy reports and materials from the tribunals' online archives; and legal analyses of cases and judicial concepts. This multisource, multi-method approach to understanding backlash helps to illuminate the complexity of backlash against human rights and criminal tribunals across multiple courts, countries, and legal cases.

As discussed above and in Chapter 1, one of the goals of this book is to move the current thinking about backlash away from single case studies and to examine, instead, backlash across a number of contexts. The rest of this section describes the case selection and scope of examples examined throughout the rest of the book. It also provides some basic information about the court systems from which the empirical cases draw.

Case Selection

The empirical chapters that follow focus on the experience of the European and Inter-American Human Rights systems and the International Criminal Court. The European and Inter-American regional systems represent the vast majority of international human rights adjudication, while the ICC is the most politically salient and far-reaching of the international criminal tribunals. It is also the only court with a global mandate. The depth and breadth of these institutions make them all targets for backlash politics, and despite the differences in their scope and mandate, each of the three systems have all experienced the four types of backlash identified in Chapter 1. Moreover, across the three systems, patterns of backlash emerge on the key drivers of backlash identified above: the effect of the tribunals' continued dependency on states; normative discontent; the courts' role as watchdogs; and the creation of domestic political gains and losses as a result of international human rights and criminal adjudication. Taken together, these three human rights and criminal tribunals provide rich examples of backlash and resistance across a range of states, stakeholders, and normative standards. Each of the following chapters provides a discussion of the individual cases selected to illustrate the multiple forms of backlash politics.

The European Court of Human Rights

The European Court of Human Rights was created in 1950 by the Council of Europe. The Council of Europe, and by extension the ECtHR, has a broad reach, with membership spanning from Russia and Azerbaijan in the east to Iceland in the west. The Court is charged with investigating and ruling on suspected violations of the European Convention on Human Rights.[74] While the Court can – and occasionally does – hear interstate petitions, the vast majority of its work focuses on petitions brought by individuals against member states. The ECtHR receives a tremendous number of such petitions each year. For example, the number of petitions the ECtHR received in 2019 topped 44,500.[75] As a result of this crushing caseload, the ECtHR has struggled to reduce delays and redundancies in its work. In 2014, the Council of Europe agreed to Protocol 14 of the European Convention, which implemented a streamlined process for reviewing clone petitions, or petitions that dealt with violations on which the Court had previously ruled. Protocol 14 has helped to reduce some of the backlog, but it continues to mask the underlying problem the Court faces: lack of compliance with its rulings. With the departure of the UK from the European Union and threats to the ECtHR from historical antagonists and supporters alike, the ECtHR is facing a new wave of backlash against its authority.

The Inter-American Human Rights System

The Inter-American Human Rights System, which is part of the Organization of American States, is comprised of two different institutions: the Inter-American Commission on Human Rights and the Inter-American Court of Human Rights. The Commission was founded in 1959 and plays a number of important roles in the region. It has quasi-judicial powers, by which it receives petitions, investigates the allegations, and hears cases. The Commission also works with the different parties to come to friendly settlement agreements. When the Commission is unable to broker a friendly settlement agreement and finds that there has been a violation of the Inter-American Convention on

---

74 "European Convention for the Protection of Human Rights and Fundamental Freedoms, as amended by Protocol Nos. 11 and 14," opened for signature November 4, 1950, *European Treaty Series* no. 5, https://www.echr.coe.int/documents/convention_eng.pdf.

75 European Court of Human Rights, "Analysis of Statistics 2019," *Council of Europe*, June 2020, https://www.echr.coe.int/Documents/Stats_analysis_2019_ENG.pdf.

Human Rights, it can ask states to take a number of measures to remedy the violation. If states fail to do so, then the Commission can hand the case up to the Inter-American Court of Human Rights.[76]

The Inter-American Court of Human Rights is a judicial body designed to adjudicate on cases of alleged violations of the Inter-American Convention on Human Rights. The Court can only adjudicate on cases after they have gone through the Inter-American Commission on Human Rights. In addition to ruling on the admissibility and merits of a case, the Inter-American Court of Human Rights can rule on the reparations needed. These reparations include monetary payment, individual measures related to the unique circumstances of the individual victims, and measures of non-repetition, which are designed to make sure that those violations are not repeated.[77]

The International Criminal Court

The International Criminal Court was established in 1998 with the passage of the Rome Statute. The Court, which is based in The Hague, is designed to try the worst perpetrators of the worst crimes. It is meant to sit at the bottom, not the top, of the national and international legal architecture, trying only those criminals whom domestic courts cannot or will not try. The ICC can hear cases involving three crimes: genocide, crimes against humanity, and war crimes. As noted above, cases come either from self-referrals, UN Security Council Referrals, or via the *propio motu* powers of the Office of the Prosecutor. The ICC has opened investigations in thirteen situations, but since it became operational in 2002, it has only handed down four convictions.[78] In addition to the open cases, the ICC has preliminary examinations open in nine countries, including a number outside of Africa.

The Vast Architecture of the International Justice Regime

The European, Inter-American, and ICC systems do not operate in isolation. Instead, they are part of a complex architecture of international justice institutions. Throughout the book, I make occasional reference to the other parts of the international justice regime, including human rights courts, quasi-judicial institutions, and criminal tribunals. The appendix provides a description of

---

[76] Inter-American Commission on Human Rights, "Basic Documents in the Inter-American System," *Organization of American States*, 2020, https://www.oas.org/en/iachr/mandate/Basics/intro.asp.

[77] Pasqualucci, *The Practice and Procedure of the Inter-American Court.*

[78] "The Court Today, ICC-PIDS-TCT-01–113/20_Eng," International Criminal Court, September 2020, https://www.icc-cpi.int/iccdocs/PIDS/publications/TheCourtTodayEng.pdf.

these other institutions. Further research can apply the definition, typology, and explanation of backlash outlined here and throughout the book to the experience of any of these institutions.

CONCLUSION

This chapter has set out the theoretical framework that informs the remainder of the book. Throughout the chapter, I suggested that backlash against international human rights and criminal tribunals is a function of four factors: the tribunals' abiding dependency on states; underlying normative schisms within the courts' member states and beyond; the creation of domestic political winners and losers as a result of international adjudication; and the likelihood of states and elites' relying on future political violence. These factors are not mutually exclusive. Instead, as the case studies in the next four chapters suggest, backlash politics is multicausal and manifold in its presentation.

The following chapters present examples of backlash from Colombia to Russia, Brazil to Rwanda. They cross both the human rights and international criminal accountability spheres, and cover multiple continents and countries. Throughout the remainder of the book, it becomes clear that backlash to international courts and human rights is not simply a one-off example of normatively bad behavior, but rather, a systematic attack on the authority of international human rights and criminal courts. Whether through withdrawals or bureaucratic maneuvering, whether prompted by the anticipation of future violence or the tribunals' abiding dependence on states, backlash in all of its manifestations seeks to undermine the tribunals' authority. Despite these threats, international justice can be, as Mr. Eboe-Osuji and Mr. Jackson remarked, diverse, permanent and, ultimately, indispensable.

3

The Politics of Withdrawal

INTRODUCTION

When Rodrigo Duterte, the President of the Philippines and an outspoken critic of the International Criminal Court, made good on his threats to leave the ICC, he became only the second head of state to usher in a withdrawal from the Rome Statute.[1] Duterte was not alone in threatening to leave the ICC. Threatening to walk out of an international court following a judgment that empowers the opposition, reveals normative discontent, or threatens a head of state's hold on power is part and parcel of international adjudicative politics. But, in the case of Duterte, it was not just an instance of a vociferous critic blowing off steam. Rather, it was an example of backlash.

As outlined in Chapter 1, backlash against international human rights tribunals has a number of distinctive features: (1) it is neither normatively "bad behavior" nor routine pushback against international courts, but rather part of a larger pattern of behavior; (2) it is directed at the authority of international human rights criminal courts; and (3) it is action that can be, but is not always, coupled with angry rhetoric. While backlash can take any number of forms, this chapter focuses on withdrawals from international human rights and criminal courts. Throughout the chapter, I pay close attention to the drivers of backlash identified in Chapter 2. In particular, I suggest that withdrawals are largely a function of regime uncertainty and the use of – or anticipated use of – violence and repression to quell domestic opposition. I also illustrate how underlying normative discontent at the courts can set the stage for withdrawals.

The chapter begins by explaining why states and elites turn to withdrawals as a form of backlash politics and then maps patterns of withdrawals from

---

[1] Regina Cabato, "Philippines Leaves International Criminal Court as Duterte Probe Is Underway," *The Washington Post*, March 18, 2019, https://www.washingtonpost.com/world/as ia_pacific/philippines-leaves-international-criminal-court-as-duterte-probe-underway/2019/03/ 18/f929d1b6-4952-11e9-93d0-64dbcf38ba41_story.html.

international human rights and criminal courts. The chapter then turns to explaining the empirical approach and offers a set of case studies designed to illustrate patterns of withdrawal (or the lack thereof) in Peru, Venezuela, and Colombia. Following the case studies, the chapter concludes.

EXPLAINING WITHDRAWALS FROM INTERNATIONAL HUMAN RIGHTS AND CRIMINAL COURTS

The agreements that establish international courts all have provisions for how states can withdraw, or abdicate, from the courts and their foundational legal instruments.[2] As such, abdicating from international human rights and criminal courts is not, by definition, illegal or even necessarily backlash. The exceptions to this, however, can constitute one of the most visible manifestations of backlash against human rights and criminal tribunals, and the international justice regime more broadly.[3]

Norms and Dependencies: Facilitating Backlash and Exacerbating Its Impacts

Withdrawals from international courts are driven, in part, by contestation about the tribunals' substantive norms, as well the very idea of human rights and criminal adjudication. As the case studies later in this chapter illustrate, normative schisms over collective versus individual rights, political versus socioeconomic rights, and the threat of individual criminal accountability spur withdrawals and attempted withdrawals.

Not only do normative schisms drive withdrawals, but withdrawals have serious implications for the tribunals' normative and moral authority. Withdrawals call into question the very premise of the universality of human rights and criminal accountability norms. When states withdraw from international human rights and criminal courts, they cast doubt on the norm of compulsory jurisdiction, the courts' ability to articulate and enforce that norm, and the value of the human rights and criminal accountability norms at the heart of these institutions.[4]

---

[2] See, for example, Stephen P. Mulligan, *Withdrawal from International Agreements: Legal Framework, the Paris Agreement, and the Iran Nuclear Agreement* (Washington, DC: Congressional Research Service, 2018), https://fas.org/sgp/crs/row/R44761.pdf.

[3] Inken von Borzyskowski and Felicity Vabulas, "Credible Commitments? Explaining IGO Suspensions to Sanction Political Backsliding," *International Studies Quarterly* 63, no. 1 (March 2019): 139–152, https://doi.org/10.1093/isq/sqy051.

[4] The principle of compulsory jurisdiction implies, of course, that once a state has accepted the jurisdiction of a tribunal, it must submit to judicial review when that court has a case against it, for example Vanda Lamm, *Compulsory Jurisdiction in International Law* (Cheltenham, UK: Edward Elgar, 2014); Yuval Shany, "Assessing the Effectiveness of International Courts: A Goal-Based Approach," *American Journal of International Law* 106, no. 2 (April 2012): 225–270,

Withdrawals also target the tribunals' structural and adjudicative authority. As explained in Chapter 2, the tribunals rely on states for material and procedural support. If states were to withdraw from the courts en masse, the courts themselves would suffer. Not only does the loss of member states mean a loss of revenue, but the drama surrounding withdrawals diverts precious resources away from casework and proactive public outreach and toward crisis management.[5] Furthermore, when a state withdraws from an international court, the court no longer has access to witnesses, victims, or evidence and the case cannot proceed because the "defendant" is no longer participating in the process. The implications are real. Justice goes unserved and victims remain without recourse.

Domestic Consequences and the Threat of Violence

As discussed in Chapters 1 and 2, when international human rights and criminal tribunals hand down adverse judgments, they or their corresponding political institutions also demand that states take a set of steps to provide reparations for the victims, publicize the rulings, and enact the policies necessary to prevent the violations from recurring, among other things. While the tribunals and their oversight bodies monitor compliance with and implementation of these mandates, compliance remains an almost inherently domestic affair.[6] Nevertheless, international court rulings have domestic consequences. In particular, when international human rights and criminal courts hand down adverse judgments, they empower domestic opposition vis-à-vis the state. These rulings serve as a tool for mobilizing against the state for policy change, and, in the case of international criminal tribunals, the rulings can even call for the removal of sitting heads of state. Withdrawing from an international court becomes a quick fix to a long-running problem. Moreover, withdrawing from an international human rights or criminal court can, at least

---

https://doi.org/10.5305/amerjintelaw.106.2.0225; Yuval Shany, *Questions of Jurisdiction and Admissibility before International Courts* (Cambridge, UK: Cambridge University Press, 2016).

5   While young courts tend to want to attract more cases – and thus withdrawals are a blow because they reduce the potential pool of cases – the regional human rights courts, especially in Europe and the Americas, are drowning in case backlogs. Case in point: in 2014, *The Guardian* reported that the backlog at the European Court of Human Rights fell *below* 100,000 cases for the first time in five years. Withdrawals from new or inchoate courts are, as evidenced in Table 3.1, essentially non-existent. Owen Bowcott, "Backlog at European Court of Human Rights Falls below 100,000 Cases," *The Guardian*, January 30, 2014, www.theguardian.com/law/2014/jan/30/european-court-human-rights-case-backlog-falls.

6   Courtney Hillebrecht, "The Power of Human Rights Tribunals: Compliance with the European Court of Human Rights and Domestic Policy Change," *European Journal of International Relations* 20, no. 4 (December 2014): 1100–1123, https://doi.org/10.1177/1354066113508591; Courtney Hillebrecht, *Domestic Politics and International Human Rights Tribunals: The Problem of Compliance* (New York: Cambridge University Press, 2014).

temporarily, eliminate the international spotlight on domestic abuses, stop the flow of cases to the courts, and signal to domestic opposition that the regime is willing and able to inflict more suffering on them.[7]

MAPPING THE SCOPE OF WITHDRAWAL

Although withdrawals can be particularly damaging for international courts, they are rather rare. Before turning to a set of comparative case studies on withdrawals from the Inter-American Court of Human Rights, this chapter maps the scope of withdrawals from the regional human rights courts and the ICC. Table 3.1 shows the universe of threatened and actual withdrawals from these courts. To be counted as a "threatened" withdrawal, there must be either high-level talks about withdrawal between an executive to the tribunal and/or domestic legislative or judicial action toward withdrawal. More specifically, withdrawal threats must satisfy one of the following criteria: the state presented withdrawal proceedings to the international court; sub-state actors initiated the domestic processes associated with withdrawal; or the court or oversight body has spoken out against the threat, deeming it serious enough to warrant a response. As with the definition of backlash presented in Chapter 1, angry rhetoric is not enough. While unhappy executives or other political elites might preach about how the tribunals violate sovereignty rights or perpetuate the ills of global governance, until those verbal threats prompt a response from the court or oversight body, that bluster is not a particularly costly signal.

The examples of withdrawals and attempted withdrawals listed in Table 3.1 have taken a variety of shapes. Some, like the experiences of the Caribbean countries of the Dominican Republic and Trinidad and Tobago, have relied on domestic constitutional courts to facilitate the withdrawals. In other instances, such as South Africa, domestic high courts have invalidated threats of withdrawal pursued by executives or legislatures.[8] In other situations, withdrawals or threats thereof have simply limited the scope of the court's

---

[7] See, for example, Abel Escribà-Folch, "Repression, Political Threats, and Survival under Autocracy," *International Political Science Review* 34, no. 5 (November 2013): 543–560, https://doi.org/10.1177/0192512113488259.

[8] Alfonso Calcaneo Sanchez, "The Dominican Withdrawal from the Jurisdiction of the Inter-American Court of Human Rights: A Legal and Contextual Analysis," Master's thesis, University of Oslo, 2015, https://www.duo.uio.no/handle/10852/46874; Natasha Parassram Concepcion, "The Legal Implications of Trinidad and Tobago's Withdrawal from the American Convention on Human Rights," *American University International Law Review* 16, no. 3 (2001): 847–890, https://digitalcommons.wcl.american.edu/cgi/viewcontent.cgi?article=1242&context=auilr; Peter Fabricius, "South Africa Confirms Withdrawal from ICC," *Daily Maverick*, December 7, 2017, https://www.dailymaverick.co.za/article/2017-12-07-south-africa-confirms-withdrawal-from-icc/.

TABLE 3.1 *Withdrawals and threatened withdrawals from international human rights and criminal courts*

Tribunal	State	Date of Threatened Withdrawal[1]	Date of Withdrawal	Other
Inter-American Court of Human Rights	Dominican Republic		2014	
	Peru	1999–2000		
	Venezuela		2012–2013	
Organization of American States & Inter-American Commission on Human Rights	Brazil			Stopped relations with IACmHR, 2011
	Trinidad and Tobago		1999	
	Venezuela		2017	
European Court of Human Rights	Hungary	2017 (under consideration)		
	Russia	2000, 2018		
African Court on Human and Peoples' Rights	Rwanda			Withdrew from cases derived from petitions from NGOs and individuals 2016
International Criminal Court	African Union	2012 (+/−)		
	Burundi		2016–2017	
	The Gambia	2016–2017		
	Kenya	2016		
	Philippines		2019	
	South Africa	2016–2017		

[1] These threats were unrealized.

authority over a state's practices, as in the case of Rwanda and the African Court on Human and Peoples' Rights.[9] Other withdrawals, such as Venezuela's most recent abrogation attempt, have included not just withdrawing from the human rights or criminal court but also the parent organization.[10] With the exception of a possible British withdrawal from the European Court of Human Rights as a result of Brexit, none of the withdrawals or threatened withdrawals have come from the tribunals' core stakeholders.[11]

CASE SELECTION AND EMPIRICAL APPROACH

In order to better understand why states withdraw from international courts and how this form of backlash politics unfolds, the remainder of the chapter offers a set of empirical examples from Peru, Venezuela, and Colombia. These case studies rely on legal analyses, newspapers of record, and policy documents, among other sources, to process trace the politics of backlash. The theoretical framework presented in Chapter 2 guides the examination of how the drivers of backlash exacerbate the threat of states' withdrawals from international courts and, in the case of Venezuela, push states over the edge toward formal abrogation.

Case Selection

The empirical cases that follow focus on the experiences of Peru, Venezuela, and Colombia. These three states share some critical commonalities: they are

9   "Rwanda's Withdrawal of Its Special Declaration to the African Court: Setback for the Protection of Human Rights," *International Federation for Human Rights*, March 17, 2016, https://www.fidh.org/en/region/Africa/rwanda/joint-civil-society-statement-on-rwanda-s-with drawal-of-its-article.

10 "Venezuela to Withdraw from OAS as Deadly Protests Continue," *BBC News*, April 27, 2017, www.bbc.com/news/world-latin-america-39726605.

11 Tobias Lock, "Reassessing the European Convention on Human Rights in the Light of Brexit," *E-International Relations*, July 10, 2017, www.e-ir.info/2017/07/10/reassessing-the-european-convention-on-human-rights-in-the-light-of-brexit/; Ben Glaze, "EU Referendum: Forget Brexit, It's the European Convention on Human Rights We Need to Quit, Says Theresa May," *Mirror Online*, April 25, 2016, https://www.mirror.co.uk/news/eu-referendum-forget-brexit-its-7829574; Anushka Asthana and Rowena Mason, "UK Must Leave European Convention on Human Rights, Says Theresa May," *The Guardian*, April 25, 2016, https://www.theguardian.com/politics/2016/apr/25/uk-must-leave-european-convention-on-human-rights-theresa-may-eu-referendum.
    This is not to suggest that these stakeholder states do not receive adverse judgments from international tribunals. Even a quick glance at the European Court of Human Right's adverse judgments suggests that key stakeholders receive their own share of rulings from regional human rights courts.

all Bolivarian states with patterns of widespread physical violence. While in Peru and Colombia that violence has centered on countering guerilla movements and rural insurgencies, in Venezuela, the violence has taken the shape of repressing opposition parties' civil and political rights.

All three countries have had active caseloads before both the Inter-American Commission and Court of Human Rights. Indeed, if the number and depth of cases before a court were the driving factor of withdrawals, Colombia should have been a prime suspect for leaving the Inter-American Court of Human Rights. Colombia has received a number of adverse judgments that deal precisely with its domestic security apparatus and its long-running internal conflict. Government troops have been implicated in aiding paramilitary forces in clearing rural villages, and the IACtHR has even put restrictions on how Colombia can engage in reparations (see the *Operation Genesis* case).[12] And yet, Colombia has *not* withdrawn from the IACtHR.[13]

In contrast, Peru, whose caseload before the IACtHR also primarily pertains to its efforts to fight a leftwing domestic insurgency, threatened to withdraw from the Inter-American Human Right System (IAHRS) in 1999–2000 but never actually did so. Peru's threatened withdrawal came in response to an IACtHR ruling that argued that three Peruvian Constitutional Court justices had been unlawfully removed because they ruled against Alberto Fujimori's attempts to seek another term as Peruvian president.[14] The IACtHR threatened Fujimori's regime security, and he threatened to withdraw from the Court in turn.

Venezuela, in contrast, did withdraw from the Inter-American Court of Human Rights. Although it was a case against prison conditions that

---

[12]   Geneviève Lessard, "Preventive Reparations at a Crossroads: The Inter-American Court of Human Rights and Colombia's Search for Peace," *The International Journal of Human Rights* 22, no. 9 (2018): 1–20, https://doi.org/10.1080/13642987.2016.1268405; Luis van Isschot, "Assessing the Record of the Inter-American Court of Human Rights in Latin America's Rural Conflict Zones (1979–2016)," *The International Journal of Human Rights* 22, no. 9 (2018): 1144–1167, https://doi.org/10.1080/13642987.2017.1382086; *Caso de las Comunidades Afrodescendientes desplazadas de la Cuenca del Río Cacarica (Operación Génesis)* v. *Colombia*, Excepciones Preliminares, Fondo, Reparaciones y Costas, Serie C No. 270 (Inter-American Court of Human Rights November 20, 2013).

[13]   Courtney Hillebrecht and Alexandra Huneeus, with Sandra Borda, "The Judicialization of Peace," *Harvard International Law Journal* 59, no. 2 (Summer 2018): 279–330, https://ssrn.com/abstract=3227107.

[14]   Anthony Faiola, "Peru Withdraws from International Rights Court," *Washington Post*, July 8, 1999, https://www.washingtonpost.com/archive/politics/1999/07/08/peru-withdraws-from-international-rights-court/bbd3415f-2a8a-4965-a7ad-2616d214be60/; Jo-Marie Burt, "Fujimori vs. the Inter-American Court," *The North American Congress on Latin America*, September 25, 2007, https://nacla.org/article/fujimori-vs-inter-american-court.

ultimately led to Venezuela's withdrawal from the IACtHR in 2012–2013, then-president Hugo Chávez argued that it was about "dignity,"[15] stressing the normative discontent at the IACtHR. More recently, in 2017, Venezuela also moved to withdraw from the IACtHR's parent organization, the Organization of American States, which means leaving the Inter-American Commission on Human Rights. The official abrogation and withdrawal process takes two years, but other member states started to exclude Venezuela from the OAS' proceedings almost immediately following the announcement of Venezuela's intended withdrawal from the organization.[16]

CASE 1: PERU AND THE (MOSTLY) REALIZED WITHDRAWAL

Today, Peru enjoys a generally collegial working relationship with the IAHRS, and Peruvians regularly seek recourse at the IACmHR and the IACtHR, leading Peru to have one of the most active caseloads before the Inter-American Commission on Human Rights and the Inter-American Court of Human Rights. Two decades ago, however, Peru's relationship with the IACtHR was very different. In 1999, then-president Alberto Fujimori initiated a withdrawal process in a last-ditch effort to secure his hold on power.

Alberto Fujimori came to power in Peru in 1990, when he secured the presidency via popular vote. Over the next few years, however, Fujimori became increasingly authoritarian. He staged an autogolpe, or self-coup, in 1992, doing away with critical checks on executive power. In addition to dissolving Congress and shuttering the Constitutional Guarantees Court, which operated as a constitutional court, Fujimori dismissed Supreme Court justices and pushed for a new constitution, which was adopted in 1993.[17] As Helio Bicudo, the former president of the Inter-American Commission on Human Rights described it, "President Fujimori instituted a regime with clear dictatorial qualities, establishing what could be classified as state terrorism."[18] Indeed, Fujimori's presidency was marked by

[15]   Burt, "Fujimori vs. the Inter-American Court."

[16]   "Peru to Maduro: You're Still Not Welcome at Summit of Americas," *Reuters*, April 3, 2018, https://www.reuters.com/article/us-peru-venezuela-politics/peru-to-maduro-youre-still-not-welcome-at-summit-of-americas-idUSKCN1HA2HS; "CARICOM Divided on Venezuela at OAS Assembly," *The New York CaribNews*, October 29, 2020, https://www.nycaribnews.com/articles/caricom-divided-on-venezuela-at-oas-assembly/.

[17]   República del Perú Constitución Política de 1993 (Republic of Peru 1993 Political Constitution) (The Peruvian Congress, 1993).

[18]   Helio Bicudo, "The Inter-American Commission on Human Rights and the Process of Democratization in Peru," *Human Rights Brief* 9, no. 2 (Winter 2002): 18–20, https://digitalcommons.wcl.american.edu/hrbrief/vol9/iss2/5/.

a devastating conflict between the state and the Marxist insurgency, Sendero Luminoso, or Shining Path. He relied on increasing levels of repression and corruption to maintain state control.

International Adjudication and Expanding Executive Authority

One of Fujimori's main points of contention was, consistent with the theoretical framework above, maintaining power in the face of international adjudication that mobilized domestic opposition and sought to limit executive power. As the theoretical framework in Chapter 2 explains, international human rights adjudication has domestic consequences. In Peru in the 1990s, these consequences centered on empowering the opposition vis-à-vis an increasingly authoritarian regime. In particular, domestic opponents tried to use the Inter-American Human Rights System to curb Fujimori's efforts to expand executive power.

Fujimori sought to retain his hold on Peruvian politics by altering Peru's rules on presidential reelection. The new 1993 constitution made an important provision for reelection, stating in Article 112: "The presidential mandate is five years. The President may be re-elected immediately for an additional period. Once a minimum of another constitutional period has passed, a former president may run for the presidency, subject to the same conditions."[19] The new constitutional provision solved Fujimori's immediate problem of seeking reelection in 1995, an election which he won handily.[20] It did not, however, solve his long-term problem of seeking reelection indefinitely. Thus, in 1996, the Peruvian Congress, which was stacked with Fujimoristas, passed Law No. 26,627, known as the "Interpretation Law." Law No. 26,627 was meant to clarify Article 112 of the Constitution by stating that the reelection provisions only took effect after the new constitution was passed. Terms served prior to the new constitution did not count against Fujimori's subsequent reelection bids.[21]

The Lima Bar Association (LBA) swiftly filed a suit with the Constitutional Court about the constitutionality of Law No. 26,627, which the Court agreed

[19] *Caso del Tribunal Constitucional* v. *Perú*, Competencia, Serie C No. 55 (Inter-American Court of Human Rights, September 24, 1999); Sally Bowen, "Peru's New Constitution Seems Sure to Satisfy the President's Desires," *The Christian Science Monitor*, July 27, 1993, https://www.csmonitor.com/1993/0727/27062.html; Constitución Política del Perú 1993 con reformas hasta 2005 (1993), https://pdba.georgetown.edu/Constitutions/Peru/per93reforms05.html.

[20] Calvin Sims, "Fujimori Wins 5 More Years at Peru Helm," *The New York Times*, April 11, 1995, https://www.nytimes.com/1995/04/11/world/fujimori-wins-5-more-years-at-peru-helm.html.

[21] Rachel Glickhouse, "Explainer: Presidential Reelection in Latin America," AS/COA, April 28, 2015, https://www.as-coa.org/articles/explainer-presidential-reelection-latin-america.

to hear. On November 20, 1996, the Constitutional Court heard the case in a public hearing. On December 27, 1996, they issued their decision: five justices supported the opinion that the Interpretation Law was nonapplicable, versus unconstitutional. Two justices voted against that ruling.[22] After the draft opinion was made public, two of the justices sent a letter to the President of the Constitutional Court alleging "inconsistencies" in how the case was decided. They became subject to what they called "political harassment." Shortly thereafter, forty members of Congress asked the Constitutional Court to issue a ruling expressly on the issue of constitutionality, which the Court rejected and called an "extremely serious attack against the jurisdictional autonomy of [the] Court."[23] One of the judges alleged that key documents were taken from the justices' offices in an intimidation campaign.

What followed next was a series of rather subtle moves and countermoves. The justices on the Constitutional Court voted again on the draft opinion. Only three, Justices Aguirre Roca, Rey Terry, and Revoredo Marsano de Mur, voted in favor of the nonapplicability opinion this time. This decision put them at odds with Fujimori, who ensured that they would pay for their disloyalty. Two other judges, Justices Acosta Sánchez and García Marcelo, signed a "judgment" that argued that the initial complaint about the law was unfounded, which the President of the Constitutional Court said lacked "legal value and effect."[24]

The following month, February 1997, Congress constituted an Investigation Committee to examine the judges' harassment claims. In the meantime, Justices Acosta Sánchez and García Marcelo, friends of Fujimori, lodged complaints against Justices Aguirre Roca, Rey Terry, and Revoredo Marsano de Mur. The Investigation Committee, also stacked with Fujimoristas, charged them with violating the Constitution. The three justices were then called before a newly constituted Evaluation Sub-Committee. The three judges saw the Sub-Committee as a reprisal for their vote on the Interpretation Law. And, indeed, the Sub-Committee recommended that

---

[22]   The rules of the Court required six votes to make an unconstitutionality ruling, thus the Peruvian Court was unable to rule that the Interpretation Law was unconstitutional. See: *Caso del Tribunal Constitucional* v. *Perú*, Competencia; *Caso del Tribunal Constitucional* v. *Perú*, Fondo, Reparaciones y Costas, Serie C No. 71 (Inter-American Court of Human Rights, January 31, 2001).

[23]   This was quoted in the court case as such: "They also said that the Constitutional Court should rule within the period of 30 working days established in article 34 of Law No. 26,435, which, they claimed had expired on January 10, 1997. This letter was rejected by the Constitutional Court, considering that it constituted an 'extremely serious attack against the jurisdictional autonomy of [the] Court' and an act of pressure" (p. 25).

[24]   *Caso del Tribunal Constitucional* v. *Perú*, Competencia.

the Congressional Permanent Committee impeach the three justices, which Congress did on May 28, 1997.[25] As a result of their dismissal, the Constitutional Court only had four sitting justices and was, therefore, technically unable to evaluate the constitutionality of laws or executive orders. Fujimori was thus able to continue to govern Peru and, critically, run for reelection for his third consecutive term in 2000.[26]

After Fujimori coerced the Peruvian Congress to clear the way for him to run for a third term, he had two remaining challenges to face: a Peruvian public that was widely opposed to a president seeking a third term and the Inter-American Human Rights System. On the first challenge, Fujimori and his allies took a number of steps to hamstring the different domestic institutions charged with ensuring free and fair elections.[27] Fujimoristas exploited their control of the media and initiated a systemic campaign of harassment against any opposition. The government also leveraged its widely used food pantries (according to the North American Congress on Latin America, NACLA, 42.5 percent of all household relied on government food aid, with 65 percent of rural families relying on such support) to advance its pro-Fujimori agenda and intimidate the general population.[28] As Human Rights Watch described in their 1999 report:

> President Alberto Fujimori and the political party he leads, Change 90-New Majority (Cambio 90-Nueva Mayoría, C90-NM), continued to undermine the rule of law and independence of the judiciary during 1998. At the same time, they impeded the exercise of political rights. Although political violence and human rights violations associated with counterinsurgency continued to decline, the incidence of criminal violence increased, provoking the C90-NM-controlled Congress to delegate powers to the executive branch to impose tough new anti-crime decrees likely to lead to violations of the rights of criminal suspects. The decrees permitted the use of military courts to try serious crimes, systematic restrictions of suspects' rights and due process guarantees, and a special coordinating role for the abusive National Intelligence Service, which was responsible for grave human rights violations committed in combatting leftist insurgencies.[29]

[25] *Caso del Tribunal Constitucional v. Perú*, Competencia.

[26] Inter-American Commission on Human Rights, "Second Report on the Situation of Human Rights in Peru, OEA/Ser.L/V/II.106, Doc. 59 rev," *Organization of American States*, June 2, 2000, www.cidh.org/countryrep/Peru2000en/TOC.html.

[27] Coletta Youngers, "Fujimori's Relentless Pursuit of Reelection," *The North American Congress on Latin America Report on the Americas* 33, no. 4 (2000): 6–10, https://doi.org/10.1080/10714839.2000.11722667.

[28] Youngers, "Fujimori's Relentless Pursuit."

[29] "Peru: Human Rights Developments," *Human Rights Watch*, 1999, https://www.hrw.org/legacy/worldreport99/americas/peru.html.

While Fujimori's campaign of undermining judicial independence, corruption, and intimidation mitigated his biggest domestic threats to reelection, he and his allies still had to contend with the Inter-American Human Rights System.

Threats to Regime Stability

By 1999, the Inter-American Court of Human Rights was considering three cases against Peru that struck right at the heart of Fujimori's control of the country and his insatiable desire to remain in power. Of the three cases – *Castillo Petruzzi et al. v. Peru*; *Ivcher Bronstein v. Peru*; and the *Constitutional Court v. Peru* – the first two dealt with the rights to nationality and due process. In the case of *Castillo Petruzzi et al. v. Peru*, the Court found that Peru had violated the rights of the Chilean petitioners by charging them with "treason against the Peruvian fatherland" and convicting them without upholding due process. With regard to the second case, *Ivcher Bronstein v. Peru*, the Court found that Mr. Bronstein had been stripped of his naturalized Peruvian citizenship in what he viewed as retaliation for the anti-Fujimori tenor of *Frecuencia Latina*, the television network he owned.[30] The Peruvian state had been relying on these repressive tactics to remain in power and fully expected to do more of the same in the future. The IACtHR rulings threatened to expose Peru's dirty laundry and mobilize domestic dissent, further contributing to a dissent–repression cycle.

In the aftermath of the *Castillo Petruzzi et al.* judgment, Peru declared that it would not comply with the Court's rulings on that case, nor would it pay the reparations awarded in a different case (*Loayza Tamayo v. Peru*) because it needed to crack down on terrorists.[31] As the former IACtHR president, Helio Bicudo, explained: "Peru's reaction was unusual. On July 15, 1999, Peru informed the Inter-American Court that the Plenary Assembly of the Supreme Council of Military Justice found the Court's sentence in the *Castillo Petruzzi et al.* case 'lacked impartiality and violated the national Constitution.'"[32] The Inter-American Court responded by reminding Peru

---

[30] *Caso Castillo Petruzzi y otros v. Perú*, Cumplimiento de Sentencia, Serie C No. 52 (Inter-American Court of Human Rights, November 17, 1999); *Caso Ivcher Bronstein v. Perú*, Fondo, Reparaciones y Costas, Serie C No. 74 (Inter-American Court of Human Rights, February 6, 2001); *Caso del Tribunal Constitucional v. Perú*, Fondo, Reparaciones y Costas; Bicudo, "The Inter-American Commission on Human Rights."

[31] *Case of Loayza-Tamayo v. Peru*, Reparations and Costs, Series C No. 42 (Inter-American Court of Human Rights, November 7, 1998); Inter-American Commission on Human Rights, "Second Report."

[32] Bicudo, "The Inter-American Commission on Human Rights."

of its obligation to comply with the ruling, by virtue of both the principles of *pacta sunt servanda* and Article 68(1) of the Inter-American Convention on Human Rights, which outlines expectations about compliance.[33]

While Peru's relationship with the IACtHR clearly deteriorated throughout the late 1990s, the *Constitutional Court v. Peru* case, dealing with the dismissal of the three Constitutional Court judges who found the "Interpretation Law" inapplicable, was the last straw. Before the *Constitutional Court* case reached the IACtHR, the Inter-American Commission on Human Rights had tried, unsuccessfully, to broker a friendly settlement between the parties. The Commission subsequently found that the justices had been unfairly dismissed and denied due process, recommending that the government reinstate them to the Court. Peru did not act, and thus, on February 1, 1999, the Commission referred the case to the IACtHR.[34]

On July 16, 1999, the Peruvian Ambassador to Costa Rica returned the application of the case, which is the diplomatic equivalent of simply refusing to acknowledge the claim or the Court's adjudicative authority.[35] The Ambassador also delivered a letter to the IACtHR on behalf of the Minister for Foreign Affairs of Peru. The letter read: "This withdrawal of recognition of the Inter-American Court's contentious jurisdiction will take effect immediately and will apply to all cases in which Peru has not answered the application filed with the Court."[36] In other words, Peru would be withdrawing from the IACtHR's contentious jurisdiction because its work in the *Constitutional Court v. Peru* case directly touched upon Fujimori's bid to stay in power and coincided with increasingly repressive tactics used to keep domestic opposition at bay.

The government's letter was met with swift resistance. The International Human Rights Law Group submitted an *amicus curiae* brief on August 27, 1999, rejecting Peru's position. The Inter-American Commission filed a brief on September 10, 1999, noting that Peru accepted the Court's jurisdiction on July 2, 1999, the date on which the Commission sent the case to the court, and thus could not unilaterally withdraw from the Court's jurisdiction on the case.

On September 24, 1999, the IACtHR issued its own ruling, finding the withdrawal inadmissible. The IACtHR ruling referred to Article 62(3) of the Inter-American Convention on Human Rights, which outlines the scope of

---

[33]   Bicudo, "The Inter-American Commission on Human Rights."
[34]   *Caso del Tribunal Constitucional v. Perú*, Competencia; *Manuel Aguirre Roca, Guillermo Rey Terry, and Delia Revoredo de Mur v. Peru*, Report No. 35/98, Case 11.760 (Inter-American Commission on Human Rights, May 5, 1998).
[35]   *Caso del Tribunal Constitucional v. Perú*, Competencia.
[36]   *Caso del Tribunal Constitucional v. Perú*, Competencia.

the Court's jurisdiction. Regarding Article 62(3), the Court noted that it is "fundamental to the operation of the Convention's system of protection" and called it "an ironclad clause to which there can be no limitations except those expressly provided for in Article 62(1)."[37] Moreover, the Inter-American Convention and, relatedly, the jurisdiction of the Court, are subject to abrogation rules. As the Court noted, the only way for a state to *not* be subjected to the Court's jurisdiction is to denounce the Inter-American Convention on Human Rights as a whole and provide one year's notice in doing so. Given those rules, the Court declared its competence to consider the case at hand.[38]

The rest of 1999 and the first half of 2000 were occupied with a back-and-forth between the Government of Peru and the IACtHR on the Court's authority to rule on the case and on a set of precautionary measures necessary to protect one of the petitioners, Justice Revoredo Marsano de Mur. On November 22, 2000, the State failed to appear at the public hearing on the merits of the case. The Court's rules of procedure allow it to proceed under such circumstances. On January 10, 2001, the Commission submitted its final arguments; again, the State failed to appear.[39]

While the *Constitutional Court* case and its attendant drama were unfolding in San José, Fujimori had his sights set on the 2000 presidential election. The first of the presidential races was held on April 9, 2000. The election was marked by missing ballots, secretive vote-counting, and other suspicious activity. By the time of the runoff on May 28, 2000, Fujimori's only remaining opponent decided to boycott the race, protesting the corruption and fraud that had marked the first race and the electoral environment. Indeed, the run-off was so fraught with fraud that the OAS election monitor left Peru two days before the election.[40] Thus, the runoff election ultimately had only one contestant – Fujimori – and was beset by what one could only generously call "irregularities."[41]

Human Rights Watch labeled the 2000 election, "an affront to the Inter-American System." In their report from the Permanent Council of the OAS, they noted: "Mr. Fujimori's long maneuver to secure a third term of office, termed unconstitutional both by Peru's Constitutional Court and by its

---

[37] *Caso del Tribunal Constitucional v. Perú*, Competencia.
[38] *Caso del Tribunal Constitucional v. Perú*, Competencia.
[39] *Caso del Tribunal Constitucional v. Perú*, Fondo, Reparaciones y Costas.
[40] Clifford Krauss, "Angry Election Monitor Leaves Peru 2 Days before Runoff Vote," *The New York Times*, May 27, 2000, https://www.nytimes.com/2000/05/27/world/angry-election-monitor-leaves-peru-2-days-before-runoff-vote.html.
[41] "Elections in Peru: Democracy at Risk," *Human Rights Watch*, May 31, 2000, https://www.hrw.org/news/2000/05/31/elections-peru-democracy-risk.

Ombudsperson, has finally been crowned with success by this year's mani-
festly irregular election."[42] Fujimori's battle with the Peruvian Constitutional
Court and the Inter-American Human Rights System was waged in service of
the 2000 election. As the theoretical framework in Chapter 2 suggests, not only
does international adjudication have domestic consequences, but leaders will
engage in backlash politics when those consequences threaten regime stability
and are accompanied by an expectation of relying on increasingly repressive
tactics to stay in power.

After the Election

Shortly after the election, which was widely condemned both in Peru and
internationally, Fujimori found himself with an unsolvable dilemma: his most
important supporter and chief of intelligence, Vladimiro Montesinos, was
caught on video offering a bribe to a member of the opposition in Congress
to switch his allegiance to the pro-Fujimori coalition. Getting caught offering
a bribe turned out to be the last straw for Montesinos, Fujimori, and his
regime. Pressure from the IAHRS, foreign allies, and domestic constituents
finally came to a head. While Fujimori could have, presumably, saved himself
by sacrificing Montesinos, his hold on power was inextricably connected to the
authority and force that Montesinos wielded as the chief of the National
Intelligence Service (SNI). It was through violence and repression that the
SNI deployed against Peru's own citizens that Fujimori was protected from
a coup or overthrow. Without Montesinos and without the apparatus of
repression behind him, Fujimori could no longer govern. And thus, on
September 18, 2000, President Fujimori declared, "After deep reflection[,]
I have decided first to deactivate the National Intelligence Service and second
to call a general election immediately."[43]

On November 20, 2000, Fujimori officially resigned, and fled the country –
and the possibility of accountability – for Japan. He submitted his resignation
from exile.[44] On January 22, 2001, the Government of Peru submitted
a legislative resolution to the Inter-American Court of Human Rights that
acknowledged the Court's jurisdiction, thus nullifying the threat of

---

[42] "Elections in Peru," *Human Rights Watch*.
[43] Jeremy McDermott, "Fujimori to Quit in Peru Bribes Scandal," *The Telegraph*, September 18,
      2000, https://www.telegraph.co.uk/news/worldnews/southamerica/peru/1355897/Fujimori-to-
      quit-in-Peru-bribes-scandal.html.
[44] Clifford Krauss, "Fujimori Resignation Sets off Succession Scramble in Peru," *The New York
      Times*, November 21, 2000, https://www.nytimes.com/2000/11/21/world/fujimori-resignation-
      sets-off-succession-scramble-in-peru.html.

withdrawal.[45] Nearly two decades later, Alberto Fujimori's legal fate remains in flux, with his post-presidency years marked by alternating periods of asylum-seeking and defiance of international accountability norms.[46]

Peru's experience with the IACtHR during Fujimori's regime illustrated the multiple drivers of backlash politics. Fundamental normative disagreement about if and how the IACtHR should adjudicate on presidential politics set the tone for an adversarial relationship between Peru and the IACtHR. Meanwhile, domestic mobilization around the Inter-American Court of Human Rights put increased pressure on the Fujimori regime, and the expectation of further violence only exacerbated Fujimori's vulnerability to the spotlight that the Inter-American Human Rights System shone on him.

CASE 2: VENEZUELA'S REALIZED WITHDRAWAL(S)

Venezuela has effectively withdrawn from the Inter-American Human Rights System twice. The first time was in 2012–2013, when, under President Hugo Chávez, Venezuela withdrew from the Inter-American Convention on Human Rights and with it the Inter-American Court of Human Rights. The second time was in 2017, when President Nicolás Maduro withdrew Venezuela from the OAS and, as a result, the Inter-American Commission on Human Rights. In both instances, the executive branch needed to rely on increasingly repressive tactics to quash dissent; the prospect of IAHRS oversight threatened their regime stability. Moreover, Venezuela had long highlighted normative discontent within the Inter-American system, arguing that the IAHRS advanced a Western, *estadounidense*[47] vision of human rights to the detriment of its Latin American neighbors.

Extending Executive Authority and a (Self-)Coup

Much like Fujimori in Peru, shortly after his election to the Presidency in 1998, Hugo Chávez called a referendum on the Venezuelan constitution. This referendum created a Constituent Assembly, which served as the main legislative organ of the government, and allowed presidents, namely Chávez, to serve a six-year term with the possibility of one reelection. Despite expanding executive control, the new constitution was progressive regarding the

---

[45] *Caso del Tribunal Constitucional v. Perú*, Competencia.
[46] "Peru's Ex-President Fujimori Ordered to Stand Trial Again," *BBC News*, February 20, 2018, www.bbc.com/news/world-latin-america-43122187.
[47] Meaning "pertaining to the United States."

integration of international law, and particularly international human rights law, into domestic canon.[48]

By 2002, however, Chávez increasingly relied on decrees and special authority granted to him by the Constituent Assembly to preside over a large range of social and economic issues previously outside the president's scope. These moves included naming a new president and board for Petróleos de Venezuela, which led to massive opposition from the oil sector and drew the IACmHR's attention. The medical and education sectors also were active in the opposition movement.

This domestic mobilization and corresponding pro-government activity led to a violent encounter on April 11, 2002, between pro- and anti-government forces in front of the presidential palace. The following day, April 12, 2002, a group of military defectors, who called themselves the "Government of Democratic Transition and National Unity," detained President Chávez and a group of civilians. The defectors then declared Pedro Carmona the President of Venezuela. As they did not have a resignation letter from Chávez, the group officially labeled their takeover a coup. Later that afternoon, the new president dissolved all of the branches of government. This decision inspired a new set of protests, demanding the reconstitution of democratic institutions and that Chávez be released. Within the military, forces still loyal to Chávez also put pressure on Carmona, who promptly resigned. In the early morning of April 14, 2002, Chávez returned to the presidential palace. By that evening, he was reinstated as president and order was restored.[49]

In the aftermath of the coup and violence, the National Assembly created a truth commission to investigate and address the human rights abuses that took place during those tumultuous days in April 2002. The Inter-American Commission on Human Rights, however, noted that the truth commission did not absolve the government from holding perpetrators accountable and, moreover, that the truth commission was not even operational. In addition, the Commission highlighted other breakdowns in accountability, including, but not limited to, additional violence in front of the Supreme Court on August 8, 2002; the dismissal of a court case against four generals accused of overthrowing Chávez; a national strike; the political assassination of a pro-Chávez politician; and the bombing of the Colombian and Spanish embassies in Caracas.[50]

---

[48] Inter-American Commission on Human Rights, "Report on the Situation of Human Rights in Venezuela," *Organization of American States*, 2003, www.cidh.org/countryrep/Venezuel a2003eng/intro.htm#BACKGROUND.

[49] Inter-American Commission on Human Rights, "Report on the Situation of Human Rights in Venezuela."

[50] Inter-American Commission on Human Rights, "Report on the Situation of Human Rights in Venezuela."

The remainder of 2002 and much of 2003 was spent attempting dialogue between the parties and addressing the questions of if/how a popular referendum could be used to recall Chávez.[51] By the end of 2003 and into 2004, Venezuela was characterized by what CNN called, "the battle of referendums."[52] Not only was there a referendum being planned in 2004 to recall Chávez, but Chávez also initiated a different set of referenda to recall his political opponents from various posts. In August 2004, Venezuela held its recall vote on Chávez's future, which Chávez handily won, re-upping his mandate until regular elections in 2006.[53] Chávez also won the 2006 election easily. In 2007, however, he held a referendum on proposed changes to the Constitution, which would have granted him new powers, but the referendum was defeated.[54] Chávez tried again in 2009, and this time he was able to pass a referendum that removed term limits and effectively allowed him to be president indefinitely.[55] By this time, Chávez had nearly complete control over the Venezuelan government, economy, and society, which in turn extended to the electoral process. He also had perfected his long-running anti-American, anti-Western rhetoric and used these normative fissures to lambast the IAHRS.

From Coup to Collapse

Three trends were obvious during the 2002–2012 period. The first was the breakdown of democratic order in Venezuela and the omnipresent threat of additional violence and repression to keep control over the country. Second, and not unrelatedly, was the Inter-American Commission's and Court's increased attention to the attendant human rights violations and the domestic consequences of the IAHRS's activity in the country. The third, and also related, trend was Venezuela's increased anti-IAHRS rhetoric and attacks on the authority of both the Inter-American Court of Human Rights and the Inter-American Commission on Human Rights.

---

[51] Inter-American Commission on Human Rights, "Report on the Situation of Human Rights in Venezuela."

[52] "Chávez Joins Venezuela's Battle of Referendums," CNN, November 22, 2003, www.cnn.com /2003/WORLD/americas/11/22/venezuela.referendums.reut/.

[53] Ruth Morris, "Venezuela: Hugo Chavez, Clutch Hitter," *Frontline World*, August 24, 2004, www.pbs.org/frontlineworld/elections/venezuela/.

[54] Simon Romero, "Venezuela Hands Narrow Defeat to Chávez Plan," *The New York Times*, December 3, 2007, https://www.nytimes.com/2007/12/03/world/americas/03venezuela.html.

[55] Simon Romero, "Chávez Decisively Wins Bid to End Term Limits," *The New York Times*, February 15, 2009, https://www.nytimes.com/2009/02/16/world/americas/16venez.html.

It was no surprise, then, that when Chávez was aiming to run for an unprecedented fourth term as president, in a campaign and administration marked by increasing levels of repression and undemocratic maneuvers, Venezuela denounced the Inter-American Convention on Human Rights. As the framework in Chapter 2 indicates, backlash politics can serve to "blind the watchdog" in the face of increasingly repressive tactics.

Venezuela's withdrawal from the American Convention on Human Rights, and thus the Inter-American Court of Human Rights, unfolded in late 2012 and throughout 2013. On September 10, 2012, the government delivered its official denunciation to the Secretary-General of the OAS. This withdrawal, which the government made pursuant to the relevant abrogation article, Article 78 of the Convention, meant that Venezuela could no longer be subject to the jurisdiction of the Inter-American Court of Human Rights.

Although Venezuela withdrew from the Inter-American Court of Human Rights, this decision also took aim at the ability of the Inter-American Commission on Human Rights to consider Venezuelan human rights abuses. Because Venezuela denounced the whole Convention, the Inter-American Commission on Human Rights could only concern itself with individual complaints related to the American Declaration of the Rights and Duties of Man, which consisted of a more limited scope of justiciable issues.[56] In fact, Venezuela's withdrawal was, in part, motivated by (1) long-standing conflict between the Chávez regime and the Inter-American Commission and (2) Chávez's need for abusive policies to remain in power to which the Commission would bear (public) witness.

As the International Justice Resource Center (IJRC) explained, the Inter-American Commission on Human Rights first raised Chávez's ire when it recognized the Carmona government. The IACmHR asked the short-lived Carmona government for information about Chávez's whereabouts and well-being, thereby officially recognizing Carmona as the executive. The Commission also made statements about the coup/resignation in 2002, condemned the resulting violence, and produced a report in 2003 about the Venezuelan government. By recognizing the Carmona government and publicly rebuking Venezuela's human rights practices, the IACmHR interjected itself – unfairly in Chávez's opinion – into domestic Venezuelan politics. From Chávez's perspective, this was a transgression that demanded punishment.

---

[56] "Venezuela Denounces American Convention on Human Rights as IACHR Faces Reform," *International Justice Resource Center*, September 19, 2012, www.ijrcenter.org/2012/09/19/vene zuela-denounces-american-convention-on-human-rights-as-iachr-faces-reform/.

In addition to withdrawing from the IACtHR and thereby limiting the adjudicative authority of the IACmHR, Chávez also targeted the IACmHR's reliance on states for access to witnesses and victims. The Chávez government prohibited *in situ* Commission visits, cutting off victims from a potential avenue for recourse and thwarting the IACmHR's ability to perform its core judicial tasks.[57]

Despite being barred from *in situ* visits, the Commission remained very active regarding the state of human rights in Venezuela. It published a report in 2009, refuting the notion that it was not allowed to report on rights conditions in the country simply because it was banned from conducting visits. The report then went on to detail systematic repression in the country, from limitations in the electoral landscape to the increase of criminal charges levied against political opponents and violent reprisals against dissenters. The report further detailed concerns about the independence of the Venezuelan judiciary; violence and intimidation against journalists and protestors; the growth of a militarized national police force; and the excessive use of state force against civilians, particularly human rights defenders, unionists, and indigenous groups. While the report noted improvement in some economic and social rights, the Commission reminded Venezuela:

> The Commission emphasizes that human rights are an indivisible whole and so the realization of economic, social, and cultural rights in Venezuela does not justify sacrificing the currency of other basic rights. In that the effective exercise of democracy demands full enjoyment of citizens' fundamental rights and freedoms, the IACHR again points out to the State its duty of meeting the international human rights obligations it freely assumed under the American Convention and other applicable legal instruments.[58]

In Section IV of its Annual Report, which is reserved for a discussion of serious human rights conditions, the Commission, again and again, detailed the deteriorating human rights conditions in Venezuela. In their 2011 report, the Commission detailed the scope of violations in Venezuela and made nine recommendations to the state, including that the state: "Refrain from taking reprisals or using the punitive power of the State to intimidate or sanction individuals based on their political opinions, and guarantee the plurality of opportunities and arenas for democratic activity, including respect for

57 "Venezuela Denounces American Convention on Human Rights as IACHR Faces Reform," *International Justice Resource Center.*

58 Inter-American Commission on Human Rights, "Democracy and Human Rights in Venezuela, OEA/Ser.L/V/II, Doc. 54," *Organization of American States,* 2009, www.cidh.org/pdf%20files/VENEZUELA%202009%20ENG.pdf.

gatherings and protests held in exercise of the right of assembly and peaceful protest."[59] In addition to the reports, the Commission granted as admissible thirty-five petitions against Venezuela and accepted twenty-five precautionary measures between 2002 and 2012.[60]

While Venezuela was busy relieving itself of any obligations to the Inter-American Convention, it leaned into other human rights institutions. As suggested in Chapters 2 and 4, states often couple withdrawal from one human rights institution with the creation or bolstering of another human rights institution that more clearly aligns with their policy preferences. Viviana Giacaman, the chief of Freedom House's Latin American programs, highlighted that Venezuela joined the United Nations Human Rights Council within days of withdrawing from the Inter-American Convention. She explained: "Venezuela's willingness to participate at the UN shows that the country is able to weaken international human rights norms by both undermining them from within international bodies, and by withdrawing from mechanisms when it's convenient. These two seemingly contradictory decisions are perfectly consistent with Venezuela's hostility to human rights."[61] Indeed, Venezuela was able to weaken, simultaneously, the IAHRS through withdrawal and the UN Human Rights Council through cooptation. Both were manifestations of backlash politics.

During this same time, the IACtHR also was actively adjudicating those cases against Venezuela that had reached its docket prior to its withdrawal. The Court issued fifteen judgments against Venezuela between 2002 and 2012. Among those were *The Barrios Family* v. *Venezuela*, *López Mendoza* v. *Venezuela*, and a provisional measure, Matter of "Globovisión" Television Station.[62] The cases concerned violations ranging from extrajudicial killings to

---

[59]   Inter-American Commission on Human Rights, "Inter-American Commission of Human Rights 2011 Annual Report, OEA/Ser.L/V/II, Doc. 69," *Organization of American States*, December 30, 2011, https://www.oas.org/en/iachr/docs/annual/2011/toc.asp; Inter-American Commission on Human Rights, "Democracy and Human Rights in Venezuela."

[60]   Inter-American Commission on Human Rights, "Statistics," n.d., www.oas.org/en/iachr/multimedia/statistics/statistics.html.

[61]   Freedom House, "Venezuela Opts out of American Convention on Human Rights," *ifex*, September 17, 2013, https://ifex.org/venezuela-opts-out-of-american-convention-on-human-rights/.

[62]   See, for example, *Case of the Barrios Family* v. *Venezuela*, Merits, Reparations and Costs, Series C No. 237 (Inter-American Court of Human Rights, November 24, 2011); *Case of López Mendoza* v. *Venezuela*, Merits, Reparations and Costs, Series C No. 233 (Inter-American Court of Human Rights, September 1, 2011); *Case of Apitz Barbera et al. ("First Court of Administrative Disputes")* v. *Venezuela*, Preliminary Objection, Merits, Reparations and Costs, Series C No. 182 (Inter-American Court of Human Rights, August 5, 2008); Matter of Certain Venezuelan Prisons, Provisional Measures regarding Venezuela, Order of the Court, Series A (Inter-American Court of Human Rights, July 6, 2011); Matter of

restrictions on political participation and, in the case of Globovisión, freedom of the press.

Nicolás Maduro, who at the time was the Chancellor of the Republic, argued that the Commission was being steered by a gang based in the United States.[63] The Chávez government also noted, as justification for the application to leave the Commission, that prior to Chávez's presidency, which began in 1998, there were only five confirmed cases against Venezuela but between 2000, that is, after the autogolpe, and 2012 there were thirty-six.[64] Of course, this uptick in cases was not unique to Venezuela or even particularly pronounced. It happened around the region, as well as in Europe, as democracy took root and the regional systems matured beyond their earlier incarnations.

Maduro's Turn

After Chávez's death in 2013, living conditions and political safeguards declined rapidly. Without the cult of personality that propped up Chávez for so many years, Maduro was forced to resort to (even more) brutalist tactics than his predecessor to retain tenuous control over Venezuela.

In 2017, Maduro moved to deepen Venezuela's isolation in the region and withdrew from the Organization of American States and, with it, the Inter-American Commission on Human Rights. Maduro called it "a break with imperialism."[65] At the time of Maduro's withdrawal from the OAS, his administration was increasingly relying on repressive measures to retain control. Venezuela's letter declaring the state's intent to withdraw from the OAS was marked by violent clashes between protestors and the police. The BBC reported that this violence led to the deaths of thirty people within the first month of Venezuela's withdrawal.[66] By then, inflation in Venezuela had reached 700 percent, and the country faced a major shortage of basic goods, including food and medicine.[67]

"Globovisión" Television Station, Provisional Measures regarding Venezuela, Order of the Court, Series A (Inter-American Court of Human Rights, January 29, 2008).

[63] "Venezuela.-Maduro asegura que la CIDH solo obedece a los intereses de la 'mafia internacional' que representa EEUU," *El Economista*, May 3, 2012, https://ecodiario .eleconomista.es/global/noticias/3937734/05/12/Venezuela-Maduro-asegura-que-la-CIDH-solo-obedece-a-los-intereses-de-la-mafia-internacional-que-representa-EEUU.html.

[64] "Venezuela.-Maduro asegura que la CIDH solo obedece a los intereses de la 'mafia internacional,'" *El Economista*.

[65] "Venezuela to Withdraw from OAS," *BBC News*.

[66] "Venezuela to Withdraw from OAS," *BBC News*.

[67] "Venezuela to Withdraw from OAS," *BBC News*.

The OAS withdrawal also came at a moment when over 60 percent of Venezuelans viewed the OAS as trustworthy.[68] Why, then, did Maduro seek to withdraw from the OAS at this time? It was clear that his hold on power was increasingly tenuous. The OAS and the Inter-American Commission were only going to further shine a spotlight on the repressive tactics his regime relied upon and legitimize domestic mobilization and dissent. Thus, as with Chávez before him, Maduro withdrew from the IAHRS in order to divert attention away from his repressive tactics and retain control, at least for the short-term. Withdrawal from the OAS cleared the path for Maduro's election in May 2018, guaranteeing him a second, six-year term as president.[69]

CASE 3: COLOMBIA'S DIFFERENT PATH

While the Peruvian and Venezuelan cases outline the conditions under which states withdraw, or at least threaten to withdraw, from international human rights courts, Colombia's decisions to not only remain in the IAHRS but also to fully engage with the Inter-American human rights regime are equally illustrative. Instead of withdrawing from the IACtHR in response to the Court's caseload, which regularly criticizes the government and inspires domestic dissent, Colombia participates fully, and generally cooperatively, with the Inter-American Court and Commission. This is not to suggest that Colombia has been a model of compliance but rather that it has not sought to limit the IAHRS's powers through withdrawals or threats thereof. Why?

A Frequent Flier at the IAHRS

Colombia has a long history with the Inter-American Court of Human Rights and is one of the countries in which the IACtHR has been the most active and the most assertive. Colombia was the respondent in 469 cases at the Inter-American Commission on Human Rights between 2006 and 2017 alone. It has been the subject of more than thirty contentious cases at the Inter-American Court of Human Rights and 110 precautionary measures at the Inter-American

---

[68] Christine Huang and Mariana Rodríguez, "As Maduro Calls for Venezuela's Withdrawal from the OAS, the Majority of Citizens Report the Organization Is Trustworthy," *Latin American Public Opinion Project*, May 17, 2017, https://www.vanderbilt.edu/lapop/insights/ITB028en.pdf.

[69] William Neuman and Nicholas Casey, "Venezuela Election Won by Maduro amid Widespread Disillusionment," *The New York Times*, May 20, 2018, https://www.nytimes.com/2018/05/20/world/americas/venezuela-election.html.

Commission on Human Rights.[70] The Inter-American Commission on Human Rights has issued four special reports on Colombia and conducted seven site visits. While the sheer number of cases and IAHRS activity involving Colombia is noteworthy, perhaps even more important are the *types* of issues on which the IACtHR has adjudicated. These include the perpetration of rights abuses as part of Colombia's long-standing conflict with the Revolutionary Armed Forces of Colombia (FARC) and the National Liberation Army (ELN), as well as cases about how to manage reparations to victims, the rights of forcibly displaced persons, and women's and indigenous rights.[71] Indeed, the bulk of these cases went directly to how Colombia was fighting its internal conflict and sought to limit the violence perpetrated by government and paramilitary forces and to require the state to pay reparations to victims of violence from all sides of the conflict.

Given the nature of the Colombian cases at the IACtHR, a very possible alternate reality would have been for Colombia to withdraw from the Court. Why, then, would the government lean into it? The answer, I suggest, is threefold. First, while Colombia's governmental system has widely relied on a strong executive, it never crossed into the personalistic regimes that Venezuela and Peru had under Chávez and Fujimori, respectively. Relatedly, despite the persistent and ongoing corruption attendant to the Colombian conflict, democratic elections have been, on the whole, free and fair. When Alváro Uribe, who served as President from 2002 to 2010, sought to seek a third term in office, the referendum allowing such a change to the constitution was struck down, and all parties accepted the agreement. Moreover, the 1993 Colombian constitution is widely considered to be one of the most robust in the hemisphere. Thus, while repression was – and is – persistent in Colombia, it was not the *only* mechanism for regime survival. This means that no single president, particularly since 2000, has had to rely on more repression than his predecessor, and no president could reasonably expect to govern Colombia *ad infinitum*.

---

[70] Statistics of the Inter-American Commission on Human Rights, www.oas.org/en/iachr/multi media/statistics/statistics.html.

[71] See, among others, *Case of the Rochela Massacre* v. *Colombia*, Merits, Reparations and Costs, Series C No. 163 (Inter-American Court of Human Rights May 11, 2007); *Case of the "Mapiripán Massacre"* v. *Colombia*, Merits, Reparations and Costs, Series C No. 134 (Inter-American Court of Human Rights, September 15, 2005); *Case of the 19 Merchants* v. *Colombia*, Merits, Reparations and Costs, Series C No. 109 (Inter-American Court of Human Rights, July 5, 2004); *Case of Caballero Delgado and Santana* v. *Colombia*, Merits, Series C No. 22 (Inter-American Court of Human Rights, January 29, 1997); *Caso de las Comunidades Afrodescendientes desplazadas de la Cuenca del Río Cacarica (Operación Génesis)* v. *Colombia*.

The second explanation is that the Government of Colombia has been able to maneuver around both the IACtHR and the International Criminal Court. While the Inter-American system cannot hold individuals accountable, it does require that the state prosecute perpetrators of human rights abuse. The ICC, of course, can and does prosecute individuals, including heads of state. Thus, the Colombian government was able to strategically comply with the IACtHR's rulings and engage with the ICC such that it protected Colombian leadership from accountability while also hamstringing the international courts.[72] As a result, these courts never truly posed a threat to incumbents' ability to govern or to their individual freedom.

Moreover, because none of the Colombian presidents ever tried, beyond Uribe's referendum, to alter the constitution to continue their hold on power, the IAHRS never posed a material threat to their presidency. To put this within the context of the theoretical framework in Chapter 2, Colombian political elites have not only been able to exploit the IAHRS's dependency on states for material, jurisdictional, and normative support, but also, in doing so, they have been able to limit the domestic consequences of international courts' rulings.

Third, unlike Venezuela, and to a lesser degree, Peru, Colombia has not taken an oppositional stance to the normative core of the Inter-American Human Rights System. With important economic and political relationships with the United States, Canada, and the European Union (EU), lobbing critiques of the IAHRS as a tool of North American hegemony would be unwise and inconsistent with Colombia's highly legalistic political culture and US-oriented foreign policy.[73]

CONCLUSION

This chapter considered why states withdraw from international human rights tribunals, paying particular attention to the cases of Peru, Venezuela, and

---

[72] Hillebrecht, *Domestic Politics and International Human Rights Tribunals*; Hillebrecht and Huneeus, with Borda, "The Judicialization of Peace"; Alexandra Huneeus and René Urueña, "Introduction to Symposium on the Colombian Peace Talks and International Law," *AJIL Unbound* 110 (2016): 161–164, https://doi.org/10.1017/S2398772300003007; Christine Bell, "Lex Pacificatoria Colombiana: Colombia's Peace Accord in Comparative Perspective," *AJIL Unbound* 110 (2016): 165–171, https://doi.org/10.1017/S2398772300003019.

[73] "Pressure Point: The ICC's Impact on National Justice," *Human Rights Watch*, May 3, 2018, https://www.hrw.org/report/2018/05/03/pressure-point-iccs-impact-national-justice/lessons-colombia-georgia-guinea-and; "Colombia," The Observatory of Economic Complexity, n.d., https://oec.world/en/profile/country/col/; John Paul Rathbone and Gideon Long, "Colombia and Corruption: The Problem of Extreme Legalism," *Financial Times*, August 14, 2018, https://www.ft.com/content/0b833ef8-9c81-11e8-9702-5946bae86e6d.

Colombia. Building on the theoretical framework in Chapter 2, the case studies here illustrate that normative discontent and the threat of governments' relying on (increasingly) repressive or corrupt tactics to stay in power can prompt backlash in the form of withdrawals from international courts. The case studies also demonstrate how international courts' adjudication can ignite domestic mobilization and inspire governmental ire, further contributing to governments' incentives to engage in backlash politics, up to and including withdrawing from international courts. Withdrawals from international courts, in turn, undermine the tribunals' structural, adjudicative, and normative authority.

Readers familiar with the threats facing the international justice regime will surely note that the most (in)famous threat of withdrawal, the ICC–AU case, is not discussed in this chapter. In Chapter 4, I consider not only the AU's threatened withdrawal from the ICC but also its plans to supplant the ICC with an alternative justice mechanism, one in which heads of state, particularly those who have reason to fear an ICC indictment, would enjoy immunity. I also revisit the Latin American states discussed in this chapter, particularly Venezuela, and consider how they tried to undermine international justice through the creation of a subregional alternative to the Inter-American human rights regime.

4

Replacing the International Justice Regime

Chapter 3 examined a set of cases in which states withdrew – or threatened to withdraw – from international human rights and criminal courts. While withdrawing from international human rights and criminal courts is a rare event, when it does happen it is sometimes coupled with another manifestation of backlash: the creation of alternate or substitute justice mechanisms. These substitute justice mechanisms are the focus of this chapter.

Throughout this book, I use the terms alternate or substitute mechanisms to mean the tribunals or quasi-tribunals that states either create or revive to act as a replacement for the human rights or criminal court they seek to undermine. Proponents of these substitute judicial mechanisms often talk about the need for "local justice," but the scope and independence of these alternative courts reveal a different aim. Efforts to supplant existing courts are aimed at subverting the authority of the original courts by offering watered-down versions of accountability and human rights, all while maintaining the façade of justice.

In the short-term, creating a new human rights or criminal court allows states and elites to say, "We are not opposed to human rights and justice, simply the version of human rights and justice offered by the international justice regime." This statement, however simplistic it might appear on the surface, reveals a great deal about the current state of the international justice regime and why states and elites engage in backlash politics against it. For example, the argument that states are working to supplant existing judicial institutions with new institutions highlights the normative discontent that characterizes the international justice regime. It suggests that the norms on which the courts are based are not universal, nor is the very idea of human rights and criminal adjudication. Instead, these norms were and are contested.

Further, by exploiting the courts' dependence on states for material, procedural, and reputational support, these substitute justice mechanisms can become appendages of their creators, offering a very limited version of "just-ice." As the plans for developing alternate justice mechanisms demonstrate, the line between dependence and usurpation can be quite narrow. These highly dependent and coopted courts also illustrate the domestic effects of international adjudication, but they flip the script. For heads of state and other elites anticipating that they will need to resort to violence to hang on to power, having an international court at their disposal for dealing with domestic political opponents and regional foes is an added benefit of creating these alternate or substitute justice mechanisms.

This chapter begins by explaining in more detail the reasons why states and elites would choose the creation of an alternate justice mechanism as a form of backlash politics. Next, the chapter turns to a discussion of the methodological approach and case selection. Third, the chapter examines the African Union's threats to withdraw from and replace the ICC. Next, I offer a brief discussion of a Venezuela-led effort to supplant the Inter-American Human Rights System with a Union of South American Nations (UNASUR) human rights mechanism. The final section concludes.

WHY ALTERNATIVE JUSTICE MECHANISMS AS A FORM OF BACKLASH?

In addition to furthering our understanding of why and how states and elites engage in backlash politics against human rights and criminal tribunals, this chapter also considers the *additional* benefit to states and elites of not only withdrawing from, but also creating alternatives to, international courts. States and elites create alternate justice mechanisms for two reasons: first, to create smokescreens of justice and human rights; and second, to create human rights and criminal courts that can be summoned if/when leaders need to prevail upon judicial actors to help solve domestic conflicts in the future.

The Proliferation of Justice and Smokescreens of Accountability

While some scholars suggest that international courts are largely epiphenomenal,[1] the rapid proliferation of the international justice regime would suggest that states view international courts as important set pieces in contemporary international politics. Indeed, the proliferation of these tribu-nals changed the international political and legal landscape to the extent that

---

[1] Jack L. Goldsmith and Eric A. Posner, *The Limits of International Law* (New York: Oxford University Press, 2005).

only the Middle East and Asia remain (largely) free of international human rights and criminal courts.[2] Yet, even there, nascent attempts at human rights courts and commissions surface with some regularity. The trend over the past thirty years has been *more* international rights adjudication, not less. As international courts became a sort of lingua franca, it follows that other states would seek to create courts, not only to fill the traditional roles of mediation and adjudication, but also to demonstrate a commitment to the language and power of international law. As Yuval Shany writes: "The reason for establishing international courts and entrusting them with these functions may be, at least in part, symbolic: international courts, like their national counterparts, are expected to confer legitimacy on the operation of the social institutions or political systems that established them."[3] In other words, the creation of courts can serve to legitimize states and illustrate their entrenchment in the new, highly adjudicated "normal" of international politics. Appearing committed to international law can provide states and elites with reputational benefits, both at home and abroad. Participation in international courts can be linked to trade agreements and earn states a seat at the international agenda-setting table.[4] If international courts are, indeed, the lingua franca of contemporary politics, then creating substitute courts allows elites and states to demonstrate a commitment to the language and power of law while also freeing themselves from authority of the tribunal(s) they seek to undermine.[5]

[2] Karen J. Alter, *The New Terrain of International Law: Courts, Politics, Rights* (Princeton, NJ: Princeton University Press, 2014).

[3] Yuval Shany, *Assessing the Effectiveness of International Courts* (Oxford: Oxford University Press, 2014), 44–45.

[4] Emilie Hafner-Burton, *Forced to Be Good: Why Trade Agreements Boost Human Rights* (Ithaca, NY: Cornell University Press, 2009).

[5] See, among others, Karen J. Alter, "Delegation to International Courts and the Limits of Re-Contracting Political Power," in *Delegation and Agency in International Organizations*, eds. Darren G. Hawkins, David A. Lake, Daniel L. Nielson, and Michael J. Tierney (Cambridge, UK: Cambridge University Press, 2006), 312–338; Alter, *The New Terrain*; Shany, *Assessing the Effectiveness of International Courts*; Yuval Shany, "No Longer a Weak Department of Power? Reflections on the Emergence of a New International Judiciary," *European Journal of International Law* 20, no. 1 (February 2009): 73–91, https://doi.org/10.1093/ejil/chn081; Leslie Johns, *Strengthening International Courts: The Hidden Costs of Legalization* (Ann Arbor: University of Michigan Press, 2015); Karen Alter, Laurence R. Helfer, and Mikael Rask Madsen, "How Context Shapes the Authority of International Courts," *Law and Contemporary Problems* 79, no. 1 (2016): 1–36, https://scholarship.law.duke.edu/lcp/vol79/iss1/1/; Jonas Christoffersen and Mikael Rask Madsen, eds., *The European Court of Human Rights Between Law and Politics* (Oxford: Oxford University Press, 2011); Andrew Moravcsik, "The Origins of Human Rights Regimes: Democratic Delegation in Postwar Europe," *International Organization* 54, no. 2 (2000): 217–252, https://doi.org/10.1162/002081800551163; Rachel A. Cichowski, "Introduction: Courts, Democracy, and Governance," *Comparative Political Studies* 39, no. 1 (February 2006): 3–21, https://doi.org/10.1177/0010414005283212.

Beyond these benefits, creating alternative justice mechanisms, and thus professing a commitment to human rights and international law, helps states and elites advance the notion that the targeted tribunals (e.g., the ICC and the institutions in the Inter-American and European human rights systems) are biased, neocolonial outfits. The premise of creating a substitute justice mechanism offers cover for this story, implying that what departing states and elites want is not to be impervious to accountability, but rather to be free from the tyranny of what they view as a neocolonial version of justice.[6]

Creating Courts for Future Conflicts

As discussed in Chapters 1 and 2, courts derive their authority from their structural relationship with states, but even the most independent international courts are heavily reliant on state support. Alternate mechanisms heighten this dependency, as the proposed justice mechanisms are designed to be structurally and politically beholden to their member states.[7] In being beholden to their member states, the courts can then serve as outgrowths of their principals, trying domestic opponents and advancing both their domestic and foreign policy aims. The tribunals' dependency on states is not a design flaw but rather a feature.

In practice, the proposed alternatives to the standing international human rights and criminal courts are unable to hand down judgments against their principals. Instead, they preserve the status quo and help political elites manage domestic disputes. For example, having a standing court in which states enjoy significant political latitude is especially beneficial for states or

---

[6] A separate question, of course, is whether or not domestic and international audiences are persuaded by this line of argument. There is a growing literature that suggests that publics generally favor international law and courts, for example Geoffrey P. R. Wallace, "International Law and Public Attitudes toward Torture: An Experimental Study," *International Organization* 67, no. 1 (January 2013): 105–140, https://doi.org/10.1017/S0020818312000343; Sarah Kreps and Geoffrey Wallace, "International Law and US Public Support for Drone Strikes," *openDemocracy*, July 2, 2015, https://www.opendemocracy.net/openglobalrights/sarah-kreps-geoffrey-wallace/international-law-and-us-public-support-for-drone-stri; Yonatan Lupu and Geoffrey P. R. Wallace, "Violence, Nonviolence, and the Effects of International Human Rights Law," *American Journal of Political Science* 63, no. 2 (April 2019): 411–426, https://doi.org/10.1111/ajps.12416; Stephen Chaudoin, "How Contestation Moderates the Effects of International Institutions: The International Criminal Court and Kenya," *The Journal of Politics* 78, no. 2 (April 2016): 557–571, https://doi.org/10.1086/684595.

[7] In their much-contested article on international adjudication, Posner and Yoo claim that more dependence makes for more effective courts: Eric A. Posner and John Yoo, "A Theory of International Adjudication," *University of Chicago Law and Economics, Olin Working Paper No. 206, UC Berkeley Public Law Research Paper No. 146* (2004), http://dx.doi.org/10.2139/ssrn.507003.

elites that need to enact the so-called legal lasso to remove domestic spoilers or otherwise lean on a weak court to do their bidding.[8] Moreover, if states and elites expect to resort to more violence in the future, they can be assured that these new courts, by design, are unable to hold them to account for their crimes.

In brief, the proposed alternatives to existing international justice mechanisms lack the structural, adjudicative, and normative authority of the tribunals they are meant to replace. Not only are they weak substitutes for the tribunals at the core of the international justice regime, but the initiatives to create these substitute justice mechanisms can inflict real damage on existing international human rights and criminal courts.

CASE SELECTION AND EMPIRICAL APPROACH

Understanding the backlash politics that lead states and elites to create alternative justice mechanisms requires careful process tracing. The following case studies rely on detailed, inferential descriptions to show *how* and *why* states and elites sought to create alternate justice mechanisms to the ICC and IACtHR.[9] Relying on a range of data, from interviews with stakeholders to newspapers of record, official reports from states and international organizations, and legal analyses of cases, the following empirical examples piece together the story of backlash politics and use the theoretical framework outlined in Chapter 2 to guide the discussion.

The empirical work in this chapter begins with the African Union's plans to withdraw, en masse, from the ICC and to create an AU-based international criminal court. The chapter focuses on this case for three reasons. First, it is the most salient example of backlash to the ICC in the past decade and, as such, it has consumed the international justice community. Second, the AU's process of proposing an alternative to the ICC illustrates the drivers of backlash politics outlined in the theoretical framework. Third, while the AU as a whole supported this initiative of withdrawing from the ICC and creating a regional alternative, some member states voiced disagreement, showing the power of stakeholder states to shore up the international justice regime.

---

[8] Courtney Hillebrecht and Scott Straus, "Who Pursues the Perpetrators?: State Cooperation with the ICC," *Human Rights Quarterly* 39, no. 1 (February 2017): 162–188, https://doi.org/10.1353/hrq.2017.0006.

[9] David Collier, "Understanding Process Tracing," *PS: Political Science & Politics* 44, no. 4 (October 2011): 823–830, https://doi.org/10.1017/S1049096511001429; James Mahoney, "The Logic of Process Tracing Tests in the Social Sciences," *Sociological Methods & Research* 41, no. 4 (November 2012): 570–597, https://doi.org/10.1177/0049124112437709.

The second empirical section offers a brief discussion of the UNASUR alternative to the IACtHR. This short discussion of UNASUR is offered both as a point of comparison to the AU example, as well as a complement to the analysis in Chapter 3.

CASE 1: THE AFRICAN UNION'S PLAN FOR THE ICC

The Judicialization of Africa

Over the course of the 1990s and early 2000s, Africa, like Europe and the Americas, ushered in a wave of regional and subregional courts, many of which have human rights-related components. The Economic Community of West African States (ECOWAS) created the Community Court of Justice (CCJ) in 1991, which became operational in 2000, and expanded its jurisdiction to include human rights-related claims in 2005.[10] In 2001, the East African Community established the East African Court of Justice (EACJ).[11] The Southern African Development Coordination Conference and the South African Development Community (SADC) similarly established a tribunal that dealt with human rights issues, although the tribunal was suspended in 2012.

In 1981 the Organization of African Unity (OAU) established the African Charter on Human and Peoples' Rights, known as the Banjul Charter, which entered into force in 1986.[12] The African Commission on Human and Peoples' Rights (ACmHPR) is charged with monitoring the Banjul Charter, which covers a broad scope of civil, political, and collective human rights.[13] In 1998, the OAU further developed its regional human rights system and adopted the Protocol to the African Charter on Human and Peoples' Rights on the

[10] "ECOWAS Community Court of Justice," Open Society Justice Initiative, June 2013, https://www.justiceinitiative.org/publications/ecowas-community-court-justice.

[11] Daniel Abebe, "Does International Human Rights Law in African Courts Make a Difference?" *Virginia Journal of International Law* 56, no. 3 (2017): 527–584, https://chicagounbound .uchicago.edu/cgi/viewcontent.cgi?article=12639&context=journal_articles.

[12] "African [Banjul] Charter on Human and Peoples' Rights," adopted June 27, 1981, *Organization of African Unity/African Union Treaties, Conventions, Protocols & Charters*, http://hrlibrary.umn.edu /instree/z1afchar.htm; Amnesty International, *A Guide to the African Charter on Human and Peoples' Rights* (Chalgrove, UK: Amnesty International Publications, 2006), https://www .amnesty.org/download/Documents/76000/ior630052006en.pdf; https://au.int/en/treaties/african-charter-human-and-peoples-rights.

[13] African Commission on Human and Peoples' Rights, "Information Sheet No. 1: Establishment," *Secretariat of the Commission on Human and Peoples' Rights*, n.d., https://archives.au.int/bitstream/handle/123456789/2073/Information%20Sheet%20no1_E.pdf?sequence=1&isAllowed=y.

Establishment of an African Court on Human and Peoples' Rights. This Protocol entered into force in 2004, thereby creating the African Court on Human and Peoples' Rights (ACtHPR).[14]

While the African Commission on Human and Peoples' Rights worked in the shadows for many years, and the ACtHPR was slow to hear admissible contentious cases, the past ten years have marked important growth and development in the Banjul Charter system. The African Commission on Human and Peoples' Rights, which serves as a clearinghouse for cases to the Court, has made decisions on nearly 250 communications alleging violations against member states.[15] The African Court on Human and Peoples' Rights issued its first decision in 2009.[16] Since then, it has heard and finalized nearly sixty contentious cases, with Rwanda and Tanzania being the two most frequent defendants. Many more cases are pending.[17] Despite this activity, only nine states – Benin, Burkina Faso, Côte d'Ivoire, The Gambia, Ghana, Mali, Malawi, Tanzania, and the Republic of Tunisia – have accepted the jurisdiction of the Court to hear petitions from NGOs and individual applicants.[18] Thus, while the Banjul system has matured remarkably over the past decade, it would be fair to say that few states and even fewer heads of state view the ACmHPR and ACtHPR as a real threat to their hold on power.[19]

Over the same period that the African human rights system was growing, so too was interest in a regional interstate dispute mechanism. In 2002, the African Union replaced the old OAU, and the following year, the AU adopted

[14] "Protocol to the African Charter on Human and Peoples' Rights on the Establishment of an African Court on Human and Peoples' Rights," adopted June 10, 1998, *Organization of African Unity/African Union Treaties, Conventions, Protocols & Charters*, https://au.int/en/treaties/protocol-african-charter-human-and-peoples-rights-establishment-african-court-human-and.

[15] African Commission on Human and Peoples' Rights, "Decisions on Communications," n.d., https://www.achpr.org/communications.

[16] Chacha Bhoke Murungu, "Judgment in the First Case before the African Court on Human and Peoples' Rights: A Missed Opportunity or Mockery of International Law in Africa?" *SSRN* (December 2009), http://dx.doi.org/10.2139/ssrn.1526539.

[17] "Contentious Matters: Pending Cases," African Court on Human and Peoples' Rights, n.d., https://en.african-court.org/index.php/cases#pending-cases.

[18] African Court on Human and Peoples' Rights, "Frequent Questions," n.d., http://en.african-court.org/index.php/faqs/frequent-questions#Criminal; "Welcome to the African Court," African Court on Human and Peoples' Rights, n.d., https://en.african-court.org/.

[19] Frans Viljoen and Lirette Louw, "State Compliance with the Recommendations of the African Commission on Human and Peoples' Rights, 1994–2004," *American Journal of International Law* 101, no. 1 (January 2007): 1–34, https://doi.org/10.1017/S0002930000002950X; Tom Gerald Daly and Micha Wiebusch, "The African Court on Human and Peoples' Rights: Mapping Resistance against a Young Court," *International Journal of Law in Context* 14, no. 2 (June 2018): 294–313, https://doi.org/10.1017/S1744552318000083.

the Protocol of the Court of Justice of the African Union. This Protocol provided for an interstate dispute mechanism to interpret AU and international law. The Court was never established, however. Instead, in 2008, the Protocol of the Court of Justice of the African Union was merged with the AU's Protocol to the African Charter on Human and Peoples' Rights on the Establishment of an African Court on Human and Peoples' Rights to establish the Statute of the African Court of Justice and Human Rights.[20] At the core of this crucible of amendments and protocols was the groundwork for the AU's proposed alternative to the ICC.

The ICC, the AU, and the Reality of Unmet Expectations

The tide of judicialization that ushered in the development of the African human rights system and efforts at an interstate justice mechanism also included many African states ratifying the Rome Statute.[21] As has been well documented and frequently lambasted, all of the thirteen situations under open investigation, bar three (Georgia, Bangladesh/Myanmar, and Afghanistan), are from Africa.[22] Two of the nine preliminary examinations (Nigeria and Guinea) are also from Africa.[23] Moreover, the ICC has gone after two African heads of state via United Nations Security Council referral (Sudan's Omar al-Bashir and Libya's Muammar Gaddafi) and two others via the prosecutor's *propio motu* powers (Kenya's Uhuru Kenyatta and Côte d'Ivoire's Laurent Gbagbo and former first lady Simone Gbagbo).

In addition to the pure number of cases concerning African states at the ICC, the UNSC referral and *propio motu* mechanisms have drawn particular ire. As many African leaders have noted, three of the five permanent members of the Security Council (P-5) have not ratified the Rome Statute and yet are allowed to refer cases to the ICC, including from other non-member states.[24]

---

[20] African Court on Human and Peoples' Rights, "Frequent Questions."

[21] "The States Parties to the Rome Statute," International Criminal Court, n.d., https://asp.icc-cpi.int/en_menus/asp/states%20parties/pages/the%20states%20parties%20to%20the%20rome%20statute.aspx.

[22] These situations include: Burundi (2017); Central African Republic (2007 and 2014); Mali (2013); Côte d'Ivoire (2011); Libya (2011); Kenya (2010); Darfur, Sudan (2005); Uganda (2004); and Democratic Republic of the Congo (2004). "Situations under Investigation," International Criminal Court, n.d., https://www.icc-cpi.int/pages/situation.aspx.

[23] "Preliminary Examinations," International Criminal Court, n.d., https://www.icc-cpi.int/pages/pe.aspx.

[24] These states are China, Russia, and the United States. Domenico Carofiglio, "To What Extent Have Politics Restricted the ICC's Effectiveness?" *E-International Relations*, December 20, 2015, https://www.e-ir.info/2015/12/20/to-what-extent-have-politics-restricted-the-iccs-effectiveness/.

Similarly, while the Office of the Prosecutor's *propio motu* powers are limited to alleged violations that took place in/by member states of the ICC, the mechanism still puts a great deal of power into the OTP's office. Thus, while the ICC has shown itself to be quite slow and inefficient when it comes to prosecuting heads of state, it poses a challenge to African leaders beyond anything that the African Court on Human and Peoples' Rights or domestic courts have done to date.[25]

As the Colombian example in Chapter 3 illustrates, the number of cases a state has at an international human rights or criminal court does not directly translate into backlash politics. Instead, backlash politics is driven by a set of normative and political factors. This has been the case with the AU and the ICC. The AU's dissatisfaction with the ICC has been a direct result of normative discontent among Rome Statute member states, especially with respect to head of state immunity. There is no domestic consequence of international adjudication quite so significant as indicting, arresting, and trying sitting heads of state, which the ICC OTP's office and the UNSC have now done on multiple occasions.

At the time African heads of state ratified the Rome Statute, it is unlikely that they believed the ICC would ever come after them.[26] In the years since the ICC entered into force, however, it became clear that the ICC was, in fact, going to pursue heads of state and other powerful players, and that it would do so in Africa. In 2005, the UNSC referred the situation in Darfur to the ICC, which subsequently indicted Sudanese President Omar al-Bashir. By this point, Uganda, the Democratic Republic of the Congo, and the Central African Republic had all spent a few years under the ICC's microscope, but the al-Bashir indictment brought together some of the ICC's most contentious features, namely a commitment to head of state accountability and UNSC referrals. Anti-ICC sentiment in the region began to intensify, and opponents of the Court started to develop a plan for undermining and ultimately replacing the ICC.[27]

The anti-ICC movement reached a fever pitch in 2008. On July 21, 2008, the African Union requested the ICC defer on issuing an arrest warrant for Sudanese President Omar al-Bashir.[28] Ignoring the request, the ICC's

---

[25] Viljoen and Louw, "State Compliance with the Recommendations"; Daly and Wiebusch, "The African Court on Human and Peoples' Rights."

[26] Beth A. Simmons and Allison Danner, "Credible Commitments and the International Criminal Court," *International Organization* 64, no. 2 (April 2010): 225–256, https://doi.org/10.1017/S0020818310000044.

[27] Kurt Mills, "'Bashir Is Dividing Us': Africa and the International Criminal Court," *Human Rights Quarterly* 34, no. 2 (2012): 404–447, https://doi.org/10.1353/hrq.2012.0030.

[28] Mills, "'Bashir Is Dividing Us'."

Prosecutor's Office issued the Court's first arrest warrant for al-Bashir on March 4, 2009.[29] Luis Moreno Ocampo, who was then Chief Prosecutor of the ICC, said about issuing the warrant, "We received a judicial mandate and we fulfilled it."[30] Human Rights Watch and other NGOs declared the importance of handing down the arrest warrant in establishing the ICC's deterrent powers.[31]

Soon thereafter, the Assembly of the African Union voted to condemn the UNSC's lack of action on their requested deferral of al-Bashir's warrant, in what was essentially a statement of noncooperation with the ICC.[32] The resolution passed. Only Chad issued a reservation, noting disagreement with the resolution, although activists, scholars, and practitioners claimed that other countries were browbeaten into remaining silent so that the AU could present a united front.[33] Indeed, in the days following the vote, Benin and Botswana expressed their disagreement with the decision, and a South African foreign ministry official claimed that al-Bashir would be arrested were he to travel to South Africa.[34]

The arrest warrant posed two challenges to African leaders. First, it showed that the ICC could – and would – issue warrants for sitting heads of state. This

[29] International Criminal Court, "Al Bashir Case," n.d., https://www.icc-cpi.int/darfur/albashir. A second arrest warrant for al-Bashir was issued on July 12, 2010. The suspect remains at large.

[30] Office of the Prosecutor, "ICC Prosecutor in New York to Meet with United Nations and African Union Officials," *International Criminal Court*, September 22, 2008, https://www.icc-cpi.int/Pages/item.aspx?name=icc%20prosecutor%20in%20new%20york%20to%20meet%20with%20united%20nations%20and%20african%20union%20officials.

[31] "Arab States: Press Sudan on Darfur Aid," *Human Rights Watch*, March 29, 2009, https://www.hrw.org/news/2009/03/29/arab-states-press-sudan-darfur-aid.

[32] Laurence R. Helfer and Anne E. Showalter, "Opposing International Justice: Kenya's Integrated Backlash Strategy against the ICC," *International Criminal Law Review* 17, no. 1 (February 2017): 1–46, https://scholarship.law.duke.edu/faculty_scholarship/3713/; "African Civil Society Urges African States Parties to the Rome Statute to Reaffirm Their Commitment to the ICC," *Human Rights Watch*, July 30, 2009, https://www.hrw.org/news/2009/07/30/african-civil-society-urges-african-states-parties-rome-statute-reaffirm-their; "President of the Assembly Meets Minister of Foreign Affairs of Kenya," *Assembly of States Parties*, September 21, 2010, https://www.icc-cpi.int/Pages/item.aspx?name=president%20of%20the%20assembly%20meets%20minister%20of%20foreign%20affairs%20of%20kenya; African Union, "Assembly of the African Union: Thirteenth Ordinary Session July 1–3, 2009 Sirte, Great Socialist People's Libyan Arab Jamahiriya: Decisions and Declarations," July 3, 2009, https://au.int/sites/default/files/decisions/9560-assembly_en_1_3_july_2009_auc_thirteenth_ordinary_session_decisions_declarations_message_congratulations_motion_0.pdf.

[33] Mills, "'Bashir Is Dividing Us'."

[34] "South Africa Reverses Course on ICC Arrest Warrant for Bashir," *Sudan Tribune*, July 31, 2018, www.sudantribune.com/South-Africa-reverses-course-on,31986; Mills, "'Bashir Is Dividing Us'"; BBC, "African Union Defies ICC over Bashir Extradition," ABC News, July 4, 2009, www.abc.net.au/news/2009-07-05/african-union-defies-icc-over-bashir-extradition/1341682.

was not what many leaders had anticipated when they deposited their ratifications of the Rome Statute.[35] Second, it underscored real normative tensions among Rome Statue member states. It put leaders in a difficult position with respect to their Rome Statute obligations. Should they try to fulfill their obligations under the Rome Statute and arrest al-Bashir if he were to travel to their country or should they defy the ICC and allow al-Bashir to travel around the region? Of course, in the intervening decade, al-Bashir has traveled throughout Africa – to Kenya,[36] Chad,[37] Malawi,[38] Uganda, South Africa, and Jordan, among others – largely without consequence.[39] States' willingness (or unwillingness) to welcome al-Bashir on their territory demonstrated internal divides within the AU that ultimately contributed to the downfall of the organization's plan to supplant the ICC. In the process of arriving at this anti-climax, however, the AU's efforts to replace the ICC cast doubt on the ICC's moral authority and hampered its ability to effectively investigate, adjudicate, and communicate about ongoing cases.

Crafting an AU Alternative to the ICC

Amidst the uncertainty and anxiety surrounding al-Bashir's travels, in 2008, the African Union adopted the Protocol on the Statute of the African Court of Justice and Human Rights, which would merge the African Court on Human and Peoples' Rights with the Court of Justice of the African Union. This proposed court would give a newly constituted African Court of Justice and Human Rights (ACJHR) jurisdiction over a range of legal instruments: the AU Constitutive Act, African Union treaties and legal instruments, the African Charter and its Protocol on the Rights of Women in Africa, the African Charter on the Rights and Welfare of the Child, and other relevant

---

[35] Simmons and Danner, "Credible Commitments and the International Criminal Court."

[36] Helfer and Showalter, "Opposing International Justice."

[37] "Pre-Trial Chamber I Informs the United Nations Security Council and the Assembly of States Parties about Chad's Non-Cooperation in the Arrest and Surrender of Omar Al Bashir," *International Criminal Court*, December 13, 2011, https://www.icc-cpi.int/Pages/item.aspx?name=pr756.

[38] "Pre-Trial Chamber I Informs the United Nations Security Council and the Assembly of States Parties about Malawi's Non-Cooperation in the Arrest and Surrender of Omar Al Bashir," *International Criminal Court*, December 13, 2011, https://www.icc-cpi.int/Pages/item.aspx?name=pr755.

[39] Helfer and Showalter, "Opposing International Justice"; "President Song Ends a Two Days Visit to Addis Ababa, Ethiopia," *International Criminal Court*, July 12, 2010, https://www.icc-cpi.int/Pages/item.aspx?name=pr558; "Kenya Refuses to Arrest Sudanese President Omar Al-Bashir," *Amnesty International*, August 27, 2010, https://www.amnesty.org/en/latest/news/2010/08/kenia-se-niega-detener-presidente-sudanes/.

international treaties ratified by the involved states. The African Court on Human and Peoples' Rights already drew on a wide range of legal instruments and the ACJHR would follow in a similar mold.[40] Mali and Libya ratified the Protocol in 2009; Burkina Faso ratified in 2010; Congo ratified in 2011; Benin ratified the Protocol in 2012; and Liberia ratified in 2014.[41]

In February 2009, however, the Assembly of Heads of State Government of the African Union called upon the African Commission on Human and Peoples' Rights to consider the implications of expanding the jurisdiction of the African Court on Human and Peoples' Rights to include war crimes, crimes against humanity, and genocide, which are the very same crimes over which the ICC has jurisdiction.[42] The Assembly was setting the stage to supplant the ICC in Africa. The AU contracted the Pan-African Lawyers Union to draft a report outlining the implications of expanding the jurisdiction of the proposed ACJHR to include individual criminal accountability.[43] An AU–EU Expert Group on the Principle of Universal Jurisdiction also endorsed studying the implications of adding international criminal accountability to the ACJHR, adding credibility to the initiative.[44] By November 2011, the AU had a draft proposal to add international criminal jurisdiction to the proposed ACJHR. This proposal would ultimately become the Draft Protocol on Amendments to the Protocol on the Statute of the ACJHR, or the Malabo Protocol.

Around this same time, the African Union decided to more forcefully reckon with the ICC's arrest warrant for Omar al-Bashir, the UNSC's decision to refer the situation in Sudan to the ICC in the first place, and the ongoing proceedings with regard to Kenya.[45] By December 2010, the ICC OTP had

---

[40] Amnesty International, *Malabo Protocol: Legal and Institutional Implications of the Merged and Expanded African Court* (London: Amnesty International Ltd, 2016), https://www.amnesty.org/download/Documents/AFR0130632016ENGLISH.PDF.

[41] More recently, The Gambia and Angola ratified the Protocol in 2018 and 2020, respectively. Twenty-six other states have signed but not ratified the Protocol.

[42] Max Du Plessis, "Implications of the AU Decision to Give the African Court Jurisdiction over International Crime," *Institute for Security Studies*, June 2012, https://issafrica.s3.amazonaws.com/site/uploads/Paper235-AfricaCourt.pdf.

[43] Don Deya, "Africa: Is the African Court Worth the Wait," *AllAfrica*, March 22, 2012, https://allafrica.com/stories/201203221081.html.

[44] Amnesty International, *Malabo Protocol: Legal and Institutional Implications*.

[45] The UNSC vote on the Darfur referral, UNSC Resolution 1593 (2005), was the first UNSC referral to the ICC. The vote was split: eleven countries voted in favor, none voted against and four abstained. Among those states that voted in favor of Resolution 1593 were AU members Benin and Tanzania. Algeria, also an AU member, abstained. The UNSC vote on Resolution 1593 would prove to be a harbinger for intra-AU divisions about the ICC and a rallying cry for anti-ICC leaders throughout Africa.

released the names of the suspects in the cases of electoral violence in Kenya. This happened despite Kenya's attempts to stop the process via a complementarity claim and by lobbying the UNSC to defer the cases.[46] In April 2012, Kenyan President Mwai Kibaki convinced the East African Court of Justice to expand its jurisdiction to include crimes against humanity, overlapping, of course, with the ICC. In response, Avocats Sans Frontières noted: "The AU and other regional blocks like the [East African Legislative Assembly] EALA are now on the road towards actualizing their resistance to the ICC by clothing existing Courts such as the African Court on Human and Peoples' Rights and the East African Court of Justice with the jurisdiction to try international crimes."[47] Kenya also lobbied the East African Legislative Assembly to request that four ICC cases, including the case against Uhuru Kenyatta, be transferred to the EACJ. The proposal was, at best, impractical and, at worst, an extremely thinly veiled attempt to circumvent the ICC.[48]

The Malabo Protocol in Context: A Smokescreen of Accountability

In May 2012, justice ministers and attorneys general from across the AU met to discuss the Malabo Protocol and plans to add a third chamber dedicated to international crimes to the proposed African Court of Justice and Human Rights.[49] The Malabo Protocol would endow the ACJHR with jurisdiction over fourteen international crimes, including genocide, crimes against humanity, war crimes, the crime of unconstitutional change of government, piracy, terrorism, mercenaryism, corruption, money laundering, trafficking in persons, trafficking in drugs, trafficking in hazardous wastes, illicit exploitation of natural resources, and the crime of aggression.[50] Of these, of course, the ICC has jurisdiction over genocide, crimes against humanity, war crimes and the crime of aggression. Unlike the ICC, however, which can hold heads of

---

[46] "Kenya to Establish Local Judicial Mechanism to Probe Violence," *The Hague Justice Portal*, December 14, 2010, www.haguejusticeportal.net/index.php?id=12321; Helfer and Showalter, "Opposing International Justice."

[47] Sharon Esther Nakandha, *Africa and the International Criminal Court: Mending Fences* (Kampala: Avocats Sans Frontières, 2012), 11, https://asf.be/wp-content/uploads/2012/08/ASF_UG_Africa-and-the-ICC.pdf.

[48] Allan Ngari, "Kenya's Ongoing Battle with Complementarity at the ICC," *International Justice Monitor*, May 16, 2012, https://www.ijmonitor.org/2012/05/kenyas-ongoing-battle-with-complementarity-at-the-icc/.

[49] Ngari, "Kenya's Ongoing Battle."

[50] Amnesty International, *Malabo Protocol: Legal and Institutional Implications of the Merged and Expanded African Court* (London: Amnesty International Ltd, 2016), https://www.amnesty.org/download/Documents/AFR0130632016ENGLISH.PDF.

state responsible, the Malabo Protocol included a convenient carve-out for executives and other senior officials, offering them immunity for these crimes.[51] Most importantly, the Malabo Protocol offered immunity to those heads of state currently serving their executive term. As such, it would operate in direct contrast to the ICC and the principles of universal jurisdiction, and offered a court that could try heads of states' political opponents but not the heads of states themselves.[52] In brief, it would be a court built on the premise of state control, exploiting the court's dependence on its member states and the political elites that controlled them. Not only did the proposed court fail to meet global accountability standards but it also served to remind the ICC, and all who were watching, that member states could not only leave the Rome Statute but also drag the ICC through the dirt in the process.

Civil society from across Africa and around the world expressed their concern about the draft of the Malabo Protocol in an open letter. These organizations wanted clarification about the relationship between the reimagined ACJHR and the ICC and how this more expansive jurisdiction would enhance the fight against impunity.[53] A lack of clarity around immunity for the fourteen international crimes for which the ACJHR would have jurisdiction would likely produce diplomatic tension between states and dilute accountability norms.[54] Thus, the proposed new court, in addition to standing in as a watered-down substitute for the ICC, could exacerbate intra-regional schisms, further dissemble already contested norms, and operate under the heavy thumb of regional leaders.

The Malabo Protocol also sought to limit the role of domestic political and civil society opponents. The inclusion of the crime of "unconstitutional change of government" (Article 28E) prompted concern that the ACJHR could be used to thwart and deter domestic opposition, including democratic governance and even self-determination.[55] Others feared that the Malabo

[51]   Ngari, "Kenya's Ongoing Battle."

[52]   "Protocol on Amendments to the Protocol on the Statute of the African Court of Justice and Human Rights," adopted June 27, 2014, *Organization of African Unity/African Union Treaties, Conventions, Protocols & Charters*, https://au.int/en/treaties/protocol-amendments-protocol-statute-african-court-justice-and-human-rights.

[53]   Amnesty International, "Africa: Open Letter to the African States Parties to the International Criminal Court," May 3, 2012, https://www.amnesty.org/en/documents/afr01/007/2012/en/; Helfer and Showalter, "Opposing International Justice"; Du Plessis, "Implications of the AU Decision to Give the African Court Jurisdiction over International Crime."

[54]   Du Plessis, "Implications of the AU Decision to Give the African Court Jurisdiction over International Crime."

[55]   Harmen Van Der Wilt, "Unconstitutional Change of Government: A New Crime within the Jurisdiction of the African Criminal Court," *Leiden Journal of International Law* 30, no. 4 (December 2017): 967–986, https://doi.org/10.1017/S0922156517000449.

Protocol restricted the role of NGOs in pursuing litigation at the proposed court to "African individuals or African non-governmental organizations with observer status with the African Union."[56] The Malabo Protocol highlighted not just international courts' dependence on states but also the drafters' keen awareness that international courts have domestic consequences. By blocking civil society from participating in the proposed court, elites could use the court to thwart their domestic opposition and remain untouchable, especially if they anticipated resorting to (more) repressive tactics to maintain their posts in the future.

The 2012 AU Summit ushered in more drama about al-Bashir's travels and debates about the Malabo Protocol. Malawi was scheduled to host the Summit but ultimately backed down, knowing that al-Bashir would be in attendance. Malawi had already lost Western aid once before when it had allowed al-Bashir to travel to the country; it did not care for a repeat perform-ance. Botswana and Zambia supported Malawi's decision, but the AU itself remained steadfast that al-Bashir attend the summit.[57] Meanwhile, the AU Assembly tabled a discussion of the Malabo Protocol, noting that they required more information on two divisive issues, namely the definition of unconstitutional change of government and the financial implications of expanding the jurisdiction of the ACJHR.[58]

By 2013, the ICC had ramped up its work on the Kenyan situation. In early May 2013, Kenya lobbied the UNSC, first via a *note verbale*, to terminate the Kenyatta and William Ruto cases at the ICC, claiming that Kenyan courts would address the matter.[59] Later that May, Kenya sent a letter to the UNSC, requesting that the Security Council discuss their earlier request(s) to defer

---

[56] Amnesty International, *Malabo Protocol: Legal and Institutional Implications of the Merged and Expanded African Court – Snapshots* (London: Amnesty International Ltd, 2017), 11, www .coalitionfortheicc.org/document/africa-malabo-protocol-legal-and-institutional-implications -merged-and-expanded-african; "Protocol on Amendments to the Protocol on the Statute of the African Court of Justice and Human Rights."

[57] Associated Press in Blantyre, "African Union Pulls Summit from Malawi in Row over Sudan's President," *The Guardian*, June 8, 2012, www.theguardian.com/world/2012/jun/08/african-union-malawi-summit-sudan; H. Thijssen, "The African Union and the International Criminal Court," *Peace Palace Library* (blog), June 22, 2012, https://www .peacepalacelibrary.nl/2012/06/the-african-union-and-the-international-criminal-court/.

[58] Amnesty International, "Malabo Protocol: Legal and Institutional Implications," January 22, 2016, https://www.amnesty.org/en/documents/afro1/3063/2016/en; Assembly of Heads of State and Government, "Decision on the Protocol on Amendments to the Protocol on the Statute of the African Court of Justice and Human Rights Doc. Assembly/Au/13(Xix)A," *African Union*, n.d., https://archives.au.int/bitstream/handle/123456789/68/Assembly%20AU%20Dec%20427 %20%28XIX%29%20_E.pdf?sequence=1&isAllowed=y.

[59] Helfer and Showalter, "Opposing International Justice."

and/or terminate the ICC proceedings against Kenyatta and Ruto. The UNSC declined to engage in such a debate and suggested that Kenya take its claims to the ICC Assembly of States Parties. The ICC labeled Kenya's effort as a "backdoor attempt to politicize the ICC process."[60]

The ICC also sought to clarify its relationship with the UNSC, stating:

> Decisions are taken independently on the basis of the law and the available evidence and are not based on regional or ethnic considerations . . . While the Rome Statute gives the United Nations (UN) Security Council powers of referral and deferral in relation to the ICC, the exercise of these powers by the Security Council is governed by the UN Charter. The ICC is autonomous from the United Nations and does not participate in the Security Council's decision-making.[61]

One week before the trials for Ruto and Joshua Arap Sang were scheduled to begin at the ICC, the Kenyan Parliament advanced a bill to withdraw from the Rome Statute. While Kenyatta did not sign this bill, the initiative shored up Kenyan-led efforts to hold an AU Extraordinary Summit on the ICC.[62] Kenyatta and his allies, particularly the presidents of Rwanda and South Africa, Paul Kagame and Jacob Zuma, respectively, won enough votes to hold the Extraordinary Summit, which took place in Ethiopia in October 2013.[63] During the Summit, Kenyatta stressed his continued cooperation with the ICC. At the same time, however, he also claimed that the ICC "stopped being the home of justice the day it became the toy of declining imperial powers."[64]

---

[60]   Helfer and Showalter, "Opposing International Justice," 14.

[61]   "ICC Underlines Impartiality, Reiterates Commitment to Cooperation with the African Union," *International Criminal Court*, May 29, 2013, https://www.icc-cpi.int/Pages/item.aspx?name=pr908.

[62]   "Case Information Sheet: Situation in the Republic of Kenya, The Prosecutor v. Uhuru Muigai Kenyatta, ICC-PIDS-CIS-KEN-02-014/15_Eng," International Criminal Court, March 13, 2015, https://www.icc-cpi.int/CaseInformationSheets/kenyattaEng.pdf; "Case Information Sheet: Situation in the Republic of Kenya, The Prosecutor v. William Samoei Ruto and Joshua Arap Sang, ICC-PIDS-CIS-KEN-01-012/14_Eng," International Criminal Court, April 2016, https://www.icc-cpi.int/CaseInformationSheets/rutosangEng.pdf; "Kenya MPs Vote to Withdraw from ICC," *BBC News*, September 5, 2013, https://www.bbc.com/news/world-africa-23969316; Sabine Hoehn, "Is ICC Withdrawal Down to Court's 'Lack of Respect' for Kenyan Cooperation and Trial Relocation Requests?" *African Arguments*, September 9, 2013, https://africanarguments.org/2013/09/09/kenya-is-icc-withdrawal-down-to-courts-lack-of-respect-for-kenyan-cooperation-and-trial-relocation-requests-by-sabine-hoehn; Helfer and Showalter, "Opposing International Justice."

[63]   "African Union Summit on ICC Pullout over Ruto Trial," *BBC News*, September 20, 2013, https://www.bbc.com/news/world-africa-24173557.

[64]   Helfer and Showalter, "Opposing International Justice," 22.

While Presidents Kenyatta, Kagame, and Zuma were able to stir up enough anti-ICC sentiment to hold the Extraordinary Summit, they were not able to gather enough votes to orchestrate a mass withdrawal of AU member states from the Rome Statute. The voting record from the 2013 Extraordinary Session remains sealed,[65] but reports suggest a Francophone–Anglophone split, with Côte d'Ivoire, Mali, and The Gambia voting to stay in the Rome Statute, and Ghana, Kenya, Malawi, Sudan, Uganda, and Zimbabwe voting to leave. Notably, Côte d'Ivoire and Mali both had active situations at the ICC, although they are situations in which the sitting heads of state have used the ICC as an international legal lasso, removing their powerful domestic opponents. In Kenya and Sudan, by contrast, those who helm the government are also those on trial.[66] Other powerful states, such as Nigeria, rejected the proposition to withdraw, as did small but vociferous Botswana.[67] As Oumar Ba suggests, there are benefits to be had, particularly for small states, by staying under the ICC's umbrella.[68]

Normative Schisms Cut Both Ways

While Kenya's efforts to derail the cases against Kenyatta and Ruto and alter the terms of accountability at the ICC failed, the AU continued to move to establish its own justice mechanism that would afford head of state immunity. In June 2014, when the AU Assembly of Heads of State and Government met in Malabo, they formally adopted the Protocol on Amendments to the Protocol on the Statute of the African Court of Justice and Human Rights, or the Malabo Protocol. In January 2015, the AU Assembly called on states to ratify the Protocol of the ACJHR as well as the Malabo Protocol, but no states acted.[69] Nevertheless, in June 2015, Zimbabwe's longtime strongman dictator, Robert Mugabe, called for another mass withdrawal of the AU from the Rome Statute, stating: "There is a view that we must distance ourselves from the ICC, but unfortunately the treaty that set it up was done not by the AU but by individual countries . . . [T]hose who signed the treaty are now regretting [it]. We didn't sign it as Zimbabwe. We won't subject ourselves to justice outside

[65] The record is sealed as of the time of writing, February 2019.
[66] Hillebrecht and Straus, "Who Pursues the Perpetrators?"
[67] "African Union Demands Changes in ICC, but Won't Withdraw from It," *International Business Times News*, October 12, 2013, Nexis Uni.
[68] Oumar Ba, *States of Justice: The Politics of the International Criminal Court* (Cambridge, UK: Cambridge University Press, 2020).
[69] African Union, "Assembly of the Union: Twenty-Fourth Ordinary Session 30–31 January 2015 Addis Ababa, Ethiopia: Decisions, Declarations, and Resolutions," January 31, 2015, https://au .int/sites/default/files/decisions/9665-assembly_au_dec_546_-_568_xxiv_e.pdf.

our country's borders."[70] Later that month, Kenyan President Kenyatta pledged $1 million to the ACJHR, calling the court "unstoppable," even though, notably, Kenya neither ratified the Protocol on the Statute, nor the Malabo Protocol.

While Kenya and the AU were pushing for the Malabo Protocol, al-Bashir's travels generated fresh controversy when South Africa refused to arrest him when he traveled to the country. South African President Zuma claimed that al-Bashir had immunity from prosecution given his status as head of state.[71] The ICC, however, viewed this as a direct challenge to their adjudicative authority, so much so in fact that the OTP asked the judges to weigh in. On July 6, 2017, the Pre-Trial Chamber II (PTCII) found that "South Africa failed to comply with its obligations by not arresting and surrendering Omar al-Bashir to the Court," but stopped short of referring South Africa to the ASP or UNSC.[72]

Over the course of the following two years, the AU made repeated calls to withdraw from the ICC. As Table 3.1 indicated, individual states, such as South Africa, Burundi, and The Gambia, made moves to free themselves from the responsibility of the Rome Statute. Thus far, however, only Burundi, which was the subject of a 2016 ICC report detailing the death, rape, torture, and forced disappearances of its citizens, made good on its threat to withdraw from the ICC.[73] Despite Burundi's withdrawal in 2017, the ICC Pre-Trial Chamber III handed down a decision allowing the OTP to open a *propio motu* investigation into the crimes committed in Burundi during the time that Burundi was a member state of the ICC (2004–2017).[74]

[70] "Zuma Assured AU al-Bashir Would Not Be Arrested - Mugabe," *News24*, June 16, 2015, https://www.news24.com/News24/zuma-assured-au-al-bashir-would-not-be-arrested-mugabe-20150616.

[71] Norimitsu Onishi, "Bid by Omar Al-Bashir of Sudan to Avoid Arrest Is Tested in South Africa," *The New York Times*, June 14, 2015, https://www.nytimes.com/2015/06/15/world/africa/bashir-sudan-international-criminal-court-south-africa.html; Marlise Simons, "South Africa Should Have Arrested Sudan's President, I.C.C. Rules," *The New York Times*, July 6, 2017, https://www.nytimes.com/2017/07/06/world/africa/icc-south-africa-sudan-bashir.html.

[72] "Al Bashir Case: ICC Pre-Trial Chamber II Decides Not to Refer South Africa's Non-cooperation to the ASP or the UNSC," *International Criminal Court*, July 6, 2017, https://www.icc-cpi.int/Pages/item.aspx?name=pr1320.

[73] Jeffrey Gettleman, "Raising Fears of a Flight from International Criminal Court, Burundi Heads for Exit," *The New York Times*, October 12, 2016, https://www.nytimes.com/2016/10/13/world/africa/burundi-moves-to-quit-international-criminal-court-raising-fears-of-an-exodus.html.

[74] "Public Redacted Version of 'Decision Pursuant to Article 15 of the Rome Statute on the Authorization of an Investigation into the Situation in the Republic of Burundi,' ICC-01/17-X-9-US-Exp, 25 October 2017," *Pre-Trial Chamber III*, November 9, 2017, https://www.icc-cpi.int/Pages/record.aspx?docNo=ICC-01/17-9-Red.

In early 2017, the AU again revisited the idea of a collective withdrawal from the ICC.[75] But, by that time, divisions within the AU over a mass withdrawal were even more apparent. Nigeria, Senegal, and Cape Verde all reaffirmed their commitment to the ICC, while Malawi, Tanzania, Tunisia, and Zambia said that they needed more to time to deliberate such a strategy.[76] During a closed-door meeting at the AU Summit in Addis Ababa in February 2017, Nigeria and Senegal, as well as Côte d'Ivoire, Mali, Burkina Faso, Tanzania, Tunisia, Cape Verde, Botswana, and Chad all reaffirmed their commitment to the ICC.[77] Again in 2018, Botswana, Nigeria, Tunisia, Senegal, and Zambia all vocalized their support of the ICC. Nigeria's president, Muhammadu Buhari, even gave the keynote address at the twentieth-anniversary celebration of the ICC in July 2018.[78] High participation rates masked significant internal disagreements. This was as true for this new AU court and as it was for the ICC itself. As a result of this discontent, plans for a new AU court fell dormant.

While African Union leaders debated the merits of withdrawing from the ICC and the contours of an alternate criminal accountability court, they touched, time and again, on the key drivers of backlash politics: the tribunals' dependency on states; the domestic consequences of international adjudication; the anticipation of relying on violence in the future; and normative discontent within and among the ICC's member states. The persistent uncertainty about if and how the AU would withdraw from and replace the ICC left scars. The ICC suffered significant reputational damage, as it appeared unable to uphold its most fundamental normative principle: a commitment to accountability. The time, money, and energy spent dealing with the potential AU withdrawal distracted from the ICC's regular adjudicative work. And,

---

[75]   Elias Meseret, "African Leaders OK Strategy for Mass Withdrawal from ICC," *Associated Press*, January 31, 2017, https://apnews.com/0e19488f91bc4ccfad1e167c6c5742d5/African-leaders-OK-strategy-for-mass-withdrawal-from-ICC.

[76]   Michelle Nel and Vukile Ezrom Sibiya, "Withdrawal from the International Criminal Court: Does Africa Have an Alternative?" *African Journal of Conflict Resolution* 17, no. 1 (2017), www.accord.org.za/ajcr-issues/withdrawal-international-criminal-court/; Brendon J. Cannon, Dominic R. Pkalya, and Bosire Maragia, "The International Criminal Court and Africa: Contextualizing the Anti-ICC Narrative," *African Journal of International Criminal Justice* 2, no. 1–2 (December 2016), https://doi.org/10.5553/AJ/2352068X2016002001001.

[77]   Cannon, Pkalya, and Maragia, "The International Criminal Court and Africa."

[78]   Frédérique Renée Zoë Gabriel Moes, "Withdrawal from the Rome Statute by the Republic of South Africa: Filling the Gaps," Master's thesis, Tillburg University, 2018, http://arno.uvt.nl/show.cgi?fid=144811; Elise Keppler, "African Members Reaffirm Support at International Criminal Court Meeting," *Human Rights Watch*, November 17, 2016, https://www.hrw.org/news/2016/11/17/african-members-reaffirm-support-international-criminal-court-meeting; Sylvester Ugwuanyi, "Full Text of Buhari's Address at International Criminal Court Event," *Daily Post Nigeria* (blog), July 17, 2018, http://dailypost.ng/2018/07/17/full-text-buharis-address-international-criminal-court-event/.

above all, the ICC showed itself to be vulnerable to attack. How much authority could a court have if a large contingent of its member states walked out and replaced it with a watered-down version of itself?

CASE 2: THE LATIN AMERICAN EXPERIENCE

In Chapter 3, I considered possible withdrawals from the Inter-American Court of Human Rights. In addition to withdrawing, or threatening to withdraw, from the IACtHR, Venezuela and allied countries also tried to create a human rights instrument within the Union of South American Nations. This section considers how Venezuela, among others, used it as a tool to lambast the West and provide political cover for their human rights shortcomings.

UNASUR was formally established in 2008, following a wave of subregional integration efforts in Latin America. UNASUR's membership includes all twelve South American states and forms a bridge across the region's two main trading blocs, the Southern Common Market (MERCOSUR) and the Andean Community (CAN).[79] The impetus for UNASUR came largely from Argentina, Brazil, and Venezuela as a way to coordinate South American states' responses to the international community and to protect the populist and quasi-populist vision of social change that gripped much of the region in the early 2000s.[80] The creation of UNASUR became not only an opportunity for increased trade among its member states, but also a way to advance an anti-hegemonic policy platform and to provide political cover for member states increasingly under fire at the IAHRS.[81] This is not to suggest that there was consensus in the primary goals of UNASUR. Indeed, the Brazilians envisioned a regional agreement focused on trade and security, while the Venezuelans instead viewed UNASUR as a way to confront the United States. As Rita Giacalone explains:

---

[79] UNASUR, United Nations, and Economic Commission for Latin America and the Caribbean, *UNASUR: Fostering South American Integration through Development and Cooperation* (Santiago, Chile: United Nations, 2014), https://repositorio.cepal.org/bitstream/handle/11362/37384/1/S1420807_en.pdf; "Tratado Constitutivo de La Uniön de Naciones Suramericanas," adopted May 23, 2008, UNASUR, https://www.cancilleria.gov.co/sites/default/files/tratado-constitutivo-unasur.pdf.

[80] Hugo Carvajal Donoso, "La UNASUR de Samper, el último brazo del Chavismo," *Cuadernos faes*, July/September 2016, 53–60, https://fundacionfaes.org/file_upload/publication/pdf/2016 0713144021la_unasur_de_samper-_el_ultimo_brazo_del_chavismo.pdf.

[81] Fabio Luis Barbosa dos Santos, "UNASUR in a Comparative Light: The Relations with Venezuela and Colombia," *Brazilian Journal of Strategy & International Relations* 5, no. 10 (July/December 2016): 229–251, https://doi.org/10.22456/2238-6912.67243; Rita Giacalone, "Venezuela en Unasur: integración regional y discurso político," *Desafíos* 25, no. 1 (January–June 2013): 129–163, www.scielo.org.co/pdf/desa/v25n1/v25n1a05.pdf.

At the same time, it implied a confrontation between the objectives of Brazil and Venezuela: while the Brazilian project needed regional peace – to expand business, trade, build infrastructure obtain energy sources and project itself globally as a guarantor of regional security – the Venezuela project rested on the inevitability of conflict with the United States and other regional governments and was based on the ideological–political affinity, ruling out commercial liberalization through development.[82]

Ultimately, the Venezuelan vision carried the day. Venezuela, Bolivia, and Ecuador shaped UNASUR as a human rights alternative to the IAHRS. Despite their efforts, however, the UNASUR human rights body never came to pass.

Circumnavigating the Domestic Consequences of International Adjudication

In 2008, Bolivia, a critical Venezuelan ally, was facing a political crisis. Governors in Bolivia's northern and eastern provinces threatened to withhold natural gas exports over La Paz's efforts to redistribute profits from its oil tax revenues. These threats quickly grew violent, as protestors seized natural gas resources, a provincial airport, and government buildings. President Evo Morales declared a state of emergency, instated martial law, and cracked down on protestors and free speech.[83] This crisis prompted Bolivia, Venezuela, and Ecuador, among others, to go on the offensive and attack the normative and adjudicative authority of the Inter-American Human Rights System, particularly its work on the freedom of expression.

Morales, Chávez, and their allies knew that litigation within the IAHRS about the social unrest in Bolivia would empower civil society actors and journalists to rise up against the state. In response, Ecuador's president, Rafael Correa, together with Venezuelan president Hugo Chávez, moved to create a mechanism within UNASUR that would protect governments from what they called "the private media," meaning journalists and others not part of their state-run media apparatuses.[84]

The idea that UNASUR could provide a viable alternative for human rights deliberation took off in 2011. In September 2011, the IACtHR handed down a ruling against Venezuela regarding the government's treatment of an

---

[82]   Giacalone, "Venezuela en Unasur," 134–135. Translation mine.

[83]   Simon Romero, "A Crisis Highlights Divisions in Bolivia," *The New York Times*, September 14, 2008, https://www.nytimes.com/2008/09/15/world/americas/15bolivia.html.

[84]   Vanessa Gómez Quiroz, "Alertan sobre nuevos controles a la prensa," *El Nacional (Venezuela)*, May 25, 2009, Nexis Uni.

opposition leader.[85] In his characteristically colorful rhetoric, Chávez had this to say: "To me, this means nothing, nothing to the left. A haircut is worth more than this court . . . Unfortunately, this 'celebrated' Court is one of the institutions of the past." Invoking his own misfortunate relationship with the Court involving the 2002 autogolpe and the Court's inaction regarding his sequestration and near-ouster, Chávez continued, "We are still waiting." Chávez finished by saying that UNASUR "should quickly, sooner rather than later, have a human rights court."[86]

North American Hegemony and Normative Fractures

In addition to trying to circumnavigate the IAHRS's jurisdiction and its mobilizing effect on the domestic opposition, Chávez and his allies stressed normative disagreements within the IAHRS and tried to align the IAHRS with North American hegemony, even though the United States does not accept the jurisdiction of the IACtHR.[87] Ecuador's Rafael Correa, for example, said that he wanted to bring radical change to the IAHRS to make it "Latin American." Correa argued: "There is a big bias in the Inter-American Commission on Human Rights and the Rapporteur for Freedom of Expression, financed by the United States and the European Union, by the Anglo-Saxon institutionalization ... They try to impose the values of the United States everywhere on the planet because they see themselves as the kings."[88]

The anti-IACmHR rhetoric ramped up even further as human rights conditions in Venezuela deteriorated, and as more neighboring states saw the value of lambasting the IAHRS. Nicolás Maduro, then Venezuela's foreign minister, argued, "Brothers from Latin America and the Caribbean: the time has come to dismantle this decadent structure of the Inter-American Court and of the Inter-American Commission on Human Rights." He then invited his audience to join Venezuela in creating an alternative. Such a body, he claimed, "would guarantee and ensure human rights from our experience, not

---

[85] "Chávez dice corte de cabello vale más que la CorteIDH que condenó a Venezuela," *Proceso Digital*, September 17, 2011, https://proceso.hn/politica/18-politica/Ch%C3%A1vez-dice-corte-de-cabello-vale-m%C3%A1s-que-la-CorteIDH-que-conden%C3%B3-a-Venezuela.html.

[86] *Proceso Digital*, "Chávez dice corte de cabello vale más que la CorteIDH que condenó a Venezuela."

[87] "Ecuador d.humanos; Ecuador cree que hay interés en la región por reformar sistema interamericano," *Spanish Newswire Services*, November 15, 2011, Nexis Uni.

[88] "Correa propone 'cambio radical' de sistema interamericano de derechos humanos," *Editorial Azeta S.A. (ABC Color)*, November 11, 2011, https://www.abc.com.py/internacionales/correa-propone-cambio-radical-de-sistema-interamericano-de-ddhh-331079.html.

from the experience of an international bureaucracy controlled from Washington."[89]

In 2013, Venezuela officially left the IACtHR. Correa called for the IACmHR to either revolutionize or disappear.[90] In 2013 Morales argued, "I consider the CIDH [the Commission's Spanish acronym] like another military base." He also notes, "I am seriously considering leaving the Commission. What does it do? Imagine, having its office in the USA when that country has not even ratified any treaties protecting human rights!"[91] The bluster continued through 2014 and allowed Latin America's most populist leaders to claim that they were not opposed to human rights, simply the version of human rights advanced by the IAHRS. Not coincidentally, it was during this time that these populist regimes were imposing increasing domestic restrictions and threatening basic human rights principles. Replacing the IAHRS and its constituent institutions was one way to blind the international watchdog as domestic politics grew more repressive.

The Resurgence of the IAHRS and the End of the Line for UNASUR's Human Rights Body

The IAHRS was not without supporters. Colombia's Juan Manuel Santos said that it would be preferable to rehabilitate rather than destroy the IAHRS.[92] Peru pushed back against Ecuador's efforts to diminish the IACmHR and the Office of the Special Rapporteur for the Freedom of Expression.[93] More importantly, perhaps, the death of Hugo Chávez in 2013 and the resulting and continued turmoil in Venezuela took much of the energy out of the anti-IAHRS initiatives. The IAHRS underwent its own set of institutional reforms (see Chapter 5), and the political tides in the region shifted to the right. The zeal behind creating a UNASUR human rights mechanism dissipated and the

---

[89] "Maduro llama a crear sistemas de DD.HH. en Unasur y CELAC frente a los de OEA," *La Prensa*, May 3, 2012, https://www.laprensa.com.ni/2012/05/03/internacionales/100194-maduro-llama-a-crear-sistemas-de-dd-hh-en-unasur-y-celac-frente-a-los-de-oea.

[90] "Canciller Venezolano insta a países Latinoamericanos a abandonar la CIDH," *Agence France Presse*, May 3, 2012, Nexis Uni; "Venezuela's Withdrawal from Regional Human Rights Instrument Is a Serious Setback," *Amnesty International*, September 6, 2013, https://www.amnesty.org/en/latest/news/2013/09/venezuela-s-withdrawal-regional-human-rights-instrument-serious-setback/.

[91] Nancy F. Verdezoto, "A tres días de la cita de la OEA, Bolivia presiona por las reformas a la CIDH," *El Comercio (Ecuador)*, March 19, 2013, Nexis Uni.

[92] Verdezoto, "A tres días de la cita de la OEA, Bolivia presiona por las reformas a la CIDH."

[93] Juan Paredes Castro, "Diplomacia a tres bandas," *El Comercio*, June 9, 2014, https://elcomercio.pe/opinion/columnistas/diplomacia-tres-bandas-juan-paredes-castro-328015-noticia/.

proposal sat dormant. At the time of writing, UNASUR itself had become defunct.[94]

In South America, as in Africa, the push for creating an alternative justice mechanism came from a desire to create a smokescreen that ostensibly provided political cover for a range of human rights abuses and to have a judicial tool at states' disposal, all while undermining the existing international justice regime. While the UNASUR human rights body was clearly a response to the IAHRS's work, it was also a way for South American states, and particularly Bolivarian states, to lock in their human rights preferences and continue to restrict their opposition. The desire to limit freedom of expression – or at least to lambast the Western version of freedom of expression – was a critical tool in restricting domestic opponents and otherwise limiting the ability of opponents and activists to promote a broader understanding of human rights. The anti-Western, counter-hegemonic sentiment was both the motivation for and the veil covering the Venezuela-led agenda to supplant the IACHR.

CONCLUSION

This chapter considered the creation of substitute justice mechanisms as one form of backlash. Driven largely by normative discontent and the domestic consequences, both good and bad, of international adjudication, these substitute mechanisms exploit international courts' dependency on member states to provide a poor simulacrum of justice. The colorful anti-tribunal rhetoric that drives the development, or threatened development, of these substitutes makes the international justice regime appear biased and trifling. Much like with withdrawals, the creation of alternate or substitute justice mechanisms is obvious and ostentatious.

In the following chapters, I consider two other, subtler, forms of backlash. Chapter 5 considers the role of institutional reforms and budget cuts. For states that cannot or will not withdraw from a tribunal, pulling the purse strings and redesigning institutions in order to hamstring their power are convenient forms of backlash. Similarly, Chapter 6 turns to doctrinal challenges that dilute the potential domestic impacts of international adjudication. All of these mechanisms share, of course, one central tenet: to undermine, directly or indirectly, the authority of the international justice regime and the institutions that prop it up.

---

[94] "Uruguay Withdraws from Unasur and Suspends TIAR," *Buenos Aires Times*, March 11, 2020, https://www.batimes.com.ar/news/latin-america/uruguay-withdraws-from-unasur-and-suspends-exit-from-tiar.phtml.

5

Bureaucrats, Budgets, and Backlash: Death by a Thousand Paper Cuts

INTRODUCTION

On April 12, 2019, Pre-Trial Chamber II of the ICC handed down a ruling saying that it would not proceed with an investigation into possible war crimes in Afghanistan. PTCII cited the current political and security conditions in Afghanistan as major impediments to successfully carrying out the investigation.[1] The Pre-Trial Chamber's decision *not* to pursue the situation in Afghanistan shed a harsh light on international courts' abiding dependence on member states (and non-member states). It also amplified growing calls for significant institutional reform at the ICC. Three former presidents of the Assembly of States Parties (ASP)[2] led this charge. In an op-ed on the Atlantic Council's blog, they wrote: "[T]he powerful impact of the Court's central message is too often not matched by its performance as a judicial institution. We are disappointed by the quality of some of its judicial proceedings, frustrated by some of the results, and exasperated by the management deficiencies that prevent the Court from living up to its full potential."[3] The former ASP presidents cited bureaucratic in-fighting and management problems as one of the ICC's ongoing challenges and called for an independent committee to assess the necessary reforms.[4]

---

[1] Merrit Kennedy, "World Criminal Court Rejects Probe into U.S. Actions in Afghanistan," *NPR*, April 12, 2019, https://www.npr.org/2019/04/12/712721556/world-criminal-court-rejects-probe-into-u-s-actions-in-afghanistan; "Afghanistan: Situation in the Islamic Republic of Afghanistan," International Criminal Court, n.d., https://www.icc-cpi.int/afghanistan.

[2] Prince Zeid Raad Al Hussein (Jordan) served as ASP President from 2002 to 2005, Bruno Stagno Ugarte (Costa Rica) served from 2005 to 2008, Christian Wenaweser (Liechtenstein) served from 2008 to 2011, and Tiina Intelman (Estonia) filled the post from 2011 to 2014.

[3] Prince Zeid Raad Al Hussein, Bruno Stagno Ugarte, Christian Wenaweser, and Tiina Intelman, "The International Criminal Court Needs Fixing," *Atlantic Council*, April 24, 2019, https://www.atlanticcouncil.org/blogs/new-atlanticist/the-international-criminal-court-needs-fixing.

[4] Al Hussein et al., "The International Criminal Court Needs Fixing"; Douglas Guilfoyle, "Reforming the International Criminal Court: Is It Time for the Assembly of State Parties to Be the Adults in the Room?" *EJIL: Talk!* (blog), May 8, 2019, https://www.ejiltalk.org/reform

Calls for bureaucratic reforms are not unique to the ICC. Instead, almost all of the justice mechanisms discussed in this book have undergone significant reform processes over the past decade. As caseloads have grown, global politics have shifted rightward, and the courts have become middle-aged, reform initiatives have become important components in determining the next decade – or more – of international human rights and criminal adjudication. While the previous two chapters examined highly visible but relatively isolated examples of backlash to the international justice regime, this chapter, in contrast, turns to a subtler form of backlash politics. It considers how states and elites use bureaucratic reforms and budgetary restrictions to control and possibly subvert the mission of international human rights and criminal courts.

Using case studies from the Inter-American Human Rights System and the ICC, this chapter illustrates how seemingly small questions about bureaucratic rules and budgets have become major battles for the future of international justice. Drawing on the theoretical propositions from Chapter 2, the cases studies explored here demonstrate how backlash, even in its subtler forms, is driven by the tribunals' dependencies on states, debates about underlying norms, the creation of domestic winners and losers as the result of international adjudication, and states and elites' anticipation of future repression.

BUDGETS AND BUREAUCRACIES AS SITES OF BACKLASH

Although international human rights and criminal courts are *courts*, they also are massive international bureaucracies. In addition to judges, these tribunals employ hundreds of people in their registries, outreach, and execution of judgments offices. The ICC alone employs over 900 bureaucrats with an operating budget of over €150,000,000 in 2020.[5] Being able to reform these bureaucracies is a powerful tool for states and other stakeholders seeking to shape the nature of international human rights and criminal justice.[6]

---

ing-the-international-criminal-court-is-it-time-for-the-assembly-of-state-parties-to-be-the-adults
-in-the-room/.

[5] "About the International Criminal Court," International Criminal Court, n.d., https://www.icc
-cpi.int/about/Pages/default.aspx; International Criminal Court, "Proposed Programme
Budget for 2020 of the International Criminal Court, Eighteenth Session, The Hague, 2–
7 December 2019, ICC-ASP/18/01," *Assembly of States Parties*, July 25, 2019, https://asp.icc-
cpi.int/iccdocs/asp_docs/ASP18/ICC-ASP-18-10-ENG.pdf.

[6] See, more broadly, Tana Johnson, "Institutional Design and Bureaucrats' Impact on Political
Control," *The Journal of Politics* 75, no. 1 (January 2013): 183–197, https://doi.org/10.1017/S002

Battling over budgets and bureaucratic rules is one way for states and governments to thwart or undermine international human rights and criminal courts without taking the egregious steps of withdrawing from the tribunals or creating alternate justice mechanisms. Whether states and elites are bound to international courts because of normative commitments, the preferences of domestic voters, or the demands of international donors, withdrawing from and threatening to replace international courts is not a policy option available to all of the states and elites that seek to undermine the international justice regime.[7] In contrast, instigating and supporting reform processes that thwart the structural, adjudicative, and normative authority of international courts generally goes unnoticed by the public, domestically and internationally.[8]

Remaining within the tribunals whilst attempting to control the courts' internal workings and financial health also allows states and political elites to claim that they are supportive of the court in question and international justice in general. By working within the framework of international justice institutions, states and elites can maintain some moral high ground. They can claim that they are working to "reform," "strengthen," and "improve" the courts and blame the failings of the tribunals on their political opponents or on the tribunals' own bureaucrats. Even in cases where efforts to undermine the tribunals under the guise of "strengthening" them is transparent, these maneuvers still provide states and elites with some political cover, both for their machinations today and as a smokescreen for any violations they might commit tomorrow.

2381612000953; Tana Johnson, *Organizational Progeny: Why Governments Are Losing Control over the Proliferating Structures of Global Governance* (Oxford: Oxford University Press, 2014); Michael Barnett and Martha Finnemore, *Rules for the World: International Organizations in Global Politics* (Ithaca, NY: Cornell University Press, 2004); Kenneth W. Abbott and Duncan Snidal, "Why States Act through Formal International Organizations," *Journal of Conflict Resolution* 42, no. 1 (February 1998): 3–32, https://doi.org/10.1177/0022002798042001001; Darren G. Hawkins, David A. Lake, Daniel L. Nielson, and Michael J. Tierney, eds., *Delegation and Agency in International Organizations* (Cambridge, UK: Cambridge University Press, 2006).

[7]   Eric Voeten, "Populism and Backlashes against International Courts," *Perspectives on Politics* 18, no. 2 (June 2020): 407–422, https://doi.org/10.1017/S1537592719000975; Laurence R. Helfer and Anne E. Showalter, "Opposing International Justice: Kenya's Integrated Backlash Strategy against the ICC," *International Criminal Law Review* 17, no. 1 (2017): 1–46 https://scholarship .law.duke.edu/faculty_scholarship/3713/,.

[8]   Helfer and Anne E. Showalter, "Opposing International Justice"; Mikael Rask Madsen, Pola Cebulak, and Micha Wiebusch, "Backlash against International Courts: Explaining the Forms and Patterns of Resistance to International Courts," *International Journal of Law in Context* 14, no. 2 (June 2018): 197–220, https://doi.org/10.1017/S1744552318000034.

Why Target Budgets and Bureaucracies?

The framework developed in Chapter 2 can help to explain why states and elites target international human rights and criminal courts' budgets and bureaucracies as a way of engaging in backlash politics against international justice. Bureaucratic and budgetary backlash is predicated on the tribunals' dependence on states, particularly for material and procedural support. This reliance on member states is easily exploited.

The tribunals and their member states are all keenly aware that the courts can only function if and when member states contribute to their budget. It is unsurprising, then, that the courts' budgets are both a source of and site for backlash politics. As Theresa Squatrito notes, courts tend to have more control over the selection of their chief administrators than over their budgets. States hold on quite tightly to the financial reigns of these institutions.[9] In the ICC, as well as the African Court on Human and Peoples' Rights, Inter-American Court of Human Rights, the International Criminal Tribunal for the former Yugoslavia, and the International Criminal Tribunal for Rwanda, states and the courts decide their budgets jointly, while states have primary control over the European Court of Human Rights' budget.[10] Omnipresent uncertainty about the institutions' financial security and the persistent threat of member states either intentionally or unintentionally falling into arrears with their contributions put the tribunals in a vulnerable place vis-à-vis the member states and elites they are meant to hold accountable.

The courts' rules and operating procedures are also targets of backlash. These rules exist to help the courts fulfill their legal functions. In the broadest sense, these rules mitigate transaction costs and provide stability both within the courts and between the courts and their member states.[11] Given the wide and potentially conflicting array of state interests at international courts, clear rules of procedure that mitigate potential conflicts are even more necessary in international institutions than in their domestic counterparts.[12] They are also more contentious.

---

[9] Theresa Squatrito, "Resourcing Global Justice: The Resource Management Design of International Courts," *Global Policy* 8, no. S5 (August 2017): 62–74, https://doi.org/10.1111/175 8-5899.12452.

[10] Squatrito, "Resourcing Global Justice."

[11] Kenneth A. Shepsle and Barry R. Weingast, "When Do Rules of Procedure Matter?" *The Journal of Politics* 46, no. 1 (February 1984): 206–221, https://doi.org/10.2307/2130440.

[12] Jochen von Bernstorff, "Procedures of Decision-Making and the Role of Law in International Organizations," *German Law Journal* 9, no. 11 (November 2008): 1939–1964, https://doi.org/10 .1017/S2071832200000705; Eric A. Posner and Alan O. Sykes, "Voting Rules in International Organizations," *Chicago Journal of International Law* 15, no. 1 (Summer 2014): 195–228, https:// heinonline.org/HOL/P?h=hein.journals/cjil15&i=199.

Bureaucratic rules can have significant distributional consequences for member states. Many of the reform processes that have marked the past decade of international human rights and criminal adjudication have centered on what outsiders would consider institutional minutiae.[13] These details are important, certainly, for the functioning of the courts and for due process, but the debates have assumed larger proportions. Indeed, these debates are fundamentally about the autonomy of the institutions and their ability to weigh in on domestic contests over human rights, accountability, and the rule of law.[14]

As the framework in Chapter 2 suggests, states and elites engage in backlash politics, including these budgetary and bureaucratic measures, in large part because of the domestic consequences of international human rights and criminal adjudication. Restricting international human rights and criminal courts through budgetary and bureaucratic maneuvering can be a way for governments to shelter their own human rights practices and policies from the spotlight of international jurisdiction and to dilute the effects of international jurisprudence on domestic politics. Shrinking a tribunal's budget or imposing Byzantine bureaucratic measures that limit the court's adjudicative authority allows states and elites to exact revenge on international courts following particularly divisive rulings and weaken the court's ability to hand down similar judgments in the future. This is, of course, particularly important for those states and elites who plan to use repressive tactics that are likely to attract the court's attention.

In brief, a hamstrung international court cannot effectively exercise its structural, adjudicative, or moral authority. It cannot expediently hear cases on, or bring attention to, domestic human rights abuses or the commission of atrocity crimes. Indeed, the more limited an international court is, either because of a restricted budget or because of arcane and arduous procedural rules, the less able it is to effectively hold states and perpetrators to account.

CASE SELECTION AND EMPIRICAL APPROACH

In order to better understand how battles over budgets and bureaucrats have emerged as a key manifestation of backlash politics, the following empirical analyses use process tracing techniques to illustrate how the factors identified

---

[13] Autumn Lockwood Payton, "Consensus Procedures in International Organizations," working paper, *Max Weber Programme, EUI Working Papers* (2010): 1–20, http://cadmus.eui.eu//han dle/1814/14381.

[14] Sam Garkawe, "Victims and the International Criminal Court: Three Major Issues," *International Criminal Law Review* 3, no. 4 (January 2003): 345–367, https://doi.org/10.1163 /157181203322584350.

in Chapter 2 – the tribunals' inexorable reliance on member states, deep-rooted normative discontent, the domestic implications of international adjudication, and state and elites' intentions to resort to more violence in the future – lead to bureaucratic and budgetary conflict. The case studies on the IAHRS's budget crisis and the ICC's reform processes that follow both draw on a range of primary and secondary data, including interviews, annual reports, social media campaigns, newspaper reporting, and NGO analyses.

The first case study, of the IAHRS's budget crisis, illustrates how budgetary restrictions and bureaucratic battles can be ways of limiting the courts' authority as part of a larger normative debate about the value of human rights and international accountability. The same tensions that helped to explain Venezuela's withdrawal from the IAHRS and subsequent attempts to create an alternate court go a long way in explaining the ways that the IAHRS's so-called "strengthening process" and budget crisis undermined the ability of the IAHRS to hold states accountable for their human rights practices.

The second case, which considers reform processes at the ICC, illustrates that duels over rules and budgets are not only waged to weaken international tribunals but are also a function of the institutions' own mismanagement. The ICC and Assembly of States Parties have struggled to get competent, well-respected judges on the bench and approve a budget that meets the Court's needs. These challenges illustrate both the efforts of some states to subvert the ICC through a series of small attacks and the way that the tribunals' own mismanagement can play directly into the hands of those that seek to undermine it.

The case studies that follow also demonstrate that despite suffering a thousand paper cuts, the courts have shown remarkable resilience. They have overcome these crises, in no small part because of the efforts of steward states and stakeholders in civil society. Indeed, these examples illustrate that while backlash to international human rights and criminal tribunals is a threat to the international justice regime, it is not a one-way fight. The tribunals and their bureaucrats have agency over how they express their authority. Revisiting best practices, calling upon powerful allies, and motivating civil society support are all ways that the tribunals and their supporters can push back against backlash. Chapter 7 offers suggestions for how internal, institutional reform can help the tribunals fight back against backlash politics.

CASE 1: REFORMS AND RESTRICTIONS AS A CANARY IN THE COAL MINE FOR THE IAHRS

On May 23, 2016, the Inter-American Commission on Human Rights announced that it was "going through a severe financial crisis that will have serious consequences on its ability to fulfill its mandate and carry out its basic functions."[15] Pending a large infusion of capital, the IACmHR was planning on laying off nearly half of its staff, suspending any planned visits to assess human rights conditions throughout the hemisphere, and canceling the two sessions of hearings on alleged human rights violations planned for July and October of that year. This fiscal emergency was not only a crisis in its own right but it also was part of a larger set of proposed reforms and restrictions that began in 2011. Both the budget crisis and the reform process that preceded it illustrate how conflicting normative commitments to international human rights accountability and the international justice system's dependence on member states can set the stage for backlash. Further, these reform processes, which were generally concurrent with the more dramatic pledges by Venezuela and other states to withdraw from the IAHRS, similarly illustrate how the domestic consequences of international adjudication and states' expectations to rely on more repression in the future can drive backlash politics. Of course, the IAHRS budget crisis and bureaucratic reform process also show that the different manifestations of backlash discussed throughout this book are not mutually exclusive but rather complementary.

Smaller Budgets, Bigger Demands

The Inter-American Human Rights System has long operated on a shoestring budget. In 2015, the year preceding the Inter-American Commission's financial crisis, the annual budget for the Inter-American Human Rights System clocked in at US$8 million. This pales in comparison to the budgets for the African Human Rights System (US$13 million), the International Criminal Court (US$27 million), and the Council of Europe, which sponsors the European Court of Human Rights (US$110 million).[16] At that time, not only was the overall Inter-American Human Rights System's budget smaller than its regional counterparts, but the Inter-American Commission's budget was shrinking over time. Its budget in 2011 was US$5.1 million; in 2016 it was US$3.6 million. The contracting budget was driven by fluctuating member

---

[15] Inter-American Commission on Human Rights, "Severe Financial Crisis of the IACHR Leads to Suspension of Hearings and Imminent Layoff of Nearly Half Its Staff," *Organization of American States*, May 23, 2016, https://www.oas.org/en/iachr/media_center/PReleases/2016/o 69.asp.

[16] Par Engstrom, Paola Limón, and Clara Sandoval, "#CIDHenCrisis: Urgent Action Needed to Save the Regional Human Rights System in the Americas," *openDemocracy*, May 27, 2016, https://www.opendemocracy.net/en/democraciaabierta/cidhencrisis-urgent-action-needed-to-save-/; https://www.corteidh.or.cr/docs/informe2019/ingles.pdf.

state contributions, a decrease in permanent observer state funding (down to US$689,500 in 2016 from an average of US$2 million per year between 2011 and 2015) and a 42 percent cut in funding from international nongovernmental organizations from the peak during that time frame.[17] While the IACmHR was facing an increasingly restrictive fiscal environment, it was in more demand than ever.[18] Recall from Chapter 2 that the IACmHR is the first stop for litigation at the Inter-American system, and the Commission essentially serves as a clearinghouse for cases. As such, the number of petitions the Commission received annually increased exponentially, including in the years leading up to the 2016 crisis.[19] The number of precautionary measures also grew during this time.[20]

Moreover, in the years leading to the 2016 crisis, the IACmHR expanded its work to include additional special rapporteurs, including a rapporteurship for Economic, Social, Cultural, and Environmental Rights to address some of the critiques lobbied by the Bolivarian states discussed in the previous chapters.[21] It also created a new Interdisciplinary Group of Independent Experts, which has tackled pressing issues such as the disappearance of forty-three students in the Mexican city of Iguala, Guerrero.[22]

More Activity Inspires More Backlash

While demand for the Commission's services was on the rise in the years between 2010 and the budget crisis in 2016, government support of the Commission and its work waned during this period. The two phenomena are not unrelated. Increased IAHRS activity encroached on domestic human

---

[17] "Specific Funds Contributions to IACHR by Donor (Amounts in Thousands of USD)," *Organization of American States*, June 30, 2016, https://www.oas.org/es/cidh/mandato/finan zas/RecursosFinancieros-2011-2016.pdf.

[18] Inter-American Commission on Human Rights, "Statistics," n.d., www.oas.org/en/iachr/multi media/statistics/statistics.html.

[19] Inter-American Commission on Human Rights, "Statistics: Petitions Received," n.d., www .oas.org/en/iachr/multimedia/statistics/statistics.html.

[20] Inter-American Commission on Human Rights, "Statistics: Precautionary Measures Granted/ Requests," n.d., www.oas.org/en/iachr/multimedia/statistics/statistics.html.

[21] Engstrom, Limón, and Sandoval, "#CIDHenCrisis."

[22] As Engstrom, Limón, and Sandoval note in "#CIDHenCrisis," the Commission's response to the forced disappearance of these students highlights the capacity of the IACHR. Many scholars and practitioners (this author included) point to the Iguala effort as one of the Commission's most important innovations of late and an example of the ever-evolving role for international justice mechanisms (Engstrom, Limón, and Sandoval, "#CIDHenCrisis."). Also note, however, that Mexico's USD$1 million contribution for the Iguala investigation did not go into the IACmHR's operating budget but rather was earmarked for this special mechanism.

rights policies and put a spotlight on practices that fell short of regional and global standards. In doing so, the IAHRS empowered domestic opposition groups, and the ensuing debates laid bare fundamental and unresolved disputes about the norms that the Inter-American Human Rights System embodied. As documented in Chapters 3 and 4, the IAHRS became a political target for neo-populist governments in the region. Critics, largely but not exclusively, from Bolivia, Brazil, Ecuador, and Venezuela, alleged that the Commission was a tool of North American hegemony. They called the IACmHR a hypocritical institution that was "not Latin American" and that espoused an overly narrow view of human rights that was limited to civil and political rights. While these criticisms, rooted in domestic political struggles as well as normative debates about the value of civil and political rights, took the more dramatic form of Venezuela's withdrawal from the IAHRS and the proposed UNASUR human rights body, they also manifested in a list of seemingly small yet nevertheless damaging reform initiatives.

One such manifestation was a long-term institutional reform process that began in 2011 with the creation of a special working group, referred to, simply, as the Working Group. The Working Group was charged with evaluating the Commission's work and proposing reforms to improve the efficacy of the Commission and the IAHRS. Alarmingly for supporters of the Commission, however, the Working Group's membership included IAHRS antagonists – Brazil, Peru, and Venezuela, as well as Colombia – and was intended, in the words of the Center for Justice and International Law (CEJIL), "to hinder the work of the Inter-American Commission. These recommendations [could] be seen as a response to specific actions of the IACHR, such as the recent admission of cases denouncing human rights violations in [the] aforementioned countries."[23]

The Working Group identified a set of agenda items: the selection of the executive secretary; precautionary measures; procedural matters in processing petitions and cases; friendly settlements; processes for developing Chapter IV of the annual report (Development of Human Rights in the Region); promotion of human rights; and the financial situation of the Commission.[24] While

[23] "700 Organizations in the Americas Denounce the OAS' Attempt to Weaken Human Rights Defense System," *Center for Justice and International Law*, March 28, 2012, https://cejil.org/en/comunicados/700-organizations-americas-denounce-oas%E2%80%99-attempt-weaken-human-rights-defense-system.

[24] Permanent Council of the Organization of American States, *Report of the Special Working Group to Reflect on the Workings of the IACHR with a View to Strengthening the Inter-American Human Rights System for Consideration by the Permanent Council* (Washington, DC: Organization of American States, December 13, 2011).

the Commission had reached a point in which some institutional reforms were – and continue to be – necessary, the Working Group's recommendations had the effect of restricting the IACmHR's adjudicative, normative, and structural authority.

As the International Justice Resource Center noted, some of the most controversial reforms the Working Group advanced included:

(a) a narrower definition of situations leading to precautionary measures and a proposal that previous precautionary measures, taken without state consultation, be reviewed in conjunction with the state;

(b) a modification of Chapter IV of the Annual Report to include *all* states, not just those with the worse human rights conditions;

(c) a reduction in the mandate of the Special Rapporteur on Freedom of Expression;

(d) reallocating the Commission's time and resources to focus more on human rights promotion and less on individual petitions;

(e) restricting the admissibility of petitions while broadening the scope of conditions for closing a petition and imposing deadlines on each procedural stage of the petition process;

(f) establishing processes to identifying each of the individual, alleged victims;

(g) providing states with more time to review and respond to petitions.[25]

These proposed reforms aligned quite closely with some of the critiques that Venezuela, Ecuador, Bolivia, and, to an extent, Brazil, lobbied against the Commission. The reforms highlighted the Bolivarian states' displeasure with the Commission's emphasis on the freedom of expression and the galvanizing effect that the Commission's rulings on the topic had on their domestic political opponents. Meanwhile, the efforts to expand Chapter IV of the Annual Report to *all* countries, rather than those experiencing extreme human rights abuses, was consistent with the Chavistas' critiques of the Commission's hypocrisy. Venezuela regularly complained that the IAHRS was hypocritical in its tough stance on Venezuela and comparatively lax approach to dealing with the United States. The proposal also attempted to weaken the IAHRS's individual dispute settlement mechanism and limit the ability of individuals to lodge complaints against member states. These reforms took aim at the IAHRS's adjudicative authority and would have hampered the IAHRS's ability to deter future repression, hold perpetrators

---

[25] "Understanding the IACHR Reform Process," *International Justice Resource Center*, last modified November 20, 2012, https://ijrcenter.org/2012/11/20/iachr-reform-process/.

accountable, promote civil and political rights throughout the regime, and, above all, provide recourse for victims.

Unsurprisingly, civil society issued a swift and full-throated denunciation of these proposals.[26] In March 2012, 700 human rights organizations in the region, represented by the International Coalition of Human Rights Organizations in the Americas, denounced these proposals.[27] At the same time, the Inter-American Commission also submitted its own report, which identified four core reform priorities: universality, resources, compliance, and effective access for victims. Importantly, the Commission's report stressed the need for additional funds to keep up with their demanding caseload, as well as the importance of the Commission's independence from regional politics.[28]

Much of 2012 and 2013 were spent in public meetings, listening sessions with civil society, and other forms of debate.[29] The final resolution on the reform or "strengthening" process did address some of the Working Group's concerns, but it also managed to preserve the Commission's independence and the robustness of the individual petitioning and precautionary measures mechanisms.[30] On March 23, 2013, the Extraordinary General Assembly of the Organization of American States approved a resolution drawing that particular "strengthening process" to a close.[31] The Commission's operating budget became the next target, leading to the aforementioned 2016 fiscal crisis.

The Commission and the IAHRS survived the 2016 budget crisis in much the same way that they survived the "strengthening" process: through civil society mobilization and the engagement of steward states. In 2016, civil

[26]   Carey L. Biron, "Pan-American Rights Commission 'Under Threat,'" *Inter Press Service*, November 1, 2012, www.ipsnews.net/2012/11/pan-american-rights-commission-under-threat/.

[27]   "700 Organizations in the Americas Denounce," *Center for Justice and International Law*.

[28]   Inter-American Commission on Human Rights, *Position Document on the Process of Strengthening of the Inter-American System for the Protection of Human Rights* (Washington, DC: Organization of American States, April 9 2012), www.oas.org/en/iachr/docs/pdf/Posicio nFortalecimientoENG.pdf; Inter-American Commission on Human Rights, *Reply of the Inter-American Commission on Human Rights to the Permanent Council of the Organization of American States Regarding the Recommendations Contained in the Report of the Special Working Group to Reflect on the Workings of the IACHR with a View to Strengthening the Inter-American Human Rights System* (Washington, DC: Organization of American States, 2012).

[29]   "Understanding the IACHR Reform Process," *International Justice Resource Center*.

[30]   The Commission also agreed to add an overview statement about human rights in the region into Chapter IV of the annual reports, while also preserving the space and authority to include country-specific reports (Permanent Council of the Organization of American States, *Report of the Special Working Group*).

[31]   Inter-American Commission Human Rights, "Process for Strengthening the IACHR: Methodology," Organization of American States, n.d., www.oas.org/En/Iachr/Mandate/Stre ngthening.Asp.

society organizations generated a strong social media presence, working under the hashtag "#CIDHenCrisis." A variety of NGOs from across the region issued statements of support for the IAHRS.[32] As James Cavallaro, the President Commissioner at the time, suggested: "The crisis announcement led to a mobilization of resources with a speed not usual in the world of international cooperation. This is further evidence that the Inter-American Commission on Human Rights has an extraordinary institutional legitimacy among Member States and other international donors, be it States and international or regional organizations."[33] Commissioner Cavallaro's statement hit on the centrality of donor and stakeholder states' support. Of course, at its root, the IACmHR needed (and needs) money, but it also needs its legitimacy reaffirmed. Indeed, if one of main sources of international courts' authority is their normative and moral standing, then reaffirming the centrality of human rights and accountability norms is a key component to fighting back against backlash. Without state support to legitimize the IAHRS, the outcome of the budget reform process and the future of the Inter-American Commission would have been very different indeed.

That said, states' moral support of the IAHRS was not enough to keep the Commission functional. The Commission needed an infusion of capital to survive. Camilo Sánchez of the Colombian human rights organization, *Dejusticia*, argued that the much-needed cash should come from the OAS general budget (of which only 6 percent goes to the IACmHR), as an illustration of the parent organization's support for the IAHRS in particular and human rights in general.[34] In 2016, however, the capital came from donors and member states. Argentina, Chile, Panama, Peru, Uruguay, and Antigua and Barbuda all made additional contributions, as did the European Commission, individual European states, and a set of private donors. Their material contributions and normative support allowed the Commission to keep its doors open and to continue its work in the face of sustained backlash.[35]

[32] "Crisis Financiera 2016," Comisión Interamerican de Derechos Humanos, n.d., https://www .oas.org/es/cidh/prensa/crisis-apoyo.asp.

[33] Inter-American Commission on Human Rights, "IACHR Overcomes Its Severe Financial Crisis of 2016 and Thanks Countries and Donors Who Made It Possible," *Organization of American States*, September 30, 2016, https://www.oas.org/en/iachr/media_center/PReleases/ 2016/145.asp.

[34] Nelson Camilo Sánchez León, "The Silent Checkmate against the IACHR," *Inter-American Human Rights Network* (blog), May 23, 2016, http://interamericanhumanrights.org/the-silent-checkmate-against-the-iachr/.

[35] Inter-American Commission on Human Rights, "IACHR Overcomes Its Severe Financial Crisis"; Inter-American Commission on Human Rights, "Panama Will Host the Ordinary

The IACHR's experience in 2016 illustrated how vulnerable international justice institutions are to manipulation, including both overt threats such as those discussed in the previous two chapters as well as subtler budgetary and bureaucratic machinations. This vulnerability, of course, stems from international courts' dependence on member states, not only for compliance and cooperation, but also for budgets and bureaucratic rules. It also illustrated that stakeholder and supporter states must remain ever vigilant if they would like to see these institutions flourish. At the time of writing,[36] Argentina, Brazil, Chile, Colombia, and Paraguay were promoting a new declaration about the IACmHR. This declaration, not unlike the ones that preceded it, called for a strengthening of the friendly settlement mechanism (a trade-off for a more limited individual petition mechanism) and offered a limited vision of subsidiarity. Both dimensions of this new proposal elevated the role of the state and subjugated the Commission to states' preferences. The declaration also called for a more conditional approach to reparations, explaining that the Commission should recognize the diverse political and socioeconomic situations of their member states and, as such, should issue reparations that heed the various constitutional and legal systems in the region.[37] Civil society has come out against these proposals, arguing that this reform process is yet another form of backlash – doctrinal challenges – which I discuss in more detail in Chapter 6.[38]

CASE 2: POLITICAL CRISES AND BUREAUCRATIC AND BUDGETARY CONFLICTS AT THE ICC

The IAHRS is not alone in trying to fend off backlash politics in the form of budgetary and bureaucratic restrictions. As the previous two chapters have documented, the ICC has been fighting a series of political battles with a number of actors, particularly the African Union. The ICC has been called biased, incompetent, and illegitimate.[39] Internal bureaucratic mismanagement,

Period of Sessions of the IACHR," *Organization of American States*, September 29, 2016, https://www.oas.org/en/iachr/media_center/PReleases/2016/144.asp.

[36]   May 2019.

[37]   La República Argentina et al., "Declaración Sobre El Sistema Interamericano de Derechos Humanos," April 23, 2019, https://repositorio.uca.edu.ar/handle/123456789/8628.

[38]   Observatorio del Sistema Interamericano de Derechos Humanos, "Posicionamiento Frente a La Declaración Sobre El Sistema Interamericano de Derechos Humanos Suscrita Por Cinco Gobiernos de América Latina," May 6, 2019, https://archivos.juridicas.unam.mx/www/site// index/posicionamiento-cidh-ibero-osidh-final-4078.pdf.

[39]   See, among many examples, "Jail Me, Hang Me: Philippines' Duterte Says Won't Answer to ICC," *Reuters*, December 20, 2019, https://www.reuters.com/article/us-philippines-drugs/jail-me-hang-me-philippines-duterte-says-wont-answer-to-icc-idUSKBN1YO184.

compounded by the ICC's dependence on member states, has contributed to the narrative that the ICC is incapable of administering justice. In response to these critiques, however, the ICC and its supporters have generally deployed a set of technical, rather than political, answers. Thus, the fight for the ICC has become a fight to capture the bureaucracy of the institution, not to resolve normative debates or address the ways in which international adjudication privileges some domestic actors' agendas over others. In Chapter 7, I discuss how this strategy simply delays the normative reckoning lurking in the shadows, but in the remainder of this chapter I discuss how two key issues – the experience and quality of judges and the Court's operating budget – have become flash points for backlash politics.

Providing Better Justice with Stronger Judges and a Cleaner Budget

The quality of judges on the ICC bench has long been a high priority for member states. Judges are, of course, the linchpin at any court, domestic or international. Both critics and advocates of the ICC alike have pointed to ICC judges with little to no experience running a courtroom; judges who never show up to work; and judges who spend the institution's money recklessly.[40] ICC judges are elected by the Assembly of States Parties and serve non-renewable nine-year terms.[41] This procedure has achieved the stated goals of gender equality and regional diversity on the bench, but it has failed to ensure that the judges nominated to the bench were actually qualified to run an international criminal tribunal.[42] The Court's normative and adjudicative authority hinges on the ability of the judges to apply the rule of law fairly and consistently. As such, electing high-quality judges in a transparent way is critical. Yet, it has proved elusive over the Court's two-decade history.[43]

The difficulty in selecting judges reveals normative cleavages about what the ICC should or should not be, particularly the degree to which the ICC should be a judicial actor versus a political promise. Article 36(3) of the Rome Statue outlines the criteria for the judges. It lists:

(a) The judges shall be chosen from among persons of high moral character, impartiality and integrity who possess the qualifications required in their respective States for appointment to the highest judicial offices.

---

[40] Interview #520, 2014; Interview #171, 2014; Interview #168, 2014.
[41] "The Judges of the Court," International Criminal Court, n.d., https://www.icc-cpi.int/Publications/JudgesENG.pdf.
[42] Interview #959, 2014.
[43] Interview #783, 2016.

(b) Every candidate for election to the Court shall:

   (i) Have established competence in criminal law and procedure, and
       the necessary relevant experience, whether as judge, prosecutor,
       advocate or in other similar capacity, in criminal proceedings; or
   (ii) Have established competence in relevant areas of international law
       such as international humanitarian law and the law of human
       rights, and extensive experience in a professional legal capacity
       which is of relevance to the judicial work of the Court;

(c) Every candidate for election to the Court shall have an excellent knowledge
    of and be fluent in at least one of the working languages of the Court.[44]

The main critique of the ICC's judges is that they lack the necessary
experience. They are elected as a function of vote-trading and political
pressure and/or the so-called "dual list system," set up in Article 36 of the
Rome Statute, that puts knowledge of international law on the same plane as
criminal law experience.[45] Article 36(5) of the Rome Statute states:

For the purposes of the election, there shall be two lists of candidates:
   List A containing the names of candidates with the qualifications specified
in paragraph 3 (b) (i); and
   List B containing the names of candidates with the qualifications specified
in paragraph 3 (b) (ii).
   A candidate with sufficient qualifications for both lists may choose on
which list to appear. At the first election to the Court, at least nine judges
shall be elected from list A and at least five judges from list B. Subsequent
elections shall be so organized as to maintain the equivalent proportion on
the Court of judges qualified on the two lists.[46]

Critics contend that the two lists contribute to the uneven set of competencies
of the judges. List A candidates are selected for their expertise in criminal
proceedings. List B candidates are selected for their competence in international law. This dual-list nominating procedure, however, means that some
candidates have nominal – if any – courtroom experience and, instead, rely on
a background in international law to get through the nominating process.[47]

44 "Rome Statute of the International Criminal Court," entered into force July 1, 2002, *United
   Nations Treaty Series* 2187 no. 38544, http://hrlibrary.umn.edu/instree/Rome_Statute_ICC/
   Rome_ICC_toc.html.
45 "Rome Statute of the International Criminal Court."
46 "Rome Statute of the International Criminal Court."
47 Guilfoyle, "Reforming the International Criminal Court"; Open Society Justice Initiative,
   *Raising the Bar: Improving the Nomination and Election of Judges to the International Criminal
   Court* (New York: Open Society Foundations, 2019), https://www.justiceinitiative.org/publica

These jurists' abilities to fulfill their responsibilities upon taking a seat on the bench are then called into question.

A second issue, vote-trading, is simply backroom politics. While civil society has called for this practice to come to an end and for states to vote for the most qualified members of the bench, the practice persists.[48] Moreover, the process of actually running for a position on the bench was described to the Justice Initiative by one sitting judge as "a circus." Backroom negotiations, meet-and-greets, and other political maneuvers are the characteristic features of the elections, not transparent debates or cost-effective campaigns.[49] Vote-trading, within the ICC and across other international organizations, is facilitated by anonymous voting. Repeated rounds of voting, necessitated by the two-thirds majority necessary for a candidate to secure a judgeship, further fuel the practice. In the words of the Justice Initiative, "This is fertile ground for *ad hoc* campaigning and vote-trading in the midst of election rounds."[50] And, of course, for backlash politics.

The Rome Statute gives the ASP, and thus member states, significant latitude in selecting judges. Prior to 2010, the job of coordinating candidates for these judicial positions fell to civil society, especially the Coalition for the ICC (CICC). In 2010, however, the ASP requested that its Bureau prepare a report into the possibility of a committee on the selection of judges. As a result, in 2011, the Advisory Committee on Nominations of Judges (ACN) came into operation.[51] The nine members of the Advisory Committee on Nominations of Judges are nationals of States Parties who represent geographic and legal system diversity, as well as gender parity.[52] The members of the ACN "should be drawn from eminent interested and willing persons of high moral character, who have established competence and experience in criminal or international law."[53] Further, the members of the ACN "would not be the representatives of States or other organizations. They would serve in

tions/raising-the-bar-improving-the-nomination-and-election-of-judges-to-the-international-criminal-court; Steven Freeland, "Judicial Decision-Making in International Criminal Courts: 'Effective' Justice?" *Griffith Journal of Law & Humanity* 3, no. 1 (2015): 59–85, https://griffithlawjournal.org/index.php/gjlhd/article/viewFile/660/597.

48   "The ICC Judicial Elections 2020: #ElectTheBest to Lead the Fight against Impunity," Coalition for the International Criminal Court, n.d., www.coalitionfortheicc.org/explore/icc-elections-2020; Open Society Justice Initiative, *Raising the Bar*.

49   Open Society Justice Initiative, *Raising the Bar*.

50   Open Society Justice Initiative, *Raising the Bar*, 39.

51   Open Society Justice Initiative, *Raising the Bar*.

52   "2019 Election for the Advisory Committee on Nominations," *Coalition for the International Criminal Court*, November 1, 2019, http://coalitionfortheicc.org/news/20191101/2019-election-advisory-committee-nominations.

53   International Criminal Court, "Reference: ICC-ASP/17/SP/03," *Assembly of States Parties*, March 14, 2018, 1, https://asp.icc-cpi.int/iccdocs/asp_docs/ASP17/NV-ASP17-ACN-ENG.pdf.

their personal capacity, and would not take instructions from States Parties, States, or any other organizations or persons."[54]

In the years that the ACN has been operational, few have been optimistic about its work. In a survey of the ACN and the selection process for ICC judges, the Justice Initiative concluded:

> Overall, the Advisory Committee's assessments have lacked rigor and the Committee's impact on the voting process has been minimal to date. Although a number of interlocutors expressed support for the Committees' purpose in principle, they noted that, in practice, it suffers from significant limitations ... There is little evidence therefore to suggest that the Committee's current practice has an appreciable influence on vote trading or political interference on the election of unqualified judges.[55]

This pessimism about the quality of judges matters, as it reinforces the narrative that the ICC is biased and incompetent, and thus undermines the ICC's adjudicative and normative authority. Whether the judges on the ICC's bench are or are not competent to do their jobs becomes almost a secondary concern when faced with the broader accusations that they are symbolic of a biased, neo-imperialist court without the authority to hold perpetrators to account for their crimes.

Restricting the Court through a Zero-Growth Budget Model

In addition to reform efforts targeted at the ways in which judges are selected, the ICC has attempted to reform and improve its budget model, particularly in the face of an expanding docket of preliminary examinations and cases. Much like other international courts, the ICC has been chronically underfunded relative to its mandate. Observers link this underfunding to stingy states and the ICC's own poor budgeting, particularly their continued underestimation of the funds they need to fulfill their mandate.[56] In their report before the 2018 meeting of the ASP, the Committee on Budget and Finance gave the following warning: "the Committee encouraged the Court to ensure [the] greatest possible accuracy in the budget forecasting so that funds are only transferred, when flexibility in budgeting requires it and in no case to circumvent resolutions of the Assembly or recommendations of the Committee, and to keep the

---

[54] International Criminal Court, "Reference: ICC-ASP/17/SP/03."

[55] Open Society Justice Initiative, *Raising the Bar*, 45.

[56] Human Rights in International Justice, "Don't Ask and You Won't Receive – Will the ICC Request the Resources It Needs in 2019?" *Amnesty International*, May 2, 2018, https://hrij .amnesty.nl/icc-zero-growth-dont-ask-and-you-wont-receive/.

Committee informed on all transfers ensuring greatest transparency."[57] The ICC is in a perennially difficult position with respect to budgeting. If the Court asks for too much, they are painted as greedy. If they ask for too little, they are unable to fulfill their legal mandate. The Court's budgetary mismanagement and miscalculations have been "unforced errors" that only add fuel to the backlash narrative that the ICC is biased and incompetent.

A zero-growth movement sprang up in 2011 to contain the Court's budget. A zero-growth model means that the Court is expected to maintain or grow its casework without any additional funds. The Court's expenditures, particularly with respect to investigations, had ballooned, and yet the investigations themselves had proven to be subpar.[58] In advance of the ASP meeting in December 2018, the Committee on Budget and Finance reported that over €110 million in contributions were outstanding, comprising nearly 29 percent of the Court's total program budget. Table 5.1 shows how this trend has grown over time.[59]

The Betrayal of Steward States

Alarmingly, the most vocal proponents of a zero-growth model were also the ICC's main financial and normative supporters: Japan, Germany, the United Kingdom, Italy, and France.[60] Not only have the G7 – Canada, France, Germany, Japan, Italy, the UK, and the USA – consistently called for a zero-growth budget model for the Court, but, as Amnesty International's Matt Cannock explains, "[w]hen the ICC has asked for more, they have used their status as the largest funders to ensure that the Court's request is cut before the budget is adopted."[61]

Supporter states' efforts to yield a zero-growth budget are derived from domestic constraints.[62] Even the Court's main stakeholders must be

---

[57] International Criminal Court, "Report of the Committee on Budget and Finance on the Work of Its Seventeenth Session, The Hague, 5–12 December 2018, ICC-ASP/17/5," *Assembly of States Parties*, May 31, 2018, 13, https://asp.icc-cpi.int/iccdocs/asp_docs/ASP17/ICC-ASP-17-5-ENG.pdf.

[58] Interview #168, 2014.

[59] International Criminal Court, "Report of the Committee on Budget and Finance on the Work of Its Seventeenth Session"; International Criminal Court, "Report of the Committee on Budget and Finance on the Work of Its Thirty-Fourth Session, Nineteenth Session, New York, 7–17 December 2020, ICC-ASP/19/5," *Assembly of States Parties*, August 24, 2020, 10, https://asp.icc-cpi.int/iccdocs/asp_docs/ASP19/ICC-ASP-19-5-ENG-CBF34%20Report-Final.pdf.

[60] Robbie Corey-Boulet, "Concern over ICC Funding," *Inter Press Service*, September 28, 2011, www.ipsnews.net/2011/09/concern-over-icc-funding/.

[61] Human Rights in International Justice, "Don't Ask and You Won't Receive."

[62] Erik Voeten, "Making Sense of the Design of International Institutions," *Annual Review of Political Science* 22, no. 1 (2019): 147–163, https://doi.org/10.1146/annurev-polisci-041916-021108.

TABLE 5.1 *Outstanding contributions to the ICC (in thousands of euros)*

Year	Program Budget	Outstanding Contributions at the End of the Period	Outstanding Contributions (percent)
2008	90,382.10	557.50	0.62
2009	101,229.90	1,093.00	1.08
2010	103,623.30	6,254.90	6.04
2011	103,607.90	2,791.60	2.69
2012	108,800.00	6,569.30	6.04
2013	115,120.30	6,980.20	6.06
2014	121,656.20	14,489.30	11.91
2015	130,665.00	20,785.70	15.91
2016	139,590.60	18,405.00	13.18
2017	144,587.30	31,047.90	21.47
2018	147,431.90	21,121.90	14.33
2019	148,135.10	25,771.80	17.40
2020 (forecast)	149,205.60	29,111.68	19.51

mindful of domestic audiences that do not support the seemingly profligate international tribunals. With headlines like "Ten Years, $900m, One Verdict: Does the ICC Cost Too Much?" and "International Criminal Court: 12 Years, $1 Billion, 2 Convictions" dominating the public conversation, it is difficult, even for supporter states, to encourage spending more money on the ICC.[63] The irony, of course, is that with an injection of capital, the ICC could, presumably, run more – and more effective – trials.

These budgetary constraints have real consequences for the ICC. The Prosecutor's office has remarked that operating in such a constrained environment is undermining the Office of the Prosecutor's prosecutorial work.[64] The defense team is underfunded compared to other units in the court and to the defense teams of other international criminal

[63] Jessica Hatcher-Moore, "Is the World's Highest Court Fit for Purpose?" *The Guardian*, April 5, 2017, https://www.theguardian.com/global-development-professionals-network/2017/apr/05/international-criminal-court-fit-purpose; David Davenport, "International Criminal Court: 12 Years, $1 Billion, 2 Convictions," *Forbes*, March 12, 2014, https://www.forbes.com/sites/daviddavenport/2014/03/12/international-criminal-court-12-years-1-billion-2-convictions-2/; Jon Silverman, "Ten Years, $900m, One Verdict: Does the ICC Cost Too Much?" *BBC News*, March 14, 2012, https://www.bbc.com/news/magazine-17351946.

[64] Human Rights in International Justice, "Don't Ask and You Won't Receive"; Office of the Prosecutor, "Statement to the United Nations Security Council on the Situation in Libya, Pursuant to UNSCR 1970 (2011)," *International Criminal Court*, November 8, 2017, https://www.icc-cpi.int/Pages/item.aspx?name=otp_lib_unsc.

tribunals.[65] An overall lack of capacity also restricts the OTP's ability to investigate cases based on the demand for justice, rather than the availability of resources. For instance, in 2016, the OTP sought a "basic size" budget increase, adding €6.5 million to its annual budget. The OTP argued that this was the *minimum* increase needed and, yet, the ICC's Committee on Budget and Finance argued that €2 million of those additional funds should *not* be offered.[66]

At the 2018 Assembly of States Parties meeting, the ASP approved a budget of €148,135,100. As the International Federation for Human Rights (FIDH) noted, not only did that represent an increase lower than the recommended 0.6 percent by the Committee on Budget and Finance, but it also did not even match the inflation rate in The Netherlands, where the ICC is based. The FIDH did, however, praise a set of ten countries, Argentina, Belgium, Costa Rica, Finland, Liechtenstein, Luxembourg, The Netherlands, Slovenia, Sweden, and Switzerland, who all advocated for more funding for the court.[67]

In brief, the ICC has found itself ensnared in the politics of backlash, which have manifested both very publicly in the form of the threatened mass AU withdrawal as well as quite quietly with continued state control over the selection of judges and efforts to limit the ICC's budget. While some states, including the largest donors, attempt to restrict the development of the ICC, others continue to promote the norm of accountability and support its growth.

CONCLUSION

The preceding case studies from the Inter-American Human Rights System and the ICC illustrate two central points about backlash to international human rights and criminal tribunals. First, they suggest that budgetary restrictions and bureaucratic reforms are one tool, among many, that states can use to undermine and usurp international tribunals. By pulling on the courts'

---

[65] Human Rights in International Justice, "Don't Ask and You Won't Receive"; Richard J. Rogers, "Assessment of the ICC's Legal Aid System," *Global Diligence*, January 5, 2017, https://www.icc-cpi.int/itemsDocuments/legalAidConsultations-LAS-REP-ENG.pdf.

[66] Elizabeth Evenson and Jonathan O'Donohue, "Still Falling Short – the ICC's Capacity Crisis," *openDemocracy*, November 3, 2015, https://www.opendemocracy.net/en/openglobal rights-openpage/still-falling-short-icc-s-capacity-crisis/.

[67] "ICC States Parties' Gathering Concludes: The Paradox of Collective Political Support for Accountability without Adequate Financial Support May Impact the Effectiveness of the ICC," *International Federation for Human Rights*, December 13, 2018, https://www.fidh.org /en/issues/international-justice/international-criminal-court-icc/icc-states-parties-gathering-concludes-the-paradox-of-collective.

purse strings or altering the rules of procedure, states and elites can reign in the authority of international courts.

Second, these cases demonstrate how the tribunals' dependence on member states for financial, jurisprudential, and political/legitimizing support can be a condition for backlash. Moreover, as the IACmHR case illustrates, as demand for international human rights adjudication increases and, as a result, empowers domestic opposition, governments can seek to limit the power of these international institutions. Underlying this tension, of course, are broader normative schisms that international human rights and criminal tribunals cannot ignore.

In addition, these cases suggest that the bureaucracies at the tribunals can be their own worst enemies. In the case of the ICC, for example, internal mismanagement has led to questions about the Court's ability to hear and try cases, staff their bench, and uphold their obligations to victims and to states. The courts' authority, however, becomes a larger issue when the debate is not only over rules of procedure and budgets but also over the tribunals' founding doctrine. In Chapter 6, I consider these doctrinal contestations and their impact on international justice.

6

Doctrinal Challenges

Diluting the Domestic Impacts of International Adjudication

INTRODUCTION

Chapter 5 considered how states and elites can undermine international human rights and criminal courts by controlling and altering their budgets and bureaucracies. This is not the only way that states and elites engage in under-the-radar backlash politics, however. States and elites opposed to international justice also try to undermine the authority of international courts by challenging the courts' main conceptual frameworks. By expanding the degree of deference that courts afford states, international justice opponents try to limit the impact that international courts have on domestic politics and judicial processes. Much like the bureaucratic and budgetary maneuvers discussed in Chapter 5, these doctrinal challenges are less ostentatious than withdrawing from international courts or creating alternate justice mechanisms.

This is not to suggest that doctrinal challenges to international human rights and criminal courts are not potentially damaging. In fact, they threaten the very foundation of the international justice system. One of the reasons that these doctrinal challenges to international courts present such a threat is that they are shrouded within the language, processes, and strictures of international adjudication. They look and sound like international justice, even if they are designed to dilute the impact of international criminal and human rights courts.

Efforts to circumscribe and undermine human rights and criminal courts' authority through doctrinal challenges center on one key question: how much latitude should domestic politicians and judiciaries have to interpret and implement international courts' rulings? The backlash politics around this question manifest as a debate about how far states and elites can attenuate the authority of international courts while still staying within the legal and conceptual confines of the international justice regime.

The Vienna Convention on the Law of Treaties dictates that while states should understand international legal instruments as legally binding obligations, they should have some latitude with respect to how they implement international law.[1] In much the same way, both critics and proponents of international courts understand that there must be some deference to domestic policy and practice in the implementation of international court rulings. Just how much deference courts should give to states is the question at the heart of the doctrinal challenges that the tribunals face today.

This chapter begins with a discussion of why states engage in backlash politics in the form of doctrinal challenges. Using the theoretical framework from Chapter 2, I explain how the same drivers of backlash politics that inspire more ostentatious forms of backlash, such as withdrawals, also can help to explain doctrinal challenges. The theoretical section of this chapter further explains that when states want to engage in backlash without drawing the attention of international or domestic audiences, doctrinal challenges can prove to be a useful tool. Following that discussion, I turn to the empirical plan and methodological approach for the chapter. Next, the chapter offers two case studies from the European Court of Human Rights that illustrate how states have attempted to expand, dilute, or otherwise undermine the margin of appreciation doctrine to challenge the authority of the ECtHR. The first empirical analysis focuses on Russia, while the second turns to reform initiatives coming from two COE founding states, the United Kingdom and Denmark. This case study also serves as an illustration of the particularly difficult task of combatting backlash wrought by long-standing supporters of the international justice system. Chapter 7 discusses the importance of supporter states' reaffirming their commitment to the international justice regime in more detail.

FROM WHENCE DOCTRINAL CHALLENGES?

Loud and vociferous debate about how much deference international courts should afford member states is a consistent feature of international adjudication. When these debates become less about how international courts should work and more about how to undermine the authority of international courts

---

[1] "Vienna Convention on the Law of Treaties (with Annex)," adopted May 22, 1969, *United Nations Treaty Series* No. 18232, https://treaties.un.org/doc/Publication/UNTS/Volume%2011 55/volume-1155-I-18232-English.pdf; Venice Commission, *Report on the Implementation of International Human Rights Treaties in Domestic Law and the Role of Courts* (Strasbourg: Council of Europe, 2014), https://www.venice.coe.int/webforms/documents/default.aspx?pdffi le=CDL-AD(2014)036-e.

as part of a broader and sustained attack, they constitute backlash politics. The dividing line between the two is perhaps quite thin, but in the case of doctrinal challenges, arguments about the degree of deference courts should afford to national authorities only thinly veil concerted efforts to attenuate the courts' impact. These arguments become backlash politics when they advocate for a degree of deference that undermines the courts' ability to hold states and perpetrators accountable, whilst only preserving the guise of justice.

This form of backlash politics has long-lasting effects on international human rights and criminal adjudication. By circumscribing the courts' adjudicative and normative authority, states can hamper both the courts' ability to hand down rulings today as well as their ability to hold perpetrators to account tomorrow. Moreover, much like the budgetary and bureaucratic backlash discussed in Chapter 5, these doctrinal challenges often go unnoticed by both domestic and international audiences. The public is often not well-versed on the inner legal workings of the ICC or ECtHR, and because doctrinal challenges take place within the framework of international courts, even foreign allies and partners can overlook this form of backlash politics. Doctrinal challenge can be both dangerous and surreptitious.

Doctrinal challenges are driven by long-standing divisions about the depth and breadth of the tribunals' authority. Disagreements about which human rights should be adjudicated and *how* reemerge in the form of doctrinal challenges about how much deference the tribunals should afford to states. These doctrinal challenges serve to reinforce the narrative that the tribunals are biased and that they do not recognize non-Western European modes of law or justice. This is a difficult narrative for the tribunals to counteract, and sometimes the tribunals take steps that make countering that narrative more difficult. For example, De Vos finds that the ICC's reluctance to accept a wider range of interpretations of complementarity has further fueled the perception and narrative that the ICC is biased against "other" forms of justice.[2]

Moreover, doctrinal challenges about how much latitude courts should afford national authorities highlight the tribunals' reliance on domestic actors. The ICC and the regional human rights courts cannot force compliance or cooperation. Instead, they depend on states for compliance and

---

[2] Liana Minkova, "Complementarity, Catalysts, Compliance Symposium: The Spectrum of Ideologies in International Criminal Justice – From Legalism to Policy," *Opinion Juris* (blog), August 3, 2020, http://opiniojuris.org/2020/08/03/complementarity-catalysts-compliance-symposium-the-spectrum-of-ideologies-in-international-criminal-justice-from-legalism-to-policy/; Christian M. De Vos, *The International Criminal Court in Uganda, Kenya, and the Democratic Republic of Congo* (Cambridge, UK: Cambridge University Press, 2020).

implementation. Indeed, states' efforts to expand the degree of deference that international courts provide national authorities exacerbate, rather than mitigate, cooperation, compliance, and enforcement problems because they invest more authority in domestic actors – the same actors on trial – to patrol and change their own behavior. No matter how progressive or advanced the courts become, they cannot untether from their stakeholders. Doctrinal challenges put this dependency into stark relief.

Further, by expanding national authorities' ability to reject, dilute, or dispute international courts' rulings, states undercut international human rights and criminal courts' ability to mobilize domestic compliance constituencies.[3] For states and elites looking to engage in further repression whilst remaining within the international legal regime, doctrinal challenges provide a form of insurance against future international adjudication.

REGIONAL COURTS, THE MARGIN OF APPRECIATION,
AND THE CONCEPT OF SUBSIDIARITY

The European Court of Human Rights' deference to states centers on the principle of the margin of appreciation. The margin of appreciation doctrine recognizes that different legal traditions, varied political and historical contexts, and divergent normative preferences render a uniform implementation of ECtHR rulings nearly impossible. The margin of appreciation is a practical solution to this problem. It acknowledges the plurality of its member states' legal systems while helping the ECtHR uphold basic standards of human rights protections.[4]

---

[3] De Vos, *The International Criminal Court in Uganda, Kenya, and the Democratic Republic of Congo.*

[4] Gary Born, Danielle Morris, and Stephanie Forrest, "A Margin of Appreciation: Appreciating Its Irrelevance in International Law," *Harvard International Law Journal* 61, no. 1 (2020): 65–134, https://heinonline.org/HOL/P?h=hein.journals/hilj61&i=71; Janneke Gerards, "Margin of Appreciation and Incrementalism in the Case Law of the European Court of Human Rights," *Human Rights Law Review* 18, no. 3 (September 2018): 495–515, https://doi.org /10.1093/hrlr/ngy017; Dean Spielmann, "Whither the Margin of Appreciation?" *Current Legal Problems* 67, no. 1 (2014): 49–65, https://doi.org/10.1093/clp/cuu012; Ronald St. J. Macdonald, Franz Matscher, and Herbert Petzold, *The European System for the Protection of Human Rights* (Dordrecht, Boston: M. Nijhoff, 1993); Yutaka Arai-Takahashi, *The Margin of Appreciation Doctrine and the Principle of Proportionality in the Jurisprudence of the ECHR* (Antwerp, Oxford, New York: Intersentia, 2002); David Harris, Michael O'Boyle, Edward Bates, and Carla Buckley, *Law of the European Convention on Human Rights*, 3rd ed. (Oxford: Oxford University Press, 2014); Howard C. Yourow, *The Margin of Appreciation Doctrine in the Dynamics of European Human Rights Jurisprudence* (Dordrecht: Martinus Nijhoff Publishers, 1996); Andrew Legg, *The Margin of Appreciation in International Human Rights Law: Deference and Proportionality* (Oxford: Oxford University Press, 2012).

Although the margin of appreciation doctrine defers to national authorities regarding the implementation of ECtHR rulings, it also places the responsibility for compliance and enforcement on domestic actors. That is, the margin of appreciation doctrine charges national authorities, and particularly domestic courts, to conduct Convention reviews in order to ensure that state practices are in line with Convention norms and to oversee the implementation of the Court's rulings.[5] Some scholars question if the ECtHR really applies the margin of appreciation doctrine or simply offers lip service to the idea.[6] In the case studies that follow, I suggest that even if the ECtHR does not regularly apply the margin of appreciation doctrine, states exploit the underlying idea of it.

A Brief Note on the Inter-American System. Although the case studies below are from the European Court of Human Rights, it is important to acknowledge the Inter-American complement to the margin of appreciation doctrine, the principle of subsidiarity. The Inter-American system's principle of subsidiarity, broadly speaking, offers less latitude than its European counterpart. As Jorge Contesse explains, "[T]he Inter-American Court embraces a maximalist model of adjudication – one that leaves very little, if any, room for states to reach their own decisions."[7] Deference to states, particularly in the early years of the Court, was unthinkable, as the Court's docket pertained nearly exclusively to cases about state-sponsored violence.[8] As the tenor of the Inter-American Court of Human Rights' casework has changed, it has opened up the possibility of more deference to the state, but the Court seems disinclined to pursue this path.

From Deference to Backlash

Broadly speaking, the margin of appreciation and subsidiarity doctrines are meant to enhance and facilitate compliance, not undermine the courts.[9] More recently, however, the challenges that the courts have faced, including

---

[5] Spielmann, "Whither the Margin of Appreciation?"

[6] Born, Morris, and Forrest, "A Margin of Appreciation: Appreciating Its Irrelevance in International Law."

[7] Jorge Contesse, "Contestation and Deference in the Inter-American Human Rights System," *Law and Contemporary Problems* 79, no. 2 (June 20, 2016): 124.

[8] Nino Tsereteli, "Emerging Doctrine of Deference of the Inter-American Court of Human Rights?" *The International Journal of Human Rights* 20, no. 8 (November 16, 2016): 1097–1112, https://doi.org/10.1080/13642987.2016.1254875.

[9] Dean Spielmann, "Allowing the Right Margin: The European Court of Human Rights and the National Margin of Appreciation Doctrine: Waiver or Subsidiarity of European Review?" *Cambridge Yearbook of European Legal Studies* 14 (2012): 381–418, https://doi.org/10.5235/1528 8871280558057o; Yuval Shany, "Toward a General Margin of Appreciation Doctrine in

the Russian challenge to the ECtHR described in more depth below, have not just advocated for giving states more latitude in implementing the ECtHR's rulings but also for granting exemptions for some types of rulings altogether.[10] In effect, the Russian government has decided that the domestic margin of appreciation extends to questions about the constitutionality of the ECtHR's decisions, endowing the Russian Constitutional Court and the Russian government with the ability to opt out of particular ECtHR decisions.

While the Russian case might be extreme, it is not alone. Italy's Constitutional Court, for example, declared that the ECtHR's rulings are not enforceable if they contradict the Italian Constitution, a decision that only the Italian Constitutional Court can make.[11] Further, as the last case study in this chapter illustrates, even Denmark and the United Kingdom, founding members of the Council of Europe, have recently attempted to expand the margin of appreciation doctrine beyond its intended contours. In each of these instances, the very core of international human rights adjudication is at stake: the sacredness of compulsory jurisdiction, the spirit of *pacta sunt servanda*, and the idea of the margin of appreciation as a mechanism for facilitating compliance, not undermining the courts' structural, adjudicative, and normative authority.

CASE SELECTION AND EMPIRICAL APPROACH

The empirical cases presented throughout the rest of the chapter rely on process tracing to illustrate if and how the different drivers of backlash politics converge to drive doctrinal challenges to international courts.[12] These analyses

---

International Law?" *European Journal of International Law* 16, no. 5 (November 2005): 907–940, https://doi.org/10.1093/ejil/chi149; George Letsas, "Two Concepts of the Margin of Appreciation," *Oxford Journal of Legal Studies* 26, no. 4 (2006): 705–732, https://doi.org/10.1093/ojls/gql030; Nasiruddeen Muhammad, "A Comparative Approach to Margin of Appreciation in International Law," *The Chinese Journal of Comparative Law* 7, no. 1 (June 2019): 212–240, https://doi.org/10.1093/cjcl/cxz008.

[10] Kirill Koroteev and Sergey Golubok, "Judgment of the Russian Constitutional Court on Supervisory Review in Civil Proceedings: Denial of Justice, Denial of Europe," *Human Rights Law Review* 7, no. 3 (July 2007): 619–632, https://doi.org/10.1093/hrlr/ngm018; Russian Federation: Judgment No. 12-П/2016 of 19 April 2016 of the Constitutional Court (Constitutional Court of the Russian Federation, 2016), https://www.venice.coe.int/webforms/documents/default.aspx?pdffile=CDL-REF(2016)033-e.

[11] *Varvara v. Italy*, No. 17475/09 (European Court of Human Rights, 2013); *Maggio and Others v. Italy*, No. 4628/09, 52851/08, 53727/08, 54486/08 and 56001/08 (European Court of Human Rights, 2011); La sentenza n. 49 of 2015 (Corte Costituzionale, 2015).

[12] David Collier, "Understanding Process Tracing," *PS: Political Science & Politics* 44, no. 4 (October 2011): 823–830, https://doi.org/10.1017/S1049096511001429; James Mahoney, "The Logic of Process Tracing Tests in the Social Sciences," *Sociological Methods & Research* 41, no. 4 (November 2012): 570–597, https://doi.org/10.1177/0049124112437709.

draw on interviews, analyses of legal doctrines and cases, and content analysis of newspapers of record, nongovernmental organization reports, and reports from the international courts themselves. The case studies pay particular attention to how and why doctrinal challenges emerged and how the courts and other stakeholders have responded to them.

The case studies chronicle the attempts of both justice insiders and outsiders to dilute the effects of the ECtHR by expanding the margin of appreciation doctrine. The first case study examines Russia's push to broaden the scope of the margin of appreciation so far as to endow domestic courts with the authority to declare some ECtHR rulings as "non-executable" or "unconstitutional." It also discusses earlier Russian attempts to pair these doctrinal challenges with procedural delays and derailments that would undermine the normative and adjudicative authority of the ECtHR.

The second case study focuses on more recent reform initiatives at the ECtHR, particularly British and Danish efforts to circumscribe the ECtHR's authority. While the UK has long adopted anti-ECtHR rhetoric, it has remained, if begrudgingly, a member and supporter of the Court.[13] But what of Denmark? Denmark's recent efforts to dilute its obligations to the European Convention on Human Rights (ECHR) are *not* characteristic of a longtime ECtHR supporter. These cases show that efforts to undermine the tribunals from within their own legal frameworks are not relegated to the most vociferous critics of the international justice regime but instead can originate with the justice regime's most ardent supporters. If, as I discuss in more depth in Chapter 7, steward states and stakeholders want to advance and uphold the international justice regime, the Danish case should be illuminating.

CASE 1: RUSSIA, THE ECTHR, AND PROTOCOL 14 OF THE ECHR

The European Court of Human Rights is the world's oldest and busiest international human rights court. By the early 2010s, it was becoming clear to staffers, stakeholders, and petitioners that the ECtHR was a victim of its own success. Its backlog of unaddressed complaints reached a peak of more than 160,000 petitions in 2011.[14] A series of reforms have lessened the backlog while, arguably, introducing a new variety of backlash politics that seeks to expand

---

[13]   Courtney Hillebrecht, "Implementing International Human Rights Law at Home: Domestic Politics and the European Court of Human Rights," *Human Rights Review* 13, no. 3 (2012): 279–301, https://doi.org/10.1007/s12142-012-0227-1.

[14]   Alice Donald, "The Remarkable Shrinking Backlog at the European Court of Human Rights," *UK Human Rights Blog* (blog), October 1, 2014, https://ukhumanrightsblog.com/2014/10/01/the-remarkable-shrinking-backlog-at-the-european-court-of-human-rights/.

the margin of appreciation whilst limiting the ECtHR's potential impact on domestic politics.

A Brief History of ECtHR Reforms

The Council of Europe introduced significant institutional reforms to the ECtHR in 1998, when, under Protocol 11 of the European Convention on Human Rights and Fundamental Freedoms, the current single court structure replaced the Commission/Court model that still exists in the African and Inter-American systems. In addition to changing the structure of the system, Protocol 11 replaced Section II of the European Convention on Human Rights and Fundamental Freedoms. Article 32 of the amended text required that all members of the Council of Europe accept the compulsory jurisdiction of the European Court of Human Rights.[15] The jump in ratifications of the ECHR does not imply that normative disputes were resolved, but rather that they were papered over, a fact which became evident by the exponential growth of the number of petitions the ECtHR received over the intervening decade.[16]

In 2004, the Council of Europe opened a new protocol, Protocol 14, for signatures. Protocol 14 made three major changes to the European system: (1) it introduced new and more stringent admissibility criteria; (2) it changed the term limits for judges to nine-year, non-renewable terms; and (3) most critically, it introduced single-judge and three-judge formations to evaluate admissibility and to rule on the merits of "repeat or clone" cases.[17] In many respects, Protocol 14 was a technical solution to a larger conceptual question about the place of the ECtHR within Europe. Laurence Helfer, writing in 2008, remarked that the addition of Protocol 14 "should be understood not as

---

[15] European Court of Human Rights, "History of the ECHR's Reforms," 2013, https://www.echr.coe.int/Documents/Reforms_history_ENG.pdf; "Protocol No. 11 to the Convention for the Protection of Human Rights and Fundamental Freedoms, Restructuring the Control Machinery Established Thereby," entered into force November 1, 1998, *Council of Europe Treaty Series* No. 155.

[16] "The ECHR in Facts & Figures 2019," *Council of Europe*, February 2020, https://www.echr.coe.int/Documents/Facts_Figures_2019_ENG.pdf.

[17] Committee of Ministers, "High-Level Conference on the 'Implementation of the European Convention on Human Rights, Our Shared Responsibility': Brussels Declaration," *Council of Europe*, March 27, 2015, https://www.echr.coe.int/Documents/Brussels_Declaration_ENG.pdf; "Protocol No. 14 to the Convention for the Protection of Human Rights and Fundamental Freedoms, Amending the Control System of the Convention," opened for signature May 13, 2004, *Council of Europe Treaty Series* No. 194; Alice Donald, "Backlog, Backlash and Beyond: Debating the Long Term Future of Human Rights Protection in Europe," *UK Human Rights Blog* (blog), April 14, 2014, https://ukhumanrightsblog.com/2014/04/14/backlog-backlash-and-beyond-debating-the-long-term-future-of-human-rights-protection-in-europe-alice-donald/.

ministerial changes in supranational judicial procedure, nor as resolving a debate over whether the ECtHR should strive for individual or constitutional justice, but rather as raising more fundamental questions concerning the Court's future identity" and particularly its relationship to domestic sociolegal and political systems.[18] By the time Protocol 14 was proposed, the domestic consequences of international adjudication at the ECtHR had become quite clear. The Court's rulings had inspired policy change and domestic mobilization around the continent.[19]

In addition to the aforementioned reforms, Protocol 14 offered an amendment to Article 46 of the European Convention regarding the supervision of judgments. The amended version of Article 46, paragraph 4, reads:

> If the Committee of Ministers considers that a High Contracting Party refuses to abide by a final judgment in a case to which it is a party, it may, after serving formal notice on that Party and by decision adopted by a majority vote of two thirds of the representatives entitled to sit on the Committee, refer to the Court the question whether that Party has failed to fulfil its obligation under paragraph 1.[20]

In other words, Protocol 14 empowered the Court to push more aggressively for domestic implementation than it ever had before and, in so doing, effectively narrowed the margin of appreciation. Protocol 14 was the sticking plaster, not the cure, for systemic noncompliance, however. Repeat and clone cases were, by definition, the result of noncompliance with previous judgments. The ECtHR had a compliance crisis, and, as a result, a caseload crisis, with Russia at the eye of the storm.[21]

---

[18]   Laurence R. Helfer, "Redesigning the European Court of Human Rights: Embeddedness as a Deep Structural Principle of the European Human Rights Regime," *European Journal of International Law* 19, no. 1 (February 2008): 125–159, 127, https://doi.org/10.1093/ejil/chn004; Bill Bowring, "The Russian Federation, Protocol No. 14 (and 14bis), and the Battle for the Soul of the ECHR," *Goettingen Journal of International Law* 2, no. 2 (2010): 589–617, https://www.gojil.eu/issues/22/22_article_bowring.pdf; Philip Leach, "Access to the European Court of Human Rights–From a Legal Entitlement to a Lottery?" *Human Rights Law Journal* 27, no. 1 (2006): 11–24; Luzius A. Wildhaber, "Constitutional Future for the European Court of Human Rights?" *Human Rights Law Journal* 23 (2002): 161–165.

[19]   Courtney Hillebrecht, "The Power of Human Rights Tribunals: Compliance with the European Court of Human Rights and Domestic Policy Change," *European Journal of International Relations* 20, no. 4 (December 2014): 1100–1123, https://doi.org/10.1177/1354066113508591.

[20]   "Protocol No. 14 to the Convention for the Protection of Human Rights and Fundamental Freedoms, Amending the Control System of the Convention."

[21]   Courtney Hillebrecht, *Domestic Politics and International Human Rights Tribunals: The Problem of Compliance* (New York: Cambridge University Press, 2014).

Russia's Margin of Appreciation Backlash

Russia's compliance with the ECtHR's general measures leading up to (and well after) the introduction of Protocol 14 was weak, contributing to the high number of cases stemming from repeat Russian violations.[22] In 2005, for example, Russian petitions accounted for 21.2 percent of the ECtHR's total petitions.[23] Protocol 14 would allow the ECtHR to more effectively move through those cases and, in turn, more effectively empower domestic opposition groups with faster and more impactful rulings.

For Protocol 14 to take effect, however, *all* COE states had to ratify it. Russia refused to do so. In fact, Russia was a holdout on Protocol 14 for many years, which was one part of Russia's larger campaign against the ECtHR. In 2006, the Russian Duma voted, 138 to 27, against Protocol 14. Vice-Speaker of the Duma, Sergey Baburin, explained the Duma's position: "The protocol is contrary to the main principles of justice. Moreover, our voluminous membership fees are being used for attacks on our country by the Council of Europe."[24]

By 2009, however, as the ECtHR's backlog continued to grow – and its reputation as being inefficient and slow grew alongside it – other member states and Council of Europe officials grew tired of waiting for Russia to ratify Protocol 14. The overwhelming number of cases the ECtHR had on its docket had thrown the Court into despair, and Protocol 14 offered much-needed respite. As Michael O'Boyle, who was the deputy registrar of the ECtHR in 2009 argued, "The credibility of the court is now in question ... We can't be held hostage by Russia."[25]

At the 119th Session of the Committee of Ministers, held in Madrid in 2009, the Committee of Ministers approved Protocol No. 14*bis* to the European Convention on Human Rights, which put important measures from Protocol 14 into effect: the use of a single-judge mechanism to decide on (in-)admissibility for clearly inadmissible cases and three-judge panels to decide on cases that did not pose unique or important legal questions. Protocol 14*bis* took effect immediately upon ratification for each state that ratified it, meaning that Russia's delaying tactics could no longer hold up critical system-wide reforms.[26]

---

[22] Hillebrecht, *Domestic Politics*.

[23] European Court of Human Rights, *Annual Report 2005* (Strasbourg: Registry of the European Court of Human Rights, 2006). https://www.echr.coe.int/Documents/Annual_report_2005_ENG.pdf.

[24] Jamie Smyth, "Council to Battle Russia on Protocol 14," *Irish Times*, May 12, 2009, https://www.irishtimes.com/news/council-to-battle-russia-on-protocol-14-1.762322.

[25] Smyth, "Council to Battle Russia on Protocol 14."

[26] Antoine Buyse, "Protocol 14 Bis – The Interim Solution," *ECHR BLOG* (blog), May 4, 2009, http://echrblog.blogspot.com/2009/05/protocol-14-bis-interim-solution.html; Council of Europe,

Throughout this multiyear debate, Russia continued to participate in trials, engage with the COE, and, above all, make claims that it was committed to human rights.[27] Moreover, holding up reforms at the ECtHR had the functional impact of neutering the Court's ability to investigate the full scope of Russian human rights violations. The Court was drowning in Russian cases. Delaying Protocol 14 translated into circumscribing the authority of the ECtHR to investigate allegations of Russian human rights abuse.

Further, hamstringing the ECtHR had the additional effect of changing the distributional politics of compliance at home. Some observers speculated that Russia's delaying tactic with respect to Protocol 14 was in response to a high-profile case involving the oil giant Yukos. The petitioner, Yukos, claimed that "irregularities" in the enforcement of its tax liability prevented the firm from repaying its debts, forcing the company to go under. The Court found that there had been violations of Yukos' rights to a fair trial and protection of property. In its decision regarding just satisfaction, the ECtHR ordered Russia to pay €1.9 billion in pecuniary damages, the largest such award the ECtHR has made to date.[28] Delaying Protocol 14 and arguing for a broader margin of appreciation directly addressed the extremely costly domestic consequences of international adjudication.

The Russian holdup of Protocol 14 also proves instructive, however, for how the courts and their stewards can weather the storm. Anton Burkov, formerly of the ECtHR registrar's office, explains that Russia's reasoning for finally ratifying Protocol 14 was twofold. He writes:

> On the one hand, Russia discovered that its attempt to block reform of the EC[t]HR was becoming ineffective, since the other 46 member states of the Council of Europe had successfully devised a route to bypass its veto. On [the] other hand, there are forces at work within the Russian judicial system and its political leadership who are committed to improving Russia's domestic judicial system. They see that the reform of the EC[t]HR could actually help that process. Why not make virtue out of necessity, as the old saying goes?[29]

"Protocol 14 – the Reform of the European Court of Human Rights," n.d., https://rm.coe.int/16807f2f4.

[27]   See, for example, Hillebrecht, *Domestic Politics*; Hillebrecht, "Implementing International Human Rights Law at Home."

[28]   "ECtHR's Largest Ever Award of Compensation – Yukos v. Russia," Monckton Chambers, August 1, 2014, https://www.monckton.com/ecthrs-largest-ever-award-compensation-yukos-v-russia/.

[29]   Anton Burkov, "Russia and the European Court of Human Rights," *Centre for European Policy Studies Commentary: Thinking Ahead for Europe*, May 10, 2010, 3, http://aei.pitt.edu/14499/1/May_Burkov_on_Russia_and_the_ECHR.pdf.

On the former point, Protocol 14*bis* offered a much-needed workaround against Russia's delaying tactic. Courts and their political organs can innovate technical solutions to political problems. These technical solutions are not necessarily long-term fixes, but they can help to span the gap when a court is under attack. Second, even when elites are set on undermining an international court, there might be domestic support for the courts. Burkov argues that a wide range of domestic stakeholders, from the Minister of Justice to the Constitutional Court, saw the connection between improving domestic law in light of the Strasbourg court's jurisprudence and reducing the number of cases before the ECtHR.

Domestic pressure slowly, and subtly, changed Russia's stance toward Strasbourg, particularly under then-President Dmitry Medvedev. In March 2010, Medvedev submitted a law that would give victims the right to a fair trial and "the right to execution of a judgment within a reasonable time."[30] In July 2010, a new law requiring Russian courts of *all* levels to publish their rulings came into effect. And, perhaps most remarkably, in 2010 at the Parliamentary Assembly of the Council of Europe (PACE), the Russian delegation joined a unanimous vote on a resolution condemning Russian activity in the North Caucuses.[31] By siding with the rest of the PACE on the situation in the North Caucuses, Russia signaled that it was turning over a new leaf. This love affair was not to last long. The ECtHR had more reforms afoot, and Vladimir Putin was soon to reclaim the presidency of the Russian Federation and resume his hostile stance toward Strasbourg.

The Annexation of Crimea and a New Phase in Russian–Strasbourg Politics

In early 2014, Russian forces entered the territory of Crimea, which is part of Ukraine, claiming that the area belonged to the Russian Federation. On March 16, 2014, Russia held a referendum in Crimea, a quick ordeal that legitimatized the annexation of the territory under the guise of a popular vote. The Council of Europe's Committee of Ministers declared both the annexation itself and the referendum illegal, noting in a press communique, "The Deputies also underlined that the illegal referendum of 16 March and the ensuing, also illegal, annexation of Crimea by the Russian Federation could in no way constitute a basis for any change in the status of Crimea and the city of

---

[30]   Bowring, "Battle for the Soul of the ECHR," 614; "Russia MPs Support Rights Reform," *BBC*, January 15, 2010, http://news.bbc.co.uk/2/hi/8460934.stm.
[31]   Bowring, "Battle for the Soul of the ECHR."

Sebastopol."[32] In retaliation for the annexation of Crimea, the Parliamentary Assembly of the Council of Europe suspended the Russian Federation's delegation's voting rights. They also suspended the Russian government's right to be represented in the Bureau of the Assembly, the Presidential Committee, and the Standing Committee, and to participate in election observation missions.[33]

Unsurprisingly, the Russian Federation did not take well to the suspension of some of their delegation's rights to the PACE. In response, the Russian government stopped participating in the activities of the Assembly and, as of mid-2017, decided to suspend payment of its dues to the Council of Europe, throwing the COE into a fiscal emergency.[34] In a letter sent to the Chair of the Committee of Ministers on July 3, 2017, the Russian Federation communicated its decision to suspend its financial contributions to the Council of Europe until its credentials were fully restored. Russian owed €33,035,000 in 2017 but, at the time it declared that it would suspend its payments, it had only paid €10,772,000 (or approximately one third) of its dues for that year.[35]

Russia is the Council of Europe's largest member state, and even though the Council of Europe was in generally good fiscal health, the loss of Russia's contributions took a bite out of the COE's ability to operate at full capacity. The European Youth Fund, the Pension Reserve Fund, and the general treasury budgets, including the Ordinary Budget, the Extraordinary Budget, the Pompidou Group, the Venice Commission, and the Group of States against Corruption (GRECO) funds all took a hit.[36] While the Rapporteur Group on Programme, Budget and Administration (GR-PBA) reported in 2017

[32] "Committee of Ministers Deems the Annexation of Crimea Illegal and Calls for Measures Concerning National Minorities," *Council of Europe Communications*, April 3, 2014, https://rm.coe.int/09000016807idb5b.

[33] Parliamentary Assembly of the Council of Europe, "Resolution 1990 (2014): Reconsideration on Substantive Grounds of the Previously Ratified Credentials of the Russian Delegation," *Council of Europe*, April 10, 2014, https://assembly.coe.int/nw/xml/XRef/Xref-XML2HTML-en.asp?fileid=20882&lang=en.

[34] Tiny Kox, "Role and Mission of the Parliamentary Assembly: Main Challenges for the Future," *Committee on Political Affairs and Democracy, Parliamentary Assembly of the Council of Europe*, April 9, 2019, http://assembly.coe.int/nw/xml/XRef/Xref-DocDetails-EN.asp?FileID=27565&lang=EN.

[35] "Statement of the Ministry of Foreign Affairs of the Russian Federation Concerning the Suspension of Payment of Russia's Contribution to the Council of Europe for 2017," *The Ministry of Foreign Affairs of the Russian Federation*, June 30, 2017, https://www.mid.ru/foreign_policy/rso/coe/-/asset_publisher/uUbe64ZnDJso/content/id/2805051; Rapporteur Group on Programme Budget and Administration, "Unpaid Contributions – Special Measures," *Committee of Ministers of the Council of Europe*, September 21, 2017, https://rm.coe.int/09000016807c2fd.

[36] Rapporteur Group on Programme Budget and Administration, "Unpaid Contributions – Special Measures."

that the Council could manage to cover the deficit in the short-term, the uncertainty about how long Russia would suspend its payments required careful and cautious financial management. The GR-PBA also lamented, "It has to be noted that a substantial part of expenditure is already committed, thus reducing the margin of manoeuver."[37] The COE's "margin of maneuver" was reduced further in November 2017 when Turkey announced that it would discontinue its status as a "major contributor" to the COE. This resulted in a €19 million reduction in contributions, €16 million of which was to be directed to the Ordinary Budget, which, of course, would have helped to offset Russia's suspended payment to that same fund.[38]

These unexpected budget cuts came at a time when the Council of Europe was promoting, much like the Assembly of States Parties to the ICC, a zero nominal growth fiscal policy. Indeed, Russia's backlash against the COE and ECtHR involved both doctrinal challenges and budgetary and bureaucratic restrictions, such as those described in Chapter 5.

In response, COE Secretary General Thorbjørn Jaglund warned against taking any steps that would cause permanent damage to the Council of Europe.[39] Russia's continued alienation from the COE and the potential for a Russian withdrawal altogether would certainly cause such damage. Indeed, even human rights groups called on the Council of Europe to repair its relationship with the Russian Federation. In a joint memorandum signed by Russian human rights defenders and endorsed by the EU-Russia Civil Society Forum, these groups called for Russia and the COE to address their increasingly tense relationship and to do so quickly. They argued that Russia should, above all, remain in the Council of Europe and noted, critically:

> It should be clear to everyone: Russia's departure from the CoE would not stop human rights violations and halt the authoritarian backslide in our country, or prevent our government's aggressive behavior in the international arena. This move would by no means contribute to the resolution of the conflict in Eastern Ukraine and the return of Crimea under Ukrainian

---

[37] Rapporteur Group on Programme Budget and Administration, "Unpaid Contributions – Special Measures."

[38] Bureau of the Congress, "Status of Turkey and Budgetary Implications," *Council of Europe*, October 3, 2018, https://rm.coe.int/09000016808e474c; Ministers' Deputies, "Progress Review Report 2017," *Committee of Ministers of the Council of Europe*, April 11, 2018, https://rm.coe.int /09000016807b7be9.

[39] "The Irish Times View on the Council of Europe: Keeping Russia in the Tent," *The Irish Times View*, June 25, 2019, https://www.irishtimes.com/opinion/editorial/the-irish-times-view-on-the-council-of-europe-keeping-russia-in-the-tent-1.3937324; Steven Erlanger, "Council of Europe Restores Russia's Voting Rights," *The New York Times*, June 25, 2019, https://www .nytimes.com/2019/06/25/world/europe/council-of-europe-russia-crimea.htm.

jurisdiction. Instead, it would have irreversible consequences, putting an end to a difficult struggle of Russian society to make the country an important part of Europe on the basis of shared norms and values of democracy, rule of law and respect for human rights. Moreover, it will turn a large territory in Europe into a legal "grey zone" for decades to come.[40]

The human rights defenders and stakeholders at the COE generally shared this sentiment, and in April 2019, the PACE adopted Resolutions 2277 and 2287, which presented a path forward for the reaccreditation of the Russian delegation.[41] In June 2019, Russia once again became a full member of the Assembly, and in July 2019, Russia paid its contributions to the 2019 Ordinary Budget in full and pledged to repay its outstanding dues as soon as possible.[42] The COE might have wrangled out of the fiscal emergency, but as that fight was ongoing, so too was a larger normative battle about the margin of appreciation and the executability of ECtHR rulings in domestic contexts.

The Russian Constitutional Court and the Nonexecutability of ECtHR Rulings

In December 2015, at the same time that the PACE was debating whether or not to ratify the Russian delegation despite the annexation of Crimea, Russia's

---

[40] Russian human rights defenders, "Addressing the Crisis in Relations between the Council of Europe and Russia: Uphold the Values and Fulfill the Mission to Protect Rights across All Europe," November 2018, 1, https://www.nhc.nl/assets/uploads/2018/12/Memorandum-on-Russia-and-CoE_November_2018_eng_signatures-as-of-30.11.18.pdf; "Russia's Departure from the Council of Europe Should Be Avoided," *Netherlands Helsinki Committee*, December 5, 2018, https://www.nhc.nl/russias-departure-from-the-council-of-europe-should-be-avoided/.

[41] Kox, "Role and Mission of the Parliamentary Assembly: Main Challenges for the Future"; Petra De Sutter, "Strengthening the Decision-Making Process of the Parliamentary Assembly Concerning Credentials and Voting," *Committee on Rules of Procedure, Immunities and Institutional Affairs, Parliamentary Assembly of the Council of Europe*, June 6, 2019, http://assembly.coe.int/nw/xml/XRef/Xref-DocDetails-en.asp?fileid=27725&lang=en; Youth Policy Team, "The Council of Europe Celebrates Its 70th Anniversary – and Quietly Prepares to Sacrifice Its Youth Sector," *Youth Policy*, May 6, 2019, https://www.youthpolicy.org/blog/youth-policy-young-people/council-of-europe-youth-sector-cuts/; Parliamentary Assembly of the Council of Europe, "Modification of Various Provisions of the Assembly's Rules of Procedure," *Committee on Rules of Procedure, Immunities and Institutional Affairs, Parliamentary Assembly of the Council of Europe*, March 25, 2019, https://pace.coe.int/en/files/27665; "PACE Proposes New 'Joint Reaction Procedure' When a State Violates Its Statutory Obligations," *Parliamentary Assembly of the Council of Europe*, April 10, 2019, http://assembly.coe.int/nw/xml/News/News-View-en.asp?newsid=7451&lang=2. Bureau of the Congress, "Meeting of the Bureau of the Congress Wednesday 11 September 2019," *Council of Europe*, October 17, 2019, https://rm.coe.int/09000016809839e6.

[42] Bureau of the Congress, "Meeting of the Bureau of the Congress Wednesday 11 September 2019."

parliament voted to amend the country's constitution. This amendment empowered the Constitutional Court to declare international rulings as impossible to execute.[43] Communist Party Member of Parliament and author of the bill, Vasily Likhachev, justified the amendment: "If the judgment is undermining the sovereignty of the country, [the] Constitutional Court would solve the situation. This decision would take effect immediately, it may not be appealed."[44]

Such an amendment stands in direct contrast to the spirit of international courts and the idea of the margin of appreciation. The central tenet of the European Court of Human Rights is that it has the authority to rule on *domestic* human rights issues. The responsibility lies with domestic courts, lawmakers, and other stakeholders to bring domestic law and practice, including national constitutions, in line with international law, not vice versa. The margin of appreciation doctrine does allow for some "wiggle room" in the domestic interpretation and implementation of international court rulings, but it does not extend so far as declaring an international court ruling "unconstitutional" and thus "nonexecutable."[45] In March 2016, the European Commission for Democracy through Law, also known as the Venice Commission, offered an interim opinion on the amendment. The Venice Commission recognized that the status of the European Convention on Human Rights in domestic contexts varies widely across the continent, but also noted this critical point:

> 84. The choice of the relation between the national and the international systems is a sovereign one for each State to make; whatever model is chosen, however, the State is bound by international law, under Article 26 of the Vienna Convention on the Law on Treaties (Pacta sunt servanda), which stipulates that "[e]very treaty in force is binding upon the parties to it and must be performed by them in good faith." Article 27 of the Vienna Convention ("Internal law and observance of treaties") further stipulates

---

[43]   European Commission for Democracy through Law (Venice Commission), "Amendments to the Federal Constitutional Law on the Constitutional Court of the Russian Federation of 14 December 2015," *Council of Europe*, January 20, 2016, https://www.venice.coe.int/web forms/documents/default.aspx?pdffile=CDL-REF(2016)006-e.

[44]   "State Duma Committee Approves Bill on Execution of International Courts' Decisions," *Russian Legal Information Agency*, November 26, 2015, http://rapsinews.com/legislation_ news/20151126/274987193.html.

[45]   See, among many others, Letsas, "Two Concepts of the Margin of Appreciation"; Shany, "Toward a General Margin of Appreciation Doctrine in International Law?"; Dominic McGoldrick, "A Defence of the Margin of Appreciation and an Argument for Its Application by the Human Rights Committee," *International & Comparative Law Quarterly* 65, no. 1 (January 2016): 21–60, https://doi.org/10.1017/S0020589315000457.

that "[a] party may not invoke the provisions of its internal law as justification for its failure to perform a treaty . . . ". [*sic*] No legal argument at national law, including constitutional law, can justify an act or omission which turns out to be in breach of international law.[46]

In April 2016, Russia's constitutional amendment was put to the test. The Russian Constitutional Court ruled that the ECtHR's final judgment in *Anchugov and Gladkov* v. *Russia* was incompatible with the Russian constitution and thus could not be executed.[47] Human rights organizations lambasted the decision. Hugh Williamson, the Europe and Central Asia director at Human Rights Watch, said, plainly, "It's very simple – Russia is violating its legal obligation to enforce rulings of the European Court of Human Rights." He continued, "The Constitutional Court's new powers risks gutting the European system of human rights protection in Russia."[48] The PACE also expressed consternation at the Constitutional Court's ruling. PACE President Anne Brasseur explained with respect to the Constitutional Court's finding on the *Anchugov and Gladkov* case:

Such a finding should in no way prompt the Russian authorities not to implement certain judgments of the European Court of Human Rights. Even now, the Russian Federation is one of the countries with the highest number of non-implemented judgments of the Strasbourg Court: it has not yet fully implemented nearly 1,500 judgments, many of which concern particularly serious human rights violations and/or complex structural problems.[49]

---

[46] Venice Commission, *Opinion No. 832/2015 Russian Federation Final Opinion on the Amendments to the Federal Constitutional Law on the Constitutional Court, Adopted by the Venice Commission at Its 107th Plenary Session (Venice, 10–11 June 2016)*, Strasbourg: Council of Europe, 2016, https://www.venice.coe.int/webforms/documents/default.aspx?pdffile=CDL-AD(2016)016-e.

[47] Marina Aksenova, "Anchugov and Gladkov Is Not Enforceable: The Russian Constitutional Court Opines in Its First ECtHR Implementation Case," *Opinion Juris*, April 25, 2016, http://opiniojuris.org/2016/04/25/anchugov-and-gladkov-is-not-enforceable-the-russian-constitutional-court-opines-in-its-first-ecthr-implementation-case/; Judgment of 19 January 2017 No. 1-П/2017 in the Case Concerning the Resolution of the Question of the Possibility to Execute in Accordance with the Constitution of the Russian Federation the Judgment of the European Court of Human Rights of 31 July 2014 in the *Case of OAO Neftyanaya Kompaniya Yukos* v. *Russia* in Connection with the Request of the Ministry of Justice of the Russian Federation (Constitutional Court of the Russian Federation, 2017), www.ksrf.ru/en/Decision/Judgments/Documents/2017_January_19_1-P.pdf.

[48] "Russia: Constitutional Court Backs Selective Justice," *Human Rights Watch*, April 19, 2016, https://www.hrw.org/news/2016/04/19/russia-constitutional-court-backs-selective-justice; Amnesty International, "A Summary of Amnesty International's Concerns in the Russian Federation," October 19, 2016, https://www.amnesty.org/download/Documents/EUR4650092016ENGLISH.pdf.

[49] Anne Brasseur, "PACE President Concerned by Decision on 'Selective Implementation' of Strasbourg Rulings in Russia," *Parliamentary Assembly of the Council of Europe*, July 16, 2015, http://assembly.coe.int/nw/xml/News/News-View-EN.asp?newsid=5720&cat=15.

But it is precisely in this larger context that the Russian Constitutional Court ruling makes sense. Russia has long bristled against the domestic implementation of ECtHR rulings. This new amendment and practice simply put a legal sheen on the problem. It also furthered the narrative that the ECtHR is a biased institution, one that is at fundamental, existential odds with Russia's legal and cultural landscape.

The following January, the Russian Constitutional Court handed down another ruling regarding the nonexecutability of an ECtHR ruling, this time with respect to *OAO Neftyanaya Kompaniya Yukos* v. *Russia*.[50] The Yukos case had long been a thorn in Russia's side. Not only is Yukos a political rival of sorts, but the required payout for the Yukos case topped €1.870 billion. The Constitutional Court's finding on the Yukos case was an act of defiance done for the benefit of both domestic audiences as well as observers and stakeholders in Strasbourg.

This normative and jurisprudential crisis prompted a new wave of questions about the role of Russia in the Council of Europe and the future of the ECtHR in Russia and beyond.[51] Writing in *EJIL: Talk!*, Philip Leach and Alice Donald noted that Russia was not the first or only country to argue that ECtHR jurisprudence ran contrary to domestic law, drawing parallels to the UK's own reluctance to comply with ECtHR rulings about prisoners' voting rights.[52] The Russian constitutional challenge to the European Convention on Human Rights and Fundamental Freedoms and ECtHR rulings, as well as the larger debate about the future of Russia in the COE hit at the core of the Council of Europe and the European Court of Human Rights. When a court's authority to hand down binding rulings is thrown into question, the whole house of cards can come tumbling down.

---

[50] *Case of OAO Neftyanaya Kompaniya Yukos* v. *Russia*, No. 14902/04 (European Court of Human Rights, 2014); Iryna Marchuk, "Flexing Muscles (Yet Again): The Russian Constitutional Court's Defiance of the Authority of the ECtHR in the Yukos Case," *EJIL: Talk!* (blog), February 13, 2017, https://www.ejiltalk.org/flexing-muscles-yet-again-the-russian-constitutional-courts-defiance-of-the-authority-of-the-ecthr-in-the-yukos-case/.

[51] Rachel M. Fleig-Goldstein, "The Russian Constitutional Court versus the European Court of Human Rights: How the Strasbourg Court Should Respond to Russia's Refusal to Execute ECtHR Judgments," *Columbia Journal of Transnational Law* 56, no. 1 (2017): 172–218, https://heinonline.org/HOL/P?h=hein.journals/cjtl56&i=176&a=dW5sLmVkdQ; Russian human rights defenders, "Addressing the Crisis in Relations between the Council of Europe and Russia"; Philip Leach and Alice Donald, "Russia Defies Strasbourg: Is Contagion Spreading?" *EJIL: Talk!* (blog), December 19, 2015, www.ejiltalk.org/russia-defies-strasbourg-is-contagion-spreading/.

[52] Leach and Donald, "Russia Defies Strasbourg"; Hillebrecht, "Implementing International Human Rights Law."

The Russian drama exemplified the vulnerability of even the most robust international justice institutions. In June 2019, when the PACE adopted Resolution 2287 allowing states voting privileges even when their credentials were being challenged, the Russian Federation finally came into compliance with the *Anchugov and Gladkov* v. *Russia* ruling.[53] Russia held both the court and the victims hostage until the PACE bowed to its political demands.

CASE 2: DOMESTIC DRAMAS, INTERNATIONAL REFORMS, AND ECtHR SUPPORTER STATES

While traditionally antagonistic states like Russia are the frequent perpetrators of backlash politics, even generally supportive states attempt to circumscribe the authority of international human rights and criminal tribunals through doctrinal challenges. This most certainly has been the case for the ECtHR, particularly after the adoption of Protocol 14, as detailed above.

Following the adoption of Protocol 14, the Council of Europe hosted a broader series of conferences aimed at further reforming the European Court of Human Rights with an eye toward reducing the backlog of cases and improving the domestic implementation of rulings. Ultimately, however, clearing the backlog of cases, particularly repeat cases, requires better compliance with existing judgments.[54]

These conferences, which took place in Interlaken in 2010, Izmir in 2011, Brighton in 2012, Oslo in 2014, Brussels in 2015, and Copenhagen in 2018, produced a set of new protocols and declarations, thereby introducing a new wave of bureaucratic and budgetary politics into the Strasbourg system. These reform processes questioned, at their core, the degree to which the central role of the ECtHR was to provide individual recourse or to serve as a forum for regional constitutional review. The overarching question was about the extent to which the ECtHR could and should defer to state practice.

The United Kingdom led the Brighton meeting in 2012 and placed an emphasis on the domestic implementation of rulings and on the nature of the Court's margin of appreciation doctrine. The final Brighton Declaration stressed the shared responsibility between states and the Court for the full realization of the rights enshrined in the European Convention on Human

---

[53] Committee of Ministers, "Action Report (27/6/2019) – Communication from the Russian Federation Concerning the Anchugov and Gladkov Group of Cases v. Russian Federation (Application No. 11157/04)," *Council of Europe*, July 2, 2019, https://publicsearch.coe.int/Pages/result_details.aspx?ObjectId=090000168095777a.

[54] European Court of Human Rights, "Reform of the Court," n.d., https://www.echr.coe.int/Pages/home.aspx?p=basictexts/reform&c=.

Rights and called for more effective and expedient domestic execution of judgments.[55] As hosts, the British delegation spearheaded early drafts of the Brighton Declaration. Their drafts privileged national judicial and political authorities, no doubt in response to the widespread criticism of the Court among politicians and the public alike in the UK.[56] In its preliminary opinion on the Brighton Declaration, however, the Court stressed the joint responsibility of states and the COE for the reform of the system. The preliminary opinion highlighted the need for the domestic implementation of rulings and the independence and full financing of the Court.[57] At the Brighton Conference, the President of the Court, Nicolas Bratza, spoke more forcefully about this joint responsibility and the importance of judicial independence. He said, "It is in part for this reason that we have difficulty in seeing the need for, or the wisdom of, attempting to legislate for it [the margin of appreciation] in the Convention, any more than for the many other tools of interpretation which have been developed by the Court in carrying out the judicial role entrusted to it."[58] Bratza was not alone. Jean-Claude Mignon, the President of the Parliamentary Assembly of the Council of Europe, further stressed how arguments about the margin of appreciation exploited the Court's dependency on member states. He argued,

> Is the Court not rather a victim of deficiencies at the national level? . . . However, the limits to this reinforcement of subsidiarity lie in the limitations of the national legal systems themselves. Let us not invert the situation. It is true that the States Parties are in principle best able to assess the necessity and the proportionality of the specific measures they have to take. However, in a way we also asked the Court, particularly following the enlargement of the Council of Europe, to make good the weaknesses of a number of member States with regard to the rule of law. It is therefore the Court that must have the last word in deciding how to interpret the Convention in each case brought before it.[59]

---

[55] European Court of Human Rights, "High Level Conference on the Future of the European Court of Human Rights: Brighton Declaration," *Committee of Ministers of the Council of Europe*, April 19, 2012, https://www.echr.coe.int/Documents/2012_Brighton_FinalDeclaration_ENG.pdf.

[56] Ed Bates, "The Brighton Declaration and the 'Meddling Court,'" *UK Human Rights Blog*, April 22, 2012, https://ukhumanrightsblog.com/2012/04/22/the-brighton-declaration-and-the-meddling-court/.

[57] European Court of Human Rights, "Preliminary Opinion of the Court in Preparation for the Brighton Conference (Adopted by the Plenary Court on 20 February 2012)," February 20, 2012, https://www.echr.coe.int/Documents/2012_Brighton_Opinion_ENG.pdf.

[58] Sir Nicolas Bratza, "High Level Conference, Brighton 18–20 April 2012," *European Court of Human Rights*, April 18, 2012, 6, https://www.echr.coe.int/Documents/Speech_20120420_Bratza_Brighton_ENG.pdf.

[59] Directorate General, Human Rights and the Rule of Law, *Reforming the European Convention on Human Rights: Interlaken, Izmir, Brighton and Beyond: A Compilation of Instruments and Texts Relating to the Ongoing Reform of the ECHR* (Strasbourg: Council of

The debates about the margin of appreciation and the independence of the European Court of Human Rights led to an amendment of the preamble of the Convention. The preamble, amended by Protocol 15, now read: "Affirming that the High Contracting Parties, in accordance with the principle of subsidiarity, have the primary responsibility to secure the rights and freedoms defined in this Convention and the Protocols thereto, and that in doing so they enjoy a margin of appreciation, subject to the supervisory jurisdiction of the European Court of Human Rights established by this Convention."[60] As Andreas Follesdal suggested, the Brighton Declaration was the beginning, not the end, of the debate about the relationship between the ECtHR, national authorities, and the politics of the margin of appreciation.[61]

In 2017, the Council of Europe prepared for the 2018 high-level conference in Copenhagen. This time, the Danish delegation led the reform initiative, and again the theme was the margin of appreciation with an emphasis on the political dynamics between member states and the Court. Denmark was dealing with a strong anti-immigrant domestic constituency and trying to balance both intense domestic political pressure pulling it away from the Strasbourg system, as well as long-standing obligations to the ECtHR.[62] The draft of the Copenhagen Declaration that was circulated in advance of the conference included strong language about the importance of subsidiarity and "national traditions." Icelandic judge and then-Vice President[63] of the Court, Róbert Spanó, also championed the early draft. Spanó called for constraints on the judicial independence of the court, which he couched in terms of judicial

Europe, 2014), 77–78, https://edoc.coe.int/en/conferences-on-the-future-of-the-european-court-of-human-rights/7308-reforming-the-european-convention-on-human-rights-interlaken-izmir-brighton-and-beyond-a-compilation-of-instruments-and-texts-relating-to-the-ongoing-reform-of-the-echr.html.

[60] "Protocol No. 15 Amending the Convention for the Protection of Human Rights and Fundamental Freedoms," opened for signature June 24, 2013, *Council of Europe Treaty Series* No. 213.

[61] Andreas Follesdal, "Squaring the Circle at the Battle at Brighton: Is the War between Protecting Human Rights or Respecting Sovereignty Over, or Has It Just Begun?" in *Shifting Centres of Gravity in Human Rights Protection: Rethinking Relations between the ECHR, EU, and National Legal Orders*, eds. Oddný Mjöll Arnardóttir and Antoine Buyse (London: Routledge, 2016); Robert Spano, "Universality or Diversity of Human Rights? Strasbourg in the Age of Subsidiarity," *Human Rights Law Review* 14, no. 3 (September 2014): 487–502, https://doi.org/10.1093/hrlr/ngu021.

[62] René Kreichauf, "Legal Paradigm Shifts and Their Impacts on the Socio-Spatial Exclusion of Asylum Seekers in Denmark," in *Geographies of Asylum in Europe and the Role of European Localities*, eds. Birgit Glorius and Jeroen Doomernik (Cham: Springer International Publishing, 2020), 45–67, https://link.springer.com/chapter/10.1007/978-3-030-25666-1_3.

[63] Spanó went on to become the President of the Court in 2020.

and political "dialogue."[64] The Copenhagen Declaration called upon states to exert more control over the Court and implementation politics. At some level, the draft of the Copenhagen Declaration threatened the independence of the ECtHR.

Unsurprisingly, this language inspired strong critiques from the Court and civil society, among others. In its preliminary opinion on the draft, the Court wrote,

> [T]he Court has concerns in particular in relation to the wording of paragraph 14 of the draft declaration. It considers that the references in this context to "constitutional traditions", and even more so to "national circumstances", may give rise to confusion. While both elements may be relevant in assessing whether a State has complied with the Convention in a particular case, that is ultimately for the Court itself to determine, as it has constantly stated in its case-law.[65]

The Court also called upon states to prioritize the domestic implementation of their rulings and stressed that deferring to national authorities was only appropriate when the case law in front of the court rendered it so, not whenever national authorities wanted it to be that way.[66]

It was not just the Court that responded to the draft of the Copenhagen Declaration. Stakeholders, including members of both civil society and steward states, adamantly rejected many of the proposals within the draft declaration. Civil society had a robust response to the Declaration, warning against the notion of "dialogue" as a code for nonimplementation. They also called on the Court, not member states, to determine the margin of appreciation in any given case.[67]

Highlighting the importance of steward states in protecting international courts, nineteen states, led by Luxembourg, refused to sign the draft declaration. They cited a number of concerns with the draft. Justice Initiative's James Goldston explains that these states argued that the draft "a) downplayed

---

[64] Geir Ulfstein and Andreas Follesdal, "Copenhagen – Much Ado about Little?" *EJIL: Talk!* (blog), April 14, 2018, https://www.ejiltalk.org/copenhagen-much-ado-about-little/#more-16106; Spano, "Universality or Diversity of Human Rights?"

[65] European Court of Human Rights, "Opinion on the Draft Copenhagen Declaration," *Council of Europe*, April 13, 2018, 2, https://www.echr.coe.int/Documents/Opinion_draft_Declaration_Copenhague%20ENG.pdf.

[66] European Court of Human Rights, "Opinion on the Draft Copenhagen Declaration."

[67] James A. Goldston, "Remarks on the Copenhagen Declaration on Reform of the ECHR," *Open Society Justice Initiative*, April 11, 2018, https://www.justiceinitiative.org/uploads/72b8dbe7-dd22-4df2-a687-fc7bb3ad5b34/james-goldston-remarks-on-copenhagen-declaration-on-reform-of-the-echr-20180411.pdf.

the Court's supervisory functions, b) questioned its independence and author-ity, c) revisited well-established principles of dynamic interpretation of the Convention, and d) undermined the principle of universality of human rights."[68] This coalition of nineteen states' refusal to sign the declaration was an important statement to the Danish delegation and to the European human rights system more broadly. As Ulfstein and Follesdal explain:

> It will be hard for the Danish government to lament the loss of democratic control when their failure to constrain the independent Court is due to other democracies' refusal to thus restrain the Court, on the basis of deliberation. Indeed, optimistic supporters of the Danish government may maintain that it got the best result it might hope for, in a two-level game partly shrouded in secrecy. The Danish government can honestly tell their voters that they tried their best to roll back the Court and push for more domestic control over issues of asylum – yet their proposal was rejected by the other European democracies.[69]

In other words, the Danish government was able to present itself as "stand-ing up" to the ECtHR to domestic constituencies who were opposed to the ECtHR, particularly with respect to immigration and asylum policy. At the same time, they were not forced to fully undermine the ECtHR because other, robust democracies stood up against this initiative and protected the Convention and the ECtHR. In effect, Denmark was able to simultaneously mount a doctrinal challenge to the ECtHR to placate domestic audiences while also shoring up the Court by relying on fellow stakeholder states to reinforce the principle of the margin of appreciation.

At the Copenhagen conference, the president of the European Court of Human Rights, Guido Raimondi, stressed that the Copenhagen Declaration, like the Brighton Declaration that preceded it, was both practical and political.[70] Raimondi's vision ultimately carried the day. The final version of the Copenhagen Declaration called for shared responsibility for the Convention system and highlighted the importance of the domestic imple-mentation of the Convention and the execution of the ECtHR's judgments. While the call for the Court to continuously and transparently rearticulate the

---

[68] Goldston, "Remarks on the Copenhagen Declaration," 3.

[69] Ulfstein and Follesdal, "Copenhagen – Much Ado about Little?" For more about the Copenhagen, please see the excellent *EJIL: Talk!* exchanges in the lead-up to and immediate aftermath of the conference.

[70] Guido Raimondi, "High-Level Conference: Continued Reform of the European Court of Human Rights Convention System – Better Balance, Improved Protection," *European Court of Human Rights*, April 13, 2018, https://www.echr.coe.int/Documents/Speech_20180412_Rai mondi_Copenhagen_ENG.pdf.

principle of subsidiarity remained in the final version of the Copenhagen Declaration, it did so in a way that made reference to the Court's case law, not political pressure.[71]

The European Court of Human Rights' reform process is illustrative in many ways. On the one hand, it illustrates that even the oldest and arguably most robust international courts are not immune to backlash. Second, and relatedly, the Copenhagen Declaration and the politics leading up to it illustrated the importance of civil society resistance, the tribunals' self-advocacy, and the critical role for supporter states in mitigating the effects of backlash. In the concluding chapter that follows, I take up the case of supporter states and civil society and identify best practices for protecting international human rights and criminal courts in the face of sustained attack.

CONCLUSION

This chapter has considered doctrinal challenges to the core principles of complementarity and the margin of appreciation. It has illustrated how states try to limit or dilute the authority of international courts by expanding the tribunals' deference to domestic actors. The factors that drive other forms of backlash – normative discontent, the tribunals' dependence on states for material, jurisdictional, and normative support, the domestic mobilizing effects of international jurisprudence, and the possibility for future violence – also push states to engage in this type of backlash politics.

As the last case study illustrated, doctrinal challenges to international courts and backlash politics are not confined to those states that have long held adversarial positions to international justice. Instead, backlash can come from within the tribunal's set of core stakeholders. Backlash from these supporter states can be particularly pernicious. The tribunals are heavily reliant on their member states in general, and on their core supporters in particular. Chapter 5 demonstrated how state support is critical for maintaining the budgets and bureaucracies of international organizations. When supporter states pull back from their fiscal and human capital commitments, the courts suffer. Similarly, when supporter states are reluctant or petulant about cooperating with the tribunals' requests for cooperation, they make the courts' jurisdictional work more difficult. They also set a bad example that other states are keen to exploit.

---

[71] Committee of Ministers, "Copenhagen Declaration," *Council of Europe*, April 13, 2018, https://www.echr.coe.int/Documents/Copenhagen_Declaration_ENG.pdf; Ulfstein and Follesdal, "Copenhagen – Much Ado about Little?"

In addition to these material and operational issues, when supporter states pose doctrinal challenges to the tribunals, or engage in other forms of backlash, they cause normative harm to both the court in question and international justice more broadly. The international justice regime relies on states' normative affirmation. When stakeholder states undermine a court, they threaten to undermine the whole idea of international justice and accountability.

In Chapter 7, I consider ways in which international justice stakeholders, from supporter states to the UN Security Council to individual activists, can shore up the international regime against the range of backlash politics discussed thus far in this book. Chapter 7 provides concrete examples of how proponents of international justice can protect the international justice regime, not just materially and procedurally, but also normatively. The task of saving the international justice regime is a formidable one, but it is one that is important for victims, for their communities, and for the global pursuit of peace and justice.

7

How to Save the International Justice Regime

INTRODUCTION

In a recent *Financial Times* profile, the International Criminal Court Chief Prosecutor, Fatou Bensouda, was asked if she feared that the whole experiment of international justice was falling into disarray. This is likely a question that the Prosecutor has pondered more than once. Indeed, this is a question that most justice proponents – and critics – have asked themselves time and again. Bensouda's answer showcased her characteristic blend of realism and optimism. She responded, "There is certainly this very vicious attack on multilateralism itself, we have seen that, and the ICC is no exception ... But what we have also seen, I believe, is a strong pushback."[1]

The previous chapters have documented the multicausal and multifaceted challenges facing the international justice regime. From withdrawals from the tribunals to conceptual challenges to the courts' doctrinal foundations, backlash politics has threatened to thwart the progress of justice, to deny victims recourse, and to provide impunity for the worst perpetrators of the worst crimes. And yet, despite these persistent and abiding challenges, the pursuit of international justice continues. The institutions that comprise the international justice regime have thus far survived the onslaught of backlash politics to serve the interests of justice and accountability.

These institutions are not perfect, surely. They have made strategic missteps that have made them vulnerable to backlash politics. They have failed to recognize the depth and meaning of the charges of bias and exclusion leveraged against them. These tribunals have overspent and underperformed. And yet, international human rights and criminal courts provide a better option for the pursuit of peace and accountability than a world that offers only war to settle disputes.

---

[1] David Pilling, "Fatou Bensouda: 'It's about the Law. It's Not about Power,'" *Financial Times*, September 25, 2020, https://www.ft.com/content/beeb8dba-ce3c-4a33-b319-3fcff0916736.

International human rights and criminal courts will always be dependent on member states for material, procedural, and normative support. Ratification rates will almost always mask deep-rooted normative divisions. International human rights and criminal adjudication will continue to privilege some domestic groups over others. The threat of repression and adjudication tomorrow will prompt backlash today. Of course, the tribunals and their supporters cannot (and do not) remain idle while the barrage of backlash comes their way. Instead, as the rest of this chapter details, the tribunals and their proponents all have a role to play in pushing back against the backlash.

In the following section, I turn to the central question of this chapter: how can supporters and the tribunals themselves save the international justice regime? I provide three answers to this question: (1) managing public opinion by engaging in targeted and effective self-marketing campaigns as a way to make the tribunals' case to a broader audience; (2) improving the rule of law and the functioning of the tribunals as judicial institutions; and (3) reaffirming the fundamental norm(s) of criminal accountability and human rights. Following that discussion, the chapter turns to outlining a future research agenda on backlash politics and international justice based on the contributions of this manuscript. The final section makes the case for why backlash against international human rights and criminal courts matters and why the international justice regime is worth fighting for.

HOW TO SAVE THE INTERNATIONAL JUSTICE REGIME

While the previous chapters documented the challenges that international human rights and criminal courts face, it is important to recognize that none of those challenges are insurmountable and that the international justice regime can continue to play an important role in international politics well into the coming years. To understand the steps that the tribunals, supporter states, and advocates for international justice can and should take to protect the international justice regime, scholars, supporters, and stakeholders must look again to the roots of the courts' authority. Chapter 1 argues that courts derive their authority from three sources: (1) their structural relationship with states; (2) the act of adjudicating; and (3) the normative and legal expertise they accrue over time.[2] If backlash is defined as sustained attacks on

---

[2] See, among others, C. Neal Tate and Torbjörn Vallinder, eds., *The Global Expansion of Judicial Power*, rev. ed. (New York: New York University Press, 1995); Ian Hurd, "Legitimacy and Authority in International Politics," *International Organization* 53, no. 2 (Spring 1999): 379–408, https://doi.org/10.1162/002081899550913; Karen J. Alter, "Agents or Trustees? International Courts in Their Political Context," *European Journal of International Relations*

international courts' authority, it holds that protecting the courts requires protecting and enhancing their political, legal, and normative authority. In the discussion that follows, I consider how the tribunals, supporter states, scholars, and activists can do precisely that.

Political Positioning: Strengthening Outreach Efforts and Flipping the Narrative

The case studies in the previous chapters illustrated how the courts' dependency on states for material, procedural, and normative support is a precondition for backlash politics. Not only do states withhold their support in the form of budgetary and bureaucratic backlash, but they also exploit the tribunals' dependency on states when engaging in other forms of backlash politics. While states can – and do – exert a great amount of control over international human rights and criminal tribunals, one thing they cannot control is the political narrative that the tribunals offer to the public. Unfortunately, the tribunals and their supporters have been particularly lax about offering a clear articulation of the value of the tribunals and their role in contemporary politics.

To understand how the tribunals get outplayed in the public relations game, consider the cases studies in Chapters 3 and 4. The Bolivarian states and the African Union threatened to withdraw from and replace the Inter-American Human Rights System and the ICC, respectively. Those states leading the charge for withdrawals and replacements relied on a narrative that linked the international courts to US hegemony and neocolonialism. These claims are debatable. On the first point, it is important to recognize that the USA rejects both the ICC and the Inter-American system, so having states participate in these courts is certainly not a top US foreign policy priority. Indeed, at various points in recent history, the USA has actively worked to *halt* state participation with the ICC.[3]

14, no. 1 (March 2008): 33–63, https://doi.org/10.1177/1354066107087769; Laurence R. Helfer and Karen J. Alter, "Legitimacy and Lawmaking: A Tale of Three International Courts," *Theoretical Inquiries in Law* 14, no. 2 (2013): 479–504, https://doi.org/10.1515/til-2013-024; Karen J. Alter, Laurence R. Helfer, and Mikael Rask Madsen, "How Context Shapes the Authority of International Courts," *Law and Contemporary Problems* 79, no. 1 (2016): 1–36, https://scholarship.law.duke.edu/lcp/vol79/iss1/1; Leslie Vinjumari, "The International Criminal Court and the Paradox of Authority," *Law and Contemporary Problems* 79, no. 1 (2016): 275–287. https://scholarship.law.duke.edu/lcp/vol79/iss1/10.

3   Judith Kelley, "Who Keeps International Commitments and Why? The International Criminal Court and Bilateral Nonsurrender Agreements," *The American Political Science Review* 101, no. 3 (August 2007): 573–589, https://doi.org/10.1017/S0003055407070426;

The second, and related charge, is perhaps harder to dismiss, largely because the courts have not done a particularly good job at even attempting to dispute claims of neocolonialism. Take the ICC as an example. While the Office of the Prosecutor of the ICC has said, time and again, that it selects cases based on their merits and not their geography, the Court's lackluster and officious public relations campaign has done little to counter this narrative. This is to say nothing of the deleterious effects of the ICC's first prosecutor's ostentatious publicity stunts, including disembarking from a helicopter in Uganda whilst wearing a white safari suit.[4] Countering these narratives requires a concerted, professional marketing strategy, something that the courts have neither the time, nor money, nor inclination for, to their detriment.

The tribunals and their supporters need to work hard to change the story. Resetting the narrative requires improving the functioning of the courts to counter arguments that they are slow, biased, and bloated institutions, which I discuss in more detail in the following section. But resetting the narrative requires more than just technical solutions. It requires that the courts do more *in situ* work and that they explain clearly and transparently what they can – and cannot – provide to victims, witnesses, and the communities in which they work.

The Limits of International Criminal and Human Rights Courts. What do victims of human rights abuses and war crimes want from international courts? My research with international justice stakeholders reveals a disconnect between the courts on the one hand and victims on the other. One former prosecutor, for example, suggested that while he was doing outreach work with victims, they regularly asked if the court with which he worked was going to help bring water or electricity back to their village.[5] The answer, of course, is no. International courts are designed to provide justice in a very particular, legalistic sense. They can hold perpetrators accountable and ask states to pay reparations, which can include individual remedies, but these courts do not provide services directly to victims. This is a problem for the

---

Michael Camilleri and Danielle Edmonds, "The Inter-American Human Rights System in the Trump Era," *The Dialogue*, June 15, 2017, https://www.thedialogue.org/analysis/the-inter-american-human-rights-system-in-the-trump-era/; "The US-ICC Relationship," ABA-ICC Project, n.d., https://www.aba-icc.org/about-the-icc/the-us-icc-relationship/.

4   David Kaye, "Who's Afraid of the International Criminal Court?" *Foreign Affairs*, May/June 2011, https://www.foreignaffairs.com/articles/2011-04-18/whos-afraid-international-criminal-court; Kai Ambos, "Room for Improvement," *Development and Cooperation*, December 13, 2011, https://www.dandc.eu/en/article/promising-change-guard-international-criminal-court.

5   Interview #505, February 2014.

courts' reputations, especially when the political elites who want to undermine them are offering a counter-narrative of elitist, bloated bureaucracies that punish the poor, not help the vulnerable.

The first step in reversing this narrative is improving the courts' work with direct victims. The courts all have victims' support units. The Inter-American Commission on Human Rights established a Legal Assistance Fund for petitioners and alleged victims who need assistance covering the costs of their legal proceedings at the IACmHR. The Legal Assistance Fund is limited to covering the expenses related to pursuing recourse at the IACmHR and can only be accessed after a case has cleared the admissibility stage. This means that victims and their advocates have to front significant costs to get their petition and supporting documents to the Commission before being able to apply for financial support.[6] The Inter-American Court of Human Rights offers a public defender option for victims unable to pay for representation and also offers resources from their Victims' Legal Assistance Fund for petitioners who are unable to cover the costs of their pursuit of justice at the IACtHR.[7] Information about both the IACmHR and IACtHR's legal assistance funds, however, is buried on their websites and difficult to access and understand.

The European Court of Human Rights offers a similarly limited legal defense fund. According to the Council of Bars and Law Societies of Europe, the ECtHR only grants legal aid in the later stages of proceedings and if applicants cannot afford a lawyer and if such legal assistance is required to conduct the case.[8] The requirements for qualifying for legal aid are hidden in the Court's "Rules of Court," a document that is nearly impenetrable to justice insiders, never mind ordinary citizens looking for recourse.[9]

The inaccessibility of this information matters for the political positioning of the courts, particularly when the courts' opponents are offering a narrative of the tribunals being biased institutions that favor wealthy Western countries at the expense of the rest of the world. By making legal assistance more accessible, not only financially but also symbolically, the regional human

---

[6] The funds can be used to retroactively cover the costs of document procurement, for example. "Legal Assistance Fund," Inter-American Commission on Human Rights, n.d., www.oas.org /en/iachr/mandate/Basics/fund.asp.

[7] "What Is the I/A Court H.R.?" Inter-American Court of Human Rights, n.d., https://corteidh .or.cr/que_es_la_corte.cfm?lang=en.

[8] "The European Court of Human Rights: Questions and Answers for Lawyers," *Council of Bars & Law Societies of Europe,* October 2018, https://www.echr.coe.int/Documents/Q_A_Lawyer s_Guide_ECHR_ENG.pdf.

[9] European Court of Human Rights, "Rules of the Court," *Council of Europe,* January 1, 2020, https://www.echr.coe.int/documents/rules_court_eng.pdf.

rights tribunals can take an important step toward reclaiming the narrative and showcasing support for the victims of human rights abuse.

Compared to either of the regional human rights systems, the ICC has a relatively well-developed, if still imperfect, victim support fund, called the Trust Fund for Victims (TFV). The TFV offers reparations to victims who have suffered from genocide, crimes of humanity, war crimes and aggression crimes, and its purpose and basic contours are outlined in the Rome Statute itself. As the cases against the perpetrators at the ICC are brought by the OTP, rather than individual petitioners, the victims and witnesses do not have legal costs, as such. Because they are not petitioners, however, there is no direct mechanism for reparations. The TFV fills this gap. It can leverage fines, funds, or property collected from the perpetrator, by order of the Court, to pay reparations directly to victims.[10] The ICC also provides practical and material support for witnesses, some of whom may also be so-called "participating victims."[11] Contributions from member states and other donors are critical for the TFV to provide adequate financial and psychosocial support for victims and witnesses. The Coalition for the ICC, as well as the TFV itself, however, regularly calls for increased state and donor support of this initiative.[12]

While the Trust Fund for Victims would benefit from more funding and a stronger political presence, it is a start at recognizing a critical step that international tribunals must take in improving their outreach and navigating their dependence on states. Rather than waiting for states to provide reparations for victims, the TFV circumnavigates the states and elites, who are also often the perpetrators of abuse, to go directly to those affected by atrocity crimes. Going directly to the victims and to the communities affected by atrocity crimes and human rights abuse is something that all international human rights and criminal courts need to do more often and more strategically.

Expanding the Impact of Outreach and Implementation Initiatives. All of the international human rights and criminal courts discussed in this book, as well as those referenced only briefly, have outreach offices. None of these outreach offices, however, can boast a particularly large public presence. The result is that international justice opponents readily fill the public relations vacuum that these outreach offices leave behind.

---

[10] "Legal Basis," The Trust Fund for Victims, n.d., https://www.trustfundforvictims.org/en/abo ut/legal-basis.

[11] "Witnesses," International Criminal Court, n.d., https://www.icc-cpi.int/about/witnesses/Pag es/default.aspx.

[12] Coalition for the International Criminal Court, "Trust Fund for Victims," n.d., www .coalitionfortheicc.org/explore/trust-fund-victims.

The Council of Europe's outreach efforts are, perhaps, the least well-known. The COE established a Human Rights Trust Fund in 2008 to provide critical funding for states to implement human rights standards and meet the obligations set forth in the European Convention on Human Rights. The goal of the Human Rights Trust Fund is to help states make the structural changes needed to stem the tide of repetitive cases at the domestic, and presumably, international levels.[13] This is a preventative, rather than reactive, measure. The Human Rights Trust Fund has facilitated a range of projects in Russia, Greece, Turkey, Georgia, and the Balkan states, among others, such as creating parliamentary oversight over the execution of judgments or establishing mechanisms for investigating allegations of torture and inhumane treatment.[14]

While the impetus and intent behind the Human Rights Trust Fund is laudable, the degree to which the public recognizes and supports its work is unclear, in no small part because the Council of Europe does not advertise the Human Rights Trust Fund's work. This is a missed opportunity to showcase the important work of international justice institutions in improving human rights. In a similar vein, the ECtHR does trainings and other outreach work, including the translation and publication of case law across the continent, but the Court itself has identified accessibility and generalizability as continued challenges for their outreach.[15] Moreover, most citizens do not read international courts' jurisprudence. The ECtHR must more readily document its relevance for European citizens, not just judges, lawyers, and activists.

The Inter-American Human Rights System, and the IACmHR in particular, has a stronger outreach program than its European counterpart, with activities ranging from trainings of government officials to hosting the Inter-American Human Rights Forum.[16] The most important tool that the IAHRS has in its toolbox for promoting the work of the Inter-American Commission and Court of Human Rights, however, is *in situ* visits. These country visits by

---

[13]   "Human Rights Trust Fund," Office of the Directorate General of Programmes, Council of Europe, n.d., https://www.coe.int/en/web/programmes/human-rights-trust-fund.

[14]   "Projects Funded," Office of the Directorate General of Programmes, Council of Europe, n. d., https://www.coe.int/en/web/programmes/projects-funded.

[15]   European Court of Human Rights, "Bringing the Convention Closer to Home," *Council of Europe*, February 2017, https://www.echr.coe.int/documents/hrtf_standards_translations_eng .pdf; European Court of Human Rights, "Bringing the Convention Home: Case-Law Information, Training and Outreach," *Council of Europe*, 2018, https://www.echr.coe.int/Do cuments/Case_law_info_training_outreach_2018_ENG.pdf.

[16]   "Institutional Strengthening," Inter-American Court of Human Rights, n.d., https://www .corteidh.or.cr/fortalecimiento_institucional.cfm?lang=en; "Promotion," Inter-American Commission on Human Rights, n.d., www.oas.org/en/iachr/activities/promotion.asp; "Foro del sistema Interamericano de Derechos Humanos," foro-sidh, n.d., https://cidhoea .wixsite.com/foro-sidh.

the Commission are integral in bringing the Inter-American Human Rights System to the people of the region. In one interview, an official at the Inter-American Commission on Human Rights noted that petitions tend to spike following *in situ* visits because these visits bring awareness of the Commission and the Inter-American Human Rights System. They also lower the costs of participation for victims and break down the barrier between an elite legal institution and the people whose rights are at risk.[17] Like the IACmHR, the IACtHR conducts training for judges, lawyers, and legal officials from around the region. The Court also conducts special sessions, during which time it hears cases in different cities across the Western Hemisphere.[18]

The ICC also has an outreach program, the goal of which is to "interact with communities affected by crimes." The ICC describes this work as follows: "The Court engages with these communities directly, in local languages, holding conversations and consultations, responding to questions, addressing concerns and providing people with information to promote understanding throughout the stages of the judicial proceedings."[19] While the ICC keeps active with these engagements, it has not published an omnibus report on its outreach activities since 2010.[20] In addition, the Pre-Trial Chambers of the ICC can order outreach and victim engagement reports with respect to certain cases. In a recent example, Pre-Trial Chamber III surveyed the work that the ICC Registry had done with respect to outreach to victims, witnesses, and communities in Myanmar/Burma. Pre-Trial Chamber III then ordered the Registry to work with the Office of the Prosecutor to create a coordinated plan for outreach and engagement with the affected communities.[21] These reports provide key insight into current situations but they are nearly impenetrable to read for anyone without a legal degree. Moreover, they are buried deep in the ICC's website, such that only stakeholders, scholars, and activists well-versed in the ICC's work would even know what to look for and where.

While the ICC, ECtHR, and, to a lesser extent, the IACmHR and IACtHR have buried their outreach work in legal jargon and bureaucracy, the states and

---

[17] Interview #464, July 2008.
[18] "Special Session," Inter-American Court of Human Rights, n.d., https://corteidh.or.cr/period o_de_sesiones_extraordinarias.cfm?lang=en.
[19] "Interacting with Communities Affected by Crimes," International Criminal Court, n.d., https://www.icc-cpi.int/about/interacting-with-communities.
[20] International Criminal Court, "Interacting with Communities Affected by Crimes."
[21] Situation in the People's Republic of Bangladesh/Republic of the Union of Myanmar, Order on Information and Outreach for the Victims of the Situation, ICC-01/09 (Pre-Trial Chamber III of the International Criminal Court, January 20, 2020), https://www.icc-cpi.int/CourtRec ords/CR2020_00138.PDF.

political elites looking to undermine the tribunals have taken their case directly – and clearly – to the public. The tribunals cannot escape their reliance on states but they can do more – or do what they are already doing more effectively – to work directly with the public and with victims. By engaging with communities and the public directly, the tribunals can circumnavigate the states and elites that try to undermine them. The research on public opinion and international human rights courts is comparatively limited, but this nascent body of work suggests that those elites opposed to international justice can leverage backlash politics against the tribunals to their own domestic advantage.[22] For example, in research on the ICC and the Special Tribunal for Lebanon, I find that elites under indictment at international courts can garner enough popular support to win elections *because of*, rather than despite, their status as indicted war criminals.[23] Similarly, Erik Voeten finds that populist leaders can leverage anti-justice rhetoric as a successful strategy for gathering domestic support.[24] The research on public opinion about human rights more broadly, however, suggests that public opinion is moveable.[25] It would serve the tribunals and their supporters well to heed that message and do more – and more impactful – outreach.

---

[22] Thomas P. Wolf, "International Justice vs Public Opinion: The ICC and Ethnic Polarisation in the 2013 Kenyan Election," *Journal of African Elections* 12, no. 1 (June 2013): 143–177, https://doi.org /10.20940/JAE/2013/v12i1a6; Kelebogile Zvobgo and Stephen Chaudoin, "Complementarity and Public Views on Overlapping Domestic and International Courts," January 2, 2020, https://www .law.uchicago.edu/files/2020-01/zvobgo_and_chaudoin.pdf; James Meernik, "Explaining Public Opinion on International Criminal Justice," *European Political Science Review* 7, no. 4 (November 2015): 567–591, https://doi.org/10.1017/S1755773914000332; Hilary Heuler, "Kenyans Split Over Kenyatta's ICC Appearance," *VOA*, October 8, 2014, www.voanews.com/content/ken yans-split-over-kenyatta-icc-appearance/2476919.html; Terrence L. Chapman and Stephen Chaudoin, "People Like the International Criminal Court – as Long as It Targets Other Problems in Other Countries," *Washington Post, Monkey Cage*, January 20, 2017, https://www .washingtonpost.com/news/monkey-cage/wp/2017/01/20/people-like-the-international-criminal-court-as-long-as-it-targets-other-problems-in-other-countries/; Kelebogile Zvobgo, "Human Rights versus National Interests: Shifting US Public Attitudes on the International Criminal Court," *International Studies Quarterly* 63, no. 4 (December 2019): 1065–1078, https://doi.org/10.1093/isq/ sqz056; Geoff Dancy, Yvonne Marie Dutton, Tessa Alleblas, and Eamon Aloyo, "What Determines Perceptions of Bias toward the International Criminal Court? Evidence from Kenya," *Journal of Conflict Resolution* 64, no. 7–8 (August 2020): 1443–1469, https://doi.org/10 .1177/0022002719893740.

[23] Courtney Hillebrecht, "International Criminal Accountability and the Domestic Politics of Resistance: Case Studies from Kenya and Lebanon," *Law & Society Review* 54, no. 2 (June 2020): 453–486, https://doi.org/10.1111/lasr.12469.

[24] Erik Voeten, "Populism and Backlashes against International Courts," *Perspectives on Politics* 18, no. 2 (June 2020): 407–422, https://doi.org/10.1017/S1537592719000975.

[25] Crow et al., "Data-Driven Optimism for Global Rights Activists," *openDemocracy*, June 29, 2015, https://www.opendemocracy.net/openglobalrights/james-ron-shannon-golden-david-crow-archana-pandya/datadriven-optimism-for-global-r; Theodore P. Gerber, "Grounds for

Adjudicative Authority: Improving the Courts' Legal Work

While improving their outreach work is one way for the tribunals and their supporters to push back against the backlash, the tribunals also derive their authority from their adjudicative work. They derive their perceived legitimacy by upholding the rule of law, providing recourse to victims, and holding perpetrators to account. As a result, some forms of backlash politics, such as bureaucratic and budgetary restrictions and doctrinal challenges, strike right to the heart of the tribunals' ability to gather evidence, hear testimony, hold trials, and rule on cases. In other instances, the courts' own bureaucratic largesse can delay and derail their legal work. The tribunals and their proponents can help to improve the legal functioning at the courts by increasing both capital and human investments in the courts, increasing transparency around case selection, and limiting the effects of conceptual stumbling blocks on the courts' legal procedures.

Increasing Investments in the Courts. Increased investment in international human rights and criminal courts is the first, and most obvious, step toward improving the tribunals' legal processes. Beyond specific, targeted examples of budgetary restrictions, the tribunals must regularly make do with limited resources. The ICC and ECtHR, for example, have been trying to

(a Little) Optimism? Russian Public Opinion on Human Rights," *openDemocracy*, January 18, 2016, https://www.opendemocracy.net/openglobalrights/theodore-p-gerber/grou nds-for-little-optimism-russian-public-opinion-on-human-right; Geoffrey P. R. Wallace, "International Law and Public Attitudes toward Torture: An Experimental Study," *International Organization* 67, no. 1 (January 2013): 105–140, https://doi.org/10.1017/S00208 1831200343; Sarah Kreps and Geoffrey Wallace, "International Law and US Public Support for Drone Strikes," *openDemocracy*, July 2, 2015, https://www.opendemocracy.net/openglo balrights/sarah-kreps-geoffrey-wallace/international-law-and-us-public-support-for-drone-stri; Dona-Gene Barton, Courtney Hillebrecht, and Sergio C. Wals, "A Neglected Nexus: Human Rights and Public Perceptions," *Journal of Human Rights* 16, no. 3 (2017): 293–313, https://doi.org/10.1080/14754835.2016.1261013; Courtney Hillebrecht, Dona-Gene Mitchell, and Sergio C. Wals, "Perceived Human Rights and Support for New Democracies: Lessons from Mexico," *Democratization* 22, no. 7 (2015): 1230–1249, https://doi.org/10.1080/13510347 .2014.950565; Erik Voeten, "Public Opinion and the Legitimacy of International Courts," *Theoretical Inquiries in Law* 14, no. 2 (2013): 411–436, https://doi.org/10.1515/til-2013-021; Shareen Hertel, Lyle Scruggs, and C. Patrick Heidkamp, "Human Rights and Public Opinion: From Attitudes to Action," *Political Science Quarterly* 124, no. 3 (Fall 2009): 443–459, https://doi.org/10.1002/j.1538-165X.2009.tb00655.x; Jeong-Woo Koo, "Public Opinion on Human Rights Is the True Gauge of Progress," *openDemocracy*, July 3, 2015, https://www.opendemocracy.net/openglobalrights/jeongwoo-koo/public-opinion-on-human-rights-is-true-gauge-of-progress; Jacob Ausderan, "How Naming and Shaming Affects Human Rights Perceptions in the Shamed Country," *Journal of Peace Research* 51, no. 1 (January 2014): 81–95, https://doi.org/10.1177/0022343313510014; Matthew Krain, "J'accuse! Does Naming and Shaming Perpetrators Reduce the Severity of Genocides or Politicides?" *International Studies Quarterly* 56, no. 3 (September 2012): 547–589, https://doi .org/10.1111/j.1468-2478.2012.00732.x.

weather no-growth budget initiatives while facing high caseloads and increased political demands.[26] The IAHRS, meanwhile, is perennially underfunded.[27]

Capital and human investments must focus on maintaining the courts' authority as judicial institutions and in decreasing their vulnerability to budgetary restrictions as a form of backlash politics. This means, on the one hand, that new or additional investments cannot simply go to large and impressive new buildings, such as the ICC's new location,[28] but also must go into the basic infrastructure of the courts, from enhancing information technology (IT) services to adding staff members to the courts' registries. Investments should focus on interventions that mitigate the severe delays in processing, hearing, and adjudicating cases. While states are often the culprits for these long impediments, the tribunals often do themselves and victims a disservice when bureaucratic inefficiencies add delays to legal proceedings.

Remove Obstacles to Processing Cases. It is not just financial support that the tribunals need in order to improve the rule of law and the functioning of the courts as judicial instruments. They also need to remove both conceptual and procedural obstacles to their ability to process cases. The example of Russia's derailment of critical reforms at the European Court of Human Rights in Chapter 6 is instructive here. By refusing to ratify Protocol 14, Russia held up reforms and affected the entire European human rights system.[29] The Kremlin benefited from the delays in the ECtHR's processing of cases, as it meant that they could prolong avoiding paying reparations to

---

[26] Theresa Squatrito, "Resourcing Global Justice: The Resource Management Design of International Courts," *Global Policy* 8, no. S5 (August 2017): 62–74, https://doi.org/10.1111/17 58-5899.12452; Assembly of States Parties, "Proposed Programme Budget for 2020 of the International Criminal Court, Eighteenth Session, The Hague, 2–7 December 2019, ICC-ASP/18/10," *International Criminal Court*, July 25, 2019, https://asp.icc-cpi.int/iccdocs/asp_d ocs/ASP18/ICC-ASP-18-10-ENG.pdf; International Criminal Court, "Report of the Committee on Budget and Finance on the Work of Its Seventeenth Session, The Hague, 5–12 December 2018, ICC-ASP/17/5," *Assembly of States Parties*, May 31, 2018, https://asp.icc-cpi.int/iccdocs/asp_docs/ASP17/ICC-ASP-17-5-ENG.pdf; Committee of Ministers, "Council of Europe Programme and Budget 2020–2021," *Council of Europe*, December 20, 2019, https://rm.coe.int/1680994ffd.

[27] "The Inter-American Human Rights System," Global Americans, n.d., https://theglobalamer icans.org/reports/inter-american-human-rights-system-fall-2016/.

[28] "The ICC Has Moved to Its Permanent Premises," International Criminal Court, n.d., https://www.icc-cpi.int/Pages/item.aspx?name=pr1180.

[29] See also, Bill Bowring, "The Russian Federation, Protocol No. 14 (and 14bis), and the Battle for the Soul of the ECHR," *Goettingen Journal of International Law* 2, no. 2 (2010): 589–617, https://www.gojil.eu/issues/22/22_article_bowring.pdf.

victims all while making the ECtHR look inefficient and incapable of rendering judgments and fostering compliance.

This example is illustrative not only of using conceptual challenges as a way to delay or derail justice, but also of how supporter states can push back against backlash politics. As documented in Chapter 6, the Council of Europe and supporter states eventually circumnavigated Russia to pass Protocol 14.[30] Could the COE have acted more swiftly? Yes. Could member states have issued a more full-throated response to Russia's obstructionism? Of course. But, their eventual action put the ECtHR on a much more sustainable path. The lesson here is that the tribunals and their supporters must take swift action to strike down doctrinal challenges that lead to the delay or derailment of justice.

The tribunals and their supporters must also ensure they are not architects of their own troubles. Consider, for example, the brouhaha at the ICC involving Judge Kuniko Ozaki, the Japanese judge who took a post as Japan's ambassador to Estonia before rescinding her seat on the ICC.[31] While Judge Ozaki ultimately stepped down, this violation of basic conflict of interest ethics brought yet more drama to the ICC. At the time of taking the ambassadorial post, Judge Ozaki was finishing her work on the bench for the trial against Bosco Ntaganda.[32] When it became known that Judge Ozaki had also taken a diplomatic post, Mr. Ntaganda's defense team argued that because she had violated conflict of interest rules, Mr. Ntaganda's conviction was invalid.[33]

[30] Antoine Buyse, "Protocol 14 Bis – The Interim Solution," *ECHR BLOG* (blog), May 4, 2009, http://echrblog.blogspot.com/2009/05/protocol-14-bis-interim-solution.html; Lucius Caflisch, "The Reform of the European Court of Human Rights: Protocol No. 14 and Beyond," *Human Rights Law Review* 6, no. 2 (2006): 403–415, https://doi.org/10.1093/hrlr/ngl007.

[31] Wairagala Wakabi, "Judge Ozaki Resigns Ambassadorial Post to Stay on Ntaganda Trial," *International Justice Monitor*, May 6, 2019, https://www.ijmonitor.org/2019/05/judge-ozaki-resigns-ambassadorial-post-to-stay-on-ntaganda-trial/; Kevin Jon Heller, "Judge Ozaki Must Resign – Or Be Removed," *Opinio Juris*, March 29, 2019, http://opiniojuris.org/2019/03/29/judge-ozaki-must-resign-or-be-removed/.

[32] Situation in the Democratic Republic of the Congo in the Case of the *Prosecutor v. Bosco Ntaganda*, Judgment, ICC-01/04-02/06 (Trial Chamber VI of the International Criminal Court, July 8, 2019), https://www.icc-cpi.int/CourtRecords/CR2019_03568.PDF.

[33] "Judge Ozaki Leaves the ICC," *International Justice Monitor*, November 26, 2019, https://www.ijmonitor.org/2019/11/judge-ozaki-leaves-the-icc/; Defence Team of Mr. Bosco Ntaganda, Public Redacted Version of "Request for Disqualification of Judge Ozaki," ICC-01/04-02/06 (The Ad Hoc Presidency of the International Criminal Court, May 21, 2019), https://www.icc-cpi.int/CourtRecords/CR2019_02885.PDF; Notification of the Observations of Judge Ozaki in Relation to the "Request for Disqualification of Judge Ozaki" dated 20 May 2019 (ICC-01/04-02/06-2347-Red) (The Presidency of the International Criminal Court, June 4, 2019), https://www.icc-cpi.int/CourtRecords/CR2019_03025.PDF; Notification of the Decision of the Plenary of Judges on the Defence Request for the Disqualification of Judge Kuniko Ozaki from the Case of the *Prosecutor v. Bosco Ntaganda*, Public with Confidential Annex, ICC-01/04-02/06 (The Presidency of the International Criminal Court, June 20, 2019), https://www.icc

These unforced errors are costly for the courts, as they must already counter a narrative that they are corrupt and biased institutions. The tribunals and their supporters must uphold excruciatingly high standards around conflicts of interest, the transparent stewardship of funds, and the rule of law.

Improving Transparency with Case Selection. A third area in which the tribunals and their supporters can improve the legal process, and the *optics* of the legal process, is in case selection. The ICC in particular has come under serious scrutiny for its case selection processes. In some instances, such as the Kenyan cases, the OTP has pursued situations where the evidence was weak or difficult to procure.[34] In other instances, such as Iraq, Syria, and Afghanistan, where the ICC's work has been slow and tentative (and met with serious resistance from the USA), the Court has come under attack for not pursuing situations more aggressively.[35]

The ICC maintains that case selection is decided solely through the legal bases set out in the Rome Statute.[36] Some scholarly research, however,

-cpi.int/CourtRecords/CR2019_03304.PDF; Defence Team of Mr. Bosco Ntaganda, Defence Appeal Brief-Part I, Public with Public Annexes A-E, ICC-01/04-02/06 A (The Appeals Chamber of the International Criminal Court, November 11, 2019), https://www.icc-cpi.int/CourtRecords/CR2019_06868.PDF.

[34] Catrina Stewart, "ICC on Trial Along with Kenya's Elite amid Claims of Bribery and Intimidation," *The Guardian*, October 1, 2013, www.theguardian.com/world/2013/oct/01/icc-trial-kenya-kenyatta-ruto; Michela Wrong, "Has Kenya Destroyed the ICC?" *Foreign Policy*, July 15, 2014, https://foreignpolicy.com/2014/07/15/has-kenya-destroyed-the-icc/; Tom Maliti, "Experts Say OTP Did Not Follow the Evidence in Collapsed Kenya Cases," *International Justice Monitor*, December 10, 2019, https://www.ijmonitor.org/2019/12/experts-says-otp-did-not-follow-the-evidence-in-collapsed-kenya-cases/; James Verini, "The Prosecutor and the President," *The New York Times Magazine*, June 22, 2016, https://www.nytimes.com/2016/06/26/magazine/international-criminal-court-moreno-ocampo-the-prosecutor-and-the-president.html.

[35] Matt Killingsworth, "Justice, Syria and the International Criminal Court," *Australian Institute of International Affairs*, December 24, 2019, https://www.internationalaffairs.org.au/australianoutlook/justice-syria-international-criminal-court/; "Iraq," International Criminal Court, n. d., https://www.icc-cpi.int/iraq; Angela Mudukuti, "Centre Stage Again – Allegations of UK War Crimes in Iraq," *Opinio Juris*, November 20, 2019, https://opiniojuris.org/2019/11/20/centre-stage-again-allegations-of-uk-war-crimes-in-iraq/; Lara Jakes and Michael Crowley, "U.S. to Penalize War Crimes Investigators Looking into American Troops," *The New York Times*, June 11, 2020, https://www.nytimes.com/2020/06/11/us/politics/international-criminal-court-troops-trump.html; "Afghanistan: ICC Appeals Chamber Authorises the Opening of an Investigation," *International Criminal Court*, March 5, 2020, https://www.icc-cpi.int/Pages/item.aspx?name=pr1516; Judgment on the Appeal against the Decision on the Authorisation of an Investigation into the Situation of the Islamic Republic of Afghanistan, ICC-02/17 OA4 (The Appeals Chamber of the International Criminal Court, March 5, 2020), https://www.icc-cpi.int/CourtRecords/CR2020_00828.PDF; David J. Scheffer, "The ICC's Probe into Atrocities in Afghanistan: What to Know," *Council on Foreign Relations*, March 6, 2020, https://www.cfr.org/article/iccs-probe-atrocities-afghanistan-what-know.

[36] Interview #296, October 2013.

suggests that power politics casts a shadow over the ICC's case selection processes.[37] The Office of the Prosecutor at the ICC and other international criminal courts is a political body as much as it is a judicial one.[38] By pretending otherwise, the ICC often invites more backlash than it mitigates. Indeed, a more transparent reckoning with the ICC's limitations to bring the largest and most powerful states under its fold would go a long way in mitigating backlash.

The ICC is not alone in needing to provide more transparency and efficiency with respect to case selection. The European Court of Human Rights, as documented in the previous two chapters, has long faced excessive delays as a result of the sheer number of petitions it receives each year. The volume of petitions, and particularly repeat petitions, is a function of poor compliance. While Protocol 14 has streamlined the admissibility process and updated the admissibility criteria, the delays that some petitioners experience during the case selection process continues to cast a pall over the ECtHR. Meanwhile, Protocol 14 has hidden, rather than addressed, systematic noncompliance through the repeat or clone case mechanism discussed in Chapter 6.[39] The Inter-American Human Rights System has a similarly vague case selection process. Like the ECtHR, the Inter-American Commission on Human Rights ultimately vets each petition it receives but some are accelerated while others sit on the shelf.[40] More capacity to process the petitions, as well as more transparent selection criteria could go a long way in fighting back against the narrative that tribunals only choose cases that will punish the Global South and privilege the powerful.

Reaffirming Fundamental Norms

In addition to improving their outreach and adjudicative work, the tribunals and their supporters must continuously and unwaveringly reaffirm the fundamental norms of human rights and accountability. The tribunals derive their normative and moral authority from their roles as guardians of human rights and accountability. No amount of capital or changes to the way the courts

---

[37] Christopher Rudolph, *Power and Principle: The Politics of International Criminal Courts* (Ithaca, NY: Cornell University Press, 2017); David Bosco, *Rough Justice: The International Criminal Court in a World of Power Politics* (New York: Oxford University Press, 2014).

[38] Alexandra Huneeus, "International Criminal Law by Other Means: The Quasi-Criminal Jurisdiction of the Human Rights Courts," *American Journal of International Law* 107, no. 1 (January 2013): 1–44, https://doi.org/10.5305/amerjintelaw.107.1.0001.

[39] Courtney Hillebrecht, *Domestic Politics and International Human Rights Tribunals: The Problem of Compliance* (New York: Cambridge University Press, 2014).

[40] Interview #464.

process cases or conduct outreach work can overcome the effects of a crumbling normative foundation.

While the tribunals have largely been able to rely on supporter states to uphold these norms, the example of Danish and British resistance to the ECtHR in Chapter 6 hinted at a larger and worrisome trend of traditionally supportive states' backtracking on their commitments to international justice. These stakeholder states, or steward states, as Emilie Hafner-Burton describes them,[41] play a critical role in protecting international human rights and criminal courts from attack and in advancing the fundamental norms that undergird the entire international justice system. Saving the international justice regime requires these stakeholder states to actively reaffirm fundamental justice norms. They can do this by mainstreaming the principles of human rights and accountability into other issue areas, expanding ratification, and by vocally supporting human rights and criminal courts and the norms they stand for in public forums.

Mainstreaming Human Rights and Accountability Norms. Mainstreaming human rights and accountability norms refers to the process that supporters and advocates can use to link human rights and accountability norms with other issue areas.[42] These efforts use a variety of tools – predominately international pressure and transnational mobilization – to change international and domestic policy and practice around human rights issues.[43] Mainstreaming hinges on proponents' belief that international organizations (IOs) are social environments.[44] International relations scholars have long suggested that IOs

---

[41]   Emilie M. Hafner-Burton, *Making Human Rights a Reality* (Princeton: Princeton University Press, 2013).

[42]   See, for example, Emilie Hafner-Burton and Mark A. Pollack, "Mainstreaming Gender in Global Governance," *European Journal of International Relations* 8, no. 3 (September 2002): 339–373, https://doi.org/10.1177/1354066102008003002; Christine Booth and Cinnamon Bennett, "Gender Mainstreaming in the European Union towards a New Conception and Practice of Equal Opportunities?" *European Journal of Women's Studies* 9, no. 4 (November 2002): 430–446, https://doi.org/10.1177/1350506802009004001; Mona Lena Krook, "Reforming Representation: The Diffusion of Candidate Gender Quotas Worldwide," *Politics & Gender* 2, no. 3 (September 2006): 303–327, https://doi.org/10.1017/S1 743923X06060107; Jacqui True and Michael Mintrom, "Transnational Networks and Policy Diffusion: The Case of Gender Mainstreaming," *International Studies Quarterly* 45, no. 1 (March 2001): 27–57, https://doi.org/10.1111/0020-8833.00181; Mona Lena Krook and Jacqui True, "Rethinking the Life Cycles of International Norms: The United Nations and the Global Promotion of Gender Equality," *European Journal of International Relations* 18, no. 1 (March 2012): 103–127, https://doi.org/10.1177/1354066110380963.

[43]   Krook, "Reforming Representation"; True and Mintrom, "Transnational Networks and Policy Diffusion"; Krook and True, "Rethinking the Life Cycles of International Norms."

[44]   Alastair Iain Johnston, "Treating International Institutions as Social Environments," *International Studies Quarterly* 45, no. 4 (December 2001): 487–515, https://doi.org/10.1111/00 20-8833.00212.

are sites of social learning. Through interacting with each other, with non-state, and transnational actors, and with the IOs themselves, states become socialized into particular norms and ideas.[45] According to True and Mintrom, the scholarship on mainstreaming typically looks at two different factors to explain mainstreaming and the success of norm diffusion: internal factors of the state "receiving" the norm, and social communications that connect the states to the norm, such as nongovernmental organizations and IOs. They suggest that a critical complement to these variables is an understanding of the individual agents that promote or reject the norm.[46] Indeed, much of the work on norm diffusion points to the role of civil society or transnational actors in promoting normative change.[47] As Park notes, even within IOs, civil society and transnational actors can play a major role in norm diffusion.[48]

Even in the midst of the backlash politics that have marked the past decade of international human rights and criminal adjudication, mainstreaming has been an important arrow in the quiver of international courts and their

[45] See, among many others, Jeffrey Checkel, ed., *International Institutions and Socialization in Europe* (New York: Cambridge University Press, 2007); Ryan Goodman and Derek Jinks, "How to Influence States: Socialization and International Human Rights Law," *Duke Law Journal* 54, no. 3 (December 2004): 621–703, https://scholarship.law.duke.edu/cgi/viewcontent .cgi?article=1240&context=dlj; Martha Finnemore, *National Interests in International Society* (Ithaca, NY: Cornell University Press, 1996); Michael Barnett and Martha Finnemore, *Rules for the World: International Organizations in Global Politics* (Ithaca, NY: Cornell University Press, 2004); Martha Finnemore, *The Purpose of Intervention: Changing Beliefs about the Use of Force* (Ithaca, NY: Cornell University Press, 2003); Jeffrey Checkel, "Why Comply? Social Learning and European Identity Change," *International Organization* 55, no. 3 (Summer 2001): 553–588, https://doi.org/10.1162/00208180152507551; Amitav Acharya, "How Ideas Spread: Whose Norms Matter? Norm Localization and Institutional Change in Asian Regionalism," *International Organization* 58, no. 2 (April 2004): 239–275, https://doi.org/10 .1017/S0020818304582024; Frank Schimmelfennig, "Strategic Calculation and International Socialization: Membership Incentives, Party Constellations, and Sustained Compliance in Central and Eastern Europe," *International Organization* 59, no. 4 (October 2005): 827–860, https://doi.org/10.1017/S0020818305050290; Jeffrey Checkel, "International Institutions and Socialization in Europe: Introduction and Framework," *International Organization* 59, no. 4 (October 2005): 801–826, https://doi.org/10.1017/S0020818305050289; Judith Kelley, "International Actors on the Domestic Scene: Membership Conditionality and Socialization by International Institutions," *International Organization* 58, no. 3 (July 2004): 425–457, https://doi.org/10.1017/S0020818304583017.
[46] True and Mintrom, "Transnational Networks and Policy Diffusion."
[47] Thomas Risse, Stephen C. Ropp, and Kathryn Sikkink, eds., *The Power of Human Rights: International Norms and Domestic Change* (Cambridge, UK: Cambridge University Press, 1999); Kathryn Sikkink, *The Justice Cascade: How Human Rights Prosecutions Are Changing World Politics*, 1st ed. (New York: W. W. Norton & Company, 2011); Kathryn Sikkink, "Human Rights, Principled Issue-Networks, and Sovereignty in Latin America," *International Organization* 47, no. 3 (Summer 1993): 411–441, https://doi.org/10.1017/S0020818300028010.
[48] Susan Park, "Theorizing Norm Diffusion within International Organizations," *International Politics* 43, no. 3 (2006): 342–361, https://doi.org/10.1057/palgrave.ip.8800149.

supporters. Perhaps no court has been the subject of more mainstreaming than the ICC, and for good reason. The campaign to mainstream the Rome Statute and accountability norms at the United Nations has been spearheaded by small or midsized countries like Argentina, Australia, Jordan, Lichtenstein, and Switzerland.[49] With the USA, China, Russia, India, and Israel, among others, being vocally opposed to both the ICC and the very norm of international criminal adjudication, the ICC's advocates and surrogates had to find a way to promote the work of the Court that could circumnavigate more powerful states while still building up the norm of accountability.

The goal of these states is to ensure that the imprint of the Rome Statute is in all of the UN Security Council's work. In interviews, stakeholders from a range of supporter states highlighted the importance of mainstreaming. These states cannot force other, more powerful states to ratify the Rome Statute or abide by accountability norms, but what they can do, as one interviewee and supporter of mainstreaming the Rome Statute noted, is put the issue of accountability on the table in *every* possible scenario. While supporter states recognize that international criminal accountability cannot, reasonably, be the first or only item on negotiating tables, they want to guarantee that it is part of each and every discussion. Moreover, according to this interviewee, the goal of supporter states is to ensure that those who support impunity have to justify their position each and every time.[50]

Mainstreaming the Rome Statute and accountability norms at the ICC follows the general contours of the previously discussed literature on mainstreaming and norm diffusion. Principled actors, particularly those at the UNSC, use their technical expertise and ability to set the organization's agenda to promote a particular norm, in this case, accountability. Particular delegations, and even individuals within those delegations, use mainstreaming to push back against backlash politics. As one interviewee explained, even at the height of the AU's threatened withdrawals from the ICC and conceptual challenges about the concept of complementarity, efforts at mainstreaming the Rome Statute and the norm of accountability meant that the UNSC discussed the ICC much more than it had in the past. Individual proponents of the ICC played an important part in (re)affirming the importance of the ICC to the UNSC.[51] Meanwhile, others, such as Lichtenstein's Stefan Barriga, assumed leadership roles in both formal and informal working groups on the ICC.[52]

---

[49] Interview #168, 2014.
[50] Interview #827, 2014.
[51] Interview #431, May 2014.
[52] Interview #959, 2014.

Mainstreaming efforts have had tangible effects on the UNSC's practices. For example, in 2014, the Commission of Inquiry for the DPRK (North Korea) explicitly referenced accountability norms.[53] The ICC's supporters applauded this move, as it marked an important integration of accountability norms into the UNSC's work, despite three of the five permanent members of the UNSC rejecting the ICC and its normative foundations.

Mainstreaming, like other efforts to promote international justice, however, is not a quick fix. Instead, it suffers regular setbacks and lacks relevance as political tides change. The Organization of American States is (in)famous for rejecting efforts at mainstreaming the work of the IAHRS into its political and diplomatic work. No matter how much work the IACmHR and IACtHR do, either in the courtroom or in the field, the OAS has proven to be impervious to efforts to mainstream human rights beyond those organs. Similarly, while the COE regularly references the European Convention on Human Rights and its norms, which are adjudicated by the ECtHR, the COE itself lacks relevance when compared to the European Union. Perhaps most importantly, while mainstreaming can be a powerful tool for not-so-powerful states to reaffirm human rights and criminal courts, it cannot overcome underlying normative divides. As one interviewee noted, how can advocates push for mainstreaming without universal norm acceptance?[54]

Focusing on Universal Ratification. One of the main drivers of backlash politics, as documented throughout this book, is the degree of normative division within the member states of international courts. High ratification rates can only hide, rather than fix, normative discontent. Nevertheless, advocates of international justice, particularly at the ICC, regularly promote the idea of universal ratification. As one interviewee explained, only two thirds of UN member states are parties to the Rome Statute, and the world's most powerful states are not among them. This gives credence to attacks on the ICC's fairness and legitimacy. Before pursuing more cases, he argued, the UNSC and the ICC must strengthen the norm of accountability through ratification.[55]

As the case studies throughout the book have illustrated, one of the main critiques of the ICC is that it offers selective – and, its critics argue, biased –

---

[53] Interview #951, 2014; Report of the Detailed Findings of the Commission of Inquiry on Human Rights in the Democratic People's Republic of Korea, Human Rights Council, Twenty-fifth Session, Agenda Item 4, Human Rights Situations that Require the Council's Attention, A/HRC/25/CRP.1 (Commission of Inquiry on Human Rights in the Democratic People's Republic of Korea, February 7, 2014), https://www.ohchr.org/EN/HRBodies/HRC/CoIDPRK/Pages/CommissionInquiryonHRinDPRK.aspx.

[54] Interview #951.

[55] Interview #951.

justice. Proponents suggest that universal ratification would help to mitigate that critique. Moreover, the fact that only 123 of 195 states have ratified the Rome Statute means that many atrocity crimes go unmonitored and perpetrators go unpunished.[56] The emphasis on expanding the reach of the Rome Statue is particularly strong among Asian and Latin American states.

Efforts at expanding the number of states that have ratified the Rome Statute are often met with resistance. State ratifications have leveled off over the past decade, with only 10 of the 123 states parties ratifying the Rome Statute in the past ten years.[57] Those that are still holding out on ratification will likely continue to do so indefinitely. The norm building must continue, however, and stakeholder states must be at the forefront of that initiative.

It is worth noting that universal ratification does not occupy the same political space in the regional human rights spheres, albeit for different reasons. In the European context, all COE states have already accepted the jurisdiction of the European Court of Human Rights, and the European Convention on Human Rights and Fundamental Freedoms enjoys universal ratification. The many and varied examples of backlash, not to mention varied rates of compliance, indicate that universal ratification is not the same at universal norm acceptance.

Advocates of the Inter-American Human Rights System have not paid much attention to universal ratification, not because they have already attained it, but rather because they know they never will. Supporters of the Inter-American Human Rights System recognize that the United States is perennially disinclined toward international human rights mechanisms, and no amount of pleading or pressure will force the USA to join the IACtHR.[58] The same is true for Canada and much of the English-speaking Caribbean. Meanwhile, IAHRS insiders sometimes whisper behind closed doors that having the USA work outside of the IAHRS provides them more latitude to pursue *their* agenda, rather than an *estadounidense* one.

Reaffirming Human Rights and Accountability Norms in the Age of Retrenchment. The past decade has ushered in a new wave of democratic retrenchment and backsliding. As discussed in Chapter 1, from the United

---

[56]   Interview #670, April 2014.

[57]   "States Parties – Chronological List," International Criminal Court, n.d., https://asp.icc-cpi.int/en_menus/asp/states%20parties/Pages/states%20parties%20_%20chronological%20list.aspx.

[58]   The USA is part of the IACmHR because it is a member of OAS and all OAS members are part of the IACmHR, although the USA generally rejects the IACmHR's individual petitioning authority. Camilleri and Edmonds, "The Inter-American Human Rights System in the Trump Era."

States to Hungary, Poland to Peru, democracy and democratic norms are facing real and sustained threats. In 2018, Freedom House declared democracy to be in "crisis."[59] In July 2020, whilst the world was in the midst of a global pandemic, and uncertainty about the forthcoming US presidential elections added to already high levels of anxiety, *The Atlantic* deemed the global order as "crumbling."[60]

These headlines, and the data that back them up, are alarming, particularly for human rights and accountability advocates and institutions. Democratic backsliding has been punctuated by attacks – physical, logistical, and legal – on human rights defenders, who are the very lifeblood of both domestic human rights change and international human rights and criminal adjudication.[61] Moreover, democracies, democratic principles, and the global order that powerful Western democracies forged out of the rubble of World War II are inextricably linked with the international justice regime.

Yet, we must be cautious about throwing out the proverbial baby with the bath water. The fact that democracy is "in crisis" and the world order is "crumbling" should be a rallying cry for supporting and protecting the international justice regime, not a white flag signaling its defeat. It is vitally important, then, for states, activists, and citizens who support the idea of human rights and accountability to stand up for international human rights and criminal courts, even, and especially, in the face of backlash politics. Academics and researchers have a key role to play in this process of resistance, and this book is just one small piece of a larger research agenda on both backlash politics and on how to shore up the international justice regime. The following section offers a brief overview of the contributions of this manuscript and outlines a research agenda for the future.

REVIEW OF THE MAIN ARGUMENT AND PATHWAYS FOR FUTURE RESEARCH

This book begins from the premise that backlash against international human rights and criminal courts is a subject worthy of rigorous academic research.

---

[59] Michael J. Abramowitz, "Freedom in the World 2018: Democracy in Crisis," Freedom House, n.d., https://freedomhouse.org/report/freedom-world/2018/democracy-crisis.

[60] William J. Burns, "The United States Needs a New Foreign Policy," *The Atlantic*, July 14, 2020, https://www.theatlantic.com/ideas/archive/2020/07/united-states-needs-new-foreign-policy/614110/.

[61] "State of Civil Society Report 2019, Part 4: Civil Society at the International Level," CIVICUS, 2019, https://www.civicus.org/documents/reports-and-publications/SOCS/2019/socs2019-year-in-review-part4_civil-society-at-the-international-level.pdf.

The novel definition of backlash, the typology of backlash politics, and the theoretical framework deployed throughout the book are all designed to begin a conversation about backlash and how the tribunals and their stakeholders can respond to it. As such, this work opens the door for a multipronged research agenda that includes additional conceptual, empirical, and practical work.

Defining Backlash

One of the contributions of this research is the definition of backlash offered in Chapter 1. As I outlined in the introduction, I understand backlash to have three defining features: (1) it is neither normatively "bad behavior" nor every instance of routine pushback; (2) it is part of a systemic, organized approach that targets the tribunals' authority; and (3) it is based in action, which can, but need not, be accompanied by anti-globalist or pro-sovereignty rhetoric. As I discuss in the introduction, without a clear definition of backlash, scholars and practitioners alike are unable to adequately identify, classify, or theorize about backlash. Absent a clear, *ex ante* definition of backlash, observers must rely on single instances of bad behavior, which limits generalizability and theorizing.

The research presented in this book also raises important questions about how backlash politics intersect with other forms of resistance, both to the courts in particular and to progressive politics and human rights and accountability norms more generally. With respect to the former, recent research has tried to differentiate between backlash and resistance, among other concepts. This is important foundational work, but understanding the full range of state responses requires not just typologies and definitions but also grounded empirical work. Incorporated into this work must also be research on cooperation, compliance, implementation, and enforcement. While the research in these areas is more developed than the research on backlash, a future research agenda could – and should – investigate the linkages across these different concepts. While researchers might consider them individually, states, elites, and the civil servants who work at international courts almost certainly do not.

Typologizing Backlash

The second main contribution of this book is its typology of backlash politics. As the previous chapters have illustrated, backlash politics can take many forms, from the more ostentatious manifestations of withdrawals from international courts to subtle conceptual challenges. Backlash also can take the form of creating alternatives to institutions within the international justice regime, or bureaucratic and budgetary restrictions. By providing a typology for backlash, this book facilitates a broad consideration of how states and elites can push back against the international justice regime and allows scholars and observers to move beyond isolated examples to consider a constellation of behaviors.

This typology also opens the door for future research about the conditions under which states choose some forms of backlash over others, when they double- or even triple-up on different forms of backlash, and how and why states sequence or time their backlash politics. While recent research has identified connections between regime type, ideology, and backlash politics,[62] the case studies in this book suggest that there is still much more to learn. In particular, the dependent variable needs to be more nuanced than a dichotomous yes/no answer. This is where the typology of backlash can inform a new wave of research on why states and elites reach for particular forms of backlash and when.

Explaining Backlash

The third contribution of this manuscript is the theoretical framework outlined in Chapter 2 and deployed throughout the book. This framework suggests that backlash is a function of four factors: (1) the tribunals' abiding dependence on states; (2) unresolved normative discontent at the tribunals; (3) the domestic consequences of international adjudication; and (4) the prospect of additional repression in the future. This framework is largely inductive, but future research can use this framework to generate testable hypotheses about why, when, and how states and elites engage in backlash politics.

In addition to the aforementioned research agenda about the form of backlash that states and elites deploy and why, the timing of backlash politics is a dependent variable rife for additional exploration. While the theoretical framework provides some guidance about when states and elites engage in backlash, future research could more closely examine the timing of backlash politics and its different forms. What role do variables such as upcoming elections, economic changes, and, particularly, salient rulings play in dictating the timing of backlash against international human rights and criminal courts?

The theoretical framework presented in Chapter 2 also suggests that the four factors that drive backlash are interrelated. A future research agenda

---

[62]   Voeten, "Populism and Backlashes against International Courts."

could consider the intersection and interaction of these four factors, as well as other variables, such as regime type, economic performance, and current human rights practices. While I suggest that the dependency of the tribunals on states and normative discontent are constant, underlying conditions, the domestic consequences of international adjudication, and the likelihood of states and elites' relying on additional repression in the future are more variable. Understanding the ebb and flow of these factors could lead to a broad research agenda that puts the framework developed here into conversation with a broader literature on the nexus between domestic and international politics.

Expanding the Scope

Perhaps the most salient and pressing topic for future study is the question of how backlash against international human rights and criminal courts is part of larger efforts at undermining multilateralism. The research presented throughout the book, particularly with respect to the creation of alternative mechanisms, or even bureaucratic and budgetary restrictions to conceptual challenges, suggests that the drivers of backlash are more complex than opposition to multilateralism or even the growth of populist and nationalist ideology on a global scale. The relationship does not appear to be as unidirectional as the contemporary narrative suggests. Future research can build on the typology of backlash to better understand the nexus between threats against multilateralism and the different types of backlash politics.

Finally, while this chapter and the case studies throughout the book have made some reference to how the tribunals and their supporters have responded to backlash politics, there is a significant amount of scholarship left to be written on this topic. Some questions that this book introduces for future research include: (1) How does the bureaucratic structure of courts influence the ways that the institutions respond to different forms of backlash? (2) How do the courts respond to backlash when it comes from long-standing opponents versus traditional supporters? (3) What role does civil society have in mitigating threats to international justice? (4) What doctrinal changes make courts more or less able to withstand these threats? Threats to international justice have been a consistent feature since the birth of the international justice regime, but justice institutions continue to evolve. As we enter into what could very well be a new era of international justice, keeping the research community active and engaged in asking and answering these questions is more important than ever.

***

LAW IS PREFERABLE TO WAR: SAVE THE INTERNATIONAL JUSTICE REGIME!

In 1947, a twenty-seven-year-old American lawyer, Ben Ferencz, walked into his first courtroom in Nuremburg, Germany. Mr. Ferencz was the Chief Prosecutor for the United States in the *Einsätzgruppen* case, which was part of the Nuremberg Trials. In Nuremberg, Mr. Ferencz secured convictions for each of the twenty-two suspects on trial. These suspects collectively murdered over two million people during the Holocaust. In his remarks to the court, Mr. Ferencz argued, "The case we present is a plea of humanity to law."[63] The decades of international human rights and criminal adjudication that followed Mr. Ferencz's groundbreaking case have made the same argument. Law is the means to resolving humanity's conflicts. It is the only path toward preserving and protecting human rights, human dignity, and world peace.

Too often scholars and policymakers point to international law's failure to stop all conflict and abuse as evidence that it is epiphenomenal at best and detrimental at worst.[64] These arguments fail to grasp the real importance of international human rights and criminal adjudication as a beacon of progress and peace. Creating, running, and preserving international human rights and criminal courts and the laws and norms that undergird them are acts of radical optimism. When put up against the challenges of state sovereignty and power politics, the fact that these courts exist at all is nothing short of amazing. That these courts can and do hold perpetrators to account, force states to pay reparations to victims, and encourage governments to change their policies is evidence of the potential for international human rights and criminal law to shape the trajectory of history. Before claiming that international justice is dead, or that the backlash is too severe for the courts to survive, we would be well-served to remember that international human rights and criminal law is, in fact, a plea of humanity against the threat of violence.

The international justice regime faces tremendous challenges. This much is obvious. But, so, too, is the dire need for accountability and human rights.

---

[63] "Biography," BenFerencz.org, n.d., https://benferencz.org/biography/; Benjamin B. Ferencz, "The Biggest Murder Trial in History," BenFerencz.org, n.d., https://benferencz.org/stories/1946-1949/the-biggest-murder-trial-in-history/.

[64] Jack Goldsmith and Stephen D. Krasner, "The Limits of Idealism," *Daedalus* 132, no. 1 (Winter 2003): 47–63, https://www.amacad.org/publication/limits-idealism; Stephen Hopgood, *The Endtimes of Human Rights* (Ithaca, NY: Cornell University Press, 2013); Samuel Moyn, *Not Enough: Human Rights in an Unequal World* (Cambridge, MA: The Belknap Press of Harvard University Press, 2018); Jack L. Goldsmith and Eric A. Posner, *The Limits of International Law* (New York: Oxford University Press, 2005); Eric A. Posner, *The Twilight of Human Rights Law* (New York: Oxford University Press, 2014).

A world without justice, or with war instead of law, is not inherently preferable to the contemporary justice regime, however flawed and incomplete it might be. Instead, international justice is worth fighting for, even amidst the backlash politics analyzed throughout this book. When facing the inevitable challenges ahead we would do well to remember another time-tested phrase from Mr. Ben Ferencz: "I prefer law to war under all circumstances."[65]

---

[65] Benjamin B. Ferencz and Katy Clark, "Benjamin Ferencz Interviewed on Radio by Katy Clark," *BenFerencz.org*, September 2001, https://benferencz.org/articles/2000-2004/benjamin-ferencz-interviewed-on-radio-by-katy-clark/.

Additional Human Rights Courts, Quasi-Judicial Human Rights Institutions, and International and Hybrid Criminal Tribunals

The international justice regime is vast. In addition to the European Court of Human Rights (ECtHR), the Inter-American Human Rights System (IAHRS), and the International Criminal Court (ICC), the courts and institutions below help to constitute the ever-evolving international justice regime.

The African Human and Peoples' Rights System (AHPRS). Like the IAHRS, the African Human and Peoples' Rights System has both a commission and a court. The AHPRS is part of the African Union (AU) and is the youngest of the regional systems. The AHPRS is based on the Banjul Charter on Human and Peoples' Rights, which is the broadest of the regional human rights conventions. Unlike the other regional human rights instruments, the Banjul Charter also endows the AHPRS with the authority to consider violations of other human rights instruments, such as the United Nations (UN) Convention against Torture (CAT).[1]

The African Commission on Human and Peoples' Rights (ACmHPR) is a quasi-judicial body, much like the Inter-American Commission on Human Rights (IACmHR), and can pass on cases to the African Court on Human and Peoples' Rights (ACtHPR), which issues binding judgments on cases. To date, the ACtHPR has had a slim docket of cases.

---

[1] "Basic Information," African Court on Human and Peoples' Rights, n.d., https://www.african-court.org/wpafc/basic-information/; African Court on Human and Peoples' Rights, "Rules of Court," *African Union*, 2010, https://www.african-court.org/en/images/Basic%20Documents/Final_Rules_of_Court_for_Publication_after_Harmonization_-_Final__English_7_sept_1_.pdf.

The International Criminal Tribunal for the Former Yugoslavia (ICTY). The ICTY was set up by the UN to deal with criminal investigations during and following the dissolution of the former Yugoslavia. The ICTY began its operations in 1993, trying perpetrators from across the former Yugoslavia and on many sides of the conflict. The ICTY closed in 2017, having completed its official UN mandate.[2]

The International Criminal Tribunal for Rwanda (ICTR). The UN established the ICTR to deal with the mass atrocity violations that took place during the Rwandan genocide in 1994. The ICTR, which is based in Tanzania, handed down seventy-one judgments. The ICTR closed in 2015 and any remaining work was shifted to the UN's International Residual Mechanism for Criminal Tribunals.[3] The ICTR, which came under fire for being far removed from the victims and for providing one-sided justice, was also part of the larger Rwandan justice system, which includes domestic criminal trials and local reconciliation mechanisms commonly known as gacaca.[4]

The Extraordinary Chambers in the Courts of Cambodia (ECCC). The Extraordinary Chambers in the Courts of Cambodia, also known as the Khmer Rouge Tribunal, was established in 2006. The ECCC's mandate is to try those most responsible for the atrocity crimes committed during the Khmer Rouge's rule in Cambodia from 1975 to 1979. Although the ECCC sits within the Cambodian justice system, it is cosponsored by the United Nations. Like the other criminal tribunals, the Khmer Rouge Tribunal has a limited scope, which includes torture, murder, religious persecution, genocide, crimes against humanity, violations of the Geneva Conventions, destruction of cultural property, and crimes against internationally protected individuals. In addition to its casework, which includes only four cases, the ECCC has a broad outreach program. This outreach program includes public hearings, study tours and court visits, among other activities. Despite the ECCC's promising outreach program,

---

[2] Owen Bowcott, "Yugoslavia Tribunal Closes, Leaving a Powerful Legacy of War Crimes Justice," *The Guardian,* December 20, 2017, https://www.theguardian.com/law/2017/dec/20/former-yugoslavia-war-crimes-tribunal-leaves-powerful-legacy-milosevic-karadzic-mladic.

[3] UN-ICTR External Relations and Communication Outreach Unit, "ICTR Expected to Close Down in 2015," *United Nations,* February 2, 2015, http://unictr.unmict.org/en/news/ictr-expected-close-down-2015.

[4] Hanna K. Morrill, "Challenging Impunity? The Failure of the International Criminal Tribunal for Rwanda to Prosecute Paul Kagame," *Brooklyn Journal of International Law* 37, no. 2 (2012): 683–712, https://core.ac.uk/download/pdf/228597499.pdf.

however, the ECCC has struggled to maintain its financial integrity and process its cases.[5]

The Special Court for Sierra Leone (SCSL). The Special Court for Sierra Leone, like the ECCC, is a hybrid court that brings together both domestic and international resources. The SCSL was established in 2002 upon the Government of Sierra Leone's request to the United Nations to create a criminal court to address the crimes that were committed during the civil war that tore through Sierra Leone from 1991 to 2002. In many respects, the SCSL was a successful court: it was the first criminal court to be headquartered in the country where the crimes were committed; it was the first court to be funded by voluntary contributions; and it was the first international court to complete its adjudicative mandate and move to a residual mechanism. The SCSL issued thirteen indictments, which led to four trials and nine convictions. Those convicted are currently imprisoned in Rwanda (except for Charles Taylor, who is serving his fifty-year sentence in the UK).[6]

The Special Tribunal for Lebanon (STL). The Special Tribunal for Lebanon is a unique international criminal tribunal in many ways. The STL is a hybrid court that draws on a combination of domestic and international law, staff, and funding. The STL was set up to find and try those accused of assassinating the Lebanese Prime Minister, Rafic Hariri, and killing twenty-one others in a February 2005 car bombing, making it the only international or hybrid court designed to deal with a singular act of terrorism.[7] The STL's roots can be traced to a UN fact-finding mission that found that the state's investigations into the assassination did not meet international standards. This, in turn, contributed to the creation of the UN International Independent Investigation Commission (UNIIIC), which was charged with facilitating the investigation into Hariri's assassination.[8] Over time, the

---

5   "ECCC at a Glance," *Extraordinary Chambers in the Courts of Cambodia*, April 2014, https://www.eccc.gov.kh/sites/default/files/ECCC%20at%20a%20Glance%20-%20EN%20-%20April%202014_FINAL.pdf.

6   "The Special Court for Sierra Leone, the Residual Special Court for Sierra Leone," The Residual Special Court for Sierra Leone and the SCSL Public Archives, Freetown and The Hague, n.d., www.rscsl.org/; Lansana Gberie, "The Special Court for Sierra Leone Rests – for Good," *United Nations Africa Renewal*, April 2014, https://www.un.org/africarenewal/magazine/april-2014/special-court-sierra-leone-rests-%E2%80%93-good; George Gelaga King, *Eleventh and Final Report of the President of the Special Court for Sierra Leone* (Freetown, Sierra Leone: Special Court of Sierra Leone, 2013), www.rscsl.org/Documents/AnRpt11.pdf. It is worth noting that the trial of Charles Taylor took place in The Hague for security reasons. He is currently in jail in the United Kingdom.

7   Ronen Bergman, "The Hezbollah Connection," *The New York Times Magazine*, February 10, 2015, https://www.nytimes.com/2015/02/15/magazine/the-hezbollah-connection.html.

8   United Nations Security Council Resolution 1595 (United Nations Security Council, 2005).

Lebanese government asked the UN Security Council (UNSC) to create a more formal body to investigate the assassination.[9] Domestically, creating a formal tribunal was fraught with delays and vetoes. Fouad Siniora, the Prime Minister who negotiated the creation of the STL with the UN, failed to get a parliamentary vote to support the passage of the tribunal and had to ask the UNSC to form the STL on its own accord. In 2007, the UNSC established the STL under the Security Council's Chapter VII powers without Lebanese parliamentary approval.[10] Hezbollah and its political affiliates in Lebanon and Iran have spent the last decade trying to undermine the STL. Despite the odds, the court continues its work.

---

[9] United Nations Security Council Resolution 1664 (United Nations Security Council, 2006).
[10] United Nations Security Council Resolution 1757 (United Nations Security Council, 2007).

Select Bibliography

"700 Organizations in the Americas Denounce the OAS' Attempt to Weaken Human Rights Defense System." *Center for Justice and International Law*, March 28, 2012. https://cejil.org/en/comunicados/700-organizations-americas-denounce-oas%E2%80%99-attempt-weaken-human-rights-defense-system.

"2019 Election for the Advisory Committee on Nominations." *Coalition for the International Criminal Court*, November 1, 2019. http://coalitionfortheicc.org/news/20191101/2019-election-advisory-committee-nominations.

"5947th Meeting (2008), S/PV.5947." *United Nations Security Council*, July 31, 2008. https://www.securitycouncilreport.org/atf/cf/%7B65BFCF9B-6D27-4E9C-8CD3-CF6E4FF96FF9%7D/Sudan%20SPV5947.pdf.

ABA-ICC Project. "The US-ICC Relationship." n.d. https://www.aba-icc.org/about-the-icc/the-us-icc-relationship/.

Abbott, Kenneth W. and Duncan Snidal. "Why States Act through Formal International Organizations." *Journal of Conflict Resolution* 42, no. 1 (February 1998): 3–32, https://doi.org/10.1177/0022002798042001001.

Abebe, Daniel. "Does International Human Rights Law in African Courts Make a Difference?" *Virginia Journal of International Law* 56, no. 3 (2017): 527–584. https://chicagounbound.uchicago.edu/cgi/viewcontent.cgi?article=12639&context=journal_articles.

Abebe, Daniel, and Tom Ginsburg. "The Dejudicialization of International Politics?" *International Studies Quarterly* 63, no. 3 (September 2019): 521–530. https://doi.org/10.1093/isq/sqz032.

Abramowitz, Michael J. "Freedom in the World 2018: Democracy in Crisis." *Freedom House*. n.d. https://freedomhouse.org/report/freedom-world/2018/democracy-crisis.

Acharya, Amitav. "How Ideas Spread: Whose Norms Matter? Norm Localization and Institutional Change in Asian Regionalism." *International Organization* 58, no. 2 (April 2004): 239–275. https://doi.org/10.1017/S0020818304582024.

Administrative Tribunal. "Reinstatement of Nine Appeals before the Administrative Tribunal." *Council of Europe*, October 14, 2019. https://www.coe.int/en/web/tribunal/news-2019/-/asset_publisher/mOvdvRaqOyoz/content/reinstatement-of-nine-appeals-before-the-administrative-tribunal.

"Afghanistan: ICC Appeals Chamber Authorises the Opening of an Investigation." *International Criminal Court*, March 5, 2020. https://www.icc-cpi.int/Pages/item.aspx?name=pr1516.

"African Civil Society Urges African States Parties to the Rome Statute to Reaffirm Their Commitment to the ICC." *Human Rights Watch*, July 30, 2009. https://www.hrw.org/news/2009/07/30/african-civil-society-urges-african-states-parties-rome-statute-reaffirm-their.

African Commission on Human and Peoples' Rights. "Decisions on Communications." n.d. https://www.achpr.org/communications.

"Information Sheet No. 1: Establishment." *Secretariat of the Commission on Human and Peoples' Rights*, n.d. https://archives.au.int/bitstream/handle/123456789/2073/Information%20Sheet%20no1_E.pdf?sequence=1&isAllowed=y.

African Court on Human and Peoples' Rights. "Rules of Court." *African Union*, 2010. https://www.african-court.org/en/images/Basic%20Documents/Final_Rules_of_Court_for_Publication_after_Harmonization_-_Final__English_7_sept_1_.pdf

    "Frequent Questions." n.d. http://en.african-court.org/index.php/faqs/frequent-questions#Criminal.

    "Contentious Matters: Pending Cases." n.d. https://en.african-court.org/index.php/cases#pending-cases.

    "Welcome to the African Court." n.d. https://en.african-court.org/.

    "Basic Information." n.d. https://www.african-court.org/wpafc/basic-information/.

African Union. "List of Countries Which Have Signed, Ratified/Acceded to the Protocol on the Statute of the African Court of Justice and Human Rights." June 18, 2020. https://au.int/sites/default/files/treaties/36396-sl-PROTOCOL%20ON%20THE%20STATUTE%20OF%20THE%20AFRICAN%20COURT%20OF%20JUSTICE%20AND%20HUMAN%20RIGHTS.pdf.

"African Union Backs Mass Withdrawal from ICC." *BBC News*, February 1, 2017. https://www.bbc.com/news/world-africa-38826073#:~:text=The%20government%20later%20announced%20that,The%20ICC%20and%20global%20justice%3A&text=Only%20Africans%20prosecuted%20so%20far.

"African Union Demands Changes in ICC, but Won't Withdraw from It." *International Business Times News*, October 12, 2013. Nexis Uni.

"African Union Summit on ICC Pullout over Ruto Trial." *BBC News*, September 20, 2013. https://www.bbc.com/news/world-africa-24173557.

Afshari, Reza. "On Historiography of Human Rights Reflections on Paul Gordon Lauren's The Evolution of International Human Rights: Visions Seen." *Human Rights Quarterly* 29, no. 1 (February 2007): 1–67. https://doi.org/10.1353/hrq.2007.0000.

Ainley, Kirsten. "The International Criminal Court on Trial." *Cambridge Review of International Affairs* 24, no. 3 (September 2011): 309–333. https://doi.org/10.1080/09557571.2011.558051.

Akande, Dap. "The African Union Takes on the ICC Again: Are African States Really Turning from the ICC?" *EJIL: Talk!* (blog), July 26, 2011. www.ejiltalk.org/the-african-union-takes-on-the-icc-again/.

Akande, Dapo, and Sangeeta Shah. "Immunities of State Officials, International Crimes, and Foreign Domestic Courts." *European Journal of International Law* 21, no. 4 (November 2010): 815–852. https://doi.org/10.1093/ejil/chq080.

Akhavan, Payam. "The International Criminal Court in Context: Mediating the Global and Local in the Age of Accountability." *The American Journal of International Law* 97, no. 3 (July 2003): 712–721. https://doi.org/10.2307/3109871.

———. "Are International Criminal Tribunals a Disincentive to Peace? Reconciling Judicial Romanticism with Political Realism." *Human Rights Quarterly* 31, no. 3 (August 2009): 624–654. https://doi.org/10.1353/hrq.0.0096.

Aksenova, Marina. "Anchugov and Gladkov Is Not Enforceable: The Russian Constitutional Court Opines in Its First ECtHR Implementation Case." *Opinion Juris*, April 25, 2016. http://opiniojuris.org/2016/04/25/anchugov-and-gladkov-is-not-enforceable-the-russian-constitutional-court-opines-in-its-first-ecthr-implementation-case/.

"Al Bashir Case: ICC Pre-Trial Chamber II Decides Not to Refer South Africa's Non-cooperation to the ASP or the UNSC." *International Criminal Court*, July 6, 2017. https://www.icc-cpi.int/Pages/item.aspx?name=pr1320.

Al Hussein, Prince Zeid Raad, Bruno Stagno Ugarte, Christian Wenaweser, and Tiina Intelman. "The International Criminal Court Needs Fixing." *Atlantic Council*, April 24, 2019. https://www.atlanticcouncil.org/blogs/new-atlanticist/the-international-criminal-court-needs-fixing.

"Al-Senussi Case: Appeals Chamber Confirms Case Is Inadmissible before ICC." *International Criminal Court*, July 24, 2014. https://www.icc-cpi.int/Pages/item.aspx?name=pr1034&ln=en.

Allain, Jean. *A Century of International Adjudication: The Rule of Law and Its Limits.* The Hague: T.M.C. Asser Press, 2000.

Allebas, Tessa. "The ICC and Victor's Justice: How to Move Away from the Stigma?" *The Hague Institute for Global Justice*, July 19, 2013. www.thehagueinstituteforglobaljustice.org/latest-insights/latest-insights/commentary/the-icc-and-victors-justice-how-to-move-away-from-the-stigma/.

Alter, Karen J. "Who Are the Masters of the Treaty? European Governments and the European Court of Justice." *International Organization* 52, no. 1 (Winter 1998): 121–147. https://doi.org/10.1162/002081898550572.

———. "Delegation to International Courts and the Limits of Re-Contracting Political Power." In *Delegation and Agency in International Organizations*, edited by Darren G. Hawkins, David A. Lake, Daniel L. Nielson, and Michael J. Tierney, 312–338. Cambridge, UK: Cambridge University Press, 2006. https://doi.org/10.1017/CBO9780511491368.012.

———. "Agents or Trustees? International Courts in Their Political Context." *European Journal of International Relations* 14, no. 1 (March 2008): 33–63. https://doi.org/10.1177/1354066107087769.

———. *The New Terrain of International Law: Courts, Politics, Rights.* Princeton, NJ: Princeton University Press, 2014.

Alter, Karen J., James T. Gathii, and Laurence R. Helfer. "Backlash against International Courts in West, East and Southern Africa: Causes and Consequences." *European Journal of International Law* 27, no. 2 (May 2016): 293–328. https://doi.org/10.1093/ejil/chw019.

Alter, Karen J., Laurence R. Helfer, and Mikael Rask Madsen. "How Context Shapes the Authority of International Courts." *Law and Contemporary Problems* 79, no. 1 (2016): 1–36. https://scholarship.law.duke.edu/lcp/vol79/iss1/1/.

eds. *International Court Authority*. Oxford: Oxford University Press, 2018.

Alter, Karen J., and Michael Zürn. "Conceptualising Backlash Politics: Introduction to a Special Issue on Backlash Politics in Comparison." *The British Journal of Politics and International Relations* 22, no. 4 (November 2020): 563–584. https://doi.org/10 .1177/1369148120947958.

Ambos, Kai. "Room for Improvement." *Development and Cooperation*, December 13, 2011. https://www.dandc.eu/en/article/promising-change-guard-international-criminal-court.

Amnesty International. *A Guide to the African Charter on Human and Peoples' Rights*. Chalgrove, UK: Amnesty International Publications, 2006. https://www .amnesty.org/download/Documents/76000/ior630052006en.pdf.

"Africa: Open Letter to the African States Parties to the International Criminal Court." May 3, 2012. https://www.amnesty.org/en/documents/afr01/007/2012/en/.

"Malabo Protocol: Legal and Institutional Implications." January 22, 2016. https:// www.amnesty.org/en/documents/afr01/3063/2016/en.

Malabo Protocol: Legal and Institutional Implications of the Merged and Expanded African Court. London: Amnesty International Ltd, 2016. https://www.amnesty.org /download/Documents/AFR0130632016ENGLISH.PDF.

"A Summary of Amnesty International's Concerns in the Russian Federation." October 19, 2016. https://www.amnesty.org/download/Documents/EU R4650092016ENGLISH.pdf.

Malabo Protocol: Legal and Institutional Implications of the Merged and Expanded African Court – Snapshots. London: Amnesty International Ltd, 2017. www .coalitionfortheicc.org/document/africa-malabo-protocol-legal-and-institutional-implications-merged-and-expanded-african.

"Arab States: Press Sudan on Darfur Aid." *Human Rights Watch*, March 29, 2009. https://www.hrw.org/news/2009/03/29/arab-states-press-sudan-darfur-aid.

Arai-Takahashi, Yutaka. *The Margin of Appreciation Doctrine and the Principle of Proportionality in the Jurisprudence of the ECHR*. Antwerp, Oxford, New York: Intersentia, 2002.

Arat, Zehra F. Kabasakal. "Global Normative Encounters: Human Rights and Their Rivals." *APSA 2020 Annual Meeting Paper* (2020).

Aregawi, Bethel. "The Politicisation of the International Criminal Court by United Nations Security Council Referral." Conflict Trends, ACCORD, no. 2 (2017). https://www.accord.org.za/conflict-trends/politicisation-international-criminal-court-united-nations-security-council-referrals/.

Assembly of Heads of State and Government. "Decision on the Protocol on Amendments to the Protocol on the Statute of the African Court of Justice and Human Rights Doc. Assembly/Au/13(Xix)A." *African Union*, n.d. https://archives .au.int/bitstream/handle/123456789/68/Assembly%20AU%20Dec%20427%20%28 XIX%29%20_E.pdf?sequence=1&isAllowed=y.

Assembly of States Parties. *Report of the Court on Human Resources Management*. The Hague: International Criminal Court, 2015. https://asp.icc-cpi.int/iccdocs/asp_ docs/ASP14/ICC-ASP-14-7-ENG.pdf#search=Japan%28DetectedLanguage%3D %22en%22%29.

"Proposed Programme Budget for 2020 of the International Criminal Court, Eighteenth Session, The Hague, 2–7 December 2019, ICC-ASP/18/10."

International Criminal Court, July 25, 2019. https://asp.icc-cpi.int/iccdocs/asp_do cs/ASP18/ICC-ASP-18-10-ENG.pdf.

Associated Press in Blantyre. "African Union Pulls Summit from Malawi in Row over Sudan's President." *The Guardian*, June 8, 2012. www.theguardian.com/world/20 12/jun/08/african-union-malawi-summit-sudan.

Asthana, Anushka, and Rowena Mason. "UK Must Leave European Convention on Human Rights, Says Theresa May." *The Guardian*, April 25, 2016. https://www .theguardian.com/politics/2016/apr/25/uk-must-leave-european-convention-on-human-rights-theresa-may-eu-referendum.

Ausderan, Jacob. "How Naming and Shaming Affects Human Rights Perceptions in the Shamed Country." *Journal of Peace Research* 51, no. 1 (January 2014): 81–95. https://doi.org/10.1177/0022343313510014.

Ba, Oumar. *States of Justice: The Politics of the International Criminal Court*. Cambridge, UK: Cambridge University Press, 2020.

Barbosa dos Santos, Fabio Luis. "UNASUR in a Comparative Light: The Relations with Venezuela and Colombia." *Brazilian Journal of Strategy & International Relations* 5, no. 10 (July/December 2016): 229–251. https://doi.org/10.22456/2238-6912.67243.

Barnett, Michael, and Martha Finnemore. *Rules for the World: International Organizations in Global Politics*. Ithaca, NY: Cornell University Press, 2004.

Barton, Dona-Gene, Courtney Hillebrecht, and Sergio C. Wals. "A Neglected Nexus: Human Rights and Public Perceptions." *Journal of Human Rights* 16, no. 3 (2017): 293–313. https://doi.org/10.1080/14754835.2016.1261013.

Bass, Gary Jonathan. *Stay the Hand of Vengeance: The Politics of War Crimes Tribunals*. Princeton, NJ: Princeton University Press, 2000.

Bates, Ed. "The Brighton Declaration and the 'Meddling Court,'" *UK Human Rights Blog*, April 22, 2012, https://ukhumanrightsblog.com/2012/04/22/the-brighton-declaration-and-the-meddling-court.

BBC. "African Union Defies ICC over Bashir Extradition." *ABC News*, July 4, 2009. www.abc.net.au/news/2009-07-05/african-union-defies-icc-over-bashir-extradition /1341682.

Beck, Nathaniel. "Is Causal-Process Observation an Oxymoron?" *Political Analysis* 14, no. 3 (Summer 2006): 347–352: https://doi.org/10.1093/pan/mpj015.

Bell, Christine. "Lex Pacificatoria Colombiana: Colombia's Peace Accord in Comparative Perspective." *AJIL Unbound* 110 (2016): 165–171. https://doi.org/10 .1017/S2398772300003019.

BenFerencz.org. "Biography." n.d. https://benferencz.org/biography/.

Bergman, Ronen. "The Hezbollah Connection." *The New York Times Magazine*, February 10, 2015. https://www.nytimes.com/2015/02/15/magazine/the-hezbollah-connection.html.

von Bernstorff, Jochen. "Procedures of Decision-Making and the Role of Law in International Organizations." *German Law Journal* 9, no. 11 (November 2008): 1939–1964. https://doi.org/10.1017/S2071832200000705.

Berti, Benedetta. "Peace vs. Justice in Lebanon: The Domestic and Regional Implications of the UN Special Tribunal." *Strategic Assessment* 13, no. 4 (January 2011): 101–111. https://strategicassessment.inss.org.il/en/articles/peace-vs-justice-in-lebanon-the-domestic-and-regional-implications-of-the-un-special-tribunal/.

Bicudo, Helio. "The Inter-American Commission on Human Rights and the Process of Democratization in Peru." *Human Rights Brief* 9, no. 2 (Winter 2002): 18–20. https://digitalcommons.wcl.american.edu/hrbrief/vol9/iss2/5/.

Biron, Carey L. "Pan-American Rights Commission 'Under Threat.'" *Inter Press Service*, November 1, 2012. www.ipsnews.net/2012/11/pan-american-rights-commission-under-threat/.

Blum, Yehuda Z. "Consistently Inconsistent: The International Court of Justice and the Former Yugoslavia (Croatia v. Serbia)." *The American Journal of International Law* 103, no. 2 (April 2009): 264–271. https://doi.org/10.2307/20535149.

von Bogdandy, Armin. "The Democratic Legitimacy of International Courts: A Conceptual Framework." *Theoretical Inquiries in Law* 14, no. 2 (2013): 361–380. https://doi.org/10.1515/til-2013-019.

von Bogdandy, Armin, and Ingo Venzke. "On the Functions of International Courts: An Appraisal in Light of Their Burgeoning Public Authority." *Leiden Journal of International Law* 26, no. 1 (March 2013): 49–72. https://doi.org/10.1017/S0922156512000647.

Booth, Christine, and Cinnamon Bennett. "Gender Mainstreaming in the European Union towards a New Conception and Practice of Equal Opportunities?" *European Journal of Women's Studies* 9, no. 4 (November 2002): 430–446. https://doi.org/10.1177/135050680200090040401.

Born, Gary, Danielle Morris, and Stephanie Forrest. "A Margin of Appreciation: Appreciating Its Irrelevance in International Law." *Harvard International Law Journal* 61, no. 1 (2020): 65–134. https://heinonline.org/HOL/P?h=hein.journals/hilj61&i=71.

von Borzyskowski, Inken, and Felicity Vabulas. "Credible Commitments? Explaining IGO Suspensions to Sanction Political Backsliding." *International Studies Quarterly* 63, no. 1 (March 2019): 139–152. https://doi.org/10.1093/isq/sqy051.

Bosco, David. *Rough Justice: The International Criminal Court in a World of Power Politics*. New York: Oxford University Press, 2014.

Bowcott, Owen. "Backlog at European Court of Human Rights Falls below 100,000 Cases." *The Guardian*, January 30, 2014. www.theguardian.com/law/2014/jan/30/european-court-human-rights-case-backlog-falls.

"Yugoslavia Tribunal Closes, Leaving a Powerful Legacy of War Crimes Justice." *The Guardian*, December 20, 2017. https://www.theguardian.com/law/2017/dec/20/former-yugoslavia-war-crimes-tribunal-leaves-powerful-legacy-milosevic-karadzic-mladic.

Bowen, Sally. "Peru's New Constitution Seems Sure to Satisfy the President's Desires." *The Christian Science Monitor*, July 27, 1993. https://www.csmonitor.com/1993/0727/27062.html.

Bowring, Bill. "The Russian Federation, Protocol No. 14 (and 14bis), and the Battle for the Soul of the ECHR." *Goettingen Journal of International Law* 2, no. 2 (2010): 589–617. https://www.gojil.eu/issues/22/22_article_bowring.pdf.

Brasseur, Anne. "PACE President Concerned by Decision on 'Selective Implementation' of Strasbourg Rulings in Russia." *Parliamentary Assembly of the Council of Europe*, July 16, 2015. http://assembly.coe.int/nw/xml/News/News-View-EN.asp?newsid=5720&cat=15.

Bratza, Sir Nicolas. "High Level Conference, Brighton 18–20 April 2012." *European Court of Human Rights*, April 18, 2012. https://www.echr.coe.int/Documents/ Speech_20120420_Bratza_Brighton_ENG.pdf.

"Brazil Breaks Relations with Human Rights Commission over Belo Monte Dam." *Latin America News Dispatch*, May 3, 2011. http://latindispatch.com/2011/05/03/ brazil-breaks-relations-with-human-rights-commission-over-belo-monte-dam/.

Brody, Reed. "Victims Bring a Dictator to Justice: The Case of Hissène Habré." *Brot für die Welt*, June 2017. https://www.brot-fuer-die-welt.de/fileadmin/mediapool/2_ Downloads/Fachinformationen/Analyse/Analysis70-The_Habre_Case.pdf.

Bureau of the Congress. "Status of Turkey and Budgetary Implications." *Council of Europe*, October 3, 2018. https://rm.coe.int/09000016808e474c.

"Meeting of the Bureau of the Congress Wednesday 11 September 2019." *Council of Europe*, October 17, 2019. https://rm.coe.int/09000016809839e6.

Bureau of Western Hemisphere Affairs. "U.S. Relations with Venezuela: Bilateral Relations Fact Sheet." *U.S. Department of State*, July 6, 2020. https://www .state.gov/u-s-relations-with-venezuela/#:~:text=Venezuela's%20Membership%2 0in%20International%20Organizations&text=Venezuela%20is%20a%20found ing%20member,(CELAC)%2C%20and%20PetroCaribe.

Burke-White, William W. "Proactive Complementarity: The International Criminal Court and National Courts in the Rome System of International Justice." *Harvard International Law Journal* 49, no. 1 (Winter 2008): 53–108. https://scholarship .law.upenn.edu/faculty_scholarship/138/.

Burkov, Anton. "Russia and the European Court of Human Rights." *Centre for European Policy Studies Commentary: Thinking Ahead for Europe*, May 10, 2010. http://aei.pitt.edu/14499/1/May_Burkov_on_Russia_and_the_ECHR.pdf.

Burns, William J. "The United States Needs a New Foreign Policy." *The Atlantic*, July 14, 2020. https://www.theatlantic.com/ideas/archive/2020/07/united-states- needs-new-foreign-policy/614110/.

Burt, Jo-Marie. "Fujimori vs. the Inter-American Court." *The North American Congress on Latin America*, September 25, 2007. https://nacla.org/article/fujimori-vs-inter- american-court.

Buyse, Antoine. "Protocol 14 Bis – The Interim Solution." *ECHR BLOG* (blog), May 4, 2009. http://echrblog.blogspot.com/2009/05/protocol-14-bis-interim- solution.html.

Cabato, Regina. "Philippines Leaves International Criminal Court as Duterte Probe Is Underway." *The Washington Post*, March 18, 2019. https://www.washingtonpost .com/world/asia_pacific/philippines-leaves-international-criminal-court-as-duterte- probe-underway/2019/03/18/f929d1b6-4952-11e9-93d0-64dbcf38ba41_story.html.

Caflisch, Lucius. "The Reform of the European Court of Human Rights: Protocol No. 14 and Beyond." *Human Rights Law Review* 6, no. 2 (2006): 403–415. https:// doi.org/10.1093/hrlr/ngl007.

Calcaneo Sanchez, Alfonso. "The Dominican Withdrawal from the Jurisdiction of the Inter-American Court of Human Rights: A Legal and Contextual Analysis." Master's thesis, University of Oslo, 2015. https://www.duo.uio.no/handle/10852/ 46874.

Çali, Başak. "Perceptions of the Authority of the European Court of Human Rights amongst Apex Court Judges in the UK, Germany, Ireland, Turkey and Bulgaria:

Summary of Findings." *University College London*, 2011. https://ecthrproject
.files.wordpress.com/2011/05/domestic-judges-ecthr-summary-findingsbw.pdf.

The Authority of International Law: Obedience, Respect, and Rebuttal (Oxford: Oxford University Press, 2015).

Çali, Başak, Anne Koch, and Nicola Bruch. "The Legitimacy of Human Rights Courts: A Grounded Interpretivist Analysis of the European Court of Human Rights." *Human Rights Quarterly* 35, no. 4 (November 2013): 955–984. https://doi.org/10
.1353/hrq.2013.0057.

Camilleri, Michael, and Danielle Edmonds. "The Inter-American Human Rights System in the Trump Era." *The Dialogue*, June 15, 2017. https://www
.thedialogue.org/analysis/the-inter-american-human-rights-system-in-the-trump-era/.

"Canciller Venezolano insta a países Latinoamericanos a abandonar la CIDH." *Agence France Presse*, May 3, 2012. Nexis Uni.

Cannon, Brendon J., Dominic R. Pkalya, and Bosire Maragia. "The International Criminal Court and Africa: Contextualizing the Anti-ICC Narrative." *African Journal of International Criminal Justice* 2, no. 1–2 (December 2016). https://doi
.org/10.5553/AJ/2352068X2016002001001.

Caplan, Lee M. "State Immunity, Human Rights, and Jus Cogens: A Critique of the Normative Hierarchy Theory." *The American Journal of International Law* 97, no. 4 (October 2003): 741–781. https://doi.org/10.2307/3133679.

Cardenas, Sonia. *Conflict and Compliance: State Responses to International Human Rights Pressure*. Philadelphia: University of Pennsylvania Press, 2007.

Carey, Sabine C. "The Dynamic Relationship between Protest and Repression." *Political Research Quarterly* 59, no. 1 (March 2006): 1–11. https://doi.org/10.1177
/1065912906059000101.

"CARICOM Divided on Venezuela at OAS Assembly." *The New York CaribNews*, October 29, 2020. https://www.nycaribnews.com/articles/caricom-divided-on-venezuela-at-oas-assembly/.

Carofiglio, Domenico. "To What Extent Have Politics Restricted the ICC's Effectiveness?" *E-International Relations*, December 20, 2015. https://www.e-ir
.info/2015/12/20/to-what-extent-have-politics-restricted-the-iccs-effectiveness/.

Carozza, Paolo G. "Subsidiarity as a Structural Principle of International Human Rights Law." *American Journal of International Law* 97, no. 1 (January 2003): 38–79. https://scholarship.law.nd.edu/law_faculty_scholarship/564/.

Carrubba, Clifford J. "Courts and Compliance in International Regulatory Regimes." *Journal of Politics* 67, no. 3 (August 2005): 669–689. https://doi.org/10.1111/j.1468
-2508.2005.00334.x.

Carrubba, Clifford James, and Matthew Joseph Gabel. "Courts, Compliance, and the Quest for Legitimacy in International Law." *Theoretical Inquiries in Law* 14, no. 2 (2013): 505–542. https://doi.org/10.1515/til-2013-025.

Cascione, Silvio. "Mercosur Suspends Venezuela, Urges Immediate Transition." *Reuters*, August 5, 2017. https://www.reuters.com/article/us-venezuela-politics-mercosur-idUSKBN1AL0IB.

Chapman, Terrence, and Stephen Chaudoin. "People Like the International Criminal Court – as Long as It Targets Other Problems in Other Countries." *Washington Post, Monkey Cage*, January 20, 2017. https://www.washingtonpost.com/news/mon

key-cage/wp/2017/01/20/people-like-the-international-criminal-court-as-long-as-it-targets-other-problems-in-other-countries/.

"Public Reactions to International Legal Institutions: The International Criminal Court in a Developing Democracy." *The Journal of Politics* 82, no. 4 (October 2020): 1305–1320. https://doi.org/10.1086/708338.

Chaudoin, Stephen. "How Contestation Moderates the Effects of International Institutions: The International Criminal Court and Kenya." *The Journal of Politics* 78, no. 2 (April 2016): 557–571. https://doi.org/10.1086/684595.

"Chávez dice corte de cabello vale más que la CorteIDH que condenó a Venezuela." *Proceso Digital*, September 17, 2011. https://proceso.hn/politica/18-politica/Ch%C3%A1vez-dice-corte-de-cabello-vale-m%C3%A1s-que-la-CorteIDH-que-conden%C3%B3-a-Venezuela.html.

"Chávez Joins Venezuela's Battle of Referendums." *CNN*, November 22, 2003. www.cnn.com/2003/WORLD/americas/11/22/venezuela.referendums.reut/.

Checkel, Jeffrey. "Why Comply? Social Learning and European Identity Change." *International Organization* 55, no. 3 (Summer 2001): 553–588. https://doi.org/10.1162/00208180152507551.

"International Institutions and Socialization in Europe: Introduction and Framework." *International Organization* 59, no. 4 (October 2005): 801–826. https://doi.org/10.1017/S0020818305050289.

ed. *International Institutions and Socialization in Europe*. New York: Cambridge University Press, 2007.

Christoffersen, Jonas, and Mikael Rask Madsen, eds. *The European Court of Human Rights between Law and Politics*. Oxford: Oxford University Press, 2011.

Chu, Yun-han, Kai-Ping Huang, Marta Lagos, and Robert Mattes. "A Lost Decade for Third-Wave Democracies?" *Journal of Democracy* 31, no. 2 (April 2020): 166–181. https://journalofdemocracy.org/articles/a-lost-decade-for-third-wave-democracies/.

Cichowski, Rachel A. "Introduction: Courts, Democracy, and Governance." *Comparative Political Studies* 39, no. 1 (February 2006): 3–21. https://doi.org/10.1177/0010414005283212.

"Civil Society and the European Court of Human Rights." *APSA 2010 Annual Meeting Paper* (2010). https://papers.ssrn.com/abstract=1643604.

CIVICUS. "State of Civil Society Report 2019, Part 4: Civil Society at the International Level." 2019. https://www.civicus.org/documents/reports-and-publications/SOCS/2019/socs2019-year-in-review-part4_civil-society-at-the-international-level.pdf.

Clark, Phil. *Distant Justice: The Impact of the International Criminal Court on African Politics*. Cambridge, UK: Cambridge University Press, 2018.

Clarke, Kamari Maxine. *Fictions of Justice: The International Criminal Court and the Challenge of Legal Pluralism in Sub-Saharan Africa*. New York: Cambridge University Press, 2009.

Clarke, Kamari Maxine, Abel S. Knottnerus, and Eefje de Volder. "Africa and the ICC: An Introduction." In *Africa and the ICC: Perceptions of Justice*, edited by Kamari Maxine Clarke, Abel S. Knottnerus, and Eefje de Volder, 1–36. New York: Cambridge University Press, 2016.

Clarke, Robert. *The "Conscience of Europe?": Navigating Shifting Tides at the European Court of Human Rights*. Vienna: Kairos Publications, 2017.

Coalition for the International Criminal Court. "Budget and Finance Background." n.d. http://iccnow.org/?mod=budgetbackground.

"The ICC Judicial Elections 2020: #ElectTheBest to Lead the Fight against Impunity." n.d. www.coalitionfortheicc.org/explore/icc-elections-2020.

"Trust Fund for Victims." n.d. www.coalitionfortheicc.org/explore/trust-fund-victims.

Cogan, Jacob Katz. "International Criminal Courts and Fair Trials: Difficulties and Prospects." *Yale Journal of International Law* 27, no. 1 (Winter 2002): 111–140. https://digitalcommons.law.yale.edu/yjil/vol27/iss1/5/.

Collier, David. "Understanding Process Tracing." *PS: Political Science & Politics* 44, no. 4 (October 2011): 823–830. https://doi.org/10.1017/S1049096511001429.

Colonna, Lucas. "El Indulto Alcanza a Ocho Militares y 17 Guerrilleros." *La Nación*, May 22, 2003. https://www.lanacion.com.ar/politica/el-indulto-alcanza-a-ocho-militares-y-17-guerrilleros-nid497951/.

Combs, Nancy. "Seeking Inconsistency: Advancing Pluralism in International Criminal Sentencing." *Yale Journal of International Law* 41, no. 1 (Winter 2016): 1–49. https://digitalcommons.law.yale.edu/yjil/vol41/iss1/2.

Comisión Interamerican de Derechos Humanos. "Crisis Financiera 2016." n.d. https://www.oas.org/es/cidh/prensa/crisis-apoyo.asp.

Committee of Ministers. "11.2 Meeting Report of the Budget Committee – May 2018 Session." *Committee of Ministers*, May 28, 2018. https://rm.coe.int/0900001680a8aea2a.

"Action Report (27/6/2019) – Communication from the Russian Federation Concerning the Anchugov and Gladkov Group of Cases v. Russian Federation (Application No. 11157/04)." *Council of Europe*, July 2, 2019. https://publicsearch.coe.int/Pages/result_details.aspx?ObjectId=0900001680095777a.

"11.1 Unpaid Contributions and Interest on Late Payments – Update of Situation as at 19 September 2019." *Council of Europe*, September 24, 2019. https://rm.coe.int/0900001680972039.

"Council of Europe Programme and Budget 2020–2021." *Council of Europe*, December 20, 2019. https://rm.coe.int/1680994ffd.

"Committee of Ministers Deems the Annexation of Crimea Illegal and Calls for Measures Concerning National Minorities." *Council of Europe Communications*, April 3, 2014. https://rm.coe.int/0900001680071db5b.

Conant, Lisa J. *Justice Contained: Law and Politics in the European Union*. Ithaca, NY: Cornell University Press, 2002.

Concepcion, Natasha Parassram. "The Legal Implications of Trinidad and Tobago's Withdrawal from the American Convention on Human Rights." *American University International Law Review* 16, no. 3 (2001): 847–890. https://digitalcommons.wcl.american.edu/cgi/viewcontent.cgi?article=1242&context=auilr.

Conrad, Courtenay R. "Constrained Concessions: Beneficent Dictatorial Responses to the Domestic Political Opposition." *International Studies Quarterly* 55, no. 4 (December 2011): 1167–1187. https://doi.org/10.1111/j.1468-2478.2011.00683.x.

Conrad, Courtenay R., and Emily Hencken Ritter. "Treaties, Tenure, and Torture: The Conflicting Domestic Effects of International Law." *The Journal of Politics* 75, no. 2 (April 2013): 397–409. https://doi.org/10.1017/S0022381613000091.

Constitución Política del Perú 1993 con reformas hasta 2005 (1993). https://pdba.georgetown.edu/Constitutions/Peru/per93reforms05.html.

Contesse, Jorge. "Contestation and Deference in the Inter-American Human Rights System." *Law and Contemporary Problems* 79, no. 2 (June 20, 2016): 124.

Corey-Boulet, Robbie. "Concern over ICC Funding." *Inter Press Service*, September 28, 2011. www.ipsnews.net/2011/09/concern-over-icc-funding/.

"Correa propone 'cambio radical' de sistema interamericano de derechos humanos." *Editorial Azeta S.A. (ABC Color)*, November 11, 2011. https://www.abc.com.py/inter nacionales/correa-propone-cambio-radical-de-sistema-interamericano-de-ddhh-3310 79.html.

Cortell, Andrew, and James Davis. "How Do International Institutions Matter? The Domestic Impact of International Rules and Norms." *International Studies Quarterly* 40, no. 4 (December 1996): 451–478. https://doi.org/10.2307/2600887.

Council of Europe. "Protocol 14 – the Reform of the European Court of Human Rights." n.d. https://rm.coe.int/168071f2f4.

Couso, Javier, Alexandra Huneeus, and Rachel Sieder, eds. *Cultures of Legality: Judicialization and Political Activism in Latin America*. New York: Cambridge University Press, 2010.

Cronin-Furman, Kate. "Managing Expectations: International Criminal Trials and the Prospects for Deterrence of Mass Atrocity." *International Journal of Transitional Justice* 7, no. 3 (November 2013): 434–454. https://doi.org/10.1093/ijtj/ijto16.

Crow, David, Shannon Golden, James Ron, and Archana Pandya. "Data-Driven Optimism for Global Rights Activists." *openDemocracy*, June 29, 2015. https://www .opendemocracy.net/openglobalrights/james-ron-shannon-golden-david-crow- archana-pandya/datadriven-optimism-for-global-r.

Dai, Xinyuan. "Why Comply? The Domestic Constituency Mechanism." *International Organization* 59, no. 2 (Spring 2005): 363–398. https://doi.org/10 .1017/S0020818305050125.

Daly, Tom Gerald, and Micha Wiebusch. "The African Court on Human and Peoples' Rights: Mapping Resistance against a Young Court." *International Journal of Law in Context* 14, no. 2 (June 2018): 294–313. https://doi.org/10.1017/S1744552318000083.

Dancy, Geoff, Yvonne Marie Dutton, Tessa Alleblas, and Eamon Aloyo. "What Determines Perceptions of Bias toward the International Criminal Court? Evidence from Kenya." *Journal of Conflict Resolution* 64, no. 7–8 (2020): 1443–1469. https://doi.org/10.1177/0022002719893740.

Danner, Allison Marston. "Enhancing the Legitimacy and Accountability of Prosecutorial Discretion at the International Criminal Court." *The American Journal of International Law* 97, no. 3 (July 2003): 510–552. https://doi.org/10 .2307/3109838.

Davenport, Christian, ed. *Paths to State Repression*. Lanham, MD: Rowman & Littlefield, 2000.

Davenport, David. "International Criminal Court: 12 Years, $1 Billion, 2 Convictions." *Forbes*, March 12, 2014. https://www.forbes.com/sites/daviddavenport/2014/03/12/ international-criminal-court-12-years-1-billion-2-convictions-2/.

Deitelhoff, Nicole. "What's in a Name? Contestation and Backlash against International Norms and Institutions." *The British Journal of Politics and International Relations* 22, no. 4 (November 2020): 715–727. https://doi.org/10 .1177/1369148120945906.

Deitelhoff, Nicole, and Lisbeth Zimmermann. "Norms under Challenge: Unpacking the Dynamics of Norm Robustness." *Journal of Global Security Studies* 4, no. 1 (January 2019): 2–17. https://doi.org/10.1093/jogss/ogy041.

——— "Things We Lost in the Fire: How Different Types of Contestation Affect the Robustness of International Norms." *International Studies Review* 22, no. 1 (March 2020): 51–76. https://doi.org/10.1093/isr/viy080.

Delbruck, Jost. "International Protection of Human Rights and State Sovereignty." *Indiana Law Journal* 57, no. 4 (Fall 1982): 567–578. https://www.repository.law.indiana.edu/c gi/viewcontent.cgi?article=2302&context=ilj.

DeMeritt, Jacqueline H. R. "The Strategic Use of State Repression and Political Violence." In *Oxford Research Encyclopedia of Politics*, edited by William R. Thompson (October 2016). https://doi.org/10.1093/acrefore/9780190228637.013.32.

Dr. Denis Mukwege Foundation. "Jurisprudence of Sexual Violence Cases." n.d. https://www.mukwegefoundation.org/jurisprudence-sexual-violence/.

De Vos, Christian M. *Complementarity, Catalysts, Compliance: The International Criminal Court in Uganda, Kenya, and the Democratic Republic of Congo.* Cambridge, UK: Cambridge University Press, 2020.

Deya, Don. "Africa: Is the African Court Worth the Wait." *AllAfrica*, March 22, 2012. https://allafrica.com/stories/201203221081.html.

Directorate General, Human Rights and the Rule of Law. *Reforming the European Convention on Human Rights: Interlaken, Izmir, Brighton and Beyond: A Compilation of Instruments and Texts Relating to the Ongoing Reform of the ECHR.* Strasbourg: Council of Europe, 2014. https://edoc.coe.int/en/conferences-on-the-future-of-the-european-court-of-human-rights/7308-reforming-the-european-convention-on-human-rights-interlaken-izmir-brighton-and-beyond-a-c ompilation-of-instruments-and-texts-relating-to-the-ongoing-reform-of-the-echr.html.

Donald, Alice. "Backlog, Backlash and Beyond: Debating the Long Term Future of Human Rights Protection in Europe." *UK Human Rights Blog* (blog), April 14, 2014. https://ukhumanrightsblog.com/2014/04/14/backlog-backlash-and-beyond-debating-the-long-term-future-of-human-rights-protection-in-europe-alice-donald/.

——— "The Remarkable Shrinking Backlog at the European Court of Human Rights." *UK Human Rights Blog* (blog), October 1, 2014. https://ukhumanrightsblog.com/2014/10/01/the-remarkable-shrinking-backlog-at-the-european-court-of-human-rights/.

Donald, Alice, Jane Gordon, and Philip Leach. *The UK and the European Court of Human Rights.* Manchester: Equality and Human Rights Commission, 2012. https://www.equalityhumanrights.com/sites/default/files/83._european_court_of_human_rights.pdf.

Donnelly, Michael P. "Democracy and Sovereignty vs International Human Rights: Reconciling the Irreconcilable?" *The International Journal of Human Rights,* (April 2018): 1–22. https://doi.org/10.1080/13642987.2018.1454904.

Donoso, Hugo Carvajal. "La UNASUR de Samper, el último brazo del Chavismo." *Cuadernos faes,* July/September 2016, 53–60. https://fundacionfaes.org/file_up load/publication/pdf/20160713144021la_unasur_de_samper-el_ultimo_brazo_del_chavismo.pdf.

Dothan, Shai. "Judicial Deference Allows European Consensus to Emerge," *Chicago Journal of International Law* 18, no. 2 (2018): 393–418.

Doty, Kathleen A. "African Union Adopts Resolution Regarding the International Criminal Court." *The American Society of International Law*, October 12, 2013. https://www .asil.org/blogs/african-union-adopts-resolution-regarding-international-criminal-court-october–12–2013.

Downs, George W., David M. Rocke, and Peter N. Barsoom. "Is the Good News about Compliance Good News about Cooperation?" *International Organization* 50, no. 3 (Summer 1996): 379–406. https://doi.org/10.1017 /S0020818300033427.

Dragu, Tiberiu, and Yonatan Lupu. "Collective Action and Constraints on Repression at the Endgame." *Comparative Political Studies* 51, no. 8 (July 2018): 1042–1073. https://doi.org/10.1177/0010414017730077.

Duhaime, Bernard. "Canada and the Inter-American Human Rights System: Time to Become a Full Player." *International Journal* 67, no. 3 (Summer 2012): 639–659. https://doi.org//10.1177/002070201206700306.

Du Plessis, Max. "Implications of the AU Decision to Give the African Court Jurisdiction over International Crime." *Institute for Security Studies*, June 2012. https://issafrica.s3.amazonaws.com/site/uploads/Paper235-AfricaCourt.pdf.

Eboe-Osuji, Chile. "ICC President's Keynote Speech 'A Tribute to Robert H Jackson – Recalling America's Contributions to International Criminal Justice' at the Annual Meeting of American Society of International Law." *International Criminal Court*, March 29, 2019. https://www.icc-cpi.int/Pages/item.aspx?name =190329-stat-pres.

"ECCC at a Glance." *Extraordinary Chambers in the Courts of Cambodia*, April 2014. https://www.eccc.gov.kh/sites/default/files/ECCC%20at%20a%20Glance%20-%2 0EN%20-%20April%202014_FINAL.pdf.

"The ECHR in Facts & Figures 2019." *Council of Europe*, February 2020. https://www .echr.coe.int/Documents/Facts_Figures_2019_ENG.pdf.

"ECtHR's Largest Ever Award of Compensation – Yukos v. Russia." *Monckton Chambers*, August 1, 2014. https://www.monckton.com/ecthrs-largest-ever-award-compensation-yukos-v-russia/.

"Ecuador d.humanos; Ecuador cree que hay interés en la región por reformar sistema interamericano." *Spanish Newswire Services*, November 15, 2011. Nexis Uni.

Ege, Jörn. "Comparing the Autonomy of International Public Administrations: An Ideal-Type Approach." *Public Administration* 95, no. 3 (September 2017): 555–570. https://doi.org/10.1111/padm.12326.

"Elections in Peru: Democracy at Risk." *Human Rights Watch*, May 31, 2000. https:// www.hrw.org/news/2000/05/31/elections-peru-democracy-risk.

Engstrom, Par, Paola Limón, and Clara Sandoval. "#CIDHenCrisis: Urgent Action Needed to Save the Regional Human Rights System in the Americas." *openDemocracy*, May 27, 2016. https://www.opendemocracy.net/en/democraciaa bierta/cidhencrisis-urgent-action-needed-to-save-/.

Erlanger, Steven. "Council of Europe Restores Russia's Voting Rights." *The New York Times*, June 25, 2019. https://www.nytimes.com/2019/06/25/world/europe/council-of-europe-russia-crimea.html.

Escribà-Folch, Abel. "Repression, Political Threats, and Survival under Autocracy." *International Political Science Review* 34, no. 5 (November 2013): 543–560. https:// doi.org/10.1177/0192512113488259.

Estrada-Tanck, Dorothy. *Human Security and Human Rights under International Law: The Protections Offered to Persons Confronting Structural Vulnerability.* New York: Bloomsbury Publishing, 2016.

European Commission for Democracy through Law (Venice Commission). "Amendments to the Federal Constitutional Law on the Constitutional Court of the Russian Federation of 14 December 2015." *Council of Europe*, January 20, 2016. https://www.venice.coe.int/webforms/documents/default.aspx?pdffile=CDL-REF(2016)006-e.

European Court of Human Rights. *Annual Report 2005.* Strasbourg: Registry of the European Court of Human Rights, 2006. https://www.echr.coe.int/Documents/Annual_report_2005_ENG.pdf.

"Preliminary Opinion of the Court in Preparation for the Brighton Conference (Adopted by the Plenary Court on 20 February 2012)." February 20, 2012. https://www.echr.coe.int/Documents/2012_Brighton_Opinion_ENG.pdf.

"High Level Conference on the Future of the European Court of Human Rights: Brighton Declaration." *Committee of Ministers of the Council of Europe*, April 19, 2012. https://www.echr.coe.int/Documents/2012_Brighton_FinalDeclaration_ENG.pdf.

"History of the ECHR's Reforms." 2013. https://www.echr.coe.int/Documents/Reforms_history_ENG.pdf.

"Bringing the Convention Closer to Home." *Council of Europe*, February 2017. https://www.echr.coe.int/documents/hrtf_standards_translations_eng.pdf.

"Bringing the Convention Home: Case-Law Information, Training and Outreach." *Council of Europe*, 2018. https://www.echr.coe.int/Documents/Case_law_info_training_outreach_2018_ENG.pdf.

"Opinion on the Draft Copenhagen Declaration." *Council of Europe*, April 13, 2018. https://www.echr.coe.int/Documents/Opinion_draft_Declaration_Copenhague%20ENG.pdf.

"Rules of the Court." *Council of Europe*, January 1, 2020. https://www.echr.coe.int/documents/rules_court_eng.pdf.

"Analysis of Statistics 2019." *Council of Europe*, June 2020. https://www.echr.coe.int/Documents/Stats_analysis_2019_ENG.pdf.

"Reform of the Court." n.d. https://www.echr.coe.int/Pages/home.aspx?p=basictexts/reform&c=.

"The European Court of Human Rights: Questions and Answers for Lawyers." *Council of Bars & Law Societies of Europe*, October 2018. https://www.echr.coe.int/Documents/Q_A_Lawyers_Guide_ECHR_ENG.pdf.

Europe's Human Rights Watchdog. "The Council of Europe." n.d. https://www.europewatchdog.info/en/council-of-europe/.

Evenson, Elizabeth, and Jonathan O'Donohue. "Still Falling Short – the ICC's Capacity Crisis." *openDemocracy*, November 3, 2015. https://www.opendemocracy.net/en/openglobalrights-openpage/still-falling-short-icc-s-capacity-crisis/.

Fabricius, Peter. "South Africa Confirms Withdrawal from ICC." *Daily Maverick*, December 7, 2017. https://www.dailymaverick.co.za/article/2017-12-07-south-africa-confirms-withdrawal-from-icc/.

Faiola, Anthony. "Peru Withdraws from International Rights Court." *Washington Post*, July 8, 1999. https://www.washingtonpost.com/archive/politics/1999/07/08/peru-

withdraws-from-international-rights-court/bbd3415f-2a8a-4965-a7ad-2616d214b
e60/.

Farer, Tom. "The Rise of the Inter-American Human Rights Regime: No Longer a Unicorn, Not Yet an Ox." *Human Rights Quarterly* 19, no. 3 (August 1997): 510–546. https://doi.org/10.1353/hrq.1997.0025.

Fearon, James. "Bargaining, Enforcement and International Cooperation." *International Organization* 52, no. 2 (Spring 1998): 296–305. https://doi.org/10.1162/002081898753162820.

Ferencz, Benjamin B. "The Biggest Murder Trial in History." *BenFerencz.org*. n.d. https://benferencz.org/stories/1946-1949/the-biggest-murder-trial-in-history/.

Ferencz, Benjamin B., and Katy Clark. "Benjamin Ferencz Interviewed on Radio by Katy Clark." *BenFerencz.org*, September 2001. https://benferencz.org/articles/200 0-2004/benjamin-ferencz-interviewed-on-radio-by-katy-clark/.

Finke, Jasper. "Sovereign Immunity: Rule, Comity or Something Else?" *European Journal of International Law* 21, no. 4 (November 2010): 853–881. https://doi.org/10 .1093/ejil/chq068.

Finnemore, Martha. *National Interests in International Society*. Ithaca, NY: Cornell University Press, 1996.

———. *The Purpose of Intervention: Changing Beliefs about the Use of Force*. Ithaca, NY: Cornell University Press, 2003.

Fleig-Goldstein, Rachel M. "The Russian Constitutional Court versus the European Court of Human Rights: How the Strasbourg Court Should Respond to Russia's Refusal to Execute ECtHR Judgments." *Columbia Journal of Transnational Law* 56, no. 1 (2017): 172–218. https://heinonline.org/HOL/P?h=hein.journals /cjtl56&i=176&a=dW5sLmVkdQ.

Folami, Olakunle Michael. "Prosecution that Never Began: An Exploration of Acceptance of International Criminal Justice in Nigeria." *International Nuremberg Principles Community*, 2017. https://www.nurembergacademy.org/fil eadmin/user_upload/Nigeria.pdf.

Follesdal, Andreas. "The Legitimacy Deficits of the Human Rights Judiciary: Elements and Implications of a Normative Theory." *Theoretical Inquiries in Law* 14, no. 2 (2013): 339–360. https://doi.org/10.1515/til-2013-018.

———. "Squaring the Circle at the Battle at Brighton: Is the War between Protecting Human Rights or Respecting Sovereignty Over, or Has It Just Begun?" In *Shifting Centres of Gravity in Human Rights Protection: Rethinking Relations between the ECHR, EU, and National Legal Orders*, edited by Oddný Mjöll Arnardóttir and Antoine Buyse. London: Routledge, 2016.

Follesdal, Andreas, and Geir Ulfstein, eds. *The Judicialization of International Law: A Mixed Blessing?* Oxford: Oxford University Press, 2018.

foro-sidh. "Foro del sistema Interamericano de Derechos Humanos." n.d. https://cid hoea.wixsite.com/foro-sidh.

Fortman, Bas de Gaay. "'Adventurous' Judgments: A Comparative Exploration into Human Rights as a Moral Political Force in Judicial Law Development." *Utrecht Law Review* 2, no. 2 (December 2006): 22–43. https://ssrn.com/abstract=991091.

Freedom House. "Venezuela Opts out of American Convention on Human Rights." *ifex*, September 17, 2013. https://ifex.org/venezuela-opts-out-of-american-convention-on-human-rights/.

Freeland, Steven. "Judicial Decision-Making in International Criminal Courts: 'Effective' Justice?" *Griffith Journal of Law & Humanity* 3, no. 1 (2015): 59–85. https://griffithlawjournal.org/index.php/gjlhd/article/viewFile/660/597.

Garkawe, Sam. "Victims and the International Criminal Court: Three Major Issues." *International Criminal Law Review* 3, no. 4 (January 2003): 345–367. https://doi.org/10.1163/157181203322584350.

Gberie, Lansana. "The Special Court for Sierra Leone Rests – for Good." *United Nations Africa Renewal*, April 2014. https://www.un.org/africarenewal/magazine/april-2014/special-court-sierra-leone-rests-%E2%80%93-good.

General Assembly of the Organization of American States. *Results of the Process of Reflection on the Workings of the Inter-American Commission on Human Rights with a View to Strengthening the Inter-American Human Rights System.* Washington, DC: Organization of American States, July 23, 2013.

Gerards, Janneke. "Margin of Appreciation and Incrementalism in the Case Law of the European Court of Human Rights." *Human Rights Law Review* 18, no. 3 (September 2018): 495–515. https://doi.org/10.1093/hrlr/ngy017.

Gerber, Theodore P. "Grounds for (a Little) Optimism? Russian Public Opinion on Human Rights." *openDemocracy*, January 18, 2016. https://www.opendemocracy.net/openglobalrights/theodore-p-gerber/grounds-for-little-optimism-russian-public-opinion-on-human-right.

Gettleman, Jeffrey. "Raising Fears of a Flight from International Criminal Court, Burundi Heads for Exit." *The New York Times*, October 12, 2016. https://www.nytimes.com/2016/10/13/world/africa/burundi-moves-to-quit-international-criminal-court-raising-fears-of-an-exodus.html.

Giacalone, Rita. "Venezuela en Unasur: integración regional y discurso político." *Desafíos* 25, no. 1 (January–June 2013): 129–163. http://www.scielo.org.co/pdf/des a/v25n1/v25n1a05.pdf.

Gilligan, Michael J. "Is Enforcement Necessary for Effectiveness? A Model of the International Criminal Regime." *International Organization* 60, no. 4 (October 2006): 935–967. https://doi.org/10.1017/S0020818306060310.

Glaze, Ben. "EU Referendum: Forget Brexit, It's the European Convention on Human Rights We Need to Quit, Says Theresa May." *Mirror Online*, April 25, 2016. https://www.mirror.co.uk/news/eu-referendum-forget-brexit-its-7829574.

Glickhouse, Rachel. "Explainer: Presidential Reelection in Latin America." *AS/COA*, April 28, 2015. https://www.as-coa.org/articles/explainer-presidential-reelection-latin-america.

Global Americans. "The Inter-American Human Rights System." n.d. https://theglobalamericans.org/reports/inter-american-human-rights-system-fall–2016/.

"#GlobalJustice Weekly–Uganda Strains Diplomatic Ties by Welcoming ICC Suspect." *Coalition for the International Criminal Court*, May 20, 2016. www.coalitionfortheicc.org/news/20160520/globaljustice-weekly-uganda-strains-diplomatic-ties-welcoming-icc-suspect.

Goldberg, Mark Leon. "Special Tribunal for Lebanon Files Indictment. Hezbollah on Notice." *UN Dispatch* (blog), January 17, 2011. https://www.undispatch.com/special-tribunal-for-lebanon-files-indictment-hezbollah/.

Goldhaber, Michael. *A People's History of the European Court of Human Rights.* New Brunswick, NJ: Rutgers University Press, 2007.

Goldsmith, Jack, and Stephen D. Krasner. "The Limits of Idealism." *Daedalus* 132, no. 1 (Winter 2003): 47–63. https://www.amacad.org/publication/limits-idealism.

Goldsmith, Jack L., and Eric A. Posner. *The Limits of International Law*. New York: Oxford University Press, 2005.

Goldstein, Judith, Miles Kahler, Robert O. Keohane, and Anne-Marie Slaughter. "Introduction: Legalization and World Politics." *International Organization* 54, no. 3 (Summer 2000): 385–399. https://doi.org/10.1162/002081800551262.

Goldston, James A. "Remarks on the Copenhagen Declaration on Reform of the ECHR." *Open Society Justice Initiative*, April 11, 2018. https://www.justiceinitiative.org/uploads/72b8dbe7-dd22-4df2-a687-fc7bb3ad5b34/james-goldston-remarks-on-copenhagen-declaration-on-reform-of-the-echr-20180411.pdf.

Goodliffe, Jay, and Darren G. Hawkins. "Explaining Commitment: States and the Convention against Torture." *The Journal of Politics* 68, no. 2 (May 2006): 358–371. https://doi.org/10.1111/j.1468-2508.2006.00412.x.

Goodman, Ryan, and Derek Jinks. "How to Influence States: Socialization and International Human Rights Law." *Duke Law Journal* 54, no. 3 (December 2004): 621–703. https://scholarship.law.duke.edu/cgi/viewcontent.cgi?article=1240&context=dlj.

Goodman, Ryan, and Thomas Pegram, eds. *Human Rights, State Compliance, and Social Change*. New York: Cambridge University Press, 2011.

Graham, Erin R. "The Institutional Design of Funding Rules at International Organizations: Explaining the Transformation in Financing the United Nations." *European Journal of International Relations* 23, no. 2 (June 2017): 365–390. https://doi.org/10.1177/1354066116648755.

Guilfoyle, Douglas. "Reforming the International Criminal Court: Is It Time for the Assembly of State Parties to Be the Adults in the Room?" *EJIL: Talk!* (blog), May 8, 2019. https://www.ejiltalk.org/reforming-the-international-criminal-court-is-it-time-for-the-assembly-of-state-parties-to-be-the-adults-in-the-room/.

Gutierrez, Jason. "Philippines Officially Leaves the International Criminal Court." *The New York Times*, March 17, 2019. https://www.nytimes.com/2019/03/17/world/asia/philippines-international-criminal-court.html.

Hafner-Burton, Emilie M. *Forced to Be Good: Why Trade Agreements Boost Human Rights*. Ithaca, NY: Cornell University Press, 2009.

Making Human Rights a Reality. Princeton: Princeton University Press, 2013.

Hafner-Burton, Emilie, and Mark A. Pollack. "Mainstreaming Gender in Global Governance." *European Journal of International Relations* 8, no. 3 (September 2002): 339–373. https://doi.org/10.1177/1354066102008003002.

Hafner-Burton, Emilie M., and Kiyoteru Tsutsui. "Justice Lost! The Failure of International Human Rights Law to Matter Where Needed Most." *Journal of Peace Research* 44, no. 4 (July 2007): 407–425. https://doi.org/10.1177/0022343307078942.

Haglund, Jillienne. *Regional Courts, Domestic Politics and the Struggle for Human Rights*. New York: Cambridge University Press, 2020.

Haglund, Jillienne, and Courtney Hillebrecht. "Overlapping International Human Rights Institutions: Introducing the Women's Rights Recommendations Digital Database (WR2D2)." *Journal of Peace Research* 57, no. 5 (September 2020): 648–657. https://doi.org/10.1177/0022343319897954.

Harris, David, Michael O'Boyle, Edward Bates, and Carla Buckley. *Law of the European Convention on Human Rights* 3rd ed. Oxford: Oxford University Press, 2014.

Hatcher-Moore, Jessica. "Is the World's Highest Court Fit for Purpose?" *The Guardian*, April 5, 2017. https://www.theguardian.com/global-development-professionals-network/2017/apr/05/international-criminal-court-fit-purpose.

Hathaway, Oona. "Do Human Rights Treaties Make a Difference?" *Yale Law Journal* 111, no. 8 (2002): 1935–2041. https://digitalcommons.law.yale.edu/cgi/viewcontent.cgi?article=1852&context=fss_papers.

Hawkins, Darren G., David A. Lake, Daniel L. Nielson, and Michael J. Tierney, eds. *Delegation and Agency in International Organizations.* Cambridge, UK: Cambridge University Press, 2006.

Hayman, Mari. "Brazil Breaks Relations with Human Rights Commission over Belo Monte Dam," *Latin America News Dispatch*, May 3, 2011. http://latindispatch.com/2011/05/03/brazil-breaks-relations-with-human-rights-commission-over-belo-monte-dam/.

Heldt, Eugénia, and Henning Schmidtke. "Measuring the Empowerment of International Organizations: The Evolution of Financial and Staff Capabilities." *Global Policy* 8, no. 55 (August 2017): 51–61. https://doi.org/10.1111/1758-5899.12449.

Helfer, Laurence R. "Overlegalizing Human Rights: International Relations Theory and the Commonwealth Caribbean Backlash against Human Rights Regimes." *Columbia Law Review* 102, no. 7 (November 2002): 1832–1911. https://doi.org/10.2307/1123662.

———. "Why States Create International Tribunals: A Theory of Constrained Independence." In *Conferences on New Political Economy: Vol. 23: International Conflict Resolution*, edited by Stefan Voigt, Max Albert, and Dieter Schmidtchen. Tübingen, Germany: Mohr Siebeck, 2006.

———. "Redesigning the European Court of Human Rights: Embeddedness as a Deep Structural Principle of the European Human Rights Regime." *European Journal of International Law* 19, no. 1 (February 2008): 125–159. https://doi.org/10.1093/ejil/chn004.

Helfer, Laurence R., and Karen J. Alter. "Legitimacy and Lawmaking: A Tale of Three International Courts." *Theoretical Inquiries in Law* 14, no. 2 (2013): 479–504. https://doi.org/10.1515/til-2013-024.

Helfer, Laurence R. and Anne E. Showalter. "Opposing International Justice: Kenya's Integrated Backlash Strategy against the ICC." *International Criminal Law Review* 17, no. 1 (2017): 1–46. https://doi.org/10.1163/15718123-01701005.

Helfer, Laurence R., and Anne-Marie Slaughter. "Toward a Theory of Effective Supranational Adjudication." *Yale Law Journal* 107, no. 2 (November 2005): 273–392. http://papers.ssrn.com/sol3/papers.cfm?abstract_id=131409.

Heller, Kevin Jon. "Judge Ozaki Must Resign – Or Be Removed." *Opinio Juris*, March 29, 2019. http://opiniojuris.org/2019/03/29/judge-ozaki-must-resign-or-be-removed/.

Henkin, Louis. "International Human Rights as 'Rights.'" *Nomos* 23 (1981): 257–280. https://heinonline.org/HOL/P?h=hein.journals/cdozo1&i=435.

———. "The Universality of the Concept of Human Rights." *Annals of the American Academy of Political and Social Science* 506 (November 1989): 10–16. https://doi.org/10.1177/0002716289506001002.

Hertel, Shareen, Lyle Scruggs, and C. Patrick Heidkamp. "Human Rights and Public Opinion: From Attitudes to Action." *Political Science Quarterly* 124, no. 3 (Fall 2009): 443–459. https://doi.org/10.1002/j.1538-165X.2009.tb00655.x.

Heuler, Hilary. "Kenyans Split Over Kenyatta's ICC Appearance." *VOA*, October 8, 2014. www.voanews.com/content/kenyans-split-over-kenyatta-icc-appearance/247 6919.html.

Heyns, Christof, and Frans Viljoen. "The Impact of the United Nations Human Rights Treaties on the Domestic Level." *Human Rights Quarterly* 23, no. 3 (August 2001): 483–535. https://doi.org/10.1353/hrq.2001.0036.

Hill, Daniel W. "Estimating the Effects of Human Rights Treaties on State Behavior." *The Journal of Politics* 72, no. 4 (October 2010): 1161–1174. https://doi.org/10.1017 /s0022381610000599.

"Why Governments Cede Sovereignty: Evidence from Regional Human Rights Courts." *Foreign Policy Analysis* 14, no. 3 (July 2018): 299–325. https://doi.org/10.1093 /fpa/orw031.

Hill, Daniel W., and Zachary M. Jones. "An Empirical Evaluation of Explanations for State Repression." *American Political Science Review* 108, no. 3 (August 2014): 661–687. https://doi.org/10.1017/S0003055414000306.

Hillebrecht, Courtney. "Rethinking Compliance: The Challenges and Prospects of Measuring Compliance with International Human Rights Tribunals." *Journal of Human Rights Practice* 1, no. 3 (November 2009): 362–379. https://doi.org/10.1093 /jhuman/hup018.

"The Domestic Mechanisms of Compliance with International Law: Case Studies from the Inter-American Human Rights System." *Human Rights Quarterly* 34, no. 4 (November 2012): 959–985. https://doi.org/10.1353/hrq.2012.0069.

"Implementing International Human Rights Law at Home: Domestic Politics and the European Court of Human Rights." *Human Rights Review* 13, no. 3 (2012): 279–301. https://doi.org/10.1007/s12142-012-0227-1.

Domestic Politics and International Human Rights Tribunals: The Problem of Compliance. New York: Cambridge University Press, 2014.

"The Power of Human Rights Tribunals: Compliance with the European Court of Human Rights and Domestic Policy Change." *European Journal of International Relations* 20, no. 4 (December 2014): 1100–1123. https://doi.org/10.1177 /1354066113508591.

"Normative Consensus and Contentious Practice: Challenges to Universalism in International Human Rights Courts." *Human Rights Quarterly* 41, no. 1 (February 2019): 190–194. https://doi.org/10.1353/hrq.2019.0010.

"International Criminal Accountability and the Domestic Politics of Resistance: Case Studies from Kenya and Lebanon." *Law & Society Review* 54, no. 2 (June 2020): 453–486. https://doi.org/10.1111/lasr.12469.

Hillebrecht, Courtney and Alexandra Huneeus, with Sandra Borda. "The Judicialization of Peace." *Harvard International Law Journal* 59, no. 2 (Summer 2018): 279–330. https://ssrn.com/abstract=3227107.

Hillebrecht, Courtney, Dona-Gene Mitchell, and Sergio C. Wals. "Perceived Human Rights and Support for New Democracies: Lessons from Mexico." *Democratization* 22, no. 7 (2015): 1230–1249. https://doi.org/10.1080/13510347 .2014.950565.

Hillebrecht, Courtney, and Scott Straus. "Who Pursues the Perpetrators?: State Cooperation with the ICC." *Human Rights Quarterly* 39, no. 1 (February 2017): 162–188. https://doi.org/10.1353/hrq.2017.0006.

Hirschl, Ran. "The Judicialization of Mega-Politics and the Rise of Political Courts." *Annual Review of Political Science* 11 (2008): 93–118. https://10.1146/annurev.polisci.11.053006.183906.

Hoehn, Sabine. "Is ICC Withdrawal Down to Court's 'Lack of Respect' for Kenyan Cooperation and Trial Relocation Requests?" *African Arguments*, September 9, 2013. https://africanarguments.org/2013/09/09/kenya-is-icc-withdrawal-down-to-courts-lack-of-respect-for-kenyan-cooperation-and-trial-relocation-requests-by-sabine-hoehn/.

Hofmann, Andreas. "Resistance against the Court of Justice of the European Union." *International Journal of Law in Context* 14, no. 2 (June 2018): 258–274. https://doi.org/10.1017/S174455231800006X.

Hopgood, Stephen. *The Endtimes of Human Rights*. Ithaca, NY: Cornell University Press, 2013.

Howard-Hassmann, Rhoda E. "Human Security: Undermining Human Rights?" *Human Rights Quarterly* 34, no. 1 (February 2012): 88–112. https://doi.org/10.1353/hrq.2012.0004.

Huang, Christine, and Mariana Rodríguez. "As Maduro Calls for Venezuela's Withdrawal from the OAS, the Majority of Citizens Report the Organization Is Trustworthy." *Latin American Public Opinion Project*, May 17, 2017. https://www.vanderbilt.edu/lapop/insights/ITB028en.pdf.

Human Rights in International Justice. "Don't Ask and You Won't Receive – Will the ICC Request the Resources It Needs in 2019?" *Amnesty International*, May 2, 2018. https://hrij.amnesty.nl/icc-zero-growth-dont-ask-and-you-wont-receive/.

"Human Rights Watch Memorandum for the Thirteenth Session of the International Criminal Court Assembly of States Parties." *Human Rights Watch*, November 25, 2014. https://www.hrw.org/news/2014/11/25/human-rights-watch-memorandum-thirteenth-session-international-criminal-court.

Huneeus, Alexandra. "Courts Resisting Courts: Lessons from the Inter-American Court's Struggle to Enforce Human Rights." *Cornell International Law Journal* 44, no. 3 (Fall 2011): 493–533. https://scholarship.law.cornell.edu/cilj/vol44/iss3/2.

"International Criminal Law by Other Means: The Quasi-Criminal Jurisdiction of the Human Rights Courts." *American Journal of International Law* 107, no. 1 (January 2013): 1–44. https://doi.org/10.5305/amerjintelaw.107.1.0001.

"Compliance with Judgments and Decisions." In *The Oxford Handbook of International Adjudication*, edited by Cesare P. R. Romano, Karen J. Alter, and Yuval Shany, 437–463. Oxford: Oxford University Press, 2014.

Huneeus, Alexandra, and René Urueña. "Introduction to Symposium on the Colombian Peace Talks and International Law." *AJIL Unbound* 110 (2016): 161–164. https://doi.org/10.1017/S2398772300003007.

Hurd, Ian. "Legitimacy and Authority in International Politics." *International Organization* 53, no. 2 (Spring 1999): 379–408. https://doi.org/10.1162/002081899550913.

Hutchinson, Michael R. "The Margin of Appreciation Doctrine in the European Court of Human Rights." *International & Comparative Law Quarterly* 48, no. 3 (July 1999): 638–650. https://doi.org/10.1017/S0020589300063478.

Huth, Paul K., Sarah E. Croco, and Benjamin J. Appel. "Does International Law Promote the Peaceful Settlement of International Disputes? Evidence from the Study of Territorial Conflicts since 1945." *American Political Science Review* 105, no. 2 (May 2011): 415–436. https://doi.org/10.1017/S0003055411 000062.

"ICC States Parties' Gathering Concludes: The Paradox of Collective Political Support for Accountability without Adequate Financial Support May Impact the Effectiveness of the ICC." *International Federation for Human Rights*, December 13, 2018. https://www.fidh.org/en/issues/international-justice/inter national-criminal-court-icc/icc-states-parties-gathering-concludes-the-paradox-of-collective.

"ICC Underlines Impartiality, Reiterates Commitment to Cooperation with the African Union." *International Criminal Court*, May 29, 2013. https://www.icc-cpi.int/Pages/item.aspx?name=pr908.

Inter-American Commission on Human Rights. "Second Report on the Situation of Human Rights in Peru, OEA/Ser.L/V/II.106, Doc. 59 rev." *Organization of American States*, June 2, 2000. www.cidh.org/countryrep/Peru2000en/TOC.htm.

Report on the Situation of Human Rights in Venezuela." *Organization of American States*, 2003. www.cidh.org/countryrep/Venezuela2003eng/intro.htm #BACKGROUND.

"Democracy and Human Rights in Venezuela, OEA/Ser.L/V/II, Doc. 54." *Organization of American States*, 2009. www.cidh.org/pdf%20files/VENEZUEL A%202009%20ENG.pdf.

"Inter-American Commission of Human Rights 2011 Annual Report, OEA/Ser.L/V/II, Doc. 69." *Organization of American States*, December 30, 2011. https://www .oas.org/en/iachr/docs/annual/2011/toc.asp.

Reply of the Inter-American Commission on Human Rights to the Permanent Council of the Organization of American States Regarding the Recommendations Contained in the Report of the Special Working Group to Reflect on the Workings of the IACHR with a View to Strengthening the Inter-American Human Rights System. Washington, DC: Organization of American States, 2012.

Position Document on the Process of Strengthening of the Inter-American System for the Protection of Human Rights. Washington, DC: Organization of American States, April 9, 2012. www.oas.org/en/iachr/docs/pdf/PosicionFortalecimientoEN G.pdf.

"Severe Financial Crisis of the IACHR Leads to Suspension of Hearings and Imminent Layoff of Nearly Half Its Staff." *Organization of American States*, May 23, 2016. https://www.oas.org/en/iachr/media_center/PReleases/2016/069 .asp.

"Panama Will Host the Ordinary Period of Sessions of the IACHR." *Organization of American States*, September 29, 2016. https://www.oas.org/en/iachr/media_center/ PReleases/2016/144.asp.

"IACHR Overcomes Its Severe Financial Crisis of 2016 and Thanks Countries and Donors Who Made It Possible." *Organization of American States*, September 30, 2016. https://www.oas.org/en/iachr/media_center/PReleases/2016/145.asp.

"Inter-American Commission on Human Rights Annual Report 2017." https://www .oas.org/en/IACHR/reports/IA.asp?Year=2017

"IACHR Presents Accountability Report for 2018 Budget." *Organization of American States*, March 14, 2019. https://www.oas.org/en/iachr/media_center/preleases/201 9/067.asp.

"Basic Documents in the Inter-American System." *Organization of American States*, 2020. https://www.oas.org/en/iachr/mandate/Basics/intro.asp.

"Process for Strengthening the IACHR: Methodology." *Organization of American States*. www.oas.org/En/Iachr/Mandate/Strengthening.Asp

"Statistics." www.oas.org/en/iachr/multimedia/statistics/statistics.html

"Promotion." n.d. www.oas.org/en/iachr/activities/promotion.asp.

"Legal Assistance Fund." http://www.oas.org/en/iachr/mandate/Basics/fund.asp.

Inter-American Court of Human Rights. "Institutional Strengthening." n.d. https://www.corteidh.or.cr/fortalecimiento_institucional.cfm?lang=en.

"Special Session." n.d. https://corteidh.or.cr/periodo_de_sesiones_extraordinarias .cfm?lang=en.

"What Is the I/A Court H.R.?" n.d. https://corteidh.or.cr/que_es_la_corte.cfm? lang=en.

International Criminal Court. "Case Information Sheet: Situation in the Republic of Kenya, The Prosecutor v. Uhuru Muigai Kenyatta, Case No. ICC-01/09-02/11 (ICC-PIDS-CIS-KEN-02–014/15_Eng)." March 13, 2015. https://www.icc-cpi.int/ CaseInformationSheets/kenyattaEng.pdf.

"Case Information Sheet: Situation in the Republic of Kenya, The Prosecutor v. William Samoei Ruto and Joshua Arap Sang, ICC-PIDS-CIS-KEN-01-012/ 14_Eng." April 2016. https://www.icc-cpi.int/CaseInformationSheets/rutosangEng .pdf.

"Report of the Committee on Budget and Finance on the Work of Its Twenty-Eighth Session, Sixteenth Session, New York, 4–14 December 2017, ICC-ASP/16/5." *Assembly of States Parties*, July 5, 2017. https://asp.icc-cpi.int/iccdocs/asp_docs/A SP16/ICC-ASP-16-5-ENG.pdf.

"Reference: ICC-ASP/17/SP/03." *Assembly of States Parties*, March 14, 2018. https:// asp.icc-cpi.int/iccdocs/asp_docs/ASP17/NV-ASP17-ACN-ENG.pdf.

"Report of the Committee on Budget and Finance on the Work of Its Seventeenth Session, The Hague, 5–12 December 2018, ICC-ASP/17/5." *Assembly of States Parties*, May 31, 2018. https://asp.icc-cpi.int/iccdocs/asp_docs/ASP17/ICC-ASP-17 -5-ENG.pdf.

"Al Bashir Case." n.d. https://www.icc-cpi.int/darfur/albashir.

"Non-Cooperation." June 28, 2019. https://asp.icc-cpi.int/en_menus/asp/non-cooperation/Pages/default.aspx.

"Financial Statements of the International Criminal Court for the Year Ended 31 December 2018, Eighteenth Session, The Hague, 2–7 December 2019, ICC-ASP/18/12." *Assembly of States Parties*, July 23, 2019. https://asp.icc-cpi.int/iccdocs/ asp_docs/ASP18/ICC-ASP-18–12-ENG.pdf.

"Proposed Programme Budget for 2020 of the International Criminal Court, Eighteenth Session, The Hague, 2–7 December 2019, ICC-ASP/18/01." *Assembly of States Parties*, July 25, 2019. https://asp.icc-cpi.int/iccdocs/asp_docs/ASP18/ICC-ASP-18-10-ENG.pdf.

"About the International Criminal Court." n.d. https://www.icc-cpi.int/about/Pages/ default.aspx.

"Cooperation Agreements." n.d. https://www.icc-cpi.int/news/seminarBooks/Coop eration_Agreements_Eng.pdf.

"Recommendations on States' Cooperation with the International Criminal Court (ICC): Experiences and Priorities." n.d. https://www.icc-cpi.int/news/seminarBooks/ 66%20Recommendations%20Flyer%20(ENG).pdf.

"The States Parties to the Rome Statute." n.d. https://asp.icc-cpi.int/en_menus/asp/ states%20parties/pages/the%20states%20parties%20to%20the%20rome%20statute .aspx.

"Report of the Committee on Budget and Finance on the Work of Its Thirty-Fourth Session, Nineteenth Session, New York, 7–17 December 2020, ICC-ASP/19/5." *Assembly of States Parties*, August 24, 2020 https://asp.icc-cpi.int/iccdocs/asp_docs/ ASP19/ICC-ASP-19-5-ENG-CBF34%20Report-Final.pdf.

"The Court Today, ICC-PIDS-TCT-01–113/20_Eng." September 2020. https://www .icc-cpi.int/iccdocs/PIDS/publications/TheCourtTodayEng.pdf.

"Preliminary Examinations." n.d. https://www.icc-cpi.int/pages/pe.aspx.

"Situations under Investigation." n.d. https://www.icc-cpi.int/pages/situation.aspx.

"Afghanistan: Situation in the Islamic Republic of Afghanistan." n.d. https://www.icc -cpi.int/afghanistan.

"The Judges of the Court." n.d. https://www.icc-cpi.int/Publications/JudgesENG .pdf.

"States Parties – Chronological List." n.d. https://asp.icc-cpi.int/en_menus/asp/states %20parties/Pages/states%20parties%20_%20chronological%20list.aspx.

"Interacting with Communities Affected by Crimes." n.d. https://www.icc-cpi.int/a bout/interacting-with-communities.

"Witnesses." n.d. https://www.icc-cpi.int/about/witnesses/Pages/default.aspx.

"The ICC Has Moved to Its Permanent Premises." n.d. https://www.icc-cpi.int/Pages/ item.aspx?name=pr1180.

"Iraq." n.d. https://www.icc-cpi.int/iraq.

International Justice Resource Center. "Understanding the IACHR Reform Process." November 20, 2012. https://ijrcenter.org/2012/11/20/iachr-reform-process/.

Interview #168, 2014.

Interview #171, 2014.

Interview #296, October 2013.

Interview #303, December 2014.

Interview #431, May 2014.

Interview #464, July 2008.

Interview #505, February 2014.

Interview #520, 2014.

Interview #670, April 2014.

Interview #783, 2016.

Interview #827, 2014.

Interview #930, 2014.

Interview #951, 2014.

Interview #959, 2014.

"The Irish Times View on the Council of Europe: Keeping Russia in the Tent." *The Irish Times View*, June 25, 2019. https://www.irishtimes.com/opinion/editorial/the- irish-times-view-on-the-council-of-europe-keeping-russia-in-the-tent-1.3937324.

Isschot, Luis van. "Assessing the Record of the Inter-American Court of Human Rights in Latin America's Rural Conflict Zones (1979–2016)." *The International Journal of Human Rights* 22, no. 9 (2018): 1144–1167. https://doi.org/10.1080/13642987.2017.1382086.

Jacobs, Dov. "Some Reactions to Douglas Guilfoyle's Posts on the Troubles of the ICC." *EJIL: Talk!* (blog), April 1, 2019. https://www.ejiltalk.org/some-reactions-to-douglas-guilfoyles-posts-on-the-troubles-of-the-icc/.

"Jail Me, Hang Me: Philippines' Duterte Says Won't Answer to ICC." *Reuters*, December 20, 2019. https://www.reuters.com/article/us-philippines-drugs/jail-me-hang-me-philippines-duterte-says-wont-answer-to-icc-idUSKBN1YO184.

Jakes, Lara, and Michael Crowley. "U.S. to Penalize War Crimes Investigators Looking into American Troops." *The New York Times*, June 11, 2020. https://www.nytimes.com/2020/06/11/us/politics/international-criminal-court-troops-trump.html.

Javonoviç, Miodrag A. "Recognizing Minority Identities through Collective Rights." *Human Rights Quarterly* 27, no. 2 (May 2005): 625–651. https://doi.org/10.1353/hrq.2005.0019.

Jeffery, Renée. *Amnesties, Accountability, and Human Rights*. Philadelphia: University of Pennsylvania Press, 2014.

Johns, Leslie. *Strengthening International Courts: The Hidden Costs of Legalization*. Ann Arbor: University of Michigan Press, 2015.

Johnson, Tana. "Institutional Design and Bureaucrats' Impact on Political Control." *The Journal of Politics* 75, no. 1 (January 2013): 183–197. https://doi.org/10.1017/S0022381612000953.

Organizational Progeny: Why Governments Are Losing Control over the Proliferating Structures of Global Governance. Oxford: Oxford University Press, 2014.

Johnston, Alastair Iain. "Treating International Institutions as Social Environments." *International Studies Quarterly* 45, no. 4 (December 2001): 487–515. https://doi.org/10.1111/0020-8833.00212.

Jones, Bruce, and Torrey Taussig. "Democracy & Disorder: The Struggle for Influence in the New Geopolitics." *Brookings Institute*, February 2019. https://www.brookings.edu/research/democracy-disorder-the-struggle-for-influence-in-the-new-geopolitics/.

Jones, Peter. "Human Rights, Group Rights and Peoples' Rights." *Human Rights Quarterly* 21, no. 1 (February 1999): 80–107. https://doi.org/10.1353/hrq.1999.0009.

"Judge Ozaki Leaves the ICC." *International Justice Monitor*, November 26, 2019. https://www.ijmonitor.org/2019/11/judge-ozaki-leaves-the-icc/.

Kastner, Philipp. "Towards Internalized Legal Obligations to Address Justice and Accountability? A Novel Perspective on the Legal Framework of Peace Negotiations." *Criminal Law Forum* 23, no. 1–3 (September 2012): 193–221. https://doi.org/10.1007/s10609-012-9174-4.

Kaye, David. "Who's Afraid of the International Criminal Court?" *Foreign Affairs*, May/June 2011. https://www.foreignaffairs.com/articles/2011-04-18/whos-afraid-international-criminal-court.

Kelley, Judith. "International Actors on the Domestic Scene: Membership Conditionality and Socialization by International Institutions." *International Organization* 58, no. 3 (July 2004): 425–457. https://doi.org/10.1017/S0020818304583017.

"Who Keeps International Commitments and Why? The International Criminal Court and Bilateral Nonsurrender Agreements." *The American Political Science Review* 101, no. 3 (August 2007): 573–589. https://doi.org/10.1017/S0003055407070426.

Kelly, J. Patrick. "Naturalism in International Adjudication." *Duke Journal of Comparative & International Law* 18, no. 2 (Spring 2008): 395–421.

Kennedy, Merrit. "World Criminal Court Rejects Probe into U.S. Actions in Afghanistan." *NPR*, April 12, 2019. https://www.npr.org/2019/04/12/712721556/world-criminal-court-rejects-probe-into-u-s-actions-in-afghanistan.

"Kenya to Establish Local Judicial Mechanism to Probe Violence." *The Hague Justice Portal*, December 14, 2010. www.haguejusticeportal.net/index.php?id=12321.

"Kenya MPs Vote to Withdraw from ICC." *BBC News*, September 5, 2013. https://www.bbc.com/news/world-africa-23969316.

"Kenya Refuses to Arrest Sudanese President Omar Al-Bashir." *Amnesty International*, August 27, 2010. https://www.amnesty.org/en/latest/news/2010/08/kenia-se-niega-detener-presidente-sudanes/.

Keppler, Elise. "African Members Reaffirm Support at International Criminal Court Meeting." *Human Rights Watch*, November 17, 2016. https://www.hrw.org/news/2016/11/17/african-members-reaffirm-support-international-criminal-court-meeting.

Kersten, Mark. "Backing the ICC: Why Botswana Stands Alone Amongst AU States." *Justice in Conflict*, June 13, 2013. https://justiceinconflict.org/2013/06/13/backing-the-icc-why-botswana-stands-alone-amongst-au-states/.

Killingsworth, Matt. "Justice, Syria and the International Criminal Court." *Australian Institute of International Affairs*, December 24, 2019. https://www.international affairs.org.au/australianoutlook/justice-syria-international-criminal-court/.

Kim, Hunjoon, and Kathryn Sikkink. "Explaining the Deterrence Effect of Human Rights Prosecutions for Transitional Countries." *International Studies Quarterly* 54, no. 4 (December 2010): 939–963. https://doi.org/10.1111/j.1468-2478.2010.00621.x.

Kim, Pauline T. "Beyond Principal-Agent Theories: Law and Judicial Hierarchy." *Northwestern University Law Review* 105, no. 2 (2015). https://scholarlycommons.law.northwestern.edu/nulr/vol105/iss2/3/.

King, George Gelaga. *Eleventh and Final Report of the President of the Special Court for Sierra Leone*. Freetown, Sierra Leone: Special Court of Sierra Leone, 2013. www.rscsl.org/Documents/AnRpt11.pdf.

Koroteev, Kirill, and Sergey Golubok. "Judgment of the Russian Constitutional Court on Supervisory Review in Civil Proceedings: Denial of Justice, Denial of Europe." *Human Rights Law Review* 7, no. 3 (July 2007): 619–632. https://doi.org/10.1093/hrlr/ngm018.

Kissinger, Henry A. "The Pitfalls of Universal Jurisdiction." *Foreign Affairs* 80, no. 4 (July–August 2001): 86–96. https://doi.org/10.2307/20050228.

Koo, Jeong-Woo. "Public Opinion on Human Rights Is the True Gauge of Progress." *openDemocracy*, July 3, 2015. https://www.opendemocracy.net/openglobalrights/jeongwoo-koo/public-opinion-on-human-rights-is-true-gauge-of-progress.

Koremenos, Barbara, Charles Lipson, and Duncan Snidal. "The Rational Design of International Institutions." *International Organization* 55, no. 4 (Autumn 2001): 761–799. https://doi.org/10.1162/002081801317193592.

Koroteev, Kirill, and Sergey Golubok. "Judgment of the Russian Constitutional Court on Supervisory Review in Civil Proceedings: Denial of Justice, Denial of Europe." *Human Rights Law Review* 7, no. 3 (July 2007): 619–632. https://doi.org/10.1093/hrlr/ngm018.

Koskenniemi, Martti. *The Politics of International Law.* Oxford: Hart Publishing, 2011.

Kox, Tiny. "Role and Mission of the Parliamentary Assembly: Main Challenges for the Future." *Committee on Political Affairs and Democracy, Parliamentary Assembly of the Council of Europe,* April 9, 2019. http://assembly.coe.int/nw/xml/XRef/Xref-DocDetails-EN.asp?FileID=27565&lang=EN.

Krain, Matthew. "J'accuse! Does Naming and Shaming Perpetrators Reduce the Severity of Genocides or Politicides?" *International Studies Quarterly* 56, no. 3 (September 2012): 547–589. https://doi.org/10.1111/j.1468-2478.2012.00732.x.

Krauss, Clifford. "Angry Election Monitor Leaves Peru 2 Days before Runoff Vote." *The New York Times,* May 27, 2000. https://www.nytimes.com/2000/05/27/world/angry-election-monitor-leaves-peru-2-days-before-runoff-vote.html.

"Fujimori Resignation Sets off Succession Scramble in Peru." *The New York Times,* November 21, 2000. https://www.nytimes.com/2000/11/21/world/fujimori-resignation-sets-off-succession-scramble-in-peru.html.

Krcmaric, Daniel. "Should I Stay or Should I Go? Leaders, Exile, and the Dilemmas of International Justice." *American Journal of Political Science* 62, no. 2 (April 2018): 486–498. https://doi.org/10.1111/ajps.12352.

Kreichauf, René. "Legal Paradigm Shifts and Their Impacts on the Socio-Spatial Exclusion of Asylum Seekers in Denmark." In *Geographies of Asylum in Europe and the Role of European Localities,* edited by Birgit Glorius and Jeroen Doomernik, 45–67. Cham: Springer International Publishing, 2020. https://link.springer.com/chapter/10.1007/978-3-030-25666-1_3.

Kreps, Sarah, and Geoffrey Wallace. "International Law and US Public Support for Drone Strikes." *openDemocracy,* July 2, 2015. https://www.opendemocracy.net/openglobalrights/sarah-kreps-geoffrey-wallace/international-law-and-us-public-support-for-drone-stri.

Krook, Mona Lena. "Reforming Representation: The Diffusion of Candidate Gender Quotas Worldwide." *Politics & Gender* 2, no. 3 (September 2006): 303–327. https://doi.org/10.1017/S1743923X06060107.

Krook, Mona Lena, and Jacqui True. "Rethinking the Life Cycles of International Norms: The United Nations and the Global Promotion of Gender Equality." *European Journal of International Relations* 18, no. 1 (March 2012): 103–127. https://doi.org/10.1177/1354066110380963.

Lamm, Vanda. *Compulsory Jurisdiction in International Law.* Cheltenham, UK: Edgar Elgar, 2014. https://www.e-elgar.com/shop/compulsory-jurisdiction-in-international-law.

Landwehr, Claudia. "Backlash against the Procedural Consensus." *The British Journal of Politics and International Relations* 22, no. 4 (November 2020): 598–608. https://doi.org/10.1177/1369148120946981.

Lauren, Paul Gordon. *The Evolution of International Human Rights: Visions Seen.* Philadelphia: University of Pennsylvania Press, 2003.

Leach, Philip. "Access to the European Court of Human Rights–From a Legal Entitlement to a Lottery?" *Human Rights Law Journal* 27, no. 1 (2006): 11–24.

Leach, Philip, and Alice Donald. "Russia Defies Strasbourg: Is Contagion Spreading?" *EJIL: Talk!* (blog), December 19, 2015. www.ejiltalk.org/russia-defies-strasbourg-is-contagion-spreading/.

"Copenhagen: Keeping on Keeping On. A Reply to Mikael Rask Madsen and Jonas Christoffersen on the Draft Copenhagen Declaration." *EJIL: Talk!* (blog), February 24, 2018. https://www.ejiltalk.org/copenhagen-keeping-on-keeping-on-a-reply-to-mikael-rask-madsen-and-jonas-christoffersen-on-the-draft-copenhagen-declaration/#more–15945.

Legg, Andrew. *The Margin of Appreciation Doctrine in the Dynamics of European Human Rights Jurisprudence*. Dordrecht: Martinus Nijhoff Publishers, 1996.

The Margin of Appreciation in International Human Rights Law: Deference and Proportionality. Oxford: Oxford University Press, 2012.

Lessa, Francesca and Leigh A. Payne, eds. *Amnesty in the Age of Human Rights Accountability: Comparative and International Perspectives*. New York: Cambridge University Press, 2012.

Lessard, Geneviève. "Preventive Reparations at a Crossroads: The Inter-American Court of Human Rights and Colombia's Search for Peace." *The International Journal of Human Rights* 22, no. 9 (2018): 1–20. https://doi.org/10.1080/13642987.2016.1268405.

Letsas, George. "Two Concepts of the Margin of Appreciation." *Oxford Journal of Legal Studies* 26, no. 4 (Winter 2006): 705–732. https://doi.org/10.1093/ojls/gql030.

Lipscy, Phillip Y. *Renegotiating the World Order: Institutional Change in International Relations*. Cambridge, UK: Cambridge University Press, 2017.

Litinski, Rotem. "Economic Rights: Are They Justiciable, and Should They Be?" *Human Rights Magazine*, November 30, 2019. https://www.americanbar.org/gro ups/crsj/publications/human_rights_magazine_home/economic-justice/eco nomic-rights–are-they-justiciable–and-should-they-be-/.

Lock, Tobias. "Reassessing the European Convention on Human Rights in the Light of Brexit." *E-International Relations*, July 10, 2017. www.e-ir.info/2017/07/10/reassess ing-the-european-convention-on-human-rights-in-the-light-of-brexit/.

Lockwood Payton, Autumn. "Consensus Procedures in International Organizations." Working paper, *Max Weber Programme, EUI Working Papers* (2010): 1–20. http:// cadmus.eui.eu//handle/1814/14381.

Lovat, Henry. "International Criminal Tribunal Backlash." In *The Oxford Handbook of International Criminal Law*, edited by Kevin Jon Heller, Frédéric Mégret, Sarah M. H. Nouwen, Jens David Ohlin, and Darryl Robinson. Oxford: Oxford University Press, 2020.

Lührmann, Anna, Seraphine F. Maerz, Sandra Grahn, et al. "Authoritarian Surges–Resistance Grows: Democracy Report 2020." *Varieties of Democracy Institute (V-Dem)*, 2020. https://www.v-dem.net/en/publications/democracy-reports/.

Lupu, Yonatan. "International Judicial Legitimacy: Lessons from National Courts." *Theoretical Inquiries in Law* 14, no. 2 (2013): 437–454. https://doi.org/10.1515/til-20 13-022.

Lupu, Yonatan, and Geoffrey P. R. Wallace. "Violence, Nonviolence, and the Effects of International Human Rights Law." *American Journal of Political Science* 63, no. 2 (April 2019): 411–426. https://doi.org/10.1111/ajps.12416.

Lutz, Ellen L., and Caitlin Reiger, eds. *Prosecuting Heads of State*. Cambridge, UK: Cambridge University Press, 2009.

Macdonald, Ronald St. J. , Franz Matscher, and Herbert Petzold. *The European System for the Protection of Human Rights*. Dordrecht, Boston: M. Nijhoff, 1993.

Madsen, Mikael Rask. "Resistance to the European Court of Human Rights: The Institutional and Sociological Consequences of Principled Resistance." In *Principled Resistance to ECtHR Judgments – A New Paradigm?*, edited by Marten Breuer, 35–52. Berlin, Heidelberg: Veröffentlichungen des Max-Planck-Instituts für ausländisches öffentliches Recht und Völkerrecht, Springer, 2019. https://doi.org/10.1007/978-3-662-58986-1_2.

Madsen, Mikael Rask, Pola Cebulak, and Micha Wiebusch. "Backlash against International Courts: Explaining the Forms and Patterns of Resistance to International Courts." *International Journal of Law in Context* 14, no. 2 (June 2018): 197–220. https://doi.org/10.1017/S1744552318000034.

"Maduro llama a crear sistemas de DD.HH. en Unasur y CELAC frente a los de OEA." *La Prensa*, May 3, 2012. https://www.laprensa.com.ni/2012/05/03/internacionales/10 0194-maduro-llama-a-crear-sistemas-de-dd-hh-en-unasur-y-celac-frente-a-los-de-oea.

Mahoney, James. "The Logic of Process Tracing Tests in the Social Sciences." *Sociological Methods & Research* 41, no. 4 (November 2012): 570–597. https://doi .org/10.1177/0049124112437709.

Maliti, Tom. "Experts Say OTP Did Not Follow the Evidence in Collapsed Kenya Cases." *International Justice Monitor*, December 10, 2019. https://www .ijmonitor.org/2019/12/experts-says-otp-did-not-follow-the-evidence-in-collapsed-kenya-cases/.

Maodza, Takunda. "Botswana Funded MDC-T." *The Herald*, August 7, 2013. https:// www.herald.co.zw/botswana-funded-mdc-t/.

Marchuk, Iryna. "Flexing Muscles (Yet Again): The Russian Constitutional Court's Defiance of the Authority of the ECtHR in the Yukos Case." *EJIL: Talk!* (blog), February 13, 2017. https://www.ejiltalk.org/flexing-muscles-yet-again-the-russian-constitutional-courts-defiance-of-the-authority-of-the-ecthr-in-the-yukos-case/.

McDermott, Jeremy. "Fujimori to Quit in Peru Bribes Scandal." *The Telegraph*, September 18, 2000. https://www.telegraph.co.uk/news/worldnews/southamerica/peru/1355897/Fujimori-to-quit-in-Peru-bribes-scandal.html.

McEvoy, Kieran. "Beyond Legalism: Towards a Thicker Understanding of Transitional Justice." *Journal of Law and Society* 34, no. 4 (December 2007): 411–440. https:// doi.org/10.1111/j.1467-6478.2007.00399.x.

McGoldrick, Dominic. "A Defence of the Margin of Appreciation and an Argument for Its Application by the Human Rights Committee." *International & Comparative Law Quarterly* 65, no. 1 (January 2016): 21–60. https://doi.org/10 .1017/S0020589315000457.

Meernik, James. "Justice and Peace? How the International Criminal Tribunal Affects Societal Peace in Bosnia." *Journal of Peace Research* 42, no. 3 (May 2005): 271–289. https://doi.org/10.1177/0022343305052012.

"The International Criminal Court and the Deterrence of Human Rights Atrocities." *Civil Wars* 17, no. 3 (2015): 318–339. https://doi.org/10.1080/13698249 .2015.1100350.

"Explaining Public Opinion on International Criminal Justice." *European Political Science Review* 7, no. 4 (November 2015): 567–591. https://doi.org/10.1017/S1755773914000332.

Merry, Sally Engle. *Human Rights and Gender Violence: Translating International Law into Local Justice*. Chicago: University of Chicago Press, 2006.

"Transnational Human Rights and Local Activism: Mapping the Middle." *American Anthropologist* 108, no. 1 (March 2006): 38–51. https://doi.org/10.1525/aa.2006.108.1.38.

"Beyond Compliance: Toward an Anthropological Understanding of International Justice." In *Mirrors of Justice: Law and Power in the Post-Cold War Era*, edited by Kamari Maxine Clarke and Mark Goodale, 28–42. New York: Cambridge University Press, 2010.

Meseret, Elias. "African Leaders OK Strategy for Mass Withdrawal from ICC." *Associated Press*, January 31, 2017. https://apnews.com/0e19488f91bc4ccfad1e167c6c5742d5/African-leaders-OK-strategy-for-mass-withdrawal-from-ICC.

Mibenge, Chiseche Salome. *Sex and International Tribunals: The Erasure of Gender from the War Narrative*. Philadelphia: University of Pennsylvania Press, 2013.

Mills, Kurt. "'Bashir Is Dividing Us': Africa and the International Criminal Court." *Human Rights Quarterly* 34, no. 2 (May 2012): 404–447. https://doi.org/10.1353/hrq.2012.0030.

Ministers' Deputies. "Progress Review Report 2017." *Committee of Ministers of the Council of Europe*, April 11, 2018. https://rm.coe.int/09000016807b7be9.

Minkova, Liana. "Complementarity, Catalysts, Compliance Symposium: The Spectrum of Ideologies in International Criminal Justice – From Legalism to Policy," *Opinion Juris* (blog), August 3, 2020. http://opiniojuris.org/2020/08/03/complementarity-catalysts-compliance-symposium-the-spectrum-of-ideologies-in-international-criminal-justice-from-legalism-to-policy/.

Mitchell, Ronald B., and Patricia M. Keilbach. "Situation Structure and Institutional Design: Reciprocity, Coercion, and Exchange." *International Organization* 55, no. 4 (Autumn 2001): 891–917. https://doi.org/10.1162/002081801317193637.

Mitchell, Sara McLaughlin and Emillia Justyna Powell. *Domestic Law Goes Global: Legal Traditions and International Courts*. New York: Cambridge University Press, 2011.

Moes, Frédérique Renée Zoë Gabriel. "Withdrawal from the Rome Statute by the Republic of South Africa: Filling the Gaps." Master's thesis, Tillburg University, 2018. http://arno.uvt.nl/show.cgi?fid=144811.

Moore, Jina. "Burundi Quits International Criminal Court." *The New York Times*, October 27, 2017. https://www.nytimes.com/2017/10/27/world/africa/burundi-international-criminal-court.html.

Moravcsik, Andrew. "The Origins of Human Rights Regimes: Democratic Delegation in Postwar Europe." *International Organization* 54, no. 2 (Spring 2000): 217–252. https://doi.org/10.1162/002081800551163.

Morrill, Hanna K. "Challenging Impunity? The Failure of the International Criminal Tribunal for Rwanda to Prosecute Paul Kagame." *Brooklyn Journal of International Law* 37, no. 2 (2012): 683–712. https://core.ac.uk/download/pdf/228597499.pdf.

Morris, Ruth. "Venezuela: Hugo Chavez, Clutch Hitter." *Frontline World*, August 24, 2004. www.pbs.org/frontlineworld/elections/venezuela/.

Moyn, Samuel. *Not Enough: Human Rights in an Unequal World*. Cambridge, MA: Belknap Press of Harvard University Press, 2018.

Mudukuti, Angela. "Centre Stage Again – Allegations of UK War Crimes in Iraq." *Opinio Juris*, November 20, 2019. https://opiniojuris.org/2019/11/20/centre-stage-again-allegations-of-uk-war-crimes-in-iraq/.

Muhammad, Nasiruddeen. "A Comparative Approach to Margin of Appreciation in International Law." *The Chinese Journal of Comparative Law* 7, no. 1 (June 2019): 212–240. https://doi.org/10.1093/cjcl/cxz008.

Mulligan, Stephen P. *Withdrawal from International Agreements: Legal Framework, the Paris Agreement, and the Iran Nuclear Agreement*. Washington, DC: Congressional Research Service, 2018. https://fas.org/sgp/crs/row/R44761.pdf.

Murray, Rachel. "The ESCR Human Rights Law Implementation Project (HRLIP)." *University of Bristol Law School*. n.d. https://www.bristol.ac.uk/law/hrlip/.

Murungu, Chacha Bhoke. "Judgment in the First Case before the African Court on Human and Peoples' Rights: A Missed Opportunity or Mockery of International Law in Africa?" *SSRN* (December 2009). http://dx.doi.org/10.2139/ssrn.1526539.

"Myanmar Rejects ICC Probe into Alleged Crimes against Rohingya." *Al Jazeera*, November 15, 2019. https://www.aljazeera.com/news/2019/11/myanmar-rejects-icc-probe-alleged-crimes-rohingya-191115180754984.html.

Nakandha, Sharon Esther. *Africa and the International Criminal Court: Mending Fences*. Kampala: Avocats Sans Frontières, 2012. https://asf.be/wp-content/uploads/2012/08/ASF_UG_Africa-and-the-ICC.pdf.

Nel, Michelle, and Vukile Ezrom Sibiya. "Withdrawal from the International Criminal Court: Does Africa Have an Alternative?" *African Journal of Conflict Resolution* 17, no. 1 (2017). www.accord.org.za/ajcr-issues/withdrawal-international-criminal-court/.

Neuman, Gerald L. "Understanding Global Due Process." *Georgetown Immigration Law Journal*, no. 2 (2009): 365–402. http://nrs.harvard.edu/urn-3:HUL.InstRepos:11339394.

Neuman, William, and Nicholas Casey. "Venezuela Election Won by Maduro amid Widespread Disillusionment." *The New York Times*, May 20, 2018. https://www.nytimes.com/2018/05/20/world/americas/venezuela-election.html.

Newton, Michael A. "The Complementarity Conundrum: Are We Watching Evolution or Evisceration?" *Santa Clara Journal of International Law* 8 (2010): 115–164. https://scholarship.law.vanderbilt.edu/faculty-publications/642.

Ngari, Allan. "Kenya's Ongoing Battle with Complementarity at the ICC." *International Justice Monitor*, May 16, 2012. https://www.ijmonitor.org/2012/05/kenyas-ongoing-battle-with-complementarity-at-the-icc/.

"Nigeria: ICC Investigation in Nigeria Now Inevitable, Further Delay a Waste of Time." *Amnesty International*, December 5, 2019. https://www.amnesty.org/en/latest/news/2019/12/nigeria-icc-investigation-in-nigeria/.

Nouwen, Sarah M. H. *Complementarity in the Line of Fire: The Catalysing Effect of the International Criminal Court in Uganda and Sudan*. Cambridge, UK: Cambridge University Press, 2013.

Observatorio del Sistema Interamericano de Derechos Humanos. "Posicionamiento Frente a La Declaración Sobre El Sistema Interamericano de Derechos

Humanos Suscrita Por Cinco Gobiernos de América Latina." May 6, 2019. https://archivos.juridicas.unam.mx/www/site//index/posicionamiento-cidh-ibero-osidh-final-4078.pdf.

The Observatory of Economic Complexity. "Colombia." n.d. https://oec.world/en/profile/country/col/.

Odermatt, Jed. "Patterns of Avoidance: Political Questions before International Courts." *International Journal of Law in Context* 14, no. 2 (June 2018): 221–236. https://doi.org/10.1017/S1744552318000046.

Office of the Directorate General of Programmes, Council of Europe. "Human Rights Trust Fund." n.d. https://www.coe.int/en/web/programmes/human-rights-trust-fund.

"Projects Funded." n.d. https://www.coe.int/en/web/programmes/projects-funded.

Office of the Prosecutor. "ICC Prosecutor Presents Case against President, Hassan Ahmad Al Bashir, for Genocide, Crimes against Humanity and War Crimes in Darfur." *International Criminal Court*, July 14, 2008. https://www.icc-cpi.int/Pages/item.aspx?name=a.

"ICC Prosecutor in New York to Meet with United Nations and African Union Officials." *International Criminal Court*, September 22, 2008. https://www.icc-cpi.int/Pages/item.aspx?name=icc%20prosecutor%20in%20new%20york%20to%20meet%20with%20united%20nations%20and%20african%20union%20officials.

"Statement to the United Nations Security Council on the Situation in Libya, Pursuant to UNSCR 1970 (2011)." *International Criminal Court*, November 8, 2017. https://www.icc-cpi.int/Pages/item.aspx?name=otp_lib_unsc.

"Report on Preliminary Examination Activities 2018." *International Criminal Court*, December 5, 2018. https://www.icc-cpi.int/itemsDocuments/181205-rep-otp-PE-ENG.pdf.

"Ollanta Humala avala propuesta de Correa de un organismo de DD.HH. en Unasur." *Editorial Azeta S.A. (ABC Color)*, February 29, 2012. https://www.abc.com.py/internacionales/ollanta-humala-avala-propuesta-de-correa-de-un-organismo-de-ddhh-en-unasur-374723.html.

Onishi, Norimitsu. "Bid by Omar Al-Bashir of Sudan to Avoid Arrest Is Tested in South Africa." *The New York Times*, June 14, 2015. https://www.nytimes.com/2015/06/15/world/africa/bashir-sudan-international-criminal-court-south-africa.html.

Open Society Justice Initiative. "ECOWAS Community Court of Justice." June 2013. https://www.justiceinitiative.org/publications/ecowas-community-court-justice.

Raising the Bar: Improving the Nomination and Election of Judges to the International Criminal Court. New York: Open Society Foundations, 2019. https://www.justiceinitiative.org/publications/raising-the-bar-improving-the-nomination-and-election-of-judges-to-the-international-criminal-court.

Paredes Castro, Juan. "Diplomacia a tres bandas." *El Comercio*, June 9, 2014. https://elcomercio.pe/opinion/columnistas/diplomacia-tres-bandas-juan-paredes-castro-328015-noticia/.

Park, Susan. "Theorizing Norm Diffusion within International Organizations." *International Politics* 43, no. 3 (2006): 342–361. https://doi.org/10.1057/palgrave.ip.8800149.

Parliamentary Assembly of the Council of Europe. "Modification of Various Provisions of the Assembly's Rules of Procedure." *Committee on Rules of Procedure*,

Immunities and Institutional Affairs, Parliamentary Assembly of the Council of Europe, March 25, 2019. https://pace.coe.int/en/files/27665.

"PACE Proposes New 'Joint Reaction Procedure' When a State Violates Its Statutory Obligations." *Parliamentary Assembly of the Council of Europe*, April 10, 2019. http://assembly.coe.int/nw/xml/News/News-View-en.asp?newsid=7451&lang=2.

"PACE Ratifies Russian Delegation's Credentials." *Council of Europe*, June 26, 2019. www.assembly.coe.int/nw/xml/News/News-View-EN.asp?newsid=7547&lang=2&cat=8#:~:text=PACE%20has%20voted%20to%20ratify,means%20of%20reaching%20lasting%20solutions%E2%80%9D.

Pasqualucci, Jo M. *The Practice and Procedure of the Inter-American Court of Human Rights*. Cambridge, UK: Cambridge University Press, 2003.

Peel, Michael. "US Threats over Afghan War Probe 'Troubling', Says ICC." *Financial Times*, December 22, 2019. https://www.ft.com/content/ecb682ec-231a-11ea-b8a1-584213ee7b2b.

Permanent Council of the Organization of American States. *Report of the Special Working Group to Reflect on the Workings of the IACHR with a View to Strengthening the Inter-American Human Rights System for Consideration by the Permanent Council*. Washington, DC: Organization of American States, December 13, 2011.

"Peru: Human Rights Developments." *Human Rights Watch*, 1999. https://www.hrw.org/legacy/worldreport99/americas/peru.html.

"Peru to Maduro: You're Still Not Welcome at Summit of Americas." *Reuters*, April 3, 2018. https://www.reuters.com/article/us-peru-venezuela-politics/peru-to-maduro-youre-still-not-welcome-at-summit-of-americas-idUSKCN1HA2HS.

"Peru's Ex-President Fujimori Ordered to Stand Trial Again." *BBC News*, February 20, 2018. www.bbc.com/news/world-latin-america-43122187.

"Peru's Fujimori Resigns." *ABC News*, January 6, 2006. https://abcnews.go.com/International/story?id=82096&page=1.

Peskin, Victor. *International Justice in Rwanda and the Balkans: Virtual Trials and the Struggle for State Cooperation*. New York: Cambridge University Press, 2008.

——. "Caution and Confrontation in the International Criminal Court's Pursuit of Accountability in Uganda and Sudan." *Human Rights Quarterly* 31, no. 3 (August 2009): 655–691. https://doi.org/10.1353/hrq.0.0093.

Petersen, Roger. "Emotions and Backlash in US Society and Politics." *The British Journal of Politics and International Relations* 22, no. 4 (November 2020): 609–618. https://doi.org/10.1177/1369148120948726.

Pilling, David. "Fatou Bensouda: 'It's about the Law. It's Not about Power.'" *Financial Times*, September 25, 2020. https://www.ft.com/content/beeb8dba-ce3c-4a33-b319-3fcff0916736.

Pisati, Maurizio. "SPMAP: Stata Module to Visualize Spatial Data." *Statistical Software Components* S456812, Boston College Department of Economics (2007), revised January 18, 2018.

Posner, Eric A. *The Twilight of Human Rights Law*. New York: Oxford University Press, 2014.

——. "Liberal Internationalism and the Populist Backlash." *University of Chicago Public Law & Legal Theory Paper Series*, no. 606 (2017). https://doi.org/10.2139/ssrn.2898357.

Posner, Eric A., and Alan O. Sykes. "Voting Rules in International Organizations." *Chicago Journal of International Law* 15, no. 1 (Summer 2014): 195–228. https://heinonline.org/HOL/P?h=hein.journals/cjil15&i=199.

Posner, Eric A. and John Yoo. "A Theory of International Adjudication." *University of Chicago Law and Economics, Olin Working Paper No. 206, UC Berkeley Public Law Research Paper No. 146* (2004). http://dx.doi.org/10.2139/ssrn.507003.

Powell, Jonathan M., and Clayton L. Thyne. "Global Instances of Coups from 1950 to 2010: A New Dataset." *Journal of Peace Research* 48, no. 2 (March 2011): 249–259. https://doi.org/10.1177/0022343310397436.

"President of the Assembly Meets Minister of Foreign Affairs of Kenya." *Assembly of States Parties*, September 21, 2010. https://www.icc-cpi.int/Pages/item.aspx?name=president%20of%20the%20assembly%20meets%20minister%20of%20foreign%20affairs%20of%20kenya.

"President Song Ends a Two Days Visit to Addis Ababa, Ethiopia." *International Criminal Court*, July 12, 2010. https://www.icc-cpi.int/Pages/item.aspx?name=pr558.

Press Unit, European Court of Human Rights. "Factsheet–Reproductive Rights." *Council of Europe*, December 2019. https://www.echr.coe.int/Documents/FS_Reproductive_ENG.pdf.

"Pressure Point: The ICC's Impact on National Justice." *Human Rights Watch*, May 3, 2018. https://www.hrw.org/report/2018/05/03/pressure-point-iccs-impact-national-justice/lessons-colombia-georgia-guinea-and.

"Pre-Trial Chamber I Informs the United Nations Security Council and the Assembly of States Parties about Chad's Non-Cooperation in the Arrest and Surrender of Omar Al Bashir." *International Criminal Court*, December 13, 2011. https://www.icc-cpi.int/Pages/item.aspx?name=pr756.

"Pre-Trial Chamber I Informs the United Nations Security Council and the Assembly of States Parties about Malawi's Non-Cooperation in the Arrest and Surrender of Omar Al Bashir." *International Criminal Court*, December 13, 2011. https://www.icc-cpi.int/Pages/item.aspx?name=pr755.

"Protocol No. 11 to the Convention for the Protection of Human Rights and Fundamental Freedoms, Restructuring the Control Machinery Established Thereby." Entered into force November 1, 1998. *Council of Europe Treaty Series* No. 155. https://www.refworld.org/cgi-bin/texis/vtx/rwmain?docid=42ef8c812&page=search.

"Protocol No. 14 to the Convention for the Protection of Human Rights and Fundamental Freedoms, Amending the Control System of the Convention." Opened for signature May 13, 2004. *Council of Europe Treaty Series* No. 194. https://www.refworld.org/cgi-bin/texis/vtx/rwmain?docid=42ef8d0b4&page=search.

"Protocol No. 15 Amending the Convention for the Protection of Human Rights and Fundamental Freedoms." Opened for signature June 24, 2013. *Council of Europe Treaty Series* No. 213. https://www.coe.int/en/web/conventions/full-list/-/conventions/treaty/213.

Public Information and Communication Section. "STL Close-Up." *Special Tribunal for Lebanon*, May 30, 2007. www.stl-tsl.org/images/stories/About/STL_Close-up_EN.pdf.

Quiroz, Vanessa Gómez. "Alertan sobre nuevos controles a la prensa." *El Nacional (Venezuela)*, May 25, 2009. Nexis Uni.

Raimondi, Guido. "High-Level Conference: Continued Reform of the European Court of Human Rights Convention System – Better Balance, Improved Protection." *European Court of Human Rights*, April 13, 2018. https://www .echr.coe.int/Documents/Speech_20180412_Raimondi_Copenhagen_ENG.pdf.

Rapporteur Group on Programme Budget and Administration. "Unpaid Contributions – Special Measures." *Committee of Ministers of the Council of Europe*, September 21, 2017. https://rm.coe.int/09000016807412c2fd.

Rathbone, John Paul, and Gideon Long. "Colombia and Corruption: The Problem of Extreme Legalism." *Financial Times*, August 14, 2018. https://www.ft.com/con tent/ob833ef8-9c81-11e8-9702-5946bae86e6d.

Report of the Detailed Findings of the Commission of Inquiry on Human Rights in the Democratic People's Republic of Korea, Human Rights Council, Twenty-fifth Session, Agenda Item 4, Human Rights Situations that Require the Council's Attention, A/HRC/25/CRP.1 (Commission of Inquiry on Human Rights in the Democratic People's Republic of Korea, February 7, 2014). https://www.ohchr.org /EN/HRBodies/HRC/CoIDPRK/Pages/CommissionInquiryonHRinDPRK.aspx.

The Residual Special Court for Sierra Leone and the SCSL Public Archives, Freetown and The Hague. "The Special Court for Sierra Leone, the Residual Special Court for Sierra Leone." n.d. www.rscsl.org/.

Risse, Thomas, Stephen C. Ropp, and Kathryn Sikkink, eds. *The Power of Human Rights: International Norms and Domestic Change.* Cambridge, UK: Cambridge University Press, 1999.

Ritter, Emily Hencken. "Policy Disputes, Political Survival, and the Onset and Severity of State Repression." *Journal of Conflict Resolution* 58, no. 1 (February 2014): 143–168. https://doi.org/10.1177/0022002712468724.

Ritter, Emily Hencken, and Courtenay R. Conrad. "Human Rights Treaties and Mobilized Dissent against the State." *The Review of International Organizations* 11, no. 4 (December 2016): 449–475. https://doi.org/10.1007/s11558-015-9238-4.

Rivera, Mauricio. "Authoritarian Institutions and State Repression: The Divergent Effects of Legislatures and Opposition Parties on Personal Integrity Rights." *Journal of Conflict Resolution* 61, no. 10 (November 2017): 2183–2207. https://doi .org/10.1177/0022002716632301.

Robert H. Jackson Center. "Robert H Jackson Biography." n.d. https://www .roberthjackson.org/article/robert-h-jackson-biography/.

"Rule of Law among Nations." n.d. https://www.roberthjackson.org/speech-and-writing/rule-of-law-among-nations/.

Rogers, Richard J. "Assessment of the ICC's Legal Aid System." *Global Diligence*, January 5, 2017. https://www.icc-cpi.int/itemsDocuments/legalAidConsultations-LAS-REP-ENG.pdf.

Roht-Arriaza, Naomi. *The Pinochet Effect: Transnational Justice in the Age of Human Rights*. Philadelphia: University of Pennsylvania Press, 2006.

Romero, Simon. "Venezuela Hands Narrow Defeat to Chávez Plan." *The New York Times*, December 3, 2007. https://www.nytimes.com/2007/12/03/world/americas/ 03venezuela.html.

"A Crisis Highlights Divisions in Bolivia." *The New York Times*, September 14, 2008. https://www.nytimes.com/2008/09/15/world/americas/15bolivia.html.

"Chávez Decisively Wins Bid to End Term Limits." *The New York Times*, February 15, 2009. https://www.nytimes.com/2009/02/16/world/americas/16venez.html.

Ron, James, David Crow, and Shannon Golden. "Human Rights Familiarity and Socio-Economic Status: A Four-Country Study." *Sur: International Journal on Human Rights* 11, no. 20 (June/December 2014). https://sur.conectas.org/en/hum an-rights-familiarity-and-socio-economic-status/.

Rosendorff, B. Peter. "Stability and Rigidity: Politics and Design of the WTO's Dispute Settlement Procedure." *American Political Science Review* 99, no. 3 (August 2005): 389–400. https://doi.org/10.1017/S0003055405051737.

Roth, Kenneth. "The Case for Universal Jurisdiction." *Foreign Affairs* 80, no. 5 (September–October 2001): 150–154, https://doi.org/10.2307/20050258.

Rudolph, Christopher. "Constructing an Atrocities Regime: The Politics of War Crimes Tribunals." *International Organization* 55, no. 3 (Summer 2001): 655–691. https://doi.org/10.1162/00208180152507588.

Power and Principle: The Politics of International Criminal Courts. Ithaca, NY: Cornell University Press, 2017.

"Russia: Constitutional Court Backs Selective Justice." *Human Rights Watch*, April 19, 2016. https://www.hrw.org/news/2016/04/19/russia-constitutional-court-backs-selective-justice.

"Russia MPs Support Rights Reform." *BBC*, January 15, 2010. http://news.bbc.co.uk/2/hi/8460934.stm.

Russian human rights defenders. "Addressing the Crisis in Relations between the Council of Europe and Russia: Uphold the Values and Fulfill the Mission to Protect Rights across All Europe." November 2018. https://www.nhc.nl/assets/uploads/2018/12/Mem orandum-on-Russia-and-CoE_November_2018_eng_signatures-as-of-30.11.18.pdf.

"Russia's Departure from the Council of Europe Should Be Avoided." *Netherlands Helsinki Committee*, December 5, 2018. https://www.nhc.nl/russias-departure-from-the-council-of-europe-should-be-avoided/.

"Rwanda's Withdrawal of Its Special Declaration to the African Court: Setback for the Protection of Human Rights." *International Federation for Human Rights*, March 17, 2016. https://www.fidh.org/en/region/Africa/rwanda/joint-civil-society-statement-on-rwanda-s-withdrawal-of-its-article.

Sánchez León, Nelson Camilo. "The Silent Checkmate against the IACHR." *Inter-American Human Rights Network* (blog), May 23, 2016. http://interamericanhu manrights.org/the-silent-checkmate-against-the-iachr/.

Sandholtz, Wayne, Yining Bei, and Kayla Caldwell. "Backlash and International Human Rights Courts." In *Contracting Human Rights: Crisis, Accountability, and Opportunity*, edited by Alison Brysk and Michael Stohl, 159–178. Cheltenham, UK: Edward Elgar, 2018.

Sandoval-Villalba, Clara. "The Concepts of 'Injured Party' and 'Victim' of Gross Human Rights Violations in the Jurisprudence of the Inter-American Court of Human Rights: A Commentary on Their Implications for Reparations." In *Reparations for Victims of Genocide, War Crimes and Crimes against Humanity: Systems in Place and Systems in the Making*, edited by Carla Ferstman, Mariana Goetz, and Alan Stephens, 243–282. Leiden, The Netherlands: Koninklijke Brill NV, 2009.

Sasaki, Sayo. "Japan Praised for ICC Backing." *The Japan Times*, November 21, 2006. www.japantimes.co.jp/news/2006/11/21/national/japan-praised-for-icc-backing/.

Schabas, William. *An Introduction to the International Criminal Court*. 3rd ed. Cambridge, UK: Cambridge University Press, 2007.

Scheffer, David J. "The ICC's Probe into Atrocities in Afghanistan: What to Know." *Council on Foreign Relations*, March 6, 2020. https://www.cfr.org/article/iccs-probe-atrocities-afghanistan-what-know.

Schimmelfennig, Frank. "Strategic Calculation and International Socialization: Membership Incentives, Party Constellations, and Sustained Compliance in Central and Eastern Europe." *International Organization* 59, no. 4 (October 2005): 827–860. https://doi.org/10.1017/S0020818305050290.

Shany, Yuval. "Toward a General Margin of Appreciation Doctrine in International Law?" *European Journal of International Law* 16, no. 5 (November 2005): 907–940. https://doi.org/10.1093/ejil/chi149.

——— . "No Longer a Weak Department of Power? Reflections on the Emergence of a New International Judiciary." *European Journal of International Law* 20, no. 1 (February 2009): 73–91. https://doi.org/10.1093/ejil/chn081.

——— . "Assessing the Effectiveness of International Courts: A Goal-Based Approach." *American Journal of International Law* 106, no. 2 (April 2012): 225–270. https://doi.org/10.5305/amerjintelaw.106.2.0225.

——— . *Assessing the Effectiveness of International Courts*. Oxford: Oxford University Press, 2014.

——— . *Questions of Jurisdiction and Admissibility before International Courts*. Cambridge, UK: Cambridge University Press, 2016.

Sharpe, Jonathan, ed. *The Conscience of Europe: 50 Years of the European Court of Human Rights*. London: Third Millennium Publishing, 2011.

Shepsle, Kenneth A., and Barry R. Weingast. "When Do Rules of Procedure Matter?" *The Journal of Politics* 46, no. 1 (February 1984): 206–221. https://doi.org/10.2307/2130440.

Sikkink, Kathryn. "Human Rights, Principled Issue-Networks, and Sovereignty in Latin America." *International Organization* 47, no. 3 (Summer 1993): 411–441. https://doi.org/10.1017/S0020818300028010.

——— . *The Justice Cascade: How Human Rights Prosecutions Are Changing World Politics*. 1st ed. New York: W. W. Norton & Company, 2011.

——— . *Evidence for Hope: Making Human Rights Work in the 21st Century*. Princeton, NJ: Princeton University Press, 2017.

Silverman, Jon. "Ten Years, $900m, One Verdict: Does the ICC Cost Too Much?" *BBC News*, March 14, 2012. https://www.bbc.com/news/magazine-17351946.

Simmons, Beth A. *Mobilizing for Human Rights: International Law in Domestic Politics*. New York: Cambridge University Press, 2009.

Simmons, Beth A., and Allison Danner. "Credible Commitments and the International Criminal Court." *International Organization* 64, no. 2 (April 2010): 225–256. https://doi.org/10.1017/S0020818310000044.

Simmons, Beth A., and Hyeran Jo. "Measuring Norms and Normative Contestation: The Case of International Criminal Law." *Journal of Global Security Studies* 4, no. 1 (January 2019): 18–36. https://doi.org/10.1093/jogss/ogy043.

Simons, Marlise. "South Africa Should Have Arrested Sudan's President, I.C.C. Rules." *New York Times*, July 6, 2017. https://www.nytimes.com/2017/07/06/world/africa/icc-south-africa-sudan-bashir.html.

"In The Hague's Lofty Judicial Halls, Judges Wrangle over Pay." *The New York Times*, January 20, 2019. https://www.nytimes.com/2019/01/20/world/europe/hague-judges-pay.html.

Simons, Marlise, and Megan Specia. "U.S. Revokes Visa of I.C.C. Prosecutor Pursuing Afghan War Crimes." *The New York Times*, April 5, 2019. https://www.nytimes.com/2019/04/05/world/europe/us-icc-prosecutor-afghanistan.html.

Sims, Calvin. "Fujimori Wins 5 More Years at Peru Helm." *The New York Times*, April 11, 1995. https://www.nytimes.com/1995/04/11/world/fujimori-wins-5-more-years-at-peru-helm.html.

Slaughter, Anne-Marie. "A Global Community of Courts." *Harvard International Law Journal* 44, no. 1 (Winter 2003): 191–219. https://heinonline.org/HOL/P?h=hein.journals/hilj44&i=197.

Smith, Jana-Mari. "ICC Withdrawal a Point of Principle." *Namibian Sun*, February 3, 2017. https://www.namibiansun.com/news/icc-withdrawal-a-point-of-principle.

Smyth, Jamie. "Council to Battle Russia on Protocol 14." *Irish Times*, May 12, 2009. https://www.irishtimes.com/news/council-to-battle-russia-on-protocol-14-1.762322.

Soley, Ximena, and Silvia Steininger. "Parting Ways or Lashing Back? Withdrawals, Backlash and the Inter-American Court of Human Rights." *International Journal of Law in Context* 14, no. 2 (June 2018): 237–257. https://doi.org/10.1017/S1744552318000058.

"South Africa Reverses Course on ICC Arrest Warrant for Bashir." *Sudan Tribune*, July 31, 2018. www.sudantribune.com/South-Africa-reverses-course-on,31986.

Spano, Robert. "Universality or Diversity of Human Rights? Strasbourg in the Age of Subsidiarity." *Human Rights Law Review* 14, no. 3 (September 2014): 487–502. https://doi.org/10.1093/hrlr/ngu021.

"Specific Funds Contributions to IACHR by Donor (Amounts in Thousands of USD)." *Organization of American States*, June 30, 2016. https://www.oas.org/es/cidh/mandato/finanzas/RecursosFinancieros-2011-2016.pdf.

Spielmann, Dean. "Allowing the Right Margin: The European Court of Human Rights and the National Margin of Appreciation Doctrine: Waiver or Subsidiarity of European Review?" *Cambridge Yearbook of European Legal Studies* 14 (2012): 381–418. https://doi.org/10.5235/152888712805580570.

"Whither the Margin of Appreciation?" *Current Legal Problems* 67, no. 1 (2014): 49–65. https://doi.org/10.1093/clp/cuu012.

Sprouse, Ian. "The Gambia's Unsurprising Renunciation of the ICC, or the So-Called 'International Caucasian Court.'" *Africa at LSE* (blog), November 10, 2016. http://blogs.lse.ac.uk/africaatlse/2016/11/10/the-gambias-unsurprising-renunciation-of-the-icc-or-the-so-called-international-caucasian-court/.

Squatrito, Theresa. "Resourcing Global Justice: The Resource Management Design of International Courts." *Global Policy* 8, no. S5 (August 2017): 62–74. https://doi.org/10.1111/1758-5899.12452.

Ssenyonjo, Manisuli. "State Withdrawal Notifications from the Rome Statute of the International Criminal Court: South Africa, Burundi and the Gambia." *Criminal Law Forum* 29, no. 1 (March 2018): 63–119. https://doi.org/10.1007/s10609-017-9321-z.

von Staden, Andreas. *Strategies of Compliance with the European Court of Human Rights: Rational Choice within Normative Constraints.* Philadelphia: University of Pennsylvania Press, 2018.

Stahn, Carsten, ed. *The Law and Practice of the International Criminal Court.* Oxford: Oxford University Press, 2015.

"State Duma Committee Approves Bill on Execution of International Courts' Decisions." *Russian Legal Information Agency,* November 26, 2015. http://rapsi news.com/legislation_news/20151126/274987193.html.

"Statement of the Ministry of Foreign Affairs of the Russian Federation Concerning the Suspension of Payment of Russia's Contribution to the Council of Europe for 2017." *The Ministry of Foreign Affairs of the Russian Federation,* June 30, 2017. https://www.mid.ru/foreign_policy/rso/coe/-/asset_publisher/uUbe64ZnDJso/con tent/id/2805051.

Steiner, Henry J., Philip Alston, and Ryan Goodman. *International Human Rights in Context: Law, Politics, Morals.* 3rd ed. Oxford: Oxford University Press, 2008.

Stephen, Chris. "Clarifying the Principle of Complementarity: The ICC Confirms Admissibility of Case despite Investigation by Kenya." *EJIL: Talk!* (blog), September 14, 2011. https://www.ejiltalk.org/clarifying-the-principle-of-complementarity-the-icc-confirms-admissibility-of-case-despite-investigation-by-kenya/.

Stephen, Matthew D. "Legitimacy Deficits of International Organizations: Design, Drift, and Decoupling at the UN Security Council." *Cambridge Review of International Affairs* 31, no. 1 (2018): 96–121. https://doi.org/10.1080/09557571 .2018.1476463.

Stewart, Catrina. "ICC on Trial Along with Kenya's Elite amid Claims of Bribery and Intimidation." *The Guardian,* October 1, 2013. www.theguardian.com/world/2013/ oct/01/icc-trial-kenya-kenyatta-ruto.

Stiansen, Øyvind. "Delayed but Not Derailed: Legislative Compliance with European Court of Human Rights Judgments." *The International Journal of Human Rights* 23, no. 8 (2019):1221–1247. https://doi.org/10.1080/13642987 .2019.1593153.

———. "Directing Compliance? Remedial Approach and Compliance with European Court of Human Rights Judgments." *British Journal of Political Science* (2019): 1–9. https://doi.org/10.1017/S0007123419000292.

Stiansen, Øyvind, and Erik Voeten. "Backlash and Judicial Restraint: Evidence from the European Court of Human Rights." *International Studies Quarterly* 64, no. 4 (December 2020): 770–784. https://doi.org/10.2139/ssrn.3166110.

Streeck, Wolfgang and Kathleen Thelen, eds. *Beyond Continuity: Institutional Change in Advanced Political Economies.* Oxford: Oxford University Press, 2005.

Subotić, Jelena. *Hijacked Justice: Dealing with the Past in the Balkans.* Ithaca, NY: Cornell University Press, 2009.

Sullivan, Christopher M. "Undermining Resistance: Mobilization, Repression, and the Enforcement of Political Order." *Journal of Conflict Resolution* 60, no. 7 (October 2016): 1163–1190. https://doi.org/10.1177/0022002714567951.

Sunstein, Cass R. "Backlash's Travels." *Harvard Civil Rights-Civil Liberties Law Review* 42, no. 2 (Summer 2007): 435–450. https://heinonline.org/HOL/P?h=hein .journals/hcrcl42&i=439.

Sutter, Petra De. "Strengthening the Decision-Making Process of the Parliamentary Assembly Concerning Credentials and Voting." *Committee on Rules of Procedure, Immunities and Institutional Affairs, Parliamentary Assembly of the Council of Europe*, June 6, 2019. http://assembly.coe.int/nw/xml/XRef/Xref-DocDetails-en.asp?fileid=27725&lang=en.

Svirsky, Meira. "Hezbollah Intimidates Witnesses in Hariri Murder Tribunal." *Clarion Project*, March 14, 2013. www.clarionproject.org/news/hezbollah-intimidates-witnesses-hariri-murder-tribunal.

Talbot, Michael. "Collective Rights in the Inter-American and African Human Rights Systems." *Georgetown Journal of International Law* 49 (2018): 163–189. https://www.law.georgetown.edu/international-law-journal/wp-content/uploads/sites/21/2018/07/GT-GJIL180005-1.pdf.

Tallberg, Jonas, Thomas Sommerer, and Theresa Squatrito. "Democratic Memberships in International Organizations: Sources of Institutional Design." *The Review of International Organizations* 11, no. 1 (March 2016): 59–87. https://doi.org/10.1007/s11558-015-9227-7.

Tate, C. Neal, and Torbjörn Vallinder, eds. *The Global Expansion of Judicial Power.* Rev. ed. New York: New York University Press, 1995.

Thijssen, H. "The African Union and the International Criminal Court." *Peace Palace Library* (blog), June 22, 2012. https://www.peacepalacelibrary.nl/2012/06/the-african-union-and-the-international-criminal-court/.

Thomas, Daniel Charles. *The Helsinki Effect: International Norms, Human Rights, and the Demise of Communism*. Princeton, NJ: Princeton University Press, 2001.

True, Jacqui, and Michael Mintrom. "Transnational Networks and Policy Diffusion: The Case of Gender Mainstreaming." *International Studies Quarterly* 45, no. 1 (March 2001): 27–57. https://doi.org/10.1111/0020-8833.00181.

The Trust Fund for Victims. "Legal Basis." n.d. https://www.trustfundforvictims.org/en/about/legal-basis.

Tsereteli, Nino, "Emerging Doctrine of Deference of the Inter-American Court of Human Rights?" *The International Journal of Human Rights* 20, no. 8 (November 16, 2016): 1097–1112, https://doi.org/10.1080/13642987.2016.1254875.

Ugwuanyi, Sylvester. "Full Text of Buhari's Address at International Criminal Court Event." *Daily Post Nigeria* (blog), July 17, 2018. http://dailypost.ng/2018/07/17/full-text-buharis-address-international-criminal-court-event/.

Ulfstein, Geir, and Andreas Follesdal. "Copenhagen – Much Ado about Little?" *EJIL: Talk!* (blog), April 14, 2018. https://www.ejiltalk.org/copenhagen-much-ado-about-little/#more-16106.

UNASUR, United Nations, and Economic Commission for Latin America and the Caribbean. *UNASUR: Fostering South American Integration through Development and Cooperation*. Santiago, Chile: United Nations, 2014. https://repositorio.cepal.org/bitstream/handle/11362/37384/1/S1420807_en.pdf.

"Understanding the IACHR Reform Process." *International Justice Resource Center*, November 20, 2012. https://ijrcenter.org/2012/11/20/iachr-reform-process/.

UN-ICTR External Relations and Communication Outreach Unit. "ICTR Expected to Close Down in 2015." *United Nations*, February 2, 2015. http://unictr.unmict.org/en/news/ictr-expected-close-down-2015.

United Nations Office of the High Commissioner on Human Rights. "Key Concepts on ESCRs–Can Economic, Social and Cultural Rights Be Litigated at Courts?" n.d. https://www.ohchr.org/EN/Issues/ESCR/Pages/CanESCRbelitigatedatcourts .aspx.

United Nations and the Rule of Law. "International and Hybrid Criminal Courts and Tribunals." n.d. https://www.un.org/ruleoflaw/thematic-areas/international-law-courts-tribunals/international-hybrid-criminal-courts-tribunals/.

"Uruguay Withdraws from Unasur and Suspends TIAR." *Buenos Aires Times*, March 11, 2020. https://www.batimes.com.ar/news/latin-america/uruguay-withdraws-from-unasur-and-suspends-exit-from-tiar.phtml.

"Venezuela Denounces American Convention on Human Rights as IACHR Faces Reform." *International Justice Resource Center*, September 19, 2012. www .ijrcenter.org/2012/09/19/venezuela-denounces-american-convention-on-human-rights-as-iachr-faces-reform/.

"Venezuela.-Maduro asegura que la CIDH solo obedece a los intereses de la 'mafia internacional' que representa EEUU." *El Economista*, May 3, 2012. https://eco diario.eleconomista.es/global/noticias/3937734/05/12/Venezuela-Maduro-asegura -que-la-CIDH-solo-obedece-a-los-intereses-de-la-mafia-internacional-que-representa-EEUU.html.

"Venezuela to Withdraw from OAS as Deadly Protests Continue." *BBC News*, April 27, 2017. www.bbc.com/news/world-latin-america-39726605.

"Venezuela's Withdrawal from Regional Human Rights Instrument Is a Serious Setback." *Amnesty International*, September 6, 2013. https://www.amnesty.org/e n/latest/news/2013/09/venezuela-s-withdrawal-regional-human-rights-instrument-serious-setback/.

Venice Commission. *Report on the Implementation of International Human Rights Treaties in Domestic Law and the Role of Courts*. Strasbourg: Council of Europe, 2014. https://www.venice.coe.int/webforms/documents/default.aspx?pdffile=CD L-AD(2014)036-e.

Venzke, Ingo. "Understanding the Authority of International Courts and Tribunals: On Delegation and Discursive Construction." *Theoretical Inquiries in Law* 14, no. 2 (2013): 381–410. https://doi.org/10.1515/til-2013-020.

Verdezoto, Nancy F. "A tres días de la cita de la OEA, Bolivia presiona por las reformas a la CIDH." *El Comercio (Ecuador)*, March 19, 2013. Nexis Uni.

Verini, James. "The Prosecutor and the President." *The New York Times Magazine*, June 22, 2016. https://www.nytimes.com/2016/06/26/magazine/international-criminal-court-moreno-ocampo-the-prosecutor-and-the-president.html.

Viljoen, Frans, and Lirette Louw. "State Compliance with the Recommendations of the African Commission on Human and Peoples' Rights, 1994–2004." *American Journal of International Law* 101, no. 1 (January 2007): 1–34. https://doi.org/10.1017 /S0002930000002950X.

Vinjamuri, Leslie. "The International Criminal Court and the Paradox of Authority." *Law and Contemporary Problems*, no. 79, no. 1 (2016): 275–287. https://scholarship .law.duke.edu/lcp/vol79/iss1/10.

Voeten, Erik. "Public Opinion and the Legitimacy of International Courts." *Theoretical Inquiries in Law* 14, no. 2 (2013): 411–436. https://doi.org/10.1515/til-2013-021.

"Making Sense of the Design of International Institutions." *Annual Review of Political Science* 22, no. 1 (2019): 147–163. https://doi.org/10.1146/annurev-polisci-041916-021108.

"Populism and Backlashes against International Courts." *Perspectives on Politics* 18, no. 2 (June 2020): 407–422. https://doi.org/10.1017/S1537592719000975.

Wakabi, Wairagala. "Judge Ozaki Resigns Ambassadorial Post to Stay on Ntaganda Trial." *International Justice Monitor*, May 6, 2019. https://www.ijmonitor.org/2019/05/judge-ozaki-resigns-ambassadorial-post-to-stay-on-ntaganda-trial/.

Wallace, Geoffrey P. R. "International Law and Public Attitudes toward Torture: An Experimental Study." *International Organization* 67, no. 1 (January 2013): 105–140. https://doi.org/10.1017/S0020818312000343.

Widener Law School Legal Studies Research Paper No. 08–29. https://ssrn.com/abstract=1103289.

Wildhaber, Luzius A. "Constitutional Future for the European Court of Human Rights?" *Human Rights Law Journal* 23 (2002): 161–165.

Van Der Wilt, Harmen. "Unconstitutional Change of Government: A New Crime within the Jurisdiction of the African Criminal Court." *Leiden Journal of International Law* 30, no. 4 (December 2017): 967–986. https://doi.org/10.1017/S0922156517000449.

Wolf, Thomas P. "International Justice vs Public Opinion: The ICC and Ethnic Polarisation in the 2013 Kenyan Election." *Journal of African Elections* 12, no. 1 (June 2013): 143–177. https://doi.org/10.20940/JAE/2013/v12i1a6.

World Justice Project. "WJP Rule of Law Index 2020." n.d. https://worldjusticeproject.org/rule-of-law-index/.

Wrong, Michela. "Has Kenya Destroyed the ICC?" *Foreign Policy*, July 15, 2014. https://foreignpolicy.com/2014/07/15/has-kenya-destroyed-the-icc/.

Youngers, Coletta. "Fujimori's Relentless Pursuit of Reelection." *The North American Congress on Latin America Report on the Americas* 33, no. 4 (2000): 6–10. https://doi.org/10.1080/10714839.2000.11722667.

Yourow, Howard C. *The Margin of Appreciation Doctrine in the Dynamics of European Human Rights Jurisprudence*. Dordrecht: Martinus Nijhoff Publishers, 1996.

Youth Policy Team. "The Council of Europe Celebrates Its 70th Anniversary – and Quietly Prepares to Sacrifice Its Youth Sector." *Youth Policy*, May 6, 2019. https://www.youthpolicy.org/blog/youth-policy-young-people/council-of-europe-youth-sector-cuts/.

"Zimbabweans Turn to Botswana for Help." *The Patriot*, June 20, 2016. www.thepatriot.co.bw/news/item/2705-zimbabweans-turn-to-botswana-for-help.html.

"Zuma Assured AU al-Bashir Would Not Be Arrested - Mugabe." *News24*, June 16, 2015. https://www.news24.com/News24/zuma-assured-au-al-bashir-would-not-be-arrested-mugabe-20150616.

Zvobgo, Kelebogile. "Human Rights versus National Interests: Shifting US Public Attitudes on the International Criminal Court." *International Studies Quarterly* 63, no. 4 (December 2019): 1065–1078. https://doi.org/10.1093/isq/sqz056.

Zvobgo, Kelebogile, and Stephen Chaudoin. "Complementarity and Public Views on Overlapping Domestic and International Courts." January 2, 2020. https://www.law.uchicago.edu/files/2020-01/zvobgo_and_chaudoin.pdf.

Index

CPSIA information can be obtained
at www.ICGtesting.com
Printed in the USA
LVHW080807251021
701445LV00009B/544

9 781009 055642